MATERIAL SUCCESS THROUGH YOGA PRINCIPLES

We are pleased to offer

MATERIAL SUCCESS THROUGH YOGA PRINCIPLES

in several different formats: print, e-book (ePub), and an unabridged audiobook read by the author, Swami Kriyananda.

MATERIAL SUCCESS THROUGH YOGA PRINCIPLES

Swami Kriyananda

CRYSTAL CLARITY PUBLISHERS   Commerce, California

> **"Be practical in your idealism."**
> (Paramhansa Yogananda)

© 2025 by Hansa Trust
All rights reserved. Published 2025
Printed in the United States of America

CRYSTAL CLARITY PUBLISHERS
1123 Goodrich Blvd. | Commerce, California
crystalclarity.com | clarity@crystalclarity.com
800.424.1055

ISBN 978-1-56589-063-3 (print) | LCCN 2024033417 (print)
ISBN 978-1-56589-579-9 (e-book) | LCCN 2024033418 (e-book)
ISBN 978-1-56589-845-5 (audiobook)

First published as a correspondence course, one lesson at a time, in 2005 and 2006.

Cover design by Tejindra Scott Tully
Interior layout and design by Michele Madhavi Molloy

 The *Joy Is Within You* symbol is registered by Ananda Church of Self-Realization of Nevada County, California.

Contents

Introduction 1
1. Dharma as the Key to Success 6
2. How to Magnetize Money 20
3. Knowledge, Inspiration, and Energy 36
4. The Importance of Right Attitude 52
5. What Is It, to Be Practical? 68
6. First Things First 84
7. Balancing Work and Meditation 102
8. Immediate Versus Long-Range Goals 120
9. The Importance of Human Values 134
10. How to Be a Good Leader 150
11. Practicality in Investments 172
12. What *Kind* of Compromises? 190
13. Keep Your Feet on the Ground 204
14. Working *with* Others 218
15. Effectiveness as an Employer 230
16. Being a Successful Employee 248
17. The Importance of a Harmonious Environment . . . 266
18. Secrets of Effective Advertising 280
19. Talk Less, Do More 294
20. Joy in Business 304
21. The Stages of Human Evolution 316
22. Dharma Versus Adharma: Truth Versus Untruth . . . 332
23. God's Place in the Business World 348
24. What Should Your Line of Work Be? 362
25. Creating Opportunities 376
26. The Right Use of Ego 388

About the Author 405
Further Explorations 406

Introduction

The three main philosophies of India were developed thousands of years ago. They are known as *Sankhya*, *Yoga*, and *Vedanta*. *Sankhya* explains why one should reject as delusive everything he perceives through the senses, and why he should seek a higher, non-material reality. *Yoga*, the second in the series, is the supreme science, for it enables one to *experience* truth for himself. And *Vedanta* explains, insofar as human reason can grasp it, the nature of that Truth.

These philosophies are best taught sequentially. People should understand, first, their need to banish delusion from their consciousness in comprehending that delusion is the source of all life's pain, uncertainty, and suffering. When they recognize their need to live by higher principles, they develop the willingness to undergo the discipline necessary for attaining a higher understanding. *Yoga*, for that reason, comes second in the series.

Beyond *Yoga* practice there lies the wisdom of *Vedanta*. One may ask why wisdom needs to be explained if it can be realized personally. The answer is that *Vedanta* shows where all true spiritual practices lead, lest people be tempted to stray off the trail to the top of the mountain by reaffirming their egos and developing, for example, the eight *siddhis* or spiritual powers. The true purpose of yoga is to bring one to the highest state of Self-realization. The *Vedanta* teachings help to keep one's aspirations directed toward that goal.

There is a story my Guru enjoyed telling about a great yogi named Baba Gorakhnath, whose life span was three hundred years. In that long time, Baba Gorakhnath developed all the yogic *siddhis*. When it was time for him at last to leave his body, he wanted to find someone highly advanced enough to receive those powers.

Gazing through the spiritual eye,* he saw a young man seated by the river Ganges in deep meditation. Here, he realized, was a fit person to receive his *siddhis*. He materialized before the young yogi and announced, "I am Baba Gorakhnath." If he, with his high renown, expected a gasp of amazement from the young man, he was disappointed. The younger one only looked at him with an expression of calm inquiry.

The old yogi continued, "I have seen that the time has come for me to leave my body. Over many years of spiritual practice I have perfected the eight yogic siddhis. Today I am here to confer them upon you, for I have seen in meditation that you are worthy of them."

Baba Gorakhnath, holding in his hand eight pellets of mud, continued: "I have infused these pellets with my yogic powers. Meditate holding them in your right hand, and their powers will be infused into you."

The young yogi took them in his right hand, looked at them for a moment, then asked, "Are these mine to do with as I choose?"

"Of course!" the other replied. "I have given them to you. They are yours."

Thereupon, the young man flung all eight pellets into the river.

"What have you done!" cried the other in horror. "It took me three hundred years to develop those powers. You have thrown away my life work!"

---

* The seat of spiritual vision, located just behind the forehead at a point midway between the eyebrows.

The young yogi gazed at him with still eyes and answered, "In delusion yet, Baba Gorakhnath?"

His words vibrated with divine realization. The ancient yogi was suddenly wakened from his lifelong fascination with powers.

"How can I thank you?" he cried. "I can do so only by leaving my body in a state of perfect freedom!" He sat down on the sand forthwith, entered into deep meditation, and left his body, a fully liberated soul.

The traditional scripture of yoga is Patanjali's *Yoga Sutras*, or aphorisms. Those *sutras* begin with a word that has probably puzzled many students over the years: "*Now* [we come to] the study of Yoga." Why did he insert that seemingly unnecessary word, *now*, in that aphorism? The answer is that, if one would comprehend the need for spiritual attainment, he must first understand the message of *Sankhya* which explains the nature of delusion. Armed with that understanding, one is ready to pursue in earnest the science of yoga.

Yoga gives the "how to" of the spiritual path. Since this is an inward journey, the main emphasis of yoga is on withdrawing one's consciousness from the body and centering it in the spine. Yoga practice enables one to *raise* his consciousness to the highest level of Self-realization.

Many obstacles confront one as he makes this inward journey. The first obstacle is the fact that human understanding is limited to the information it receives from the senses of sight, hearing, smell, taste, and touch. Man's understanding is limited, next, by reason's fumbling attempts to process that information.

From birth onward, the human being sees the world, as revealed to him through the senses, as the only reality. Even before birth, one's energy flows outward from his inmost center to create the embryo. At birth, on entering this world, his energy must immediately be engaged outwardly to sustain his body by breathing, eating, and keeping his muscles activated.

Growing children relate ever more, and more *specifically*, to the world around them. This need to do so takes precedence over every other consideration, including the soul's call within to remember the eternal, ever-blissful reality.

We have entered, without realizing it, into a house of mirrors. Everything we see and experience in the world is only a reflection of our own awareness. We see, first, only what we are capable of seeing. We understand only what we are capable of understanding. Happiness, which everyone craves, is reflected back to us, only, from the surrounding world: we project it outwardly from our center. If we lack inner joy, we will find not a hint of it outside. Melodies of a lost happiness pluck on our heartstrings, but sound faint and far away until we recognize that their source is ever inside ourselves.

It is only in our egos that we experience happiness or sadness. What *is* the ego—*ahankara* is the Sanskrit word—anyway? It is not our true self. Paramhansa Yogananda defined ego as *the soul identified with the body*. Man reaches out to the world through his senses, trying ever to grasp the joy which he intuits to be his birthright. Ego-consciousness is a delusion. It imprisons joy instead of letting it flow out toward infinity. Man's every thought and gesture affirms his own separate individuality to be his reality. He fails to realize how cramped his self-identity becomes, in consequence. Aspirations that arise from ego-consciousness seize possession of his mind. "I am this body," he affirms. "I am a man. I am a woman." And so it goes on.

As the child grows, it develops in the awareness of its surroundings. If, when the person grows to adulthood, he clings to self-involvement, the adult may remain immature. A child's self-preoccupation is natural—even necessary. It is its way of getting a firm purchase on outer realities, even as a person learning to walk on a tightrope must be exaggeratedly aware of his every movement. In an adult, however, excessive self-preoccupation betrays childishness. In exaggerated cases, indeed, such self-preoccupation may even lead to madness. The awareness of the super-egotist is expansive only insofar as it reaches out to take what he can for himself. He wants more and more wealth, more and more power, more and more self-importance, indifferent to the needs and interests of others.

Thus, we see that there are two outward directions in which the ego can grow: toward mature acceptance of objective realities; or toward a desire for possession and dominion over others.

Expanding sympathy helps the ego to be aware of its subtle identity with other people and with the universe. One's own happiness, in consequence, expands exponentially. If, on the other hand, the ego grows more self-centered, this "expansion" of self-consciousness becomes suffocating. Any happiness one experiences shrinks, in time, to virtual nonexistence. Selfish people imagine that the more they possess, the happier they will be. This is a delusion: What they accomplish is quite the opposite, for they squeeze their ever-dwindling happiness in a tightening grip that becomes even physically painful at last, owing to the tension that they build up in themselves.

When the ego's sympathy for others expands, and it grows in appreciation for the world around it, it relaxes from exaggerated consciousness of its body, and expands effortlessly into ever-clearer awareness of the indwelling soul. Ego—the soul, as I said earlier, identified with the body—discovers its identity, in this case, with the Infinite Spirit. One sees one's self no longer as the little self (with a small *s*), but as identified with the infinite Self (written with a large *S*).

There is another way that self-awareness can grow: not by outward expansion, but by withdrawing the energy altogether from outward consciousness. One realizes, thus, that the essence of life is unitive. All things, so distinct in appearance from one another, are then realized to be expressions of the one, changeless reality.

It is possible to grow spiritually in both ways: by sympathetic expansion into a sense of one's relationship with the world; and, alternatively, by withdrawing inwardly and realizing all reality as a manifestation in consciousness of the one, infinite Self. Both directions are necessary for those who want to practice yoga most effectively. The hermit-yogi, seeking only to withdraw from outwardness, may find himself not expanding at all, but diminishing, rather, in his self-involvement.

Those who are highly enough realized to be in breathless *samadhi* for indefinite periods at a time no longer need to balance their inward union with God by outward service. For those who are not so highly realized, however, it is important to serve outwardly as well as inwardly—the inward service being a self-offering of their whole existence into the ocean of divine love. One's life should be balanced, inwardly and outwardly. If he withdraws too unilaterally from the world, he may find himself excluding God in creation from his sympathies. Yet the world, too, is a manifestation of God and, therefore, of His love.

God's presence is everywhere. To despise creation is self-limiting. The yogi should behold all things as part of the one, infinite Self. Even evil people are struggling, albeit ignorantly at present, to find happiness, which they will realize at last is their own, true nature.

Everything one does has a certain potential, however slight, for danger. People have died from slipping in their bathtubs! The danger on the path of meditation is that the yogi may become absorbed, not in his true Self, but in his little ego. Such a person becomes ego-centered instead of God-centered. This is why devotion to God as a separate Reality from oneself is advised even in the Vedanta teachings. An "I-Thou" relationship helps one to avoid the trap, yawning wide for the unwary, of identifying their egos with the Infinite Self. Adi Swami Shankaracharya himself, the supreme *advaitin* or non-dualist, wrote poems expressing adoration to the Divine Mother.

A serious problem for those who seek fulfillment only in their little egos, rejecting completely their true identity with the Infinite Self in which ego-consciousness disappears, is that they lose touch with true principles. Such a person inclines to take more and more whatever he can from others, forgetting that he shares with all beings the same, universal reality.

Most people, in fact, are not aware that a nonmaterial reality exists. The world calls to them in silvery, siren tones: "Come! Make your own pleasure your entire reality!" When suffering comes to them—as it must in this world of duality—they have no notion of where to turn for help—unless it be some "professional" who is powerless to bring them the true solace they need. They've lost conscious contact with their inner homeland of joy and freedom. They feel themselves swept along, therefore, like pebbles down a raging stream, tumbled helplessly about by events over which they have no control. Young people may imagine sometimes that they'll be able to manipulate the outer events in their lives. As they grow older, however, they find themselves involved, instead, in a dog-eat-dog fight for survival.

"How can I be honest," they ask themselves, "with so many people doing their utmost to take advantage of me? How can I live by high principles, and still make an adequate living? How can I, on my wages, put my son through college so that he, in turn, can help to support our family? How can I be scrupulously truthful, when I know there are many who would eagerly use the very truths I tell to do me harm?"

A shopkeeper may sell a product in the knowledge that it is unreliable or even defective. Perhaps he hopes that his customer won't be too disappointed. Indeed, he may not really care one way or the other, justifying his misdeeds by reasoning, "Well, a person has to live, doesn't he?" In the struggle to keep his head above water as he swims with the stream, his motto becomes, *"Me first."* Like the rat in that children's fable, *Charlotte's Web*, his criterion in every circumstance is, "What's in it for me?"

The pebbles in a stream become gradually rounded by rubbing against one another. Wisdom too, shines more and more clearly as the little pebble of the ego gets smoothed by the constant rubbing together of success and failure, joy and disappointment, gain and loss. The maturing ego comes in time to understand the ancient Sanskrit saying, *"Yato dharma, tato jaya*: Where there is right action, there is victory." Unrighteous behavior brings only failure, disappointment, and grim karmic retribution in the end.

The *Sankhya* philosophy analyzes and exposes the errors of delusion. *Vedanta* teaches the eternal nature of reality, yet states that philosophy alone cannot bestow the certainty that is born of experience. Only *yoga* teaches the way out of delusion: how to walk firmly, without stumbling, in the raging waters of *maya*, in full command of one's life and inwardly singing with joy.

Yoga principles applied to the field of action will be the primary focus of these lessons. Lofty teachings need to be externalized in daily life, and not taken inside only, in meditation. This need for balance is important especially in modern life. The purpose of this course, then, is to bridge the gap between two realities—the inner and the outer.

For material success to be more assured and lasting, it must be paired with high principles. The science of yoga proves these principles to be dynamically valid. In these lessons you will learn how to direct your activities from your inner center, and to control your whole life from that center. In a word, as you practice these lessons you will find yourself becoming a *cause*, and no longer a passive *effect*. You will cease being a pebble tumbled helplessly down the stream of life by circumstances.

The yoga teachings offer principles and practices, not pious maxims. They show convincingly why everyone should practice them. And they offer practical guidelines to a better, more fulfilled life, both outwardly and inwardly.

Such was the message which my great Guru, Paramhansa Yogananda, brought to the world. The yoga he taught was twofold: the path to inner enlightenment, and important secrets, also, for achieving outer success.

It is my hope—indeed, my fond expectation—that these lessons will help you to be successful in every aspect of your life.

LESSON ONE

DHARMA AS THE KEY TO SUCCESS

> The primary purpose of karma is to instruct people, by punishment and reward, . . . in the way of upward evolution. . . . *Dharmic*, or righteous, action on the one hand, and *adharmic*, or unrighteous, action on the other, affect *present-day* success or failure.

The Principles

Swami Sri Yukteswar Giri, my Paramguru, was quoted in Paramhansa Yogananda's *Autobiography of a Yogi* as making the statement, "So long as you breathe the free air of earth, you are under obligation to render grateful service."

Sri Yukteswar himself, under other circumstances, might have asked, "Who is serving whom?" The "air of earth" is simply there; it comes with living on this planet. Where then—he might have asked rhetorically also—is the need for gratitude? The fact is, everything in the universe is consciously manifested, and with love. Nothing in it is irrational, though sometimes it seems so to human intelligence. To man there seems no reason for disease, for example, or for a baby being born blind, or for someone to fail financially who is capable and intelligent—or, for that matter, for someone else to achieve outstanding success who seems not to have done anything to earn it. One naturally asks, Why be grateful without reason?

The answer is twofold: First, as we shall see, there is indeed cause in the sense that there is a consciousness which receives our gratitude and responds to it; and, second, because to express gratitude is self-ennobling.

Sri Yukteswar said also that karmic law, though it functions to a great extent automatically, is also guided by a universal intelligence, and love, and can also be intelligently manipulated or diverted. Hence the concept of divine grace—*kripa*, in Sanskrit—is common to most religions. *Kripa* can be won above all by divine devotion and love.

Finally, we should be grateful for life itself. Gratitude, in this case, transcends reason; after all—one might say—we exist: why be grateful for the fact? Gratitude, properly understood, has no *reason*: It is simply an aspect of the pure joy of our existence—so much a part of it that one can hardly be distinguished from the other.

Success in life depends on how faithfully we follow the principles of karmic law. The primary purpose of karma is to instruct people, by punishment and reward, and also in a general way to lead all life, in the way of upward evolution. There is no animus or favoritism in the functioning of karma. Whatever happens in life, and even in lifeless-seeming matter, is a response to energy projected. Karma is simply, in this sense, the working of Newton's law: for every action there is an equal and opposite reaction.

The difficulty modern man has is with accepting, for animate creatures, laws that seem to him to apply only to mechanisms. Modern science has biased people in favor of viewing the whole universe as inanimate and unconscious. Modern biology, for example, has strengthened this bias by making evolution itself out to be an accident, and by demonstrating that inert matter reacts to stimuli in essentially the same way as nerves do. In approaching this proven fact with a materialistic bias, one naturally concludes that nothing, really, is either conscious or alive.

The weakness of this conclusion lies in its absurdity: the obvious self-contradiction that it takes *consciousness* to arrive at that conclusion, and, furthermore, that it takes *living beings* to be interested in this point in the first place!

It is easier, however, for people to believe that the law of karma works on a human level than that it works on inanimate objects. It is not difficult to see the possible justice of a baby being born blind—especially if, along with the law of karma, we accept its companion principle, the law of reincarnation. It is more difficult to see karma working in apparently automatic matters, such as the fall of a shooting star. Yet Newton's laws of motion point to cause and effect working also on apparently "inanimate" objects.

Newton was a religious-minded man. He was hampered in giving voice to that fact because his beliefs contradicted many of the dogmas both of formal religion and of science, which already had begun to manifest signs of the bigotry until then encountered primarily in religion. (It wasn't religion itself, of course, nor politics, nor science, nor any other system of belief that engendered bigotry and dogmatism: It was, simply, human nature!) Any spiritual overtones in Newton's "equal and opposite force" theory would have been totally excluded by the scientists of his day, as they would have been "on principle" by the religionists.

The real problem with religion, from a scientific viewpoint, has been its anthropomorphism: giving the Infinite Lord the human form of Lord Krishna, for example, or equating Him to His "son," Jesus Christ—none of which is compatible with modern findings that the universe contains countless billions of galaxies, each of them composed of many billions of stars. Newton himself did not doubt the existence of a divine consciousness in the universe. Nor did the ancient teachings of India, of which Vedanta is, in this case, a prime example. Newton was obliged by the dogmas of modern science to exclude God from his reckoning. Otherwise, everything he taught would simply have excluded him from both groups: scientific, and religious.

His findings fitted into the scientific system of discovery by investigation, which automatically excluded the religious system of beliefs that were based entirely on scripture-based dogmas. Therefore, he could make his discoveries blend in with only one of these groups; obviously, his natural milieu was that of the physicists of his day.

When it comes to a sophisticated understanding of such cosmic matters, the ancient wise men, or *rishis*, of India were far more knowledgeable than modern science. This truth is observable in the fact that modern science is moving closer and closer to that same ancient knowledge, which for centuries was rejected in the West as both irreligious and unscientific.

J.H.F. Umbgrove, the geologist, in his scientific work, *Symphony of the Earth*, wrote, "Nobody can foresee whether these modern speculations [on the problems of life and matter] will ever be susceptible to condensation into a social or religious system. Remarkably enough, however, they remind one of certain aspects of the Brahmanese Upanishads."

The concern of modern science has always been with proofs, based on investigation and experimentation. On this level, it is easy enough to prove that Newton's laws work: They are valid. They also express, on a material level, many aspects of the law of karma. It is more difficult to see Newton's laws at work in those aspects of karmic law that apply to human beings and to other forms of conscious life. Is it possible that a law of recompense deals with human activities? On a level both of Newton's laws and of man's own sense of justice, karmic law is surely worth more than a few idle moments of casual contemplation. Modern science has a long distance to travel before it will even consider the merits of karmic law as applied to human life. Yet the experience of wise men in India for thousands of years, and a close view of human history as we know it from careful investigation, surely provide enough factual evidence to make anyone who aspires to material success consider very seriously whether *dharmic*, or righteous, action on the one hand, and *a-dharmic*, or unrighteous, action on the other, affect *present-day* success or failure. For there are many *observable* facts that cannot be airily dismissed on dogmatic grounds.

I add to those facts my own Guru's wisdom, which I soon recognized was profound, though much of it contradicted my own thoroughly Westernized education. I do not offer what he, and what many other great yogis, declared as proof of my thesis. I offer it as impressive *additional support* for a law that I propose to present in evidential terms.

America's material success is an example of the karmic law working in man's favor. Many people believe that America's success has been due entirely to her material efficiency. Efficiency *is* important, no doubt. It is also, in its own way, a divine principle, for we see it displayed, for example, in the very process of evolution, which sifts that which works from that which doesn't work. (Hence, Darwin's "law of natural selection.") America's success is due also, far more than most of her citizens themselves realize, to two mental attitudes: faith in God, and a generous spirit.

A South American friend of mine pointed this fact out to me years ago. "Your country was started," he said, "by the Pilgrim Fathers, who came to your shores in a quest for spiritual freedom. Spain's motivation in invading Latin America, by contrast, was men's desire for gold. Your country has prospered from the beginning, but our countries have suffered for centuries from chaos and poverty."

During the 1960s, when America and Russia were competing to be the first to put a man on the moon, someone proposed an amusing suggestion. "What America should do," was the claim, "is spend enough money to put a dog on the moon and keep it alive there long enough for Americans to become aware of the poor creature's plight. They'll be so concerned for that animal's survival, they'll raise the money to bring it back to Earth again."

Karmic law is fair in the way it works. It is neither positive nor negative; in a sense, it is indifferent in the way it responds to human action by punishment and reward. There is an important indication, however, that its seeming indifference is only outward. Karmic law is, in fact, an expression of divine love. Thus, karma serves the true purpose of encouraging all beings—especially humans—to evolve spiritually.

Consider, as examples of the working of karma, the relative destinies of England and India. Marco Polo, who lived in the thirteenth century, traveled from his home in Venice, Italy, to China. On his return journey he passed through India, which he described in his book of travels as "the richest country in the world." Isn't it strange that England, soon after her mercantile adventurers arrived in India, became a great and powerful nation? India, during that same time period, sank to relative poverty. Does it seem superstition merely, to see in this seesawing of destinies a cause-and-effect relationship? England's centuries of absorbing wealth from other nations, and of returning to them hardly a tithe of the benefits she reaped from them, has surely been the karmic cause, at last, of her undoing. From the beginning of World War II, Paramhansa Yogananda said, "You will see, the karmic reason for this war is the abolition of the colonial system." As early as 1915, or thereabouts, he had already predicted, "India will be liberated in my lifetime, by peaceful means."

In 1950 I asked my Guru, "What is England's destiny?"

"England is finished!" he replied firmly. When I tried to get him to qualify that statement, he only repeated, "Finished!" England's good karma, dating possibly to ancient times, gave her the global success she achieved for some centuries. That good karma, however, seems now exhausted in the sense that—comparing her to a clock—she seems to be running down, her energy dwindling, and her very self-confidence, as evidenced in numerous novels that have been written in that country since World War II, ebbing.

Meanwhile, what about India? Have her recent centuries of poverty been karmic also? Yes, of course they have! What other reason could there be? Both success and failure are ruled by karmic law. India's downward course in recent centuries was due also, I believe, to the natural disintegrating influences of time. India had to experience the disruption through which all ancient civilizations passed. India alone however, out of all of them, has survived. The tallest mountains are eventually reduced by time to the level of lowland plains, and the low plains are raised up, again by time, to mountain heights.

Karma rules not only over human beings, but over stars, planets, and every living species. That karma which rules whole nations is known as mass karma. That which rules individual destiny is known as personal karma. Other kinds of karma there are: group karma, for example, which rules the destinies of less evolved creatures, and even, as I mentioned, those of seemingly inanimate objects. Consciousness it is, ultimately, that rules everything. It would be wise, then, in the pursuit of one's material ambitions, to accept that a cause-effect principle really does determine the consequences of how you treat others, and of how conscientiously you adhere, in your life, to truth and honesty.

A very positive example of group karma is evident in India's millennial history. Her devotion to spiritual truth has greatly strengthened her, karmically. India today is once again rising. Someday, my Guru said, India will join hands with America; the two countries, together, will lead the world on the path to material and spiritual prosperity.

The Law of Karma demands that whatever benefits one receives be, in some way, returned. One of those ways is by what Swami Sri Yukteswar counseled: "by rendering grateful service." Whatever goodness a person, or a nation, offers to others will bring expansion of consciousness in return: an expansion of sympathy, understanding and success. When one helps others to achieve prosperity, he attracts greater prosperity to himself. When he helps others to grow in understanding, he finds understanding deepening in himself. When one helps others to grow spiritually, that action brings him closer, himself, to spiritual enlightenment. The law works infallibly. Thus, in comparable measure, to *harm* others attracts similar harm to oneself.

One can offset a negative karma by generating an equal and opposite karma which thereby either deflects that negative energy or absorbs and nullifies it. Thus, if people for some reason turn against you and try to cause you harm, you can deflect or nullify their action by treating them kindly, instead of seeking revenge on them. A deflected karma may rebound on them, or, if you give it to God, it may serve you, yourself, as a *tapasya* (austerity, or penance), giving you great spiritual strength. Both to deflect and nullify that karma, the most important thing is not to let it affect your ego. This is done most completely by attaining the state of *jivan mukta*, which is the state in which no ego-consciousness remains to be affected. The karma generated by trying to harm you may, in that case, be simply dissolved in cosmic consciousness—even as a pebble, if dropped into the ocean, causes waves that expand indefinitely, but if dropped into a little pond of ego-consciousness, may create ripples that visibly expand until they reach the bank, then return, still visible, going back and forth until they subside altogether. If the people who tried to harm you did so with personal animus, they will attract that harm back to themselves, but if, on your side, you offer their animus to God, and return no negative energy of personal animus back to them, the consequence to them will be determined by how much their egos were engaged in their initial action.

I received dramatic corroboration of these various types of karma many years ago. Certain people tried, with a fury I'd had no notion they even felt, to destroy me by false accusations. Reflecting on the counsel of my Paramguru Sri Yukteswar to "render grateful service," it seemed to me that the only way to preserve my own integrity was to respond with gratitude—if not to them, then to life for helping me to grow spiritually no matter how they treated me. I made up my mind, indeed, to respond not only with gratitude, but with love. Was there some lesson I myself needed to learn? I knew of none, since it was my Guru himself who had given me the instructions they were controverting. Nevertheless, there *had* to be some benefit accruing to me from what must otherwise have been an unmitigated tragedy.

Strange to relate, over the years since then their anger toward me has increased. It has been as though my very forgiveness were, in their eyes, an insult revealing a major defect in my character. For myself, firm adherence to my Paramguru's and my Guru's teaching has brought me peace of mind, and a steady increase of inner joy. Moreover, I've been able to accomplish all that my Guru told me to do—activities which they'd done their best to block.

I have written many books in compliance with his personal instructions to me: eighty of them in all, so far. I have composed over 400 pieces of music, which he didn't commission specifically, though they helped advance his main instructions, which were to inspire people, and draw them to the spiritual path and to his teachings. I have also created seven spiritual communities, first in America and then in Europe—an activity that deeply interested him. Indeed, he pleaded repeatedly in public that people found such communities. (When, in response to his oft-repeated plea, I vowed I would do my utmost to fulfill that wish, he said to me, "You have a great work to do, Walter.") My present hope is to create similar communities in India.

All the profit from my books and recordings has gone toward building those communities, where at present some one thousand people live together in great peace and harmony.

In recent years, those friends (as I sincerely view them) who tried to engineer my undoing have made greater efforts than ever to complete their efforts by legal action. At a time when our Ananda communities were in great need of funds with which to combat these efforts, we somehow managed not only to survive, but to flourish.

In response to their more recent efforts, I wrote and published a little book called *Do*

---

* Walter was his "pet" name for me. [Publisher's note: "Walter" was a variation on Kriyananda's family name of "Walters." "Kriyananda" was a monastic name assumed after Yogananda's passing.]

It NOW!, which offers spiritual and practical sayings for every day of the year. Though our monetary needs were urgent, I felt inspired all the same to get this book read by as many people as possible. Therefore I decided to give it away free, and invested my own money for the printing of 5,000 copies, which were distributed free.

Was it wise of me—and, in light of the subject of these lessons, was it *practical*—to be generous when our needs were so desperate? Some people might well consider my deed irresponsible. However, I knew I could reach 5,000 people directly—people who knew and appreciated what Ananda was doing. Therefore, I myself don't call it at all impractical! Indeed, I can add that *something* did work for us, for Ananda Sangha emerged from that struggle stronger than ever. People appreciated that gift of the book, and Ananda Sangha, over the years, has become widely respected.

It is always good to be generous. Yet—to answer the question I posed in the last paragraph—one *must* be practical. That is to say, one should do what *works*, and one should also be generous *within his means*. What I want to say above all, then, is, *Keep a generous attitude* even if you haven't the means to be generous in other, more material ways.

I have sought steadfastly over the years to put into practice my Guru's and my Paramguru's advice to "render grateful service." Life has shown me that generosity works much better than the modern advice to "be competitive!" Indeed, I've come to prefer another word: "comparative." Yes, one should be practical; when pricing an item, for example, that you as a merchant may want to sell, take into account the cost of similar products on the market, the location of your shop, the prosperity (or lack thereof) of your customers, and other mundane considerations. Pricing, in this case, must be *comparative*. To price items *competitively*, however, suggests to mind a will to beat down the opposition. Why do that? He never truly flourishes who tries to harm others.

Sometimes I reflect on the karma created not by trying to harm others, only, but also by trying to get as much as possible out of them for *nothing*. There are people, as we know, who beg for a living. Such people try to get something for nothing. This is the unspoken desire of many if not of most people. Whether one is literally a beggar or not, anyone who tries to get something for nothing is also, in a sense, a beggar. To try to get something for nothing is bad karma. Naturally, it is unfortunate for anyone to be poor, but poverty is also a consequence of bad karma, and generates, in turn, more bad karma. It is important to try to change that downward spiral. One way of stopping it is to show compassion actively toward those who are less fortunate than oneself.

In India, many people believe that spiritual teaching is an exception to this rule. Such teaching, they insist, should always be given freely. This belief is a misunderstanding of karmic Law. To insist on one's *right* to receive *anything* without offering anything in return depletes one, karmically. What *should* be free is the willingness to *help* others through spiritual teaching, without the desire for recompense. If one receives such teaching freely, he should at least have an attitude, and better still offer some expression, of appreciation.

Forty-five years ago in East Patelnagar, a district of New Delhi and at least at that time a wealthy neighborhood, I gave a Kriya Yoga initiation. One of the envelopes offered as "*dakshina*" revealed its contents, afterward, to be only one *naya paisa*. Apart from the insult implied by such a minuscule donation, I couldn't help wondering whether that person had received any blessing from God. I myself felt I had sinned by allowing anyone to cheapen the great blessing of that initiation. My error, which needs to be included in this story, was not first to have tested that person's sincerity. Afterward, of course, I had no way of knowing who that person was, and could only pray that God would forgive him and give him blessings anyway.

The "quid pro quo" attitude that is commonly attributed to merchants demeans, in a sense, both the one who gives and the one who receives. I have often, in order to affirm my own integrity, given teachings to people who told me they could not afford to pay for them. Generally, I have found out later that they could easily have afforded the cost. Though I have never stopped this practice, it has been for my own conscience. I suspect it was only I who gained, in such cases.

To give freely is to practice *nishkam karma*: "action without desire for the fruits of one's action." Such was the teaching of Lord Krishna in the Bhagavad Gita. To demand that one be *given* spiritual teachings, however, as one's right, and to give nothing in return, is a karmic mistake. Nothing should ever be accepted without giving *something* in return. It is not wrong even to charge money for spiritual lessons, provided the fees are reasonable, and go to help a good cause.

My Guru charged for the lessons he gave. He charged only a reasonable amount, and used the money toward building his spiritual work in America. Moreover, he always took into account a person's ability to pay. When they told him they could pay nothing, he charged nothing.

I also have followed his practice. Over many years, however, I have observed that those who gave nothing also received nothing of real value to them.

In the case of merchants, of course, they are obviously, and quite properly, working for a profit. Their *attitude*, however—as I shall discuss in later lessons—should be one of service to others as well as seeking personal gain. Business itself should, in addition to being for profit, serve the additional purpose of returning gratitude to the universe for, as Sri Yukteswar put it, "the free air of earth."

I remember a time, when I was eighteen years of age, deciding I would like to learn the art of singing. Many had urged me to take up singing as a career. Thinking at least to "test the waters," I went to a singing teacher of high repute. She was an old lady who, years earlier, had been a well-known singer of classical music. I was impressed when she declared firmly in advance, "The lessons will be five dollars each. It isn't that I need the money: I don't. It is *you* who need to pay it."

Babaji Maharaj, the paramguru of Swami Sri Yukteswar, also instructed Lahiri Mahasaya (Sri Yukteswar's guru) to charge Rupees five for Kriya Yoga initiation. It was the students themselves who needed to pay, not Lahiri Mahasaya who needed the money. Indeed, the money he received went toward helping the poor.

In my own case, though I wanted to study singing, and didn't have those five dollars a week to pay for them, I didn't like asking my father to pay that money. I therefore took a job waiting tables one evening a week at a local restaurant. Thus, I managed to cover the cost of tuition.

In the ancient *Gurukul* system of India, students paid for the teaching they received in accordance with their ability to pay. The more a person gives generously of himself—to God, to life, to the very universe, and not to individuals only—the more karmic law supports him in return.

Years ago, an interviewer on a television program asked me, "What have you done in 'practical' ways to make Ananda successful?" I had been speaking of our spiritual ideals.

With conviction born of long experience I replied: "Faith *is* practical. As a matter of fact, the basic purpose of the yoga teachings is to make religion itself *practical*. Even material success is most likely to be assured when one applies spiritual principles to whatever one does. To answer your question then, yes, we *have* been practical. We've created businesses, offered retreats, published books, traveled around the country giving lessons. All these things have helped us materially, as a community, as well as giving help to others. But to return to my first theme this evening, I have also learned by experience that faith, if one exercises it for the benefit of others and not only for himself, is the most practical thing of all."

The Application

The following four paragraphs are excerpted from my book, *Hope for a Better World!* They are a commonsense analysis of Adam Smith's philosophy of free enterprise.

Adam Smith's general thesis was that every human being is motivated primarily by self-interest. A nation's prosperity, he said, will soar if it gives people the freedom to improve their own lot. "It is not," he wrote, "from the benevolence of the butcher, the brewer, or the baker that we expect our dinner, but from their regard to their own interest. We address ourselves, not to their humanity, but to their self-love, and never talk to them of our own necessities, but of their advantages." Passages like this caused an outcry among *soi-disant* champions of morality, though in fact Smith had simply stated an obvious truth. He was comparing self-interest to false morality, which bases generosity and benevolence entirely on self-denial. Smith was right, of course. Morality, as people usually define it, is hypocrisy. No one will really help another if, in doing so, he expects only to become miserable. Self-sacrifice for others should be for the sake of a greater good. If it benefits oneself also—perhaps only in terms of inner satisfaction—it is not a sacrifice, so much, as a joy. Smith erred only, as many self-styled moralists have done, by not humanizing his subject enough. He didn't focus with sufficient clarity on the people's actual needs, as human beings.

He gave us specific examples—the butcher, the brewer, the baker—to support his argument. What he didn't give were human beings. He gave us two-dimensional tradesmen. It might have helped had he given those tradesmen names, personalities, families.

Let us make up for this "sin of omission." We'll name the baker, William—surname, Baker. And we'll assume the presence of another one in town, whom we'll name Joe—surname, Crumpet. Let us be even more specific. William concentrates only on the advantages accruing to himself while he sells bread, whereas Joe, though fully aware that he is earning a living, has other considerations besides. He greets you with a smile, treats you as a friend, asks after your family, hopes that you've enjoyed his products, and perhaps solicits your advice on how to improve them.

Let us now assume—what is probably the case anyway—that William wears a perennially grim expression, that he has poor digestion, and is always bitter about something. Joe, on the other hand, is warmhearted, healthy, and happy. Isn't it likely that, quite apart from economic considerations—since their products must surely be priced more or less the same—you'll shop at Joe's, and will shun William's as a bad omen?

These are human, not merely mercantile, considerations. We must remember that even in monetary matters we are usually, in the last analysis, dealing with human beings. If we think only of our cash profits, and pay little or no attention to the service we render others, we may well find our cash inflow becoming reduced to a trickle.

I had an interesting experience on these lines several years ago. I entered a shop in Taormina, Italy. The owner, a woman slightly advanced in age, displayed along with other items a selection of hats. The weather was chilly, and I thought it might be good to get some sort of covering for my head.

"Which of these hats," I asked her, "do your customers like the best?"

"How should I know?" she asked indifferently. "I take their money, and they leave. That's an end to it as far as I'm concerned." Even her hat display showed none of the care one might expect of a shopkeeper who wanted her customers to like what they bought. The thought occurred to me, "This poor lady needs help!"

"My goodness!" I exclaimed. "Here you sit all day, thinking only of the cash you take in? How do you expect to be happy? Wouldn't your life be more enjoyable if you viewed each customer as a potential friend?"

Interestingly, I met this same woman again a year later during a return visit to Taormina. I hadn't meant to go into her shop, but she was standing outside it as I passed. She saw me, and greeted me effusively. Much to my surprise, she then gave me a big welcoming hug, in the Italian fashion.

The hotel where I and a few friends were staying had given us a bottle of wine as their way of thanking us for returning to them. None of us drank alcohol, but I thought, "Perhaps that lady will appreciate this gift." I took the bottle to her, and as I handed it to her she actually burst into tears. Then, again in the Italian fashion, she kissed me on both cheeks. Evidently, my words to her the year before had, with God's grace, affected her profoundly.

What about *you*, then, no matter whether you earn your living as a shopkeeper or by some other means? The same principles apply; they are universally valid. The more you think in terms of serving others rather than of using them to your own advantage, the more you will find these high principles working *for* you. Please, try it!

As my Guru often said, "If a thousand businessmen would view their work as a service to others, each would have nine hundred and ninety-nine friends. But if, instead, they all chose to see one another as competitors, each of them would have—at least potentially—nine hundred and ninety-nine enemies."

MEDITATION

While practicing the following exercise, don't think of people as individuals, lest their facial expressions distract you from the feelings you are to project. Think, rather, of the energy that *you* are sending out.

Visualize yourself centered in the heart. Mentally polish your heart like a silver orb, until it shines.

Now, see rays of light reflected off the surface of that orb radiating outward in all directions. Mentally see those rays reaching out and touching the hearts of human beings everywhere. See the light filling each person, and all life forms, with radiance and joy.

Meditate on the divine light shining outward from your heart to all souls, everywhere.

Now, see that light as a reflection coming to you from above, from its true source in God. The light you share is His gift to all, through you.

AFFIRMATION

"I will serve Thee in all, as extensions of my own true Self."

POINTS TO REMEMBER

1. "So long as you breathe the free air of earth, you are under obligation to render grateful service."

2. Karmic law, though it functions to a great extent automatically, is also guided by a universal intelligence and love, and can be intelligently manipulated or diverted. Divine grace, or *kripa*, can be won above all by divine devotion and love.

3. The primary purpose of karma is to instruct people, by punishment and reward, in the way of upward evolution. *Dharmic*, or righteous, action on the one hand, and *adharmic*, or unrighteous, action on the other, affect *present-day* success or failure.

4. America's example of material success is due, far more than most realize, to two mental attitudes: faith in God, and a generous spirit.

5. Karmic law is fair in the way it works. Karmic law is, in fact, an expression of divine love.

6. The Law of Karma demands that whatever benefits one receives be, in some way, returned. When one helps others to achieve prosperity, he attracts greater prosperity to himself. Thus, in comparable measure, to *harm* others attracts similar harm to oneself.

7. One can offset a negative karma by generating an equal and opposite karma which thereby either deflects that negative energy or absorbs and nullifies it. The most important thing is not to let the karma affect your ego.

8. It is always good to be generous *within your means. Keep a generous attitude* even if you haven't the means to be generous in other, more material ways.

9. In business matters, be "comparative" instead of "competitive." To be "competitive" suggests trying to beat down the opposition. He never truly flourishes who tries to harm others.

10. Anyone who tries to get something for nothing is, in a sense, a beggar. To try to get something for nothing is bad karma.

11. Spiritual teachings should be offered in a spirit of *nishkam karma*: "action without desire for the fruits of one's action." It is a karmic mistake, however, to *receive* that teaching without offering something in return. It is not wrong even to charge money for spiritual lessons, provided the fees are reasonable, and go to help a good cause.

12. The more a person gives generously of himself—to God, to life, to the very universe—the more karmic law supports him in return.

13. Faith *is* practical. Even material success is most likely to be assured when one applies spiritual principles to whatever one does.

14. The more you think in terms of serving others rather than of using them to your own advantage, the more you will find these high principles working *for* you.

WORKBOOK IDEAS
by Joseph Bharat Cornell

Life Responds in Kind

Paramhansa Yogananda appeared in a dream some time ago to a young Brazilian woman named Roberta during a visit she paid to Ananda Village. The Master spoke only *one* word to Roberta, but it changed her life and countless others. A year later, Roberta invited an Ananda minister to lecture at her university. During his visit, that minister heard many times from Roberta's graduate faculty advisors and colleagues about how her presence and loving nature had transformed her university department.

What was the one word Yogananda spoke to Roberta? It was . . . *"Give!"*

Roberta took Paramhansa Yogananda's advice to heart, and decided to dedicate herself to serving others. The fruits of her giving were many, from the loving atmosphere she created to the profound loyalty she inspired in others. The most important benefit of all, however, was the expanded consciousness and happiness that the act of giving gave to her.

"When one helps others achieve prosperity, he attracts prosperity to himself."

ACTION ITEMS:

- Focus more on giving than receiving.
- Make the word "Give" your mantra.
- At the beginning of every day, ask yourself, "How can I help a specific person or situation?" Then act on your inspiration.
- Throughout the day, ask yourself continually, "How can I contribute uplifting and positive energy to this situation?"
- Observe how acts of service expand your consciousness and sense of identification with others. Note how people and situations respond to the energy you project.

Offer the Most Value

Focus less on your competition and more on perfecting the usefulness of your service or product. If you do this, your energy will be directed inward and will remain positive and expansive. Your customers, too, will appreciate your thoughtfulness and will reciprocate loyalty to you.

ACTION ITEMS:

Ask yourself the following questions:

- How can I make my product and service more useful to others?
- How can I create the most enjoyable environment and experience for my customers?

- People will pay for value, but value can mean many things. What can I do to add value beyond the benefits themselves of the product or service that I offer?

Ananda's East West Bookshop customers often visit the store just to be in its uplifting atmosphere. Many customers tell us that the store is, for them, like a place of pilgrimage!

Change Your Karma

The best way to overcome one's karma is to meet it calmly and pleasantly. In the midst of karmic difficulties, concentrate not on your problem or present situation, which will only strengthen it, but on generating a strong flow of positive energy.

ACTION ITEM:
1. Avoid blaming others, or Life, for what happens to you.
2. See people or events as merely the instruments of your karma, to teach you.
3. Accept responsibility for your actions, past and present.
4. Generate an equal and opposite karma which will deflect any negative energy.
5. Remember, the more conscious energy you generate, positively, the sooner your bad karma will be nullified.
6. Ask God to bless your efforts.

LESSON TWO

HOW TO MAGNETIZE MONEY

One thing I can say with confidence: Success begins, certainly, by having the *right* attitude, and by putting forth the *right* energy.

The Principles

Money is a thing, merely—a medium of exchange. We give it energy by the expectations we project onto it. Otherwise, it has no energy or magnetism of its own. To some people, it comes effortlessly. I remember a well-to-do lady from Australia remarking to me quite casually, "Money's easy to make. It's never been a problem for me." The way she said that might make many people envy her "luck," though it wasn't really luck at all. She simply had good money karma. Many other people, to their misfortune, have quite the opposite: No matter how hard they work, prosperity, for them, remains elusive.

The father of a friend of mine in college made his living by advising people on their investments. A number of his clients became wealthy by following his advice. He himself, however, although never poor, could not achieve their level of financial success. Success in every field is determined, ultimately, by karmic law. My friend's father, although fully conversant with the principles of investment, and able to make others rich, hadn't the personal karmic magnetism to attract wealth.

Considering the important role karma plays in these matters, some people ask, "What's the use of even *trying* to be successful? Isn't success just 'written in the stars'—an inevitability?" Is there truth in that question? Is success-karma, as people like that believe, a decree of *kismet*?

Emphatically not!

The power of a particular karma is determined by two factors: energy, and will power. Those same two factors can change our karma. We set it in motion in the first place by our own energy and will power: We can change that motion, again, by our own energy and will power. In fact, because karma means action, it may also be *described* as motion. We need not be its passive recipients, unless we choose to be: We can be those who determine what it shall be. We can, for example, mitigate it by developing a new, good karma in some other field of activity. We can nullify it by using our very flaws of the past in a new and better way.

For instance, if in the past we tried to hurt people by unkind acts, we can devote all our energy and will power to helping and uplifting others. If we fought with armies to conquer countries in battle, we can work intensely, now, to bring peace to mankind by "fighting" for it in non-violent ways, like the heroic feats, in our times, of Mahatma Gandhi.

Indeed, it is entirely possible that Gandhi himself was expiating past deeds of violence by his extraordinary example of non-violence in the present life. It is more likely, however, that he paid off those old sins several times over in former lives, for it takes lifetimes of good karma to develop the power he showed in going into hostile places and converting people, contrary to their desires and convictions, to paths of kindness, tolerance, and love.

Never forget that the worst of sinners can—indeed, must—become a saint someday: not because God will *force* him to become good, but because he himself will at last recognize, in the search for happiness that is everyone's quest in life, that what he has really been seeking is not outward gratification, but the inner joy of his own being. The happiness he has sought in things has been with him always, inside his own Self. Such is the destiny of every human being—and, in the long span of cosmic time, of every creature. We came from the Infinite: Someday, we will *ourselves* want to rediscover our identity with the Infinite.

If someone was a merchant in a past life who cheated people, in this life he can burn up that bad karma by devoting great energy and will power to using the skills he developed in the business world to helping others in the present.

Karma can be mitigated, or lessened, but if one wants really to change it and to nullify its harmful effects, there is a simple principle to remember: The more *energy* and *will power* you put into changing that karma, the sooner and the more completely you'll be able to wipe the slate clean.

Think of the example of Valmiki. He was an evil man, but he was also strong in his evil. What he did, in the end, was use that very strength to cling the more ardently to God. And because he couldn't even call to God at first, he was taught how to turn his very rejection of God into an obsession with Him, which—because God is Love itself—caught him up in the whirlwind of divine love!

Whatever skills you have, and however you developed and used them in the past, use them now for good. The more energetically you do that, with will power, the more quickly you will expiate any wrongs you may have done in the past, to become a shining example for all.

For there is another feature of this inner transformation: The more positive energy you put out, the more positive energy it will attract to itself. What seems difficult to develop in the beginning becomes easier and easier, until the slowest nag plodding heavily through busy streets becomes a racehorse: the sinner becomes a saint, and the failure in life becomes a radiant example of success!

Don't imagine that any goal you set yourself in life will be the end of the story once you achieve that end. Don't fix your sights with blinders, like those on horses, seeing only the road ahead. There are many wonderful discoveries to be made on your way to perfection. Even your present material ambitions will be achieved more gloriously if you don't tie them all to a single post.

Bad karma can be overcome above all by *rechanneling* the energy it once directed inward toward oneself. It can be overcome by expanding it outward by helping others.

The effects of bad karma can be changed by removing the subconscious blocks of uncertainty and doubt, placed there by inner conflicts as to what you really want in life, and what you really were. Once your energy is turned and directed one-pointedly toward that which you want to do, you can release great energy within yourself for constructive action.

I remember a fellow disciple of mine whose brother, an intelligent, capable man, had never been able to achieve success in his work. Our Guru "de-jinxed" him by removing a certain energy block from the man's consciousness. From then on, the man's business flourished. Guruji never explained to us what that block had been, nor even why he had seen fit to remove it: These are subtle matters which can be best understood by introspection. We need, that is to say, to apply them to our own lives. What blocks are there in ourselves, for example, that prevent us from fulfilling our desires?

In the end, we usually discover that the solution required embodies universal principles, and is not so difficult to sift out. Any block to positive energy can be removed by focusing energy *concentratedly* in the direction you want your energy to flow. Consider the laser: Even light, intensely concentrated, can perform, for instance, wonders of surgery.

That story about the man my Guru "de-jinxed" raises several interesting questions: Was this man simply ready to receive added assistance in a struggle that he was already winning? Another person might not have been ready for that assistance. For it is ever the divine way to work *with* man's will, never *against* it. There must be complete consent *in the subconscious* before a saint will consent to assist him. Certainly it isn't that my Guru went about scattering success-karma, like largesse to the multitudes!

At the same time, I do recall that when people prayed to him for help, things often did go extraordinarily well for them. My wish in this course of lessons, however, is not to steer you to some saint so that you can give him all your problems. My wish is to show you how you can strengthen *your own success karma*. I want, in addition, to give you faith that you *can* do so! God Himself, however, needs the complete consent of your own will before He can bless you. The secret of all understanding is to work outward from the center of every situation, not from the periphery.

Karma is not a road down which one coasts as far as it will take him. "Coasting" will accomplish nothing for you. A memory springs to mind that fits this image perfectly. Years ago I was driving up Skyline Drive to San Francisco from the peninsula to the south. Suddenly my car started "coughing" and making stuttering sounds, such as cars make when their petrol tanks are nearly empty. Ahead of me I saw an off-ramp, and took it hoping for the best. I found myself on a stretch of road leading a long distance downhill; I must have coasted down it for at least two miles. No traffic lights or stop signs intervened, fortunately.

Just as the road was starting to level off, I saw a petrol station on the other side. This meant I'd have to cross the road, possibly meeting cars coming in the opposite direction. No such difficulty presented itself. The moment I reached the petrol pump and was just about to apply the brakes, the petrol ran out completely; the car stopped of its own accord, right by the pump. Miraculous? More likely, a coincidence, albeit a most pleasing one. I've found that amazing "coincidences" like that do happen when I call on God for help, which I was doing then.

It is always a question of *focused energy*: not of coasting, but of intensely generating the power to direct your own life. Even in that story, which involved coasting literally, I myself had to steer the car, to look for solutions, to remain in neutral gear (I forgot to mention that) so as not to use petrol unnecessarily, and, finally, to pray strongly, with faith, and not in a lackluster manner.

Another occasion springs to mind: I had a reservation to fly from Los Angeles to Oakland to give a lecture, and was meditating in a darkened room. In another hour (so I thought) a friend was going to drive with me to the airport. The telephone rang. This was on a weekend, at an hour when no one usually phoned me. I thought it was my friend who must have mistaken the time. Because the room was in darkness, I looked at the luminous dial on my watch; it reassured me that I still had an hour before our departure for the airport. The phone rang two or three more times. Finally I turned on the light, to discover that I had turned my forearm the wrong way: It was well *past* the time I had planned to leave. I hastily telephoned two more friends to come with us to the airport—one to look out the back window for police cars, the second out the left window, the third out the right window. Then, as the saying goes, "I drove like mad." I also prayed—though not, I hope, "like mad"! There were about seventeen traffic lights on the way—lying in ambush, possibly? Every one of them was green! I rushed into the airport lobby spilling coins out of my pocket as I took out the ticket. I was told at the counter that the gate was just about to close, but the people at the gate agreed to hold everything two more minutes—enough time for me to get there if I sprinted. I arrived just in time to stumble up the steps onto the plane!

It is easy to think that this, too, was just a coincidence, and not the result of some special good karma, or of divine intervention. After a lifetime, however, of many and even far more extraordinary events, it has become increasingly easy for me to believe that special blessings *are* part of the equation of success. One thing I can say with confidence: Success begins, certainly, by having the *right* attitude, and by putting forth the *right* energy.

People don't realize that faith simply means working *with* an energy and a will *that are already there*. There is a subtle power in the universe that we can lock in to, like plugging an electric cord into a wall socket. An all-important point to consider is *motivation*. When one does anything with ulterior motives, he dissipates his energy by pretending to be doing a thing while really doing or wanting something else. Few people, I suspect, have considered the story of Valmiki as he relates it himself in the *Ramayana*, how very straightforward he was even in his villainy.

Let us review that account briefly without going into it at length, since that story is so well known. Valmiki set out in life as a highway robber. One day he encountered a group of saints, and demanded their money. When he found they hadn't any, he told them that they'd left him no choice but to kill them.

Why, they asked, had he chosen this sure path to perdition? When he explained that he had a wife and family to support, and that this was his way of doing it, they inquired further, "Why don't you ask them if they are willing to share not only your ill-gotten gains, but also the bad karma you're reaping?" Valmiki, after extracting a promise from them to remain at that spot until he returned, went home and asked his family how they felt about that question the saints had put him. They were outraged that he would want them to share his bad karma as well. "How you earn your money is your business, not ours," was their reply. Valmiki, equally outraged by their response, returned to the saints and asked to be converted to their company.

I can't help suspecting a certain amount of hyperbole in this story, as well as a radical abbreviation of what really happened. Nevertheless, Valmiki's straightforward sincerity even in his villainy showed a singleness of purpose that helped him, eventually, to become a saint and the author of one of India's great spiritual legacies. One cannot succeed in life without single-minded purpose. Whatever you are doing, do it with all your heart. When earning money, do that also the same way, following the principles presented in these lessons. For if when dealing with a customer, for example, you pretend to be helping him, but in your mind you are thinking, "Money! Profit!" you will be working at cross purposes with yourself. You might as well sit in the street and hold out a hand, begging without even smiling in thanks to your generous donors.

True, the beggar's motivation seems single, but there is another rule here: Energy must be directed *outward*, away from one's self. Valmiki's was, for even when he was a robber he was thinking only of supporting his family. Later, when he redirected that outward-flowing energy expansively to God, he advanced quickly on the spiritual path. So also a person seeking material success will go much farther and much faster toward his goal if he doesn't think "Me—Me—Me!" all the time. In fact, it isn't possible to be single-mindedly selfish: Everyone who thinks only of personal gain will also be roaming restlessly in his mind in search of opportunities. What one achieves by single-mindedness is just the opposite: inward, calm determination.

Karma is energy that we ourselves set in motion, whether long ago or recently. The power of karma is determined by the *energy* we put into creating it in the first place. Strong will and energy create a strong karma. A deed, on the other hand, that is done without any real interest or feeling creates a relatively feeble karma. An action, moreover, in which the ego is not involved at all has very different consequences even if there is a mighty will behind it. Such is the case with *jivan muktas*: saints who have become free from all sense of "I and mine," and whose actions, therefore, attract no results back to themselves. Since the jivan mukta never does anything from ego-consciousness, the power of his actions flows outwardly, resulting in great benefit for all. Those karmas are not drawn magnetically back to their doer.

Karma can also be deflected, as I said, even as a steep downhill ski run can be done relatively safely if the skier goes down the slope crosswise, instead of straight down it. Bad karma can also be offset by intelligently creating an opposite, good karma. For such action to be directed wisely, a true guru, or spiritual teacher, is almost essential.

All action, finally, depends on the energy and strength of the *intention* behind it. In *Autobiography of a Yogi* there is a passage where Mukunda (Paramhansa Yogananda's boyhood name), in his anxiety to follow strictly the teaching of Patanjali on *ahimsa* (harmlessness), restrained his impulse to kill a mosquito. His guru Swami Sri Yukteswar asked him, "Why didn't you finish the job?"

"Master!" the disciple replied. "Do you advocate taking life?"

"No, but the deathblow already had been struck in your mind. Patanjali's meaning," the guru went on to explain, "was the removal of the *desire* to kill." (The disciple's thought processes had been an open book to him.) "This world," he added, "is inconveniently arranged for a literal practice of *ahimsa*. Man may be compelled to exterminate harmful creatures. He is not under similar compulsion to feel anger or animosity."

Karma depends above all, as I said, on the *intention* behind the deed. The debt of a minor sin, Sri Yukteswar explained, is incurred every time one finds it necessary to kill any of God's creatures. It is nevertheless right, he stated also, for man to keep pests like mosquitoes under control, for they can be a danger to human life. Human beings are more highly evolved, and for that reason must be considered first.

The contemplation of karmic law, with all its ramifications, is endlessly fascinating. I've given a few examples particularly for another reason: to show that the more conscious and intense the will *behind* an act, the stronger its consequences. The question of karma is, in fact, secondary to our present discussion. The point I want to make is that actions *now* can shatter old karmic patterns with fresh energy. Thus, they can change *any* obstructing influence in one's life.

No matter how skeptical a person is of karmic law, he surely will not challenge the scientifically demonstrated phenomenon of energy, for this phenomenon is known everywhere in the world. It seems self-evident, in light of this discussion, that in order to succeed one must put energy into whatever he wants to accomplish. No one can fly to the top of a mountain by merely wishing to be up there.

Think back to the example in Lesson One of William Baker and Joe Crumpet. Wouldn't Joe be far more successful in his work than William? Joe puts more energy into what he is doing. It is his energy that makes all the difference. My college friend's father couldn't succeed to the same degree as did those who followed his advice. There was a block in his energy-flow. In fact, recalling to mind the man himself, I remember him as being rather a low-energy person. Probably there was a certain unwillingness to put out energy, personally, that constituted his chief block to success. Often, a general lack of energy will manifest itself as lack, in a general sense. High energy, on the other hand, produces talent in many fields: in art, in music, in business, and virtually in anything in which one is interested. My friend's father had enough energy to give advice, but not enough to be single-minded in a sense of being productive.

Perhaps at some time in the past he had been successful, but selfish. If so, that could mean that in this life, if he was to achieve success he would first have to channel his energy outward once again in service to others.

It seems strange that the path outward into the world should show single-mindedness, and the path inward should show quite the opposite. This is one of the fascinating anomalies on the path of yoga. Inwardness, in meditation, really indicates an upward direction—a kind of shooting star, so to speak, soaring *upward* with intense focus into the heavens. Inwardness that is motivated by selfishness takes the mind *downward*, shrinking one inward upon the ego. When one thinks in terms of serving others, his inner energy becomes focused rightly.

Perhaps that father once deceived others in *their* investments. If so, then again, by helping others in the present he would "make good" on those past mistakes. These are suppositions, merely. The important thing in any case is that one's karmic blocks are best removed, not by exhausting that karma, but by generating *the right energy to offset them*. Thus, a talented and educated person who for some reason has not been successful in life can achieve the success his abilities merit by giving service to others, and, if possible, by giving the kind of service that is geared to offsetting his particular past mistakes.

Energy is the key, always. It must be generated consciously. An important teaching of Paramhansa Yogananda's was, "The greater the will, the greater the flow of energy." So as not to confuse the will with a furrowed brow and inner tension, one could substitute in certain circumstances the expression, "The greater the *willingness*. . . ." When you really want to succeed at something, you have the necessary *willingness* to do it well.

There is a valuable corollary to this principle: *"If you want to be fortunate, don't wait for good luck to come to you: Go out with energy; meet it halfway!"*

The results of bad karma are not necessarily a destiny chiseled in stone. There are strong karmas, both bad and good. Their strength depends on the amount of energy, generated by will power, that went into creating them. To overcome a bad karma, one has only to oppose it with an equal and opposite good karma. There is nothing absolute in any prediction based, let us say, on your horoscope. There is no *kismet* looming so overpoweringly that it can never be changed. Sri Krishna, in the Bhagavad Gita, declares that even the worst of sinners, if he meditates steadfastly, "speedily comes to Me."

Several questions remain: Is it even *good*, always to eliminate the *effects* of bad karma? That karma may provide a much-needed lesson. In this case, to have its effects simply removed might not be helpful.

In India, many years ago, I met a young woman saint who never spoke, but did respond in writing to requests for healing prayers. Her prayers, someone told me, were invariably effective. Interestingly, her own father had a chronic illness, but she wouldn't pray for him. Her mother repeatedly asked her to do so.

After some time, the mother raised an unanswerable objection: "It's because he's your own father that you won't pray for him. You think that if you pray, people will interpret it as a sign of personal attachment, which to you would be wrong. But what is this refusal of yours except attachment to people's good opinion of you?"

The young saint, thus forced, scribbled a reply: "You'll see what will happen if I pray." The mother kept on insisting, however. Finally, the daughter relented.

The father was healed. Soon afterward, however, he began to live immorally. His illness, until then, had kept him living a more balanced life. It would have been far better, in his case, *not* to have had a physical healing.

How was the universe created? It is a manifestation of consciousness. Even in the material sciences it is now known that matter, seemingly so solid, is really only a vibration of energy. Energy itself, in turn, is a vibration of thoughts. And thoughts, finally, are manifestations of absolute, undifferentiated consciousness. This truth has been explored only superficially, so far, by modern science. The much deeper explanation of how all things were created was taught ages ago by the great rishis of India. It is hinted at in the teachings of Vedanta.

I don't suggest that anyone try *literally* to materialize money! This is not to say that such a feat is impossible. Swami Nityananda, the guru of Swami Muktananda of Ganeshpuri, did exactly that. The police came to him one day and demanded that he show them his printing press. They had learned that he was giving money away freely, and figured that he could not have acquired it normally. Obviously, then, he must be printing it!

The swami replied, "Come, and I'll show you." He led them to a nearby lake, walked into the water, became submerged to the point of disappearing from sight. He then emerged with wads of rupee notes in his fists. "Come down with me," he said with a smile. "I'll show you my 'press.'" The police thereupon prudently decided to leave well enough alone. They stopped bothering him!

It isn't necessary for you to become like Swami Nityananda before you try to put these teachings into practice! Not everybody can *manifest* money by materializing it, but *everybody* can generate the energy that will *attract* money. When the energy-flow is right, it will be like electricity flowing through an electric wire; that is to say, it will generate a magnetic field. The stronger that field, the stronger also the magnetism it generates.

The kinds of karma, and the kinds of magnetism that generate it, are infinitely varied. I remember—incidentally, only—my Guru commenting about a disciple who had what he called "commotion-karma."

Obstacles to the energy-flow are whatever produces mental "static," such as doubt, anxiety, fear, self-interest, lack of self-confidence, and a self-narrowing focus on results.

Doubt can be simply resolved: Test it! Science in modern times has blazed a trail by demonstrating the existence of energy. We have only to learn the different directions that trail can lead. Don't attempt to manifest vast sums of money all at once! Aspire to smaller, more sensible victories. If you keep your aspirations within the bounds of reason, you'll be surprised at how practical this principle really *is*.

Self-confidence is best developed when it isn't centered in ego-consciousness, but expands in self-surrender to divine consciousness. Man's own ability is severely limited, but *there are no limits to the power of God for those who invite that power to flow through them.*

Attachment to specific results is, as I said, self-narrowing. It changes one's focus from energy to things. The energy is transformed in the mind from a fluid stream to a firm substance; it ceases to flow. To release one's powers of accomplishment from narrow fixation, concentrate on the energy-flow itself, not on its intended objective. This is another reason why the teaching of the Bhagavad Gita on *nishkam karma* is so wonderful: "Action without desire for the results." Action, to be self-freeing, must not be self-defining. Thus do great yogis manifest their so-called "miracles." I say "so-called" because their feats, however amazing, are simply the consequence of a *flow* of consciousness, through energy, to its final, material condensation. The flow itself is facilitated by one's not being identified with substance—by the fact, indeed, of being centered within one's self—in that awareness which is the *essence* of everything manifested.

The Application

I have read advice in books that when one wants to fulfill a desire, he should give the object of that desire a definite shape and color. "If you want a new car," they say, "visualize the exact model you want. Imagine it sitting in your driveway with the key in the ignition. See the front door standing open invitingly." Somehow, this advice has always struck me as limiting; I have found that another method works far better. It is based on results that I have observed in other people's lives, and in my own. Let me illustrate my meaning with a story:

A Christian died and went to heaven. Saint Peter welcomed him, and showed him around the place. When they'd taken in a few sights, Saint Peter took his charge to what he described as the "heavenly junkyard."

"Here," he said, "are all the things that the people on earth rejected."

The newcomer, looking about him, was amazed to see so many shiny, new-looking objects. This place didn't look to him like a "junkyard" at all! "How," he asked, "could people have rejected so many wonderful objects? For instance, just see that beautiful car over there. I can't imagine anyone rejecting anything so beautiful!"

"It's interesting that you should ask about that particular object," Saint Peter said. "As it happens, the person who sent it back was *you*!"

"Why, that isn't possible!" exclaimed the newcomer. "I'd never have sent back anything so wonderful!"

"Oh, but you did!" St. Peter insisted. "That car was intended for you, but whenever you prayed for a car, you visualized a small Volkswagen."

The point of this amusing but insightful anecdote is, Don't place any limits on your aspirations or you'll block an energy-flow that might produce even greater wonders for you.

In my experience, the best "system" is to offer whatever I visualize into the divine flow. I then pray, "Lord, this is what I'd like generally to accomplish. *You*, please, decide *what* You want done specifically, and *how* it should be done."

Years ago, at our first Ananda community outside Nevada City, California, we held a meeting to invite our members to help with the enhancement of what we euphemistically called "downtown Ananda." Members were invited to pledge different amounts of money according to their ability: ten dollars for a sapling; five dollars for a potted plant; twenty dollars for a movable tree. One request was made in the hope that some Ananda business might be able to pledge that amount. (All of our businesses, I should add, were fairly new.) The sum was $2,500 to pave the entrance driveway.

When I saw that relatively high sum, although I knew that there was a need, I thought, "No one is going to pledge so much." Ananda was still young then, and, financially, still struggling. I decided to pledge that whole amount myself. I had nowhere near that kind of money, but experience had shown me that Divine Mother, as I address God when I pray to "Him," can perform miracles when one asks Her lovingly—for others, not for oneself. Confidently, therefore, I pledged the amount asked. We'd been given two weeks to submit the money. How was I to meet that deadline? I had no idea! I had faith, only, that the money *would* come somehow. This was a specific request, but I was concentrating on the *energy* of the prayer itself. I didn't visualize specifically how the driveway should look, or how the money might come. Instead, I thought, "Divine Mother knows more than I, and will take care of that end of things!"

I told no one of my pledge; I simply focused all my energy on telling Divine Mother that this was something we needed. I then prayed, "You *have to* come through with this!"

One morning when I got up, nearly two weeks later, I saw an envelope lying on the floor inside my front door. Opening the envelope, I found a brief letter from a friend who had lived for some time at Ananda, and had returned for a brief visit. The letter said, "My mother died a few months ago, and I've long been wanting to express to you my gratitude for what you've done for me. This check is from the inheritance she left me." Enclosed was a check for $3,000. Our driveway became a reality!

That was by no means an isolated event: I've seen this principle work again and again in my life, and I don't remember ever being disappointed. I've found that the "system" works best when I concentrate on the flow of energy, rather than on any specific thing I want. That was what I did in the case I've just described: I didn't think, "Driveway! Driveway!" I prayed, "Divine Mother, You know what I want. All I can add to that is, We really *need* it!"

What I recommend is that you focus your demand, first. Then project it upward, with great will power and energy, from your heart and out through the spiritual eye. That flow of energy, like electricity passing through a wire, will generate a magnetic field, which will attract to itself consequences that match the thought and the strength of the energy.

I've found that it also helps to think of that energy as a ray of light. Rotate around that ray the magnetism you want to create. Whatever your need is, send the ray outward, not as an appeal, but (to use my Guru's expression) as a "loving demand."

Your consciousness is a unique expression of the Infinite. What *you yourself* can do is narrowly limited, but what God can accomplish *through you* is limitless. Offer your thoughts up into that infinite flow.

Karmic blocks to success may for a time prevent what you want from coming to you, but they cannot stop it forever. "If at first you don't succeed"—surely you've heard this advice—"try and try again." Success depends on your force of will. Use that will, directing the flow of energy toward whatever you want to attract.

MEDITATION

Visualize a cascade of gold coins pouring down like a waterfall. See the cascade land, then flow outward to form a shining stream. Do not think of the individual coins so much as of the shining light that has condensed into those golden forms. Reach out lightly, and touch that luminous flow of light. Hold your hands up to it; let it run freely through your fingers. Be one with its radiance, for it is *yours*. You have within you all the wealth you need to fulfill every dream.

Remember always, what *you* can do is limited, but what God can accomplish through you has no limits as long as you hold yourself open to that flow.

AFFIRMATION

"Thy wealth flows into me and through me. Its strength and power of accomplishment are unlimited, for Thou art infinite. Thy power, within me, is infinite."

POINTS TO REMEMBER

1. Money is a thing, merely. We give it energy by the expectations we project onto it

2. Our ability or inability to be successful is *not* "written in the stars"—an inevitability! Energy and will power created our karma and can be used to change it.

3. The more *energy* and *will power* you put into changing a karma, the sooner and the more completely you'll be able to wipe the slate clean.

4. Whatever skills you have, use them now for good. The more energetically you do that, with will power, the more quickly you will expiate any wrongs you may have done in the past.

5. The more positive energy you put out, the more positive energy it will attract to itself. What seems difficult to develop in the beginning becomes easier and easier.

6. Don't imagine that any goal you set yourself in life will be the end of the story once you achieve that end.

7. Any block to positive energy can be removed by focusing energy *concentratedly* in the direction you want your energy to flow.

8. It is the divine way to work *with* man's will, never *against* it. There must be complete consent *in the subconscious*. Even God needs the complete consent of your own will before He can bless you.

9. Faith simply means working *with* an energy and a will that already exists in the universe.

10. When one does anything with ulterior motives, he dissipates his energy by pretending to be doing one thing while really doing or wanting something else. Whatever you are doing, do it with all your heart.

11. What one achieves by single-mindedness is inward, calm determination.

12. When one thinks in terms of serving others, his inner energy becomes focused rightly.

13. "The greater the will, or *willingness*, the greater the flow of energy."

14. "*If you want to be fortunate, don't wait for good luck to come to you: Go out with energy; meet it halfway!*"

15. *Everybody* can generate the energy that will *attract* money. When the energy-flow is right, it will be like electricity flowing through an electric wire—it will generate a magnetic field.

16. Obstacles to the energy-flow are doubt, anxiety, fear, self-interest, lack of self-confidence, and a self-narrowing focus on results.

17. Don't attempt to manifest vast sums of money all at once! If you keep your aspirations within the bounds of reason, you'll be surprised at your success.

18. Man's own ability is severely limited, but *there are no limits to the power of God for those who invite that power to flow through them.*

19. To release one's powers of accomplishment from narrow fixation, concentrate on the energy-flow itself, not on its intended objective. Practice *nishkam karma*: "Action without desire for the results."

20. Don't place any limits on your aspirations or you'll block an energy-flow that might produce even greater wonders for you. Concentrate on the flow of energy, rather than on any specific thing you want.

21. Focus your demand. Then project it upward, with great will power and energy, from your heart and out through the spiritual eye. Think of that energy as a ray of light. Rotate around that ray the magnetism you want to create. Whatever your need is, send the ray outward as a "loving demand."

22. Success depends on your force of will. Use that will, directing the flow of energy toward whatever you want to attract.

WORKBOOK IDEAS
by Joseph Bharat Cornell

Focused Energy: Key to Success

In eighteenth-century Japan, mountain travel was often perilous. On the island of Honshu, passage through the Yamakuni River Gorge was especially so—every year travelers fell where the trail crossed its sheer walls. Hearing of the many lives lost there, a mendicant priest named Ryokai vowed he would carve a long tunnel through the solid rock cliff. With just a chisel and hammer, Ryokai began chipping away at the mountain.

At first travelers and local villagers laughed at Ryokai and said he was a fool. After several years of observing Ryokai's unstinting labor, however, the villagers became inspired by his devoted efforts and began to help. But soon they became discouraged, thinking the project impossible.

Several more times workers came, stayed for a while, then left. Their coming and going didn't matter to Ryokai. For him, now, only the rock wall existed—his eyes and mind saw only his chisel and the fall of his hammer. Years later, when the priest had dug halfway through the mountain, thirty masons helped him finish. During this time, Ryokai was virtually unaware of their presence, so single-minded was he in pursuing the task God had given him.

ACTION ITEM:
Dynamic energy focused in one direction attracts success. The magnetism generated from concentrated effort also draws opportunities and help from the universe.

1. Choose something you want to accomplish.
2. Watch your energy as you work.
3. Does it remain steadfast and concentrated? Or does it become easily diverted?
4. If you become sidetracked, refocus your energy on your purpose.
5. Continue refocusing your attention as needed.
6. Observe how Life helps you when your energy is strong and positive.
7. Remember, the only thing you have control over is the quality and focus of your energy. It is your most important asset!

Overcoming Karmic Blocks

In the above story, the priest's motivation for building the tunnel was also for karmic reasons. As a young man, Ryokai had taken lives, and he knew now he had to save lives if his karma was to be expiated. After his crimes, Ryokai, filled with remorse, had almost surrendered to the authorities. But a saintly priest told him that he would surely be executed if he did. This priest suggested instead that Ryokai begin earnestly serving and saving the lives of others. Dying now wouldn't help his victims, or himself. Only by denying himself and helping others could Ryokai become free of his karma.

Awareness of one's faults should lead to direct, positive action. The way to mitigate one's karma is not to outlast it, or feel guilty about it, but to consciously generate positive energy to offset it.

ACTION ITEM:
Although few of us have karma like Ryokai's, we all have karmic impediments that prevent us from achieving our goals. Blocks like fear, doubt, and lack of self-confidence siphon off a tremendous amount of energy. Removing subconscious blocks frees our energy for more worthwhile pursuits.

1. Ask yourself: Is there a part of me that paralyzes my efforts, that acts counter to what I want to do or accomplish?

2. Meditate on what it is, and after its consequences become very clear, think of a way to redirect this blocked energy positively and expansively.

3. Devote yourself energetically to this new direction.

LESSON THREE

KNOWLEDGE, INSPIRATION, AND ENERGY

Outstanding success comes from working with *our own* understanding, and not by repeating the thoughts and actions of others. It comes, moreover, from sensing our link with others' needs, desires, and aspirations.

The Principles

For those who want to follow well-worn paths, familiarity with what has been done before is important. This is the path of tradition, which to a great extent means a path of imitation. To follow this path, one needs knowledge, but doesn't particularly need inspiration or energy. For success in any tradition, one needs the necessary education taught by people competent to instruct others in the basic "rules of the game."

I remember the organist at the church where my mother's funeral was held. The purpose of the ceremony was to comfort the bereaved and to send blessings to the departed. The organist's job was simply to play a piece of music for the event. What I asked her to play was a composition of my own. She was graceless enough to tell me that she wouldn't play it because, as she pointed out firmly, "This melody doesn't end on the tonic note." In fact she was right according to the "rules of the game." Had she played the piece first, however, and listened with her heart, she would have seen that, in this case, she was wrong.

In musical tradition, a melody must end on the tonic, which is the first note of the scale. There is a good reason for this tradition: If a piece doesn't end on that note, the listener will wonder, "What statement is being made here?" Had that lady really listened to the piece, however, instead of merely looking at it printed out on a music sheet, she would have understood that the mood of this particular melody was not to make a statement, but to ask a question.

I should conclude that little story by saying that I did persuade her to play this music since it was my own mother's death we were commemorating. Though she relented at last, it was grudgingly!

The difficulty with following any set of rules too rigidly is that one rarely if ever asks the simple question, "Why?" In Nazi Germany, many basically good people accepted Hitler's hate-filled slogans; they even repeated them fervently, themselves. Such is the power of mass suggestion. People were not willing to oppose what was popular. Had they withdrawn into themselves even a little bit, and separated their understanding from the mass hypnosis around them, many would have been horrified at what they were endorsing. People tend to view discrimination as less important than acceptance by their contemporaries.

Tradition represents "the done thing": the endorsement of long usage. Such endorsement is proffered unquestioningly. People who go that route often reject new ideas, even in anger, simply because "That just isn't done." The danger of this policy is that it gains an obsessive momentum of its own. It urges people not to question generally approved premises, nor ever to think for themselves.

Years ago, I served on the board of directors—and was also the vice president—of a large corporation. The president once said to me, "Our focus must be on centralizing the work."

"I agree," I answered. "Centralized authority is, in many cases, a necessity. It seems to me, however, that there is a need also for *de*centralization. People who live and work far from the center of things won't feel encouraged to serve intelligently if they aren't listened to. Besides, their understanding of the local scene may be clearer, sometimes, than anything that can be achieved at a distance. To be unresponsive to those needs might have a *dis*couraging effect."

The president replied peremptorily: "The Board feels differently. Don't you think you should go along with the Board?" The fact that I, too, was on the Board, and was also the vice president, didn't seem to count. She wanted rubber stamp approval from all of us. For this style of leadership, a board of directors is hardly necessary. It is one of the best ways to corporate paralysis.

Another Board member, much senior to me, told me after I'd been "elected" (in rubber-stamp fashion) to high position, "In a corporation, no one has a right *even to think* except the members of the board of directors." The way of tradition, of society, of the world and its leaders, and of people to whom success means glorious mediocrity, the rule—though rarely expressed so blatantly—is, "Don't think at all." Fortunately for me, that "Board" came to realize something I didn't, which was that I simply didn't "belong."

Years ago, an interesting experiment was performed in psychology classes at various American universities. Two lines were drawn on a blackboard, the upper one being slightly longer than the lower one. Students were then separated into groups of five. In advance of the experiment itself, four members of each group were instructed to say that the *lower* line was the longer.

When all five were assembled for the test, the first four were asked, "Which of those lines is the longer?" and they responded dutifully, "The lower one." In an astonishing *eighty percent* of the groups, the fifth member, when asked that question, gave the same verdict: "The lower one is the longer." What emerged from that experiment was the discovery that most people, even among the educated, support more or less any opinion that is held by the majority. Rarely will they champion a different idea unless they feel confident that there exists somewhere another, and generally larger, body of opinion. They dare not say what they can see with their own eyes to be true!

A story is told, perhaps apocryphally, of Franklin Delano Roosevelt, who (as you probably know) was for some years the president of the United States of America. The story is that one time, in his younger days, he attended a cocktail party. There, he moved among the guests, saying to each person he encountered, "I just killed my mother."

No one really heard or listened to him. (Few do, on those occasions.) The responses he got were interesting. "*Really!*" said one. "How wonderful. You *must* tell me about it some time." Another one cried, "How *interesting*! I wish I could say I'd done as much!" Another remarked with enthusiasm, "Well, I must say it's high time someone did *something* about it!"

What I am saying here is that most people treat whatever they know as though it were information programmed on a computer. What many people gain from education is, essentially, only that: information. They learn the "rules of the game," and any success they achieve in life comes largely from repeating what they've been taught. Success of this sort demands only the intelligent use of knowledge. For the sort of success, however, which serves real needs and brings satisfaction to oneself, one must enhance that knowledge with *energy*, which, if used intelligently, gives rise to *inspiration*.

I am writing these lessons for that small twenty percent who think for themselves. Such were the people who in that psychology experiment might have answered: "But that's absurd! Can't you *see* that the upper line is the longer?" Lacking the courage to think for oneself, one cannot achieve that kind of success which provides true satisfaction. To the student of this course I say, Don't go along with the "norm" to the extent that you'll never dare to stand up for what you really believe.

Success, to be really meaningful, means more than a stable income: It means inner happiness and satisfaction. There is nothing so ultimately *dis*satisfying as the lackluster quality of mediocrity. Yet mediocrity is all one will achieve if what he learns in school is not combined with inspiration and energy.

We live today in a fact-finding age. Everyone's assumption seems to be that if there are enough facts at one's disposal, he will be—ta *da*!—a success in life.

I remember an architect student of mine in Patiala, Punjab, an exceptionally gifted man and the acting chief architect for the city. What I saw of his buildings were, in my opinion, more suitable to the more "rounded" consciousness of ancient India than the harshly angled, modern city of nearby Chandigarh. (This was in 1959. Perhaps things have changed in Chandigarh since then, though I don't imagine the public buildings have changed very much.) The public buildings I'd seen in Chandigarh were designed by the famous French architect Le Corbusier. I couldn't help feeling that my Patiala friend deserved appointment as Patiala's chief architect, a position he was holding only in trust, so to speak, until someone with better credentials could be found.

To me, it seems pure nonsense to consider a mere diploma to be the only qualification when a person has already demonstrated full competence and also the inspiration and energy for getting a job done well. This man's single shortcoming was that he didn't have that diploma.

Those who are best at whatever they do rely on their own inner strength and discrimination. The success that is achieved by complete reliance on the "wisdom" of others, or on the information gathered, sifted, and passed on as the ultimate word of authority, produces a color no more interesting than gray. There have been countless people in the past whose reputation in the present is owed largely to the patina of antiquity.

As an employer, use your own judgment of situations and people. In that way, you'll develop your own intuition and, as a result, your own creativity. As an employee, support your employer energetically, above all by tuning in intuitively, as much as possible, to what he is trying to accomplish. Try to develop your own knowledge in that field. In a later lesson I will discuss at some length the roles played by employers and employees.

The real keys to success are three in number: knowledge, intuition, and energy. Many highly educated people, lacking the other two qualities, plod along more or less mindlessly. Their labor is soulless. Whether they earn a good living, or work at low-paying jobs, they will never succeed in developing their own higher potential.

There is a saying in the Bible: "With all thy 'getting,' get understanding." Intellectual knowledge is important, yes, but if it is not accompanied by understanding, it will no more show him the road to success than a dictionary can give him solutions to life's problems.

Many very successful people have had very little formal education. They achieved success for two reasons: They were hard workers, and they were inwardly inspired.

What made them hard workers was their strong energy. What inspired them inwardly was that very energy. Ants too are hard workers, after all, but can do only what Nature has "programmed" them to do. Human drudges, too, may be hard workers, but, almost by definition, they are not likely to be inspired. They will probably remain drudges all their lives.

Consider Thomas Edison's prescription for genius: "Genius is one percent inspiration, and ninety-nine percent perspiration." That oft-quoted statement was not the whole story, however. That one percent is the real essence of genius; it is the most important part of that equation.

The human body, we learn, consists mainly of water. If you were to dismiss as "insignificant," however, the part that isn't water, you'd have nothing left but a puddle. What Edison meant by *perspiration*, of course, was not sitting out in the sun, steaming: Put more accurately, he meant "hard work." That one percent inspiration is what raises the commonplace to the level of genius. What Edison demonstrated in his own life was inspiration, attracted and magnetized by *high energy*.

Many really successful people in this world were actually earmarked by teachers in their schools as future failures. Edison's first teacher sent him home from school with the message that it wasn't possible to teach him. Albert Einstein's professors predicted that he'd be a failure at anything he tried his hand at. Ramanujan, the famous Indian mathematician (I'll mention him again later in this lesson), flunked out of college because of his single-minded absorption in mathematics. History gives us countless similar examples: people who seemed, in their youth, to be complete duffers, but who were eventually recognized as great geniuses.

Genius and exceptional ability of any kind never move along well-worn tracks. I am not teaching you how to be a genius, but I do urge you not to trudge along deeply rutted tracks, either. If you want to be *really* successful in any field, never let your first question be, "What has been done already in this field?" Ask, rather, "What are the greatest present *needs* in this field?" Outstanding people live not in the past, but in the present tense. Intellectual knowledge is based on past discoveries. Because such knowledge inclines people to look backward in time, it doesn't often invite present inspiration. Passive dependence on knowledge is both limited and self-limiting.

Exceptional individuals know very well from experience that most people consider it "normal" to walk on well-paved roads. They must have the courage to trust inner clarity. Indeed, the divine Spirit in man can create everything anew, never repeating itself twice.

Consider our thumbprints: In each of us they are unique. Again, consider the snowflakes that fall each year in countless billions: Every one of them is, in some minute way, different from all the others. Every moment of our lives, similarly, is unique. Were we to live for hundreds of years, all those moments would continue to be unique.

It is important to understand that there is a subtle connection between the countless outward manifestations of consciousness. Every person, though like every thumbprint uniquely himself, is also an expression of that general phenomenon: man. The diverse-seeming snowflakes, similarly, are all manifestations of one thing only: water. No one can succeed notably in life without this understanding. The reason is that, his attention being wholly outward, he will see no uniting principles, nor will he be conscious that the solution to any one problem may be, in some special way, the solution to many other problems. Notable success demands an inward gaze. It comes not by drawing on other people's insights and discoveries, but by raising up from within oneself insights that are uniquely one's own.

Originality is wrongly taken to mean thinking or doing something that has never been thought of or done before. The meaning of that word *original*, however, is to act from one's *point of origin* in himself. Think how many times, in every country and in all centuries, lovers have spoken to each other the simple words, "I love you." The words never become trite, so long as the feeling behind them is deep and sincere. Any statement, similarly, that is expressed with a full heart, is worth more than a library crammed with intellectual knowledge. To understand your own motivations is to understand the motivations of others. It is *within* that one must look for insights that are forever new, and, at the same time, forever true. Outstanding success comes from working with *our own* understanding, and not by repeating the thoughts and actions of others. It comes, moreover, from sensing our link with others' needs, desires, and aspirations.

When I was in college, I enrolled in a course on ancient Greek. At that time in my life I was rapidly becoming disillusioned with formal education, which, I realized, emphasized knowledge at the expense of inspiration and high energy. Throughout the second semester of that course, in fact, I rarely came to class, and even more rarely completed an assignment.

As the time approached for the final exam, our eminent professor, Dr. Post, began coaching us for it carefully. Even then, I seldom appeared in the classroom, and when I did, and was asked to translate a passage from the original Greek, the results were embarrassing.

I would recognize a few simple words like "*adelphos*" (meaning brother), and "*philos*" (meaning love)—this being no great feat for me, considering that Philadelphia, the "city of brotherly love," was the nearest big city to us. After a few more pathetic attempts, the professor began remarking, "There are certain students in this class who might as well not bother to come for this exam." (The others would glance in my direction, and chuckle surreptitiously.)

For some inexplicable reason, I had every intention of passing the exam. As I was to state years later in my autobiography, *The Path*,* "I can't imagine anyone in his right mind endorsing these roseate expectations."

One week before the exam, never doubting that I would pass, but admitting finally to myself that I'd better begin to apply myself in earnest to this subject, I picked up my book on Greek grammar, glanced at it listlessly, then put it down with a combination of rebelliousness and disgust. "Tomorrow," I assured myself, "*tomorrow* I will study *twice* as long."

"Tomorrow," however, found me as little interested as on the previous day. The third day was the same; also the fourth. Suddenly, the final evening loomed over me like a menacing cloud. I realized with horror that I had done no studying that entire week! Desperate now, I asked myself what I must do. In *The Path* I wrote, "Necessity is said to be the mother of invention. Fortunately for me, my present extremity displayed the right, maternal instinct. Out of the blue an inspiration appeared."

In fact, I had stumbled onto an important truth. After all, the Greeks are no different, really, from you and me. We all have the same needs and basic interests, the same patterns of ups and downs in life, the same desire for

---

* Publisher's note: Years later he edited the book extensively, and reissued it as *The New Path: My Life with Paramhansa Yogananda*.

happiness. The only thing that separates us from one another, really, is that we express ourselves differently. Suddenly it occurred to me that Greek speech patterns *cannot be* wholly foreign to my own! In whatever way they spoke, they had to be expressing essentially the same thoughts and feelings as you and I.

"I'm a Greek!" I told myself firmly. All of a sudden my mind fell naturally into new—in fact, into Greek!—ways of thinking. No longer did I encounter inwardly any resistance to the idea of expressing my thoughts in Greek. It was as if I had discovered an underlying bond that linked me and the Greek people together. Their way of thinking became my way. Thus, I eliminated one of the great problems that people face when trying to absorb new and alien information. With intense concentration I went through my book of Greek grammar, absorbing it like a sponge.

This story has another aspect, equally interesting—and equally important. We'd been studying the New Testament of the Bible in the original Greek. The next morning I saw that there was enough time for me to read one chapter of the New Testament in English. "If I put out positive energy," I told myself, "this may be the very chapter we are called upon to translate."

It was! As things turned out, the exam that year was exceptionally difficult. Only two students passed it. By honoring an important principle, I was one of them!

Dr. Post commented to me later, "It just shows the importance of studying." I didn't have the courage to explain to him just *how* I'd studied! I hadn't allowed myself to think, as an American, "Of what use will Greek be to me? What does it really matter if I pass this exam?" I approached learning Greek with the thought that I *was* Greek; I connected my consciousness to that universal consciousness in man of which Greek is simply an expression.

In this way I have, to varying degrees of fluency, learned nine languages in my life. In later years, while living in Italy, I learned Italian simply because so few of the people I met knew English. One day, after I had in fact become fairly fluent in Italian, I and a small group of American friends were in a shop in Florence. The shopkeeper asked me in Italian, "Where are you all from? I know *you're* Italian, but what about your friends?" One day, again, in the city of Bastia, a shopkeeper, on hearing me speak English with my friends, exclaimed to me, "Why, you speak *good* English!"

One might call an aptitude for languages a special skill, but where do we get our skills? They are natural gifts only to the extent that we probably attuned our minds to them at some time in the past. People are usually born with some understanding they developed in the past. Not to boast, therefore, but simply to illustrate a valuable truth, let me share one or two more examples with you.

Forty years ago the inspiration came to me to express the yoga philosophy in song. My thought was that the melodies might remain in people's minds, and the words would, as a result, become fixed there more firmly. From this inspiration I ended up writing many songs, to which I have given the generic name, "Philosophy in Song."

I didn't know music composition when I began. I think I must have had inner help. That, however, is my point. Understanding comes to us, more than we ourselves realize, from states of consciousness with which our egos are only vaguely in touch. By now I've written over 400 pieces of music. Recordings of some of them have been played on international airlines, in restaurants, and in other public places. Some of the music has won prizes. To my happy surprise, even Indians, raised as they've been in a very different cultural milieu from the Western, have expressed delight on listening to this music.

Several years ago, a group of about fifty singers came from America to Italy to perform an oratorio of mine. They sang in six cities; wherever they went, they received standing ovations. In the town of Assisi, an old man came up to me after the concert with tears in his eyes. In French he said to me, "I don't know any Italian or English, but I have to say that, as I listened to this music, I felt that I was understanding every word!"

I should add an important fact: There *are* rules in music. I had to learn them by experience, since I didn't know them. I had to discover them by sheer hard work (which, as in Edison's case, meant concentrated energy). As a matter of fact, my unfamiliarity with the rules may have been my good fortune, for I wasn't able to fall back on facile solutions that I knew would work musically, but that in other ways might be inappropriate to what I was trying to convey. I had to look for the one, right solution to any problem I faced at the moment.

I've told these stories in order to make it clear that I know, from my own experience, what I'm talking about. Knowledge is only part of the triad necessary to true achievement. I shall attempt, later on, to apply these insights to the subject of earning money.

Many years ago, I decided to study astrology. The decision was inspired by something I'd read in one or two books on yoga, which claimed that certain aspects of yoga can be understood only with the additional knowledge of astrology. Intrigued, I decided to explore the merits of this statement.

I didn't go into the subject deeply, for this wasn't a serious interest of mine. After a year, however, I felt the inner guidance to write a book on astrology. I named it, *Your Sun Sign as a Spiritual Guide*. A well-known astrologer in Hollywood, to whom movie stars often went for consultation, commented on this book to a friend of mine: "It's the best book I've ever read on astrology. If Kriyananda hadn't written it, it would have had to be written. I might even have tried writing it myself!"

No, I am not an astrologer. Two or three times, in fact, as I was working on that book the thought came to me, "I've bitten off more than I can chew!" I prayed for guidance. Each time, suddenly, I understood. Years later I discovered in books on ancient wisdom that what I'd written was taught in ancient times.

What I want to emphasize here is that any knowledge we require can be ours, if we seek it not only through rational channels, but from our own superconscious. Everything you want is inside you. I don't mean to say, therefore, "Don't study." Intellectual knowledge can be made meaningful, however, if you attune yourself inwardly with what you are studying.

The way to do that, as I wrote in the last lesson, is to *send energy* toward anything that you are doing. Energy, projected with a strong and focused will, can attract everything one wants—including money, success, inspiration, and even specific knowledge. You are part of the great web of life. *Attunement* in every field is more important than intellectual study.

Again, to achieve that attunement, direct your energy *with will power* toward the goals to which you aspire.

Successful people—far more so even than most of them realize—depend on intuitive insight. This gift is latent in everyone; it enables us to *know* what decision to make, what to say, even the what, where, and when of it. One never hears people who possess this insight say, "Well, in situations like this I've found that such and such a solution worked best." Men and women of developed insight look at every situation as unique in itself. With that attitude they ask themselves, "What is trying to happen here?" This kind of knowing is impersonal. Those who have achieved it do not identify themselves with whatever role they play. All they want is the truth in every situation, and in any particular moment. They realize completely that this insight may bear little or no relationship to anything that has ever been done before.

As the American philosopher Ralph Waldo Emerson put it, "A foolish consistency is the hobgoblin of little minds." What does it matter if you yourself are inconsistent, sometimes? You *will be* consistent on a deeper level, for what you express will be your own, deeper Self. Outwardly, this Self may express itself in endlessly different ways, as the snowflakes do.

The Application

In attuning yourself to any subject, focus your gaze and attention in the forehead at a point midway between the eyebrows. Behind this point, in the frontal lobe of the brain, is centered your own latent superconsciousness.

You have another center, equally important for the development of intuition. It is in your heart — or, rather, in what yogis call the *anahat chakra*, which is located in the spine just behind the physical heart. This *chakra*, or center, is not one of those knobs on the backbone. It lies in the true spinal column, which passes through the center of the body.

Interestingly, the physical heart may also be involved in deep, "heartfelt" intuitions. Medical science has discovered that the heart contains as many nerves as the brain. Obviously, then, the heart is more than a blood-pumping mechanism. It also has a strong connection with the medulla oblongata, where the *ahankara*, or ego, resides.

To be inspired in any desired subject, form a clear concept, first, of what you want. Focus that concept at the point between the eyebrows; then, mentally and with love (this feeling is important), demand that the inspiration be given to you. "Ask, and you shall receive," Jesus Christ said. A poet will receive inspiration in the form of words, rhymes, and rhythms; a mathematician, in mathematical terms; a businessman, in terms of sound, profitable ideas.

Ramanujan, a famous Indian mathematician of humble origins, who had had a poor education, attracted the attention and subsequently the friendship of Godfrey Harold Hardy, England's foremost mathematician. Hardy once visited Ramanujan, who at that time was seriously ill, and was staying in a country house in England. The way I first read the story, Hardy noted the license plate number on the taxi, thinking that Ramanujan, with his fascination for numbers, might ask him for that number. Ramanujan did indeed ask that question. When Hardy told him, Ramanujan exclaimed, "What a *wonderful* number! It is the smallest number expressible as the sum of two cubes in two different ways."

Ramanujan's intimate knowledge of numbers in general could only have come through an intuitive connection with them. There was nothing in any book that could have supplied that information.

Concentrate, then, at the point between the eyebrows. Next, try to sense in your heart—to "listen" there, as it were—for the response. When it comes, it is in the heart that you will feel it.

Intuition can be developed with practice. In this sense, it is like using a muscle. Don't be afraid of using it. To seek intuitive guidance doesn't necessarily mean to enter into seclusion and practice deep meditation. With practice you can call on your own intuition effectively in an instant.

At the same time, don't presume beyond your actual powers. Test in little ways, first, what you receive. See if your feeling really *is* valid. See if it *works*. Then learn, with practice, to distinguish between different kinds of feeling. Learn when a feeling really *is* right, and when you merely feel it *just has to be right* because you want it so! An important point, indeed, is to exclude rigidly from this process any personal wishes you might have on the subject.

I have found it helps very much also to form a clear idea, first, of what sort of inspiration you want to receive. Years ago I wrote nine pieces of music, including the lyrics for five of them. Later, I named this suite, "Mediterranean Magic." The melodies express a wide variety of moods and feelings. They pass, for example, from a gay song about the island of Capri to a rather melancholy melody, for flute, inspired by the ruins of Pompeii, then on to a rollicking "Tarantella" inspired by the gay Neapolitan dance of that name, and, immediately after that, to a song called "Cloisters," expressing deep longing for God.

The melodies were written to accompany color slides that I'd taken of the area around Naples and Sorrento, Italy. This last melody, "Cloisters," was written for color slides of a monastery. Monks live no longer there; the melody itself, therefore, needed to pass from the traditional Gregorian mode to a more worldly mood, consonant with the fact that the monastery has become a tourist attraction.

Recently I asked a friend of mine, "How long do you think it took me to write 'Mediterranean Magic'?"

"I don't know," she replied, then hazarded a guess, "A week?"

"It took me an hour," I told her. I had needed, however, to be utterly focused in each case on both mood and theme.

When composing, I never enter into that mood personally. Only in this way could I pass quickly from one mood to another in that suite. What I do is "play the host" to inspiration, inviting it to express what I ask of it. Once the concept becomes clearly focused in my mind, I hold it up to the point between the eyebrows and ask my superconscious, "Give me a melody that expresses this concept." Instantly the melody appears, full-blown. I've had no need, later, to edit or change. The melody was simply itself.

From experiences like these I've become deeply convinced that none of the music I have written is my own. I've simply asked for it, and refused to allow ego-motivation to intrude by asking, for example, "In what direction do *I* want this melody to go?" All I've asked is, "Is this true to my request?"

Vitally important to the process of seeking intuitive guidance is the need to "listen" in the heart. The answer must *feel* right. It isn't enough that it merely "make sense"—musically or in any other way. In fact, for true success in any undertaking it is necessary for the head and the heart to work together.

Thus, when it comes to making money, feel an inner connection between the desires and needs of others, and what you want to do for them. Ask this guidance in any field that interests you. Then try to *feel* what would work best for you. Ask that the solution be given to you *right now*. Don't be afraid if the suddenness of the inspiration startles you. Most true inspiration *is* startling!

As a simple illustration, at the Metropolitan Mall in Gurgaon, near New Delhi, there is a delightful innovation in the mall concept. Malls originated (as far as I know) in America, but in no American mall have I seen something so obviously needed as a children's play area! This area is fairly large, located on the ground floor toward the back as one enters. It occupies a well-lit space under a high, translucent ceiling. The first time I saw it I was delighted, thinking, "Why hasn't this concept been thought of before? It is so clearly needed by both parents and children who come here." The mall itself is climate controlled—very helpful, both during Delhi's intensely cold winter and during its almost unbearable summer heat. A friend of mine said to me, "I used go to the mall, in the beginning, just to take my children there. Later on, I began looking at the shops, and now I go also for the shopping, which is excellent!"

Inspirations of this kind are what I'm talking about. I'm not saying, "Become another Mozart or Michelangelo." I'm not saying, "Become another Thomas Edison." In your own work, whatever that may be, look within as often as you can for your answers.

MEDITATION

Visualize a vast web, similar to a spider's web but without the lethal connotations. See yourself on this web as a single, glistening dewdrop. The drop that is your self is not directly connected to any other drop, though every dewdrop on the web is connected to every other by subtle filaments that suggest the universality of infinite consciousness.

Feel your kinship with all life and all knowledge. Nothing in the universe is alien to you. All truth is yours. All things belong to your own, eternal reality.

AFFIRMATION

"I am one with everything in existence. Truth itself is mine. And I am part of all truth."

POINTS TO REMEMBER

1. For true success, which serves real needs and brings satisfaction to oneself, one must enhance knowledge with *energy*, which, if used intelligently, gives rise to *inspiration*.

2. Don't go along with the "norm" to the extent that you'll never dare to stand up for what you really believe.

3. Success, to be really meaningful, means more than a stable income: It means inner happiness and satisfaction.

4. Those who are best at whatever they do rely on their own inner strength and discrimination.

5. As an employer, use your own judgment of situations and people. In that way, you'll develop your own intuition and, as a result, your own creativity.

6. As an employee, support your employer energetically, above all by tuning in intuitively, as much as possible, to what he is trying to accomplish.

7. *The real keys to success are knowledge, intuition, and energy.*

8. Intellectual knowledge without understanding cannot lead to success.

9. Many very successful people have had very little formal education. They achieved success because they were hard workers, and they were inwardly inspired.

10. High energy magnetizes inspiration. Inspiration is the essence of genius.

11. If you want to be *really* successful in any field, ask, "What are the greatest present *needs* in this field?"

12. Seek to discover the uniting principles among people and situations; see how the solution to any one problem may be the solution to many others.

13. It is *within* that one must look for insights that are forever new, and, at the same time, forever true. Outstanding success comes from working with *our own* understanding, and from sensing our link with others' needs, desires, and aspirations.

14. Any knowledge we require can be ours if we seek it not only through rational channels, but from our own superconscious.

15. Intellectual knowledge can be made more meaningful if you attune yourself inwardly with what you are studying.

16. *Send energy* toward anything that you are doing. Energy, projected with a strong and focused will, can attract everything one wants—including money, success, inspiration, and even specific knowledge.

17. You are part of the great web of life. *Attunement* in every field is more important than intellectual study.

18. Men and women of developed insight and intuition look at every situation as unique in itself, asking, "What is trying to happen here?"

19. Intuitive people do not identify themselves with whatever role they play. All they want is the truth in every situation.

20. To be inspired in any desired subject, form a clear concept of what you want. Focus that concept at the point between the eyebrows; then, mentally and with love (this feeling is important), demand that the inspiration be given to you. Next, try to sense in your heart—to "listen" there—for the response. When it comes, it is in the heart that you will feel it.

21. Intuition can be developed with practice.

22. Test in little ways what you receive. See if your feeling *works*. Then learn to distinguish between when a feeling really *is* right, and when you want it so! Exclude rigidly any personal wishes you might have on the subject.

23. When it comes to making money, feel an inner connection between the desires and needs of others, and what you want to do for them. Ask that the solution be given to you *right now*.

WORKBOOK IDEAS
by Joseph Bharat Cornell

Conscious and Superconscious Inspiration

George Washington Carver, the great American scientist of the early 1900s, was once trying to make sandpaper, but wasn't successful. That afternoon, Professor Carver fell asleep and dreamed he was in a wagon shop, where a man was working on a wheel. Carver asked the wheelwright if *he* knew how to make sandpaper. The workman said, "Yes," then continued to work in silence. Finally Carver enthusiastically told him, "This is how *I* would do it," and described the sandpaper-making process he'd been using. "You did all right," said the workman, "but you need to boil the sand." Carver woke up and immediately went to his laboratory and boiled the sand. His sandpaper was perfect.

Just as Carver received his answer after generating high energy himself, we draw inspiration from the superconscious when we express our requests with will power and receptivity. The secret of creativity is raising one's energy in the spine. This lifts our awareness above conscious, everyday thinking, to the superconscious. The following Action Items will help you experience the dramatic difference between conscious and superconscious insight.

ACTION ITEMS:
Materials needed: pen and paper

1. Think about something in your life for which you really need an answer. Spend a few moments and see if you can gain greater insight into the situation. Write down any thoughts that come to you.

2. Now practice the following techniques to interiorize and raise your energy. At the end of this sequence you will hold your request up to the spiritual eye for an answer. Before starting, form a clear idea of what you want. Clarity prevents mental vagueness!

3. Body Recharging: Stand upright. Inhale slowly, and gradually tense the whole body to the point where it vibrates. Hold the tension for a few moments, and consciously fill the whole body with energy. Then exhale and slowly relax, feeling the energy as it withdraws from the body parts. Repeat five times.

Now sit comfortably. . . .

Say a Prayer

4. Ask for God's blessings and guidance. Pray for perfect openness to His presence and will.

5. Repeat a Devotional Affirmation: Command your mind's attention by saying an affirmation like: "I am Thine, be Thou mine" or "Reveal Thyself, Reveal Thyself." Say it with deep concentration and feeling; out loud at first, then more quietly.

6. Measured Breathing: Inhale slowly counting one to eight, hold your breath for the same number of counts, then exhale for the same count. This is one round of "measured breathing." You may either lengthen or shorten the number of counts according to what is comfortable, but keep the inhalation, retention, and exhalation equal. Do five rounds.

7. Stimulate Your Spiritual Eye: Inhale slowly and deeply, and feel that your breath is acting as a magnet to draw the energy up to the point between the eyebrows. Holding the breath, concentrate your energy at that point to a mental count of twelve. Exhale. Then repeat the process, concentrating at the spiritual eye a little longer (twenty-five counts, if you can do so comfortably); focus your entire being at that point. Exhale.

8. Again inhale, then concentrate still longer (forty counts, if this is not too long for comfort).

9. Forget the breath and body, and think only of focusing your energy and awareness ever more deeply at the Christ center.

Ask for Inspiration

10. Present the concept of what you want at the point between the eyebrows; mentally and with love demand that inspiration be given to you.

11. Receive Inspiration: Listen in your heart for the response. When it feels right to do so, record your insights.

12. Did you experience a difference in the answers in these two approaches: one, thinking over the problem consciously, and the other, attuning to the superconscious?

LESSON FOUR

THE IMPORTANCE OF RIGHT ATTITUDE

Right attitude is not merely *produced* by success: it actually *attracts* success. Within ourselves we have the power to emerge smiling from the greatest defeat, and to go on to achieve shining victory.

The Principles

The following episode actually occurred, though I no longer remember the names of the participants.

A certain gold prospector in America lived with his wife in a humble cabin in the mountains. For years he found only enough gold to "keep the wolf from the door." Undaunted, he kept on with his prospecting, hoping someday to strike it rich. Throughout all that time, he and his wife always kept a cheerful outlook on life.

One evening the husband came home in triumph, his arms around a large bag of money. He'd struck gold at last! That very day he had sold his claim to a mining company. He and his wife were now rich beyond their wildest dreams!

The prospector handed the precious parcel to his wife, then, with her consent, went out to celebrate with a few of his cronies. His wife, meanwhile, hid the money in the only safe spot she could think of: the wood stove, which they rarely used because of their straitened circumstances. Satisfied that no thief would ever think to look there, she went off to bed.

Her husband, meanwhile, having had a few drinks with his friends, returned home with them late at night and invited them in to do a little more celebrating. It was late, and the air was chilly. Anxious not to disturb his wife, he placed a few logs in the stove as quietly as possible, and built a fire. Their entire hoard of newly gained wealth went up in flames!

The man and wife were horrified the next morning, on discovering the disaster. The woman was devastated. Her husband, fortunately, was made of stern stuff.

"Never mind, Honey," he said consolingly. "I'll just find us some more gold." He went out after breakfast, and *that very same day* struck another vein, much richer than the first. They now found themselves rich beyond the dreams of avarice.

Two morals, especially, can be drawn from this amazing account. The first is the glimpse it gives into the workings of karma. When any karma is powerful enough, it can overcome seemingly insuperable odds. Indeed, how extraordinary: to find enough gold to make them both rich for life, to lose all of it that very day, and then immediately to find another source of even greater wealth! I have never heard anything comparable to this account of what is so often called, "luck"!

Obviously, more than skill was involved in this success story. For years that man had been devoting any skills he had to seeking gold. To attribute *both* those finds, one right on the heels of the other, to luck alone seems as superstitious as crying, "Baby needs new shoes" before one throws dice. Surely it is more reasonable to explain such good fortune as being due to some kind of consciousness working behind the scenes. Life repeatedly shows us, though seldom with such clarity, that we are in the hands of a power higher than ourselves, one which we may be able to channel wisely, but one over which we have very little actual control.

The second moral in that episode teaches an even more important lesson—namely, the importance of exerting one's will when faced with adversity no matter how appalling. Sometimes we seem to be confronted by an implacable-seeming fate. If we meet it indomitably, however, even the harshest karma can be defeated, and any lingering good karma that is still present can be reaffirmed.

Had that man lacked courage, he might have given up mining altogether in a mood of utter defeat. Many people would have done so. Even if he didn't abandon hope utterly, but after some time summoned his will power once again until it was strong enough to return to the "fray," someone else might, in the meantime, have discovered that second vein. For the gold was there all the time, ready to be found. It wasn't that the gold itself was *fated* to be found, or to be found by any person in particular. That man had the karma to become wealthy. He also had the karma to lose his wealth. The two karmas vied together, for and against him. It was his indomitable will that decided which side would predominate.

Years ago, a Swiss friend of mine told me that he had once been an alpinist—a man, that is to say, who enjoys climbing high mountains and braving steep cliffs. He said that he once went mountain climbing with two friends. One of them slipped and fell to the bottom of a cliff. The others climbed down immediately to see what hope there was for him. They found him dead, as they'd been very much fearing. My friend's surviving friend insisted that both of them make the same climb again immediately. "Otherwise," he said, "our will power will be broken, and we may never have the courage to climb again."

Usually, the first essentials for success are a positive attitude, and a strong will. I say "usually," because people do strike it rich often enough, not because of their present mental attitude, but because they had strong money karma brought over from past lives. In the present life, they may not have demonstrated either a strikingly positive attitude or remarkable strength of will. Past good karma without supportive present attitudes can bestow success, but without the support of present right attitudes that karma will soon dissipate itself. Good past karma, moreover, without present right attitude and strong self-effort, represents no real victory in life. That which comes too easily can even become, in a sense, a misfortune. I have often observed that young people, for example, who inherited large fortunes from their parents often frittered their lives away with partying and having a good time, accruing no further good karma, but preparing themselves unconsciously, but laughingly, for a future fall.

I remember many years ago seeing a group of beggars gathered together outside the train station in Howrah, West Bengal. Most of them had developed a begging attitude, consonant with their way of life. I was struck to observe one of them, however, a young woman who stood somewhat aloof inwardly as if thinking, "What am I doing in this impossible situation?" I had the strong impression that she had been a queen in a former life, or someone prominent, who had wasted away her good karma by selfishness and indifference to the sufferings of those less fortunate than herself.

In the case of that prospector's gold discovery, though it resulted also from long years of patience and hardship, it was, as far as I know, the grand finale of their story. The wife went on to become a society "*grande dame*." The man continued to live quietly in their little mountain cabin.

His wife did have further adventures, for she was among those who were rescued from the famous ship, Titanic, when it sank after hitting an iceberg. (Let me intrude an interesting personal note: I crossed the Atlantic on an ocean liner many years later. Our ship passed over that same part on the Atlantic Ocean at exactly the same time of year. Thanks to modern technology the passage was without incident, but an iceberg *was* reported to be "lying in wait" twenty miles to the north of us.)

I once knew a man to whom wealth came all of a sudden, not because of any great effort on his part, but owing only to some right effort he had made in the past. All he had done in this life to earn it was to insist, astutely, that a clause be inserted into a certain agreement guaranteeing him a percentage if he was fortunate enough to find oil. I don't remember him as anyone noteworthy in either ability or energy. Apart from that one brief demonstration of astuteness, he seemed a rather ordinary person. What became of him I can't say. I lost touch with him more than sixty years ago. Judging by his lackluster energy, however, I imagine that his was not a glowing future.

My own experience in life has convinced me that right attitude is actually even *more* important than good karma. For although good karma can ensure success, no one, generally speaking, can say whether, when, or for how long that good karma will last before it crashes again, washing up onto the beach—a spent wave. True success produces a well-rounded human being. If one reaps a monetary windfall but retains, or even becomes deep-set in, a basically dour attitude, one might consider him still a failure in life.

My purpose in writing these lessons is to show you how, by the sheer power of your own will, you can succeed in *every* aspect of your life. Well-rounded success must above all bring happiness. That happiness should include inner serenity in confrontation with any situation no matter how testing. It should affect one harmoniously in mind and heart: that is to say, it should bring inner satisfaction, not only outer victory. Well-rounded success should increase one's appreciation for true values, spiritual as well as material. Indeed, success without an increase of understanding is an empty cornucopia: reaching into it for its benefits, one's hands come out empty.

To succeed materially at the cost of inner happiness means that one is, in fact, in terms of what he *really* wants in life, a failure.

Right *attitude* is, then, for all of the above reasons the most important ingredient in any struggle for success. Right attitude is not merely *produced* by success: it actually *attracts* success. Within ourselves we have the power to emerge smiling from the greatest defeat, and to go on to achieve shining victory.

Why be like those social misfits who, even when things go well for them, manage to find something to grumble about? Disgruntlement becomes a habit. A positive attitude depends far less on things going right outwardly than on an inner determination to *be happy always*. More often, such an attitude is the *cause* of good fortune, not merely a result of it. A strong, positive attitude, finally, is most effective when it is self-generated.

People whose outlook on life is, by contrast, basically negative can actually *attract* failure! The stronger a person's attitude, whether positive or negative, the stronger the *magnetic field of energy* it generates, drawing good or bad fortune to oneself.

True success is his already, indeed, who clings determinedly to right attitudes, for in the long run success means victory over one's self. Merely to stumble onto success, like someone finding buried treasure in the garden of his ancestral home, is delusion's way of softening one up for another plunge into failure! Above all, true success means self-mastery. What can anyone accomplish more than that? Complete mastery awaits you within yourself. Money, fame, worldly power, and other outward achievements are evanescent: they bring no lasting satisfaction. Whatever you do, think above all in terms of what success will make of *you*, both as a human being and as an instrument of Higher Truth.

Consider this modern example of the importance of happiness to true success: Elvis Presley's spectacular singing career brought him world fame and fabulous wealth. Yet the more famous and wealthy he became, the more desperately *un*happy he was. And the more impressive his public success, the more happiness eluded him, slipping through his fingers like mercury.

Howard Hughes—another telling example—was reputed to be the richest man in the world. Toward the end of his life, though he was famous by then as a recluse, a journalist managed to interview him. "Have you found happiness?" The journalist asked him.

"Nah!" exclaimed the billionaire sourly. "I can't say that I've found happiness."

An important secret for achieving true success is not to allow yourself to be burdened with an excess of anything.

Indeed, the truest wealth is *inner* happiness. That is why rich people generally find so little happiness: They confuse success with outward accomplishments.

This world is a laboratory. The creatures in it—human beings, especially—are like specimens in test tubes for experimentation, the experiment being to help everyone to find what brings success and happiness, and what, universally, deprives one of these desired ends. Testing in this "laboratory" reveals the existence of certain constants. Human behavior, no matter how varied, yields the same results universally, no matter what the circumstances. When a person seeks the best for everyone, actively and generously, and doesn't seek only to benefit himself, his chances of finding happiness are great. When a person makes personal benefit his primary goal, on the other hand, happiness flees from his grasp. This truth has been demonstrated so many times, without any exceptions to it, that no one of common sense would ever think seriously of contradicting it. Yet people's desires cause them to stumble repeatedly on the jagged rock of disappointment. Nature proclaims boldly and openly that selfishness is a "sucker's game." Yet people's motto remains unchanged so long as their conscious center is the ego: "Me first!"

I myself have seen these truths demonstrated so consistently that I know by now: This is a law of nature.

The ego is the greatest stumbling block to true success. If ego is overemphasized, it becomes a vortex which draws all energy into one's self, suffocating at last one's power to accomplish *anything* worthwhile. "Pride," my Guru said, "is the death of wisdom."

The ego can also be the key to highest attainments, however, spiritually as well as materially. The secret is to change one's direction of awareness: away from an inwardly spinning vortex, squeezing in upon one and filling his demitasse cup with a sense of glowing self-importance, and outward, releasing it in a relaxed *expansion* of consciousness in affirmation of a greater reality than one's own. Happiness that embraces everything and everyone turns to joy, and then bliss.

We must *desire* freedom from self-involvement, and *desire* to relinquish the delusion of self-importance. Once we understand this need, we begin to want to swim forcefully out of the vortex that was created by our deluded self ("self" written with a small *s*), and cease affirming our self-importance. At this point, the ego is a great blessing, for it gives us the incentive to soar in divine freedom.

The awareness of ego is what separates us from the lower animals. In this separation, the ego is a blessing even for people who are completely ego-centered. The lower animals, though fortunate in their relative lack of *self*-awareness because it makes them feel less personally the afflictions of pain and suffering, are less fortunate in another all-important respect: Their diminutive sense of ego keeps them from having any incentive to escape whatever suffering they experience, and to attain higher states of consciousness. Ego, which produces an awareness of *personal* suffering, is what produces in man, after countless incarnations, the desire for freedom from ego-consciousness altogether by merging in God. When the ego sees that it is only a drop in the ocean of cosmic awareness, composed of the same element—not water, but *consciousness*—it longs for freedom from all limitation.

True success in life comes with realizing that the ego actually *minimizes* one's own importance! What truly gives us value is the fact that each of us is a unique expression of Infinite Consciousness. Man is *not* important for his egoic personality, nor for anything he does, however well he does it. To his own inner gaze, the emperor, the craftsman, and the beggar are all manifestations of his own expanded Self.

Those who affirm their self-importance egoically do in fact sometimes rise to the top of their little anthills of ambition. Because they accomplish their victories in a spirit of competition, however, they find themselves anxious to protect themselves from the slightest challenge to their own "high" position. They become, in consequence, increasingly tense inwardly, and aware of a growing mental and emotional discomfort. The more tightly they grasp their happiness, the more likely is it, they find, to fly out of their fists.

If one gives loving support to others, he wins their support in return. If one gives *them* importance, he finds them spontaneously respecting him in return. His generosity of spirit in appreciating others, instead of demanding appreciation for himself, renders him smilingly unaffected even when people, misunderstanding, exaggerate their own importance by belittling him. And when he offers himself up in grateful recognition to a higher reality, he finds nature herself, like a sounding board, *amplifying* in resonance whatever musical instrument he has chosen to play in life. For life has given each of us its own special melody to sing or to play. The special impact that God designed for each of us to have on the world gains power only when we invite *Him* to sing, or play, through us.

Human nature contains two contrasting movements of energy: centripetal, and centrifugal. The first movement contracts inward upon the ego. The second is self-expansive, seeking an ever-broader ocean of reality, in which the ego exists as but a drop.

The philosophical niceties involved in these thoughts need not concern us here, though they are fascinating. More immediately important is the question: How to achieve success in this world without sacrificing dharma, or right spiritual action? Most people, in their craving for success, imagine that universal truths are not germane to their quest anyway. No matter. The facts remain the same in either case, and are easily verified. One who thinks primarily in terms of *receiving*—whether from others, or from life, or from the world—finds his self-identity shrinking and becoming, at last, insignificant. His happiness, also, becomes suffocated. One, however, who thinks primarily in terms of *giving*—to others, to life, to the world—finds his happiness and even his self-identity constantly expanding.

Another profoundly practical principle enters the picture here. People who think *expansively* are more likely to succeed in every way, even materially. On the other hand, people who think, "What's in it for me?" often blunder in matters both trifling and important. Tunnel vision prevents them from being aware of opportunity even when it stands like a visitor on their doorstep, ringing the doorbell. An expansive outlook opens the mind to many possible alternatives. Truly successful people are naturally sensitive to the subtle tremors of opportunity in the great web of life.

We have seen the two directions, expansive and contractive, that our energy can take. There is another way to define these opposing directions: They can be spoken of also as positive and negative. There is a special way, one easy to discern, to distinguish the positive from the negative directions. For they correspond to upward and downward movements of energy in the spine.

Few people's energy is unilaterally upward or downward. A certain portion of their energy moves up toward the brain, and another portion tries to cancel that upward-flowing energy by flowing downward to the base of the spine. A person's predominant attitude in life can be discerned more easily by the apparent direction of his energy in the spine. Does his energy seem to flow more upward, or more downward? Sri Krishna describes these directions in the Bhagavad Gita as the upward path toward enlightenment, and the downward path toward increasing darkness and delusion.

A downward-moving energy distances people from clarity of any kind—whether material, mental, or spiritual. An upward-moving energy, on the other hand, brings increasing clarity and an enhanced ability to succeed at whatever one attempts. Clarity brings intuitive understanding. With that understanding comes certainty at last as to what one should or should not do in every circumstance, even the most prosaic.

Success or failure depend to a great extent on the *direction* taken by the energy in the spine. A physicist who is idealistic by nature, even if he never thinks about God, will find his spinal energy flowing upward more than a wholly materialistic physicist. Neither of them aspires to any spiritual heights, but the one whose energy flows upward will comprehend Nature's laws more easily than the other, who may be equally brilliant, if his energy flows mostly downward because his basic attitude in life is selfish.

Extending these principles to the business world, the businessman whose energy in the spine flows primarily downward will approach the question of investments as mere questions of profit and loss, ignoring the interdependence of countless factors: for instance, the needs and desires of people generally, and over-all directions in the economy. Thus, he will be more likely to make mistakes than the businessman who approaches investments with the understanding that they all depend on numerous seemingly extraneous considerations.

A good example of the need for broad vision was the arrival on the market, several years ago, of the cell telephone. It created a worldwide demand for cell phones, and, hence, a need for signal-transmission stations. Investors who didn't look ahead to a probable future demand for this method of communication, but saw only the immediate figures of profit and loss, failed to take advantage of an opportunity that made many other businessmen rich.

The businessman should always ask himself, in other words, "What are the over-all trends in the marketplace?" He should not leap impulsively in any direction without first studying those trends. It might be difficult to perceive them correctly, but if he keeps in mind the yogic teachings on energy in the spine, he will find that this principle often applies also to right and wrong decisions. How so? By sensing his own inner reaction in the spine to the alternatives before him: Shall I? or shan't I? The more he tests this reaction, the more he will find the degree to which he can rely on it: whether his inner reaction is emotional, or calmly intuitive.

Here is an example: Many years ago, the owner of a bookstore in Palo Alto, California, which I frequently visited while staying with my parents, asked me one day, "How would Ananda like to buy my bookstore? I'm getting old, and am thinking of retiring."

Her request was unanticipated, and because she had said only, "I'm *thinking* of retiring," I didn't take her question seriously. It wasn't as though Ananda *needed* a bookstore in Palo Alto. "Do you really want to retire?" I asked her, then dropped the subject.

A few months later, I was in the same area again, and went to the bookstore. This time, the proprietress asked me the same question, more seriously. I decided to consult my own inner feelings, going within quickly to see if the energy in my spine flowed upward in response to this offer, and if it was calm, not emotional. I thought of God also, of course. Immediately, in this case, I felt an upward surge. "Yes," I answered her at once. "We'll accept your offer."

The store, since then, has been one of the needed moneymakers for our communities. It is among the top one percent of book shops of its kind in America.

One can easily discern the movement of spinal energy in other people by the effect it has on them outwardly. Observe little children especially, since there are few or no inhibitions in their expression of feelings. See how instantly a little child will reveal the direction of the energy-flow in the spine, whether upward or downward. When he rejoices, he jumps up and down enthusiastically as if wishing he could fly. When he laments, just see how he stoops forward, beats his feet on the ground, exhales heavily, and gazes dolefully downward. His entire body expresses a simple refusal to be happy.

A downward movement of energy in the spine has a clouding effect on the mind, robbing it of clarity. So, then, what should we make of the tendency these days to define realism by negativity? Doesn't this reflect a downward flow in the mass energy?

Reflect again on that example in Lesson One of the two bakers, William Baker and Joe Crumpet. Isn't it obvious that it is because Joe Crumpet's energy-flow is upward that he is more likely than William to succeed in his trade? William Baker's energy *cannot but* flow downward, for his glum attitude is an expression of a downward flow of energy in his spine.

When that energy moves upward, the mist of incomprehension gradually lifts from human consciousness.

In the yoga writings, especially the *Yoga Sutras* of Patanjali, what I've described as a mist is described as "sheaths," or *koshas*. These *koshas* enclose man's consciousness, and even more so the consciousness of lower creatures. In man's case they act like too much dust on a pair of glasses, which prevents one from seeing anything clearly.

Take an example from a much lower level of evolution than mankind's: the common earthworm. The worm's potential for comprehension is—I think one may safely assume—almost wholly obscured, revealing nothing outside its own extremely circumscribed periphery: the earth with which it is actually in touch. We don't think of the earthworm as minutely interested even in its immediate environment, except possibly to question whether it is edible. The worm's understanding is enclosed as if in a cocoon, by the thick layers of its *koshas*.

More highly evolved animals experience happiness with increasing clarity. Somewhere up the evolutionary ladder they begin to cognize what we know as happiness as pleasant tastes and physical comfort. Thus, they are vaguely aware of *un*happiness also, in the form of distaste and physical discomfort.

Pleasures and displeasures like these may never be experienced by the earthworm. In vertebrates, whose energy is able to move upward or downward in the spine, the cocoon-forming sheaths, or *koshas*, become gradually removed as the energy becomes centered higher up in the spine. In man, the sheaths are much fewer. And in one who attains enlightenment, the sheaths disappear altogether.

It is up to man whether, and how much, he chooses to remove those sheaths. He can remove them bit by bit, through the right use of will power, through discrimination, and by devotion, all of which direct energy up toward the higher *chakras*. Eventually the soul, released from all surrounding *koshas*, perceives its natural state to be oneness with the Infinite.

Here is the best way to develop attitudes that will ensure success of every kind: Breathe deeply, keeping your posture erect, and send out thoughts of kindness and goodwill. Bring the energy upward in the spine by these attitudes. Try to focus that energy in the spiritual eye between the eyebrows.

When you exhale, feel the energy going down to the base of the spine, preparing itself so that, when you inhale again, you will raise the energy with ever-greater intensity toward the brain.

It is important in life to develop positive attitudes, and to exclude negativity as much as possible from your thoughts. Make it a point to *expect* to succeed, and to expect the best from life and from other people. Never allow fear of failure to weaken your will, even if failure looms over you as a possible reality. Remember, *for the soul, failure is impossible*.

Don't be attached to the outcome of your acts. Disappointment, often, is only the result of a mistaken concept as to the true nature of success. Try to maintain an inner sense of freedom. In that way, you will be able to rise above discouragement altogether. Keep trying, until success is at last assured.

Learn also to be *solution-oriented*, not *problem-oriented*. This doesn't mean to be blissfully *unaware* of any problems before you. Look at your problems, rather, with a view to overcoming them. In this world of duality, where a problem exists there *must* be a solution to it. That is a law of nature herself. Aboriginal Americans (the so-called American Indians) learned, for instance, that where a poisonous plant grows there is always in its vicinity another plant that acts as an antidote. Direct your thoughts fearlessly toward whatever seems to you most likely to work. Finally, know that if anything you do doesn't work, something else *has to* work for you; such is the nature of duality. Keep on trying, therefore. Shun the very thought of failure. Ultimate failure is, in your true Self, an impossibility.

A positive attitude demands energy, but it also *uplifts* the energy. Yoga practice shows *how* to uplift it, and how to raise your consciousness upward, thereby raising your whole awareness to superconsciousness.

The Application

To bring the energy up the spine, make it a point *to think* in an upward direction also. I suggested this earlier: Inhale deeply, and fill the lungs with air all the way to your upper chest. Look upward. *Affirm upwardness.* As you fill your chest with air, you will draw any lower energy up to the heart level.

Next, concentrate your mind at the point between the eyebrows. Make it a habit to keep your thoughts centered there.

Live more also in the heart. Imagine your heart, known in yoga teachings as the *anahat chakra*, as a lotus. Mentally turn its petals gently upward, directing it toward the brain. Invite God's power and guidance to flow down into your heart from the spiritual eye. Then hold the heart's lotus turned upward in joyful readiness to receive a response. Pray with aspiration, knowing for a certainty that the answer *must* come.

Many years ago, when I was twenty-two years old and had been with my Guru only three months, I was feeling an intense desire to be in his presence. Word came one day from upstairs that a bottle of drinking water was needed for the Master's kitchen. Eagerly I appropriated the task to myself.

When I'd carried the five-gallon bottle upstairs, I heard him dictating a letter in the next room. "Perhaps I can attract his attention!" I thought. So thinking, I rattled the bottle, making as much noise as I felt I decently could for a job that required a minimum of tumult. (I knew already from experience that he knew my inmost thoughts even at a distance.) "Surely," I thought, "he *must* know how I've missed him."

And what was the response? Silence—at least as far as any greeting from him was concerned!

Suddenly I found myself plunging into a depression. "He doesn't care about me!" the thought came. I was upset with myself for allowing such a thought to enter my mind, but it went churning away just the same. The more I tried to reason with it, the greater grew its power over me.

"Do you *like* this feeling?" I demanded of my thought population indignantly, distressed at my own childishness.

"Not at all!" was the response. "Who likes being ridiculous?"

"Well then, let's see what we can do about it. Reason isn't doing the job, so let's try another tactic." When I returned to my room, I sat down and, meditating, raised my level of consciousness. Determinedly I focused my attention firmly at the point between the eyebrows.

Five minutes: that's all it took! Suddenly I found my attitude entirely changed!

"*Of course* he wouldn't interrupt his work for anything so trivial!" I thought. "*Of course* he has other things to do!" I almost laughed at myself for having held such an absurd expectation. "Why did you think he should stop everything"—I demanded of my ego (it was muttering in the background)—"just for *you*?" Positive reasons fairly tumbled over one another to submit arguments convincingly to my mind. For Master to take time out for me at that time, I realized, would have been entirely unsuitable!

If, then, you want to develop a positive attitude, remember: it requires an uplifted energy in the spine. Live more in the upper *chakras*—particularly at the *Kutastha*, the "Christ center" between the eyebrows. Whenever you find your energy and consciousness sinking downward toward the lower *chakras*, inhale and exhale deeply several times; magnetically draw the energy up to your heart. And concentrate forcibly, then, at the point between the eyebrows, directing energy from the heart to the spiritual eye.

You may have learned from certain yoga teachers to keep your energy centered in the heart. That is good, but only provided that, once the energy is centered there, you direct it on upward. Otherwise, deep feelings aroused in the heart can take the mind and energy downward again.

There is another way to keep a consistently good attitude: Make good company your priority. Mix more, and *attentively*, with people whose attitude in life is basically positive—people whose will power is strong, and who at least *try* to face their difficulties cheerfully. Avoid negative people like a disease, which in fact their negativity is.

A final word of advice: Keep a good sense of humor. The ability to laugh will help you to see things in correct proportion. Above all, try not to take *yourself* too seriously! Learn, instead, to laugh at yourself. After all, isn't it ridiculous to consider yourself so all-important in the infinite scheme of things? Nothing man does in this world can have lasting importance.

I think of myself today, at the age of seventy-eight, and reflect on the great amount of water that has flowed under the bridge all these years. So many world-famous people, perhaps admired by myself and by many others, today are all but forgotten! In a London book shop not so long ago I wanted to find a book by a famous author who had died only a few years earlier. Not a single one of the salespeople I asked about her books even recognized her name!

Become aware of how little this egoic self—so important to you, but otherwise so wholly insignificant!—means to the rest of the world! Laugh at the sheer comedy of thinking you deserve anything more.

You are important to only one person really: your own self. The beautiful thing about that truth is that your true Self—outwardly so insignificant—is an integral part of the Infinite Self: the Supreme Lord who dwells *within you*, and is at the center of every atom in the universe! To Him, everything has infinite importance, for everything and everyone is an expression of His Infinite Consciousness!

MEDITATION

Visualize a ray of sunlight slanting down through a cloud-covered sky and shining on you, illuminating your consciousness. Think of the happiness of receiving that blessing from Infinite Light.

Rise mentally on that shaft of light. Soar in divine aspiration, to become one with the Source of light, of which *you* are a part! Feel the light penetrating your being. Release your ego to merge into it. No lingering corner of darkness, of fear or doubt exists anywhere. You are the infinite Light Itself.

AFFIRMATION

"I am the divine light, shining into everything that I undertake in life, filling it with bliss and truth."

POINTS TO REMEMBER

1. If we meet fate with a positive attitude and a strong will, even the harshest karma can be defeated.

2. Good past karma, without present right attitude and strong self-effort, will soon dissipate itself.

3. By the sheer power of your own will, you can succeed in *every* aspect of your life. Well-rounded success must above all bring happiness, inner serenity, and inner satisfaction. Well-rounded success should increase one's appreciation for true values, spiritual as well as material.

4. Right *attitude* is the most important ingredient in any struggle for success. Right attitude actually *attracts* success.

5. A positive attitude depends far less on things going right outwardly than on an inner determination to *be happy always*.

6. The stronger a person's attitude, whether positive or negative, the stronger the *magnetic field of energy* it generates, drawing good or bad fortune to oneself.

7. True success means self-mastery. Whatever you do, think above all in terms of what success will make of *you*, both as a human being and as an instrument of Higher Truth.

8. An important secret for achieving true success is not to allow yourself to be burdened with an excess of anything.

9. When a person seeks the best for everyone, actively and generously, and doesn't seek only to benefit himself, his chances of finding happiness are great.

10. If ego is overemphasized, it becomes a vortex which draws all energy into one's self, suffocating at last one's power to accomplish *anything* worthwhile.

11. We must *desire* freedom from self-involvement, and *desire* to relinquish the delusion of self-importance.

12. Those who affirm their self-importance egoically find themselves increasingly tense inwardly, and aware of a growing mental and emotional discomfort

13. Invite God to flow through you if you want to discover your special influence in the world.

14. One who thinks primarily in terms of *giving*—to others, to life, to the world—finds his happiness and even his self-identity constantly expanding.

15. People who think *expansively* are more likely to succeed in every way, even materially. Truly successful people are naturally sensitive to the subtle tremors of opportunity in the great web of life.

16. Expansive and contractive, or positive and negative, energies correspond to upward and downward movements of energy in the spine. A downward-moving energy distances people from clarity of any kind. An upward-moving energy brings increasing clarity and an enhanced ability to succeed at whatever one attempts.

17. The businessman should always ask himself, "What are the over-all trends in the marketplace?" He should sense his own inner reaction in the spine to the alternatives before him.

18. Man can remove the mist of incomprehension, or *koshas* or "sheaths," through the right use of will power, discrimination, and devotion, all of which direct energy up toward the higher *chakras*.

19. Make it a point to *expect* to succeed, and to expect the best from life and from other people. Never allow fear of failure to weaken your will.

20. Learn to be *solution-oriented*, not *problem-oriented*. Look at your problems with a view to overcoming them. Where a problem exists there *must* be a solution to it.

21. A positive attitude demands energy, but it also *uplifts* the energy.

22. Breathe deeply, keeping your posture erect, and send out thoughts of kindness and goodwill. Try to focus that energy in the spiritual eye between the eyebrows. Make it a habit to keep your thoughts centered there.

23. Live more also in the heart. Invite God's power and guidance to flow down into your heart from the spiritual eye. Pray with aspiration, knowing for a certainty that the answer *must* come!

24. Mix more, and *attentively*, with people whose attitude in life is basically positive—people whose will power is strong, and who at least *try* to face their difficulties cheerfully.

25. Keep a good sense of humor. The ability to laugh will help you to see things in correct proportion. Above all, try not to take *yourself* too seriously!

26. Your true Self is an integral part of the Infinite Self. To Him, everything has infinite importance, for everything and everyone is an expression of His Infinite Consciousness!

WORKBOOK IDEAS
by Joseph Bharat Cornell

I Am the Mountain Meditation

The purpose of yoga is to withdraw the consciousness from the body and center it in the spine. The following exercise, *I Am the Mountain*, will help you become more aware of your spine. It is an excellent practice for internalizing your awareness and learning to relate to life intuitively. The *I Am the Mountain* meditation can be practiced alone or with another person. To begin, look for a place outdoors where it is beautiful; if this isn't possible revisit such a place in your mind and use your imagination. Then meditate a few minutes to become calm and interiorized.

How the exercise works when done alone:

Quietly repeat the words *I Am*. After each time you say *I Am*, look for something in nature that captivates you—perhaps a cloud sailing across the sky or the wind playing music in the forest. Whatever it is, *feel* its living reality inside of you, in your spine. Enjoy it there for a few moments, and then quietly whisper a simple word or phrase that describes your experience of what you were observing. For example, it might go like this:

I Am . . . *the drifting cloud*. . . . I Am . . . *the waving branches*. . . . I Am . . . *the exhilaration of the wind racing across the lake*.

You can also substitute *I Love* or *I Receive* for *I Am*, as in I Love . . . *the serenity I feel*. . . . I Love . . . *the blue flowers*. . . . I Receive . . . *a wonderful joy in my heart*.

Feel a sense of communion with everything you see.

Be also aware of the energy in your spine. Sensitively feel, for example, how sensing a tall tree in your spine stimulates your energy.

Repeat *I Am, I Love*, and/or *I Receive* for five minutes, then relax and enjoy the serenity of nature within and all around you.

How to share *I Am the Mountain* with a friend:

Decide who will be the prompter, who says *"I Am,"* and who will be the responder. The prompter sits behind to allow the responder an unobstructed view. Having one person repeat *I Am* (or *I Love, I Receive*) keeps the other focused and in the present moment. Doing *I Am the Mountain* with a friend creates a shared sense of communion with nature and with each other.

Switch roles when desired.

It is wonderful how nature is a part of us. The sun shines not on us, but in us. The rivers flow not past but through us.
—JOHN MUIR

Energy Awareness

Success or failure depends to a great extent on the direction taken by the energy in the spine.

ACTION ITEMS:
1. Spend today observing how different things affect your consciousness. You can determine whether something has a positive or negative influence by whether it draws the energy in your spine upward or downward. To become more aware of your spinal energy, practice the following exercise every hour: Inhale deeply and fill the lungs completely with air, while concentrating at the point between the eyebrows. Exhale normally. Do this six times.
2. Throughout the day, sensitively feel in your spine how people, thoughts, music, and the environment affect your energy.

What About Me?

When the Berlin Wall was being torn down by wildly celebrating Germans, ending the partition of their country, a journalist asked East German border guards how they felt about it. Their reply, "This isn't right. If they remove the wall, we'll lose our jobs!" was a classic example of contractive thinking. We, like the guards, become blind to life's greater flows and opportunities when we focus only on our needs.

ACTION ITEM:
- When you find yourself asking *What about me?* immediately start thinking of the needs of the other people involved. This will broaden your perspective and most likely enlist their cooperation, for everyone likes to be understood.

LESSON FIVE

WHAT IS IT, TO BE PRACTICAL?

To live determinedly by high principles is the surest road to material security — and beyond that, to glowing material success.

The Principles

Often, people use the need to be practical as an excuse for being unimaginative and uncreative. They contrast the word *practical* to unrealistic schemes born of a visionary attitude that is forever dreamy and undisciplined. When people say "Let's be practical," they generally assume that a chasm exists between idealism and the way things really are. It was this attitude, to a great extent, that kept mankind trapped for centuries in dark ages. The word, "practical," must be understood more intelligently: not to discourage innovation, but to *test* new ideas reasonably and see whether they are workable.

People who reject novelty, and are unwilling to see it even tested, view the world almost like a train traveling along fixed tracks. How can such people even consider the new discovery that matter is really a manifestation of fluid energy? To them, matter is the fundamental reality of everything they know. Ideals may be inspiring, but here on solid earth, they consider, we must accept prosaic reality, which includes the fixed ways of tradition. They cannot seriously believe that matter is not the final arbiter. To them, human ideation is wholly dependent on matter.

They overlook, in their belief, the simple fact that what is traditional was once, in another time, *new* and original. It began as a dream, a vision, or a revelation in the consciousness of some one person. Buddha springs to mind as an outstanding example of a truly innovative spirit.

America, in its openness to new concepts, sets a dynamic example for our own times. For we are living today in an age of energy: no longer an age of matter. Though all things are still material, the essence of our age is the discovery by science that matter is, itself, a vibration of energy.

The pioneering spirit in America exemplified this new awareness from the beginning. Energy may have been a thing unknown before oil was discovered seeping up out of the ground in Romania, late in the nineteenth century. Thereupon, some years later my father was sent there to find it underground. It wasn't the discovery that opened up this new age of energy. It was a new spirit in the air that made the discovery.

In 1894 Swami Sri Yukteswar, in his book, *The Holy Science*, declared that cosmic forces are now bringing a more enlightened awareness to the world. For centuries, people had observed in Romania that natural seepage of oil, and probably saw it as only a nuisance. It was the new *awareness* entering human consciousness that was opening up human minds, and that suggested to a few people the practical possibilities in that oil.

It was an *awareness* of energy that prompted scientists to recognize energy as the true basis of matter. New awareness must precede new discovery and invention. Another example of this truth is simple bread mold, which had been observed regretfully for centuries. Only when medical science had advanced to the point where it could *recognize* the uses of that mold was the discovery of penicillin made.

What seems ideal and right is not necessarily a dream in an undisciplined mind. It may simply be a reality waiting to be found. Practicality is not limited to what is known as workable today: It is what trial and error have shown actually to work. That which people call practical is only what they have experienced to date, not what some creative spirit may discover and turn into a new revelation. What a few daring pioneering spirits test and demonstrate in action (often against considerable public opposition) is not unusually the beginning of a new tradition.

Let us not, then, equate what is practical merely with what has been done before, lest, even while walking toward a beautiful sunset, our eyes look backward into a graying twilight.

One recalls America's history with covered wagons rolling over desert wilderness in search of new, fertile land. One recalls the Pilgrim Fathers, landing in the New World, confronting, and overcoming, numberless hardships in their effort to create a new and better way of living, with freedom to worship God according to their own conscience. One recalls the pioneering spirit blazing new trails of invention, again in America, by men like Cyrus McCormick (inventor of the McCormick Reaper), Benjamin Franklin (discoverer of electricity), and Thomas Edison (inventor of the electric light).

Invention and discovery are not by any means limited to America, though it was probably the pioneering spirit in America that first encouraged people throughout the world to welcome a new spirit: a spirit of inquiry that sought new ways of doing things in disregard of the paralyzing statement of tradition: "This is the way things are. This is how they have always been. And this is how they shall always be, time without end. Amen." The credit for this new spirit sweeping across the world belongs not to America, but to one simple fact: new influences in the world are producing a new age, an age of *energy*. America, being a new country, has been able more easily to welcome insights previously unknown.

The universe itself was created not by insensate surgings of unconscious, inanimate substance, but deliberately, wisely, and by a vastly superior divine *consciousness*.

Paramhansa Yogananda greatly admired the "go-getter" spirit he found in America. It is, he said, the spirit of a new age! To define as practical only what has been done before is to close one's mind to fresh opportunities. This new spirit is not "newfangled" in the sense of being a passing fad. Rather, it is how things are now on our planet, as it whirls through cosmic space.

The worst aspect of the common understanding of what is practical is the attitude that says, "A chasm yawns between idealism and reality. You can have your ideals, but don't relate them to business matters, or to getting things done in this real world." *Realpolitik* is an expression invented in Germany: politics based on a hardheaded and cynical attitude toward reality, as perceived by narrow minds. That slogan once justified, in the name of material expediency and dogmatic bigotry, the imprisonment and gassing to death of countless human beings in the 1930s and 1940s.

"Practicality" has been waved like a banner to declare that spirituality and high ideals belong in the temple, mosque, and church, but not in the "real" world of business. Hardheaded business practices are perceived too often as having nothing to do with ideals: they are purely a matter of making money. Into this thinking there creeps very easily the consciousness that dishonesty in business is perfectly justifiable—the sort of consciousness that justifies itself by saying, "One can't make an omelet without breaking a few eggs." This thinking creates a serious problem for businessmen who want to live by higher principles. It was voiced to me recently by a doctor friend in India. "I *believe* in high principles," he said to me earnestly. "*Practically speaking*, however, how can I follow them? Life makes demands of me that I simply cannot meet unless, occasionally, I cut a few corners ethically. I have a son to put through college. I *want* to live by dharmic principles, but if I did so always I couldn't survive."

It was that question which inspired me to write this course of lessons. For what I have seen from personal experience to be true is the exact opposite: To live determinedly by high principles is the surest road to material security—and beyond that, to glowing material success. My hope in these lessons has been to convince people that by giving high ideals the highest priority in their lives, they will succeed *far better* at anything they try in life than if they think—in the name of a practicality that can see only the solid ground at their feet—that, by cheating someone today, one has made his profit and needn't worry about tomorrow.

My observation has been that many people—in India nowadays especially—share that doctor's concern. The solution to his question depends first of all on another simple question: What is it doing *for you*? I couldn't easily ask my friend to look in a mirror and ask himself that question, though in fact his face showed some of the ravages of his inner conflict. The truth is, when people "cut corners" ethically, they cannot help creating an inner war—as at Kurukshetra—which pits the two selves within them, the higher and the lower, in heated combat together.

"What is it doing for you?" See whether it is giving you more inner peace, or—instead—more inner anguish. The very fact that my friend asked that question showed that he was suffering this anguish. A more hardheaded materialist might say, "What nonsense! *I* feel no such anguish!" That is because he has surrendered to the pull of his lower self. Let him ask himself then, instead, "Am I happy?" I don't believe his answer will be in the affirmative!

Many people make the gross mistake of equating practicality with greed. They may prevaricate to obtain an unfair advantage over someone; or to cheat a customer by selling him a product they know to be defective; or to damage a competitor's reputation by belittling his products and services.

Many years ago, in India, I tried to cancel a flight by telephone. The ticket agent told me I must come in person to make the cancellation. To make the journey there, however, meant a long taxi ride across New Delhi to resolve what seemed to me a most trivial matter.

"Why can't we simply conclude this thing over the phone?" I asked. She finally admitted to me, reluctantly, that businessmen had been known sometimes to cancel the reservations of their rivals to prevent them from making an important journey!

Cunning of that sort may pass among some for practicality, but it certainly is not in keeping with the principles of yoga or of dharma! Guile of that sort, moreover, generally proves counterproductive in the end. For once people begin entertaining suspicions as to who it was that tricked them, they will never again trust that person. "Straight shooters" will avoid him, certainly. He'll gradually find that the people around him have become limited to "slippery characters" like himself. And then he himself will point an accusing finger at the world with the denunciation, "You can't trust anybody!" It was that person himself first, however, who had become untrustworthy.

"Honesty is the best policy." We often hear

that phrase. It is no mere truism: It is the truth.

Take another example: Many years ago, I built the first of our several Ananda Sangha retreat centers. It was located a few miles outside the little town of Nevada City, California. During the building process I developed a friendly relationship with the owner of the building supply company where I bought my lumber. Indeed, he invited me to his home occasionally to pick fruit from his trees.

After several months, a time came when my expenses—greater than I'd expected—exceeded my savings for the project. I wasn't greatly concerned, for I was earning enough at that time through classes in the cities to cover within three months any further debts. Nevertheless, I was eager to finish the job before winter came, lest its storms ruin everything. I went therefore to those to whom I owed money and asked them if they would let me pay them five hundred dollars a month until my debt to them was discharged. Everyone, including that building supplies owner, agreed to this proposal. Fortunately, as a teacher I was popular, and at that time was attracting about 300 students a week.

My building materials supplier, however, thought he spied a chance here (perhaps with his lawyer's recommendation) to make a quick profit from my predicament. A week later his lawyer placed a lien on my property. A scant week later, a letter came from the lawyer threatening to foreclose on my property if I didn't pay off my entire debt in two weeks. We'd had a verbal agreement and I'd been honoring it. I phoned the owner. He sounded embarrassed, but blustered in a conciliatory tone of voice, "Well, you see, Don,* a person has to be practical." To him, obviously, to be *practical* meant to be *greedy*! I went then and spoke with his lawyer, who shouted at me, "What agreement? I know nothing of any agreement! Show it to me in writing." Evidently, my "friend" was more interested in gaining possession of a valuable piece of property than in the little matter of verbal agreements, or even in the relatively small amount of money I owed him.

I've seen many miracles in my life, and I believe in the power of faith. I am not proposing, however, that you leave such matters passively in the hands of God. To exert faith effectively takes a certain amount of experience. Nevertheless, I do strongly believe in the ancient teaching, "*Yato dharma, tato jaya*: Where there is adherence to right action, there is victory." And I believe, on the basis of many years of experience, that actions offered to God do receive a special blessing. When one acts rightly, moreover, everything really does turn out for the best, eventually. Still, with a situation as time-sensitive as this one was, that word "eventually" cannot but raise a certain doubt, which offers but little comfort!

Well, whether what happened was a miracle or not, it is essential always, and especially at such times, to put out all the energy one can, *dharmically*: only thus can one turn the tide of karma in his own favor. In the present instance, I can only say that what saved me *did seem* like a miracle.

What happened was this: A few days after receiving that devastating threat from the lawyer, I happened to be in a student's home giving a show of colored slides that I'd taken in India. I said nothing about my financial predicament; to do so, I felt, would not be appropriate to that occasion.

I should interject here that life has taught me that an important key to receiving divine assistance is to be inwardly non-attached—not

---

* An abbreviation for Donald, my birth name and the name by which many people still knew me.

indifferent, please note, but willing to let God handle the outcome and to accept whatever He sends. Throughout that evening, though I said nothing, I prayed mentally to God to show me what to do.

After the event, a young man who was unknown to me followed me outdoors. I was getting into my car when he said, "I like what you're doing. Would you accept a donation to help with it?"

"Yes, of course!" I replied, thinking he might give me five dollars, or even ten. Instead, leaning on the hood of my car, he wrote out a check for $3,000! This amount was more than sufficient to pay off my remaining debt to that building supplies owner.

I deposited the check the next day. Then it occurred to me that my erstwhile friend, that company's owner, needed a stern lesson in fair dealing. I telephoned him and said, "I have the money now to pay you off fully. However, I won't pay any of it until the very last moment, which your lawyer tells me won't come for another two months owing to the paperwork involved. Meanwhile, because you refused to honor our agreement, I'll let you incur all the legal fees your lawyer can charge you."

"Oh, in that case, Don," he cried, "pay me the whole amount right now and I'll give you a big discount." He'd dug a pit for me, then fell into it himself! I did pay him immediately. I was left at the end of the month, after paying my various bills, with a little over one dollar in my bank account!

Well, all of us need a few lessons in life. One lesson I myself learned from this experience (though I admit it took a little longer for the lesson really to sink in) was to put my business agreements in writing, and to get them properly signed. Such a careful precaution is offensive to my nature. I prefer to trust people, and like to consider everyone a friend with whom I have any dealings. Anyone of common sense, however, will understand the need at least to keep one's transactions clear and open. This man, meanwhile, not only fell into the pit he'd dug for me, but lost a good customer in the bargain. Not I alone, but many others at Ananda in later years have avoided going to him for their housing supplies. Worst of all, perhaps, from his point of view, was that by playing that little game of greed he lost a friend who could have supported him in other ways, in the future.

So, then—how "practical" had he really been?

I don't think he really feared that I wouldn't be able to pay him. Until then I'd always been prompt with my payments. Even if he thought he had some good reason to doubt my bona fides, could his action be called honorable? "Gentlemen's agreements" are not unheard of even in the business world, though the question obviously rests on whether both parties really *are* gentlemen! The question turns, surely, on whether *anything* is justifiable that is without honor.

What if he'd obtained that land by unscrupulous means? What *else* would he have won along with that ill-gotten gain? Inner self-reproach, certainly, though he seems to have been prepared for that. What about inner tension, and a shrinking sense of self-worth? What about a diminished trust in others, and his own dwindling trust in his own integrity? What about his consequently narrowing circle of friends?

After toting up the account, even the obvious objection to wrong action—namely, karmic retribution—begins to seem only a small part of the disadvantages incurred.

If being practical means to ask oneself,

What will work? it is apparent that what actually works may not always be something measurable by the yardstick of material values. The human dimension is, and should always be considered to be, part of the cost. Beside that consideration, monetary gain must be seen as temporary and, in most cases, unsatisfactory.

It is wise always to keep life's longer rhythms in mind. It is also wise to be sensitive to other people's realities. Selfishness has a way of blinding us to the larger picture. If that aspect gets shut out of one's reckoning, however, one develops a kind of tunnel vision which, in time, will prevent him from making good decisions even in perfectly ordinary matters.

That building supplier's selfishness prevented him from seeing that Ananda was already promising to flourish over the years. Today, it is home to hundreds of people. They, in turn, for the very slight price of common trust, would have become that man's customers also for many of their housing needs. He was never in any danger, but let us ponder this possibility: Even if I'd failed, and he'd beaten others to "the punch" in rescuing what was possible to be retrieved from the shambles, he'd have lost incalculably in ways many people would have considered important also.

To understand what *will* work, and therefore what is practical, means to consider everything in a broad context, and not merely in terms of *immediate* profit. There is a way to make this discernment. We'll discuss it in the next section, "The Application." First, however, let us consider other theoretical considerations.

For example, what if one's reason for "cutting corners" ethically is motivated by generous motives? Let us say a person wants—as my doctor friend did—to put his son through college, and feels that he must pit the boy's future against whatever little harm might result from cheating a stranger. In many people's eyes, this might seem more like generosity than selfishness. It would take someone of greater-than-usual understanding to see that, if he harms even a stranger, however slightly, he still harms himself. To that extent, indeed, he harms those as well, consequently, who are his dependents.

Valmiki, in his account of the *Ramayana*, asked his wife and children, on the prompting of a group of saints, if they'd be willing to bear the burden of his sins, committed only to support them. They responded with outrage at the suggestion. "That's *your* karma!" they cried. "Why should we have to share it with you?" Thereupon, he renounced his family as strangers to him, and left them to seek God.

In the present context, it should be stated that whatever mistakes a man commits to support others certainly draws them, too, into the karmic orbit of those mistakes, for they've benefited willingly from his sins.

Many people need to approach subjects like this with the question, "What's in it for me, *really*?" If, with the best of intentions, I draw harm to those whom I love in my efforts to help them, will not the results—assuming they support those efforts—entail eventual misfortune for them?

The truth is that a straightforward and honorable attitude develops the magnetism, in time, to become a victor under *every* circumstance. The time required to achieve this glorious end depends on how many obstacles you have to overcome in your own nature. By right action we straighten out our subconscious "kinks." The fact may be, however, that this inner transformation will take longer than that man's son has, for instance, in his present need for an education. Again, the *truth* is that no one will ever be able to transform himself without first passing through the tests that are hurled at him by the forces of *maya*, or delusion. Those forces range themselves *consciously* against every effort toward spiritual upliftment.

Will you argue, "I can't wait that long. I have *immediate* problems to face!"? So be it. I will not try to persuade you against your will and present understanding. All I will say is, Think well, before making an investment of money, time, and energy that you know must bring you grief, someday. Someday? That "someday" will be very much *this* day—someday! Meanwhile, whatever karmic mistakes, or sins, you carry in your heart will, in ways not even evident to you, diminish you as a human being. That is a burden one notices only when he has been relieved of it. Otherwise, delusion convinces him, meanwhile, that his lack of happiness and of inner satisfaction is "perfectly normal."

It would help everyone to realize that the reality behind all existence is consciousness, not a blindly operating law. This thought leads us to subtle metaphysical levels, and may seem merely theoretical to some people. It would be wise, in any case, to give these concepts at least a chance to "do their stuff." I promise you, they will prove themselves to you many times over if you sincerely give them a chance. I have some experience in these matters, long and varied.

One of the most inspiring chapters in *Autobiography of a Yogi* by Paramhansa Yogananda is "Two Penniless Boys in Brindaban." Mukunda, as my Guru was then known, receives a challenge by his materialistic older brother Ananta, who says to him, "Suppose I suggest that your vaunted philosophy be put to the test in this tangible world?"

"I would agree!" my Guru answered. "Do you confine God to a speculative world?"

What follows is one of the most thrilling episodes in the entire book. "Mukunda" abundantly demonstrates the practicality of depending on God even in this "hard" material world. I won't give away the story if you haven't yet read this book, but I do urge you, if you don't own a copy, to buy one and read it now! I will add only that this chapter helped to change my life so completely that I took the next bus nonstop across the American continent—a journey of four days and four nights—to become the author's disciple. I have, moreover, to the best of my ability lived up to my commitment to him for almost sixty years.

Nor are the miraculous-seeming events described in his book confined only to the workings of God-realized masters. I have tested and proved the claims in that one chapter again and again in my far more ordinary life. *Those principles work!* Dependence on God wins an actual, loving response from the Lord!

I remember once, many years ago, feeling that the Divine Mother wanted me to return to India. I had saved up the money I'd need for the journey, from classes that I had given and from gifts that a few kindly-disposed people had made me. It was enough to get me to India and back.

Two weeks before my scheduled departure, however, the rod on my car went out. I realized that the time had come for me to sell the car and exchange it for another, better one. A used car was all I could afford at the time, but even that would make a dent in my savings, resulting in my having to cancel my trip to India.

I asked the Divine Mother, "What shall I do?" No answer came. I was in San Francisco at that time, and the only "church" or "temple" to which I could withdraw to pray for guidance was the restaurant where I and a few friends were eating lunch.

"Divine Mother," I prayed finally, "common sense tells me I shall have to return to America in two months. On my return, living as I do in the hills, I will need a car. Since You won't answer me, what can I do but follow the dictates of common sense? If You really do want me to go to India, You'll just have to reimburse me!"

That was a Friday evening. I wrote out a check for eleven hundred dollars ($1,100) toward a good used car. The rest of the amount needed was covered by what I received by trading in my old car.

The following Monday morning, three days later, a letter came in the mail. Enclosed with it was a check for $1,000. The letter, from someone I'd never heard of, said, "Please use this money as Divine Mother wants you to."

Now, how many Americans even think of God as their Divine Mother? Very few, indeed. (I've often wished there were more!)

Many, many times have similar experiences come to me. They corroborate the testimony in my Guru's book—adding the useful evidence, perhaps, that divine faith works even for common people like me. It is evidence, furthermore, that I *know* what I am talking about when I say that God listens to any sincere demand His children address to Him, and will respond in kind. Perhaps I'll include other stories like this one in future lessons, for this is an important truth. Although God is infinite, He/She is aware of every tiny ripple of thought and feeling in our consciousness.

To return, then, to the question of *maya*'s tests, designed as they are to test our resolve to move forward on the path to truth: There *will* be tests, certainly, placed consciously, deliberately, and sometimes with seeming indifference to impede your way. Yes, you will have to prove yourself to the Divine Mother, or to any form in which you worship the Infinite Consciousness. This testing has a divine purpose: to stiffen your mettle. If you remain true to your principles, everything will work out in the end—beyond "imagination of expectancy" as my Guru put it—for your good, and will be the right thing also for all who depend on you.

Your son in college, for instance, may actually benefit from having to work part time to put *himself* through college. Or it may be that his highest success lies in some other direction, and in a different kind of training altogether. Or perhaps, again, you'll find an unexpected financial windfall coming to you.

Tests *must* come to us; sometimes they may seem to deluge us. It remains an infallible truth, however, that the law protects all who abide determinedly by truth. *Yato dharma, tato jaya!*: "Where there is adherence to right action, there [alone] lies victory!"

The Application

For some time in my life I worked under someone who, to my considerable frustration, began responding to my every proposal with the statement, "It just isn't *practical*!" I imagine she was as frustrated with me as I came to be with her predictable reply. I *knew* my ideas were good. I knew they *were* practical. If they were novel, I saw this as their main virtue. Years later I had many opportunities to prove that my ideas did work. Her unvarying judgment, however, was based on the common assumption that if a thing hasn't been tried before, it would be unsafe to try it ever.

Nothing new or better is ever accomplished by following well-trodden paths. Lack of daring may guarantee a certain smooth safety, but it also ensures mediocrity. "They laughed at Fulton" is a popular saying in America. Robert Fulton was the man who first proved that a metal steamboat could actually float on water, and would travel faster than wooden ships. People who succeed greatly in this world almost always do things in new ways. I therefore plead with you, who are studying these lessons: If you can afford to take a chance, don't be afraid to try!

What you must do when you face any problem is withdraw first, mentally, into your spine—even for just a moment. Your spine is the center of your body. Pause there, briefly if necessary, and ask yourself in a consciousness of inner balance what, considered from every angle, is the best solution.

Another secret of effective, *practical* action is to draw upon your own inmost natural resource: superconscious intuition. To receive higher guidance, don't think you must first engage in long meditation. Clarity doesn't depend on the time you spend seeking it. What is important is the *energy* you focus on coming to your decision. Some people deliberate painstakingly for hours, days, or even weeks; even then they are only tentatively hopeful of having reached a satisfactory conclusion. By contrast, really successful people make better decisions on what may seem like the spur of the moment. Let me repeat: It isn't a question of time. It is a question of focused energy.

In the last lesson, I mentioned an important truth. A strong flow of energy, I said, generates a magnetic field. That magnetism can actually *attract* inspiration, according to its animating consciousness. The slow deliberation involved in most decision-making has dim energy. The time it takes doesn't justify the results, for it seldom or never reaches any inspired conclusions.

I remember an occasion years ago, by contrast, when a quick decision was forced upon me. I would have liked nothing better just at that moment than to devote time to deliberating the matter. The matter itself was important, and seemed to call for input from a number of people. Moreover, on a personal note, I had just finished giving a great deal of energy to teaching and to being with people. I was to see several more visitors who had asked for interviews. Moreover, I had, for the moment, closed my mental doors against any further activity, and was sitting down to enjoy a leisurely lunch.

At that moment one of our members hurried into the dining room, huffing and puffing in her haste, and announced, "We've just located a printing press in Texas." We were in need of a press, and this one, she said, was for sale at a good price. "Shall we get it?" was her urgent question.

"Please," I said, "let me enjoy these few moments of peace. I really don't want to put my mind on any problems just now. And, to be honest, I really don't know what to say in reply to your question. Isn't this a matter to be deliberated over in a group before any decision is reached?"

"But we can't wait!" she replied. "The man is on the phone now, and needs our answer *immediately*! Otherwise, he says, he has another customer waiting to buy."

Well, whether or not the answer really was needed "immediately" was something I could not ascertain. If we lost this chance, however, we might not find such a good opportunity again. I realized that I had no choice but to make a decision on the spot. What about the time one ought to take in such matters, for leisurely deliberation? This, I thought, was time we all needed. Truthfully, I had no clear idea anyway as to the right decision. Time, however, was the one thing I wasn't being given.

I therefore put aside for the moment the thought of that meal I'd been looking forward to enjoying. Instead, I sat up straight, concentrated at the point between the eyebrows, and directed the question, with energy, to my superconsciousness: "Shall we get it?" Strange to relate, I knew the answer *instantly*. It wasn't as though this seemed *possibly*, only, a good idea—one maybe worth pursuing. I *really did know* what had to be done.

"Tell him we will take it," I said. My friend went off to conclude her telephone conversation, and I sat back to enjoy my lunch. Future events proved me right. Though the decision represented a major investment for us, it was the right decision for our needs at that time.

I'm reminded of a similar occasion—similar in the opposite sense. Concentrated energy-output would have accomplished so much more than the time actually involved in doing the job. An Ananda member put together a slide show about the community. It took her a whole month simply to write the script. I didn't tell her so, but the thought came to me, "My goodness, I wrote a script for a very similar project recently—a better script, too. And all it took me was an afternoon!" I didn't fault my friend for having taken so long; she hadn't had my years of practice at writing. Still, my point is that the reason it took her so long was that she didn't put forth the *energy* to get the job done more quickly. The amount of energy she expended in a month could have been expended in an afternoon, and more effectively, had it been *concentrated*. Had it been my project, I would not have allowed my thoughts to drift down winding pathways of slow deliberation.

A strong thought not only speeds up the process of finding a solution, but is more certain to draw upon the source of all truly creative effort: superconscious intuition. To reiterate this important principle: A strong thought sends out energy which, generating magnetism, *attracts* to itself whatever inspiration or insight it requires. Time has nothing to do with the process. As Paramhansa Yogananda stated, "Inspiration can be controlled by the will." There is no excuse for the "dry spells" often experienced by artists, writers, and composers. The intuitive faculty is with us always. We have only to summon it in the right way: with an uplifted attitude.

The way to approach the question is with what I call "solution-consciousness." To approach anything with this consciousness, give only minimal consideration to any difficulties confronting you. *Know*, rather, that the solution is there already, simply awaiting your recognition.

First, then, *form in your mind a clear idea as to what kind of solution you want*. Don't ask vaguely for an answer. At the same time, don't pray in blind hope that some sort of answer will appear. Rather, tell your superconscious specifically what you want.

Once, as I've mentioned earlier, I wanted to write music to accompany a showing of color slides I'd taken of the ancient Italian city of Pompeii. Pompeii, as you may know, was destroyed over two thousand years ago in an eruption of Mount Vesuvius. Before asking for a melody, therefore, I began with the thought, "What do I *want* this melody to say? I want it to do no more than *suggest* that ancient tragedy, so as not to emphasize the sins that must have been the karmic reason for that tragedy. I don't want *too* sad a melody, therefore; that disaster took place long ago, and—one hopes—was itself an *expiation* for the people's sins. Let the melody, therefore, be *reminiscent*, only, of ancient suffering. Finally, let it suggest hope for a better future."

I offered this request clearly to God and my own superconscious—not so much in those words as in the form of specific concepts. A tall order, perhaps? Well in any case, all I did after forming the ideas was pray, "Give me a melody that says all that." Instantly, the melody came. It expressed everything I wanted.

I don't suppose anyone who has heard the flute recording of this melody has been conscious, specifically, of all that the melody expresses. Many people have told me, however, that what they felt while listening was a sadness tinged with unexpected joy and upliftment. What more could any composer want for a reaction from his listeners?

It takes, energy, I repeat, not time and deliberation to arrive at solutions that *work*.

How, then, to *practice* decision-making? First, withdraw into your center, in the spine. Let nothing outside you sway your deliberation. From that inner *danda*, as we might call it, or rod of inner balance, try to *sense* a direction that will somehow express the whole spectrum of whatever is involved.

Next, focus your mind deeply at the point between the eyebrows. Lovingly demand, there, an answer to your question. Make the demand *with solution-consciousness*, in the full expectation of receiving an immediate answer. Don't say, for example, "Here is my problem. What on earth can I do about it?" Say, rather, "I need an answer, and that answer is. . . ." Await the answer with instant expectation. The answer, if your demand is made with one-pointed faith, will appear instantly and clearly in your mind.

More is involved after that, certainly. For one thing, you will need to *know* whether the answer that comes is the *right* one, and not one concocted by your imagination. But that problem must await a later lesson.

I haven't even touched on aspects of practicality that are less directly related to yoga principles: for example, how to keep your expenses within your income. There are commonsense points that might be considered here, such as being careful to control your small, daily expenses, which can mount up quickly! As Swami Sri Yukteswar put it, "Be comfortable within your purse." This aspect of our subject, however, opens up a wide territory, and might easily be the material for a book. More to the point: For this lesson, it really *isn't* to the point!

MEDITATION

Remember, what works in practice will depend *first of all* on the kind of energy you put out, not on the energy others have put out who trod that same path before you.

Imagine the consciousness of humanity in all its variety as represented by the seven colors of the rainbow. Within that spectrum of colors numerous shades of color may be discerned—from clear, bright colors to almost muddy hues.

Imagine the people you meet as projecting to you, with varying degrees of intensity, their own particular colors. The colors they project are what is called the human aura, which surrounds everyone. It indicates their magnetic field. The auras of most people are thin, and project only a feeble light. Still, in their number and variety even that feeble light can affect you, whether positively or negatively. It is not easy to protect your integrity under the impact of so many influences. How can you defend yourself against colors that are disharmonious? Even more to the point, perhaps: how can you cling to your principles in a world that, so often, equates lack of principle with being "practical"?

The answer is, Strengthen your own aura. Imagine a bright light in your heart. Radiate that light upward to the spiritual eye, and outward from there into the world. Let it radiate in every direction. Make yourself a *cause* in life, not an effect. Feel your aura extending outward from your spiritual eye into the world around you, protecting you from every discordant influence in a balloon of light. No weaker light will be able to penetrate the magnetic field you generate by your strong will. Any aura that is compatible with your own, on the other hand, will find itself strongly attracted to you.

Fill your light with joy and love. Know that these divine qualities are yours eternally.

AFFIRMATION

"In Thee alone I am truly free. Freedom is forever mine in Thy light."

POINTS TO REMEMBER

1. To define as practical only what has been done before is to close one's mind to fresh opportunities.

2. To live determinedly by high principles is the surest road to material security—and beyond that, to glowing material success.

3. When people "cut corners" ethically, they cannot help creating an inner war which pits the two selves within them, the higher and the lower, in heated combat together.

4. Honest people will avoid the dishonest businessman. He'll gradually find the people around him limited to "slippery characters" like himself.

5. "Honesty is the best policy."

6. Practicality is not always measurable by the yardstick of material values. The human dimension is, and should always be considered to be, part of the cost.

7. It is wise always to keep life's longer rhythms in mind. Selfishness has a way of blinding us to the larger picture, and preventing us from making good decisions.

8. A straightforward and honorable attitude develops the magnetism, in time, to become a victor under *every* circumstance.

9. Whatever karmic mistakes, or sins, you carry in your heart will diminish you as a human being. That is a burden one notices only when he has been relieved of it.

10. The reality behind all existence is *consciousness*, not a blindly operating law. Dependence on God wins an actual, loving response from the Lord!

11. There *will* be tests, with a divine purpose: to stiffen your mettle. If you remain true to your principles, everything will work out in the end for your good.

12. The law protects all who abide determinedly by truth. *Yato dharma, tato jaya!*: "Where there is adherence to right action, there [alone] lies victory!"

13. *Nothing* new or better is ever accomplished by following well-trodden paths. If you can afford to take a chance, don't be afraid to try!

14. A strong thought sends out energy which, generating magnetism, *attracts* to itself whatever inspiration or insight it requires. Time has nothing to do with the process. The intuitive faculty is with us always.

15. To practice decision-making: First, withdraw into your center, in the spine. Let nothing outside you sway your deliberation. From that rod of inner balance, try to *sense* a direction that will somehow express the whole spectrum of whatever is involved.

16. Next, focus your mind deeply at the point between the eyebrows. Lovingly demand, there, an answer to your question. Make the demand *with solution-consciousness*, in

the full expectation of receiving an immediate answer. Say, "I need an answer, and that answer is. . . ." Await the answer with instant expectation. The answer, if your demand is made with one-pointed faith, will appear instantly and clearly in your mind.

17. Strengthen your aura. Imagine a bright light in your heart. Radiate that light upward to the spiritual eye, and outward from there into the world. Feel your aura extending outward from your spiritual eye into the world around you, protecting you from every discordant influence in a balloon of light. Any aura compatible with your own will find itself strongly attracted to you.

WORKBOOK IDEAS
by Joseph Bharat Cornell

Give God a Chance

A wealthy devotee of Shiva was passing through a forest, when a robber suddenly appeared. The devotee called on the Lord to save him. Shiva, hearing His devotee's cry, rushed to his defense. By the time Shiva arrived, however, the devotee had already picked up a stone to protect himself. Seeing this, Shiva turned back. "Why did You return so soon?" Parvati asked Shiva. He replied, "My devotee no longer needed me."

The Lord, who gave us free will, waits to see if we really want His help. If we insist on doing things ourselves, He won't intrude.

ACTION ITEM:
Give God a chance to work in your life, by offering Him a situation, project, or even a whole day. Invite His presence and guidance on whatever you choose, and with an effort of will, pray, "Whatever You give me, is fine." Concentrate on trusting God, and leaving the results to Him. Let Him surprise you.

Don't presume on God, however. Choose something no more than one step beyond your experience of God's help and presence.

Make God your partner in this experiment. Share and do everything *with* Him. Constantly ask for His guidance. This will keep you actively attuned to Him, and add your energy to His.

Pay attention. God's guidance is often subtle and happens over time!

Choose something you want to offer completely to God. Say to Him, this is Yours, I just want to become closer to You through this experience.

Receive an Answer—Right Now!

A disciple of Yogananda had to decide whether to take a risky treatment for a serious illness. For three years he had avoided doing so because of the severe side effects. After years of no improvement, however, his doctors began to think the treatment might be the lesser of two evils. During a hospital exam the specialist wasn't able to decide. So he left the room to look at the x-rays again before giving his recommendation. Meanwhile the devotee, knowing a decision had to be made in a few minutes, prayed intensely to God for guidance. The doctor returned with sudden assurance, and with great conviction told the devotee, "I *definitely* don't think you should do the treatment, I definitely don't!" Before, there was uncertainty; now, clarity. God had answered the devotee through the doctor. Months later the devotee's health improved; the treatment was indeed unnecessary.

Clarity doesn't depend on the time spent seeking answers; it depends on the amount of energy focused while making a decision. When we are desperate for an answer, our sense of urgency naturally concentrates and increases our energy. The secret to receiving guidance anytime is to create a strong flow of energy, by dynamically offering your request up to the spiritual eye.

ACTION ITEM:

- Think of something you want answered. Magnetize a reply immediately, by generating a dynamic flow of energy at the spiritual eye with your request. If your thoughts wander, keep concentrating until only your loving demand exists.

LESSON SIX

FIRST THINGS FIRST

You, at the center of all your activities, need to be balanced as a human being. Whatever you do should receive your full concentration, but try always, at the same time, to work *from your center*. Be centered in yourself, always, and never fully identified with anything outward that you do.

The Principles

There is an expression in America today: "the bottom line." I don't know if this expression is used in England or in other countries where, as in India, English is widely spoken. Usually the expression refers to monetary profit. By extension, it also indicates something of fundamental importance to an undertaking. Because profit is so often people's concern, unless they make it clear that they mean something different it is generally understood that they are talking about money.

Let me clarify what I mean, then, in naming this lesson as I have. For this course of lessons serves a dual purpose, and may be said, in this sense, to have *two* "bottom lines." First, it accepts the common equation of material success with *monetary profit*. It also attempts to show, however, that monetary profit, without corresponding inner satisfaction, is a hollow victory. As the Bible puts it, "What shall it profit a man if he gain the whole world, but lose his own soul?"

People for whom the entire issue is monetary profit often fail to achieve what they *really* want, even materially. As a fairly common example, they may sacrifice the subtler satisfaction of esthetic good taste. Their coffers may be overflowing with gold, while their homes are monstrosities that declare only, with puffed-up pride, "See how *rich* I am!" They seem to shout the news. Tunnel vision has deprived their proud creators of refinement.

Tunnel vision also deprives people of spiritual satisfactions that are more important than esthetic pleasure: happiness, for example, and peace of mind. Worst of all, from a standpoint of what interests businessmen particularly: They may blind themselves to unusual opportunities for success that would enliven their very pursuit for money. One-pointed concentration on anything, including money, if directed with will power and energy, generates, as I have said, a magnetic field which can attract to itself whatever one desires. Thus, by energetic concentration on making money one ought indeed to become rich. In the process, however, he may lose that creative flair which lends special interest to moneymaking. If he pursues it merely as "the bottom line," that goal may lose all charm for him and become merely an obsession. Even moneymaking cannot really be anyone's real goal in life. How can bulging coffers radiate happiness? They and their contents are inert.

A collector of anything, be it money or stamps or antiques or fine porcelain, may exult in what he amasses. His exultation, however, will be a poor imitation of the happiness he desires most deeply in his heart. His collection may easily awaken negative emotions in him, moreover: envy of others who possess more, fear of robbery or breakage, or (worst of all) vain pride of possession which, robbing him of an innocent (because guileless) sense of freedom, makes true happiness impossible.

Many years ago, in New Delhi, I visited the ambassador (or "plenipotentiary," as he was titled) of a country in South America. He served me tea on priceless porcelain; its beauty was a pleasure to behold. I wasn't able to enjoy it completely, however, for my host didn't share my pleasure at all. Before, during, and after we were served he kept on exhorting his servant fearfully, "*For God's sake be careful!*" Most of our time together was filled with his lamentations about how careless servants were "nowadays." Later on, after the table had been cleared, his cautionary shouts followed that tray and its precious contents all the way to the kitchen. Was my host's refined taste really worth his excessive apprehension? I somehow doubt it.

Money is something I myself have never sought for personal gain. Yet I have certainly had to earn it for the benefit of others. The spiritual communities I founded could not have come into being without money, and it was I myself who, in the early years, had to earn almost all of it. There were times, in fact, when my financial needs must have been as pressing as any family man faces whose interests are focused entirely on his personal needs. Indeed, mine may have been heavier, for hundreds of people came, in time, to depend for their material security on my activities, and thousands more for their spiritual well-being. The pressures on me to "perform" were sometimes, to my sighs of regret, intense.

I say all this only to clarify the following point: Always, in spite of these pressures, I have never allowed my "bottom line" to become monetary. That place of priority was given to my inner peace. When merchants stood in line, figuratively speaking, demanding payment, and when people tried to block whatever I attempted (as not a few did), I never allowed my inner peace to become affected. Peace was my priority. Being a swami didn't exempt me, unfortunately, from the pressures of modern life. I had a work to develop, and had therefore to place myself willingly under a stress not so different from that of the "business tycoon" whose way of life I had renounced for God!

With God's grace I succeeded. I don't believe it would have been possible, however, had I not made inner peace my priority.

Let me sort through a few of the deliberate choices I was obliged to make, only to preserve my inner peace. These few hints may be of help to you whenever you face similar circumstances in your life, as you almost certainly will.

One choice I made was never to let myself be drawn into other people's priorities. Perhaps, among the many letters I received, there were a few that I didn't answer promptly—or, in some cases, at all. I paid my bills promptly, and met all my important obligations, but I simply accepted, with a sense of inner freedom, that I was not the legendary Atlas: I could not carry the whole world on my shoulders! If, then, someone wrote me a letter that I didn't feel to answer, even though that person was obviously anxious to hear from me, I sometimes didn't answer him. "Well," I told myself, "I didn't *ask* him to write!" Only if someone's well-being was concerned did I try conscientiously to help him as soon as possible. What use would I have been to anyone, however, had I done everything that was asked of me, but sacrificed my inner peace? Interestingly, I found that if I didn't address an issue that to others seemed urgent, it usually resolved itself anyway within a couple of months!

Something else I did was develop a team of assistants who could act on my behalf. I gave executive powers to those who showed an understanding of what I was trying to accomplish, and I also helped them to develop their own executive skills. In other words, I never allowed myself to think that, as the founder of Ananda, I had to make every decision. Many people in my place have felt they owed it to the integrity of their work to oversee *everything*, and to make every decision—important or unimportant. Often they've involved themselves in the most minor matters. Perhaps they've done so out of habit, or perhaps their thought was that faithfulness in little matters is needed if one would be faithful greatly. Thus, unfortunately, they've often become busybodies, and as a result of their "scrupulosity" they've concluded, finally, that everyone under them was incompetent. The result, of course, for those who work under them is that they come to *feel* as incompetent as they are adjudged to be. They become, in fact, incapable of making necessary decisions, all of which have to be decided "at the top," and are therefore delayed indefinitely. Alternatively, they rebel, and often leave the organization altogether. Such organizations attract, after a time, only people of second-rate capability.

My duty, as I saw it, was to make sure that those who served under me represented, not me as a person, but the ideals we were seeking to represent. I tried mainly to help them understand those ideals and to be true to them. Beyond that, I considered it my duty to encourage anyone who showed promise of becoming, himself, a good leader in this mold. I encouraged especially those who sought the well-being of everyone, and who showed no interest in their own importance. *How* they addressed specific problems was less important to me than that they address it in the right spirit: with humility, cooperation, and intelligence. If they showed themselves in that sense competent, the addition of kindness, devotion to truth and to God, and respect for others was enough, in my eyes, to earn them my trust.

Finally, what I learned was the necessity for devoting all my energy and attention to everything I did. Having decided on peace as my "bottom line," I refused to worry over decisions that were important but couldn't be faced yet. Rather, I addressed them with full concentration only *when the time came* to do so. Meanwhile, I concentrated more on keeping my inner peace and joy, while doing whatever needed to be done at present.

My "bottom line" has actually helped me to accomplish far more in my life than would have been the case had I allowed problems to engulf me. If I'd sacrificed my inner peace, but succeeded thereby in getting more done, I would not only have ended by accomplishing less in the long run, but would have diluted my powers of concentration and creativity. I might well have ended, therefore, simply "spinning my wheels."

I knew a very successful American businessman—a multimillionaire, indeed—and a disciple of my Guru. This man was exceptionally busy, being the chairman of several boards of directors. Yet his practice was often not to come to work until sometime in the afternoon. His morning hours were devoted to meditation. Colleagues would sometimes remonstrate with him, "With all your responsibilities, how can you afford to be away from your office so long?"

"Because I have so many," he answered, "I need those morning hours to deepen my peace. In that way, I can handle matters more efficiently when I do address them, and can accomplish more in a minute than would be possible for me if I were to sit at my desk all day long. Decisions that some people take weeks to make I am able to make almost instantly."

I want, similarly, to do more than urge you in this lesson to make your inner peace a priority: I want to show you how, by preserving that peace, to succeed *better* at whatever you do than would be possible if you were always on the job. The sacrifice of inner peace would disturb your concentration. Success at anything, as I've pointed out before, depends much more on concentrated energy than on the amount of time one spends in thinking about a project.

It is important also, however, not to divide your life into airtight compartments: business, personal life, family interests, social obligations, and spiritual practices. You, at the center of all your activities, need to be balanced as a human being. Whatever you do should receive your full concentration, but try always, at the same time, to work *from your center*. Be centered in yourself, always, and never fully identified with anything outward that you do. It is *you* who do it; don't become a mirror to anything that you accomplish. Don't let competing priorities enter your mind, lest you become fragmented.

I met a wealthy man in Canada years ago who was also a spiritual seeker. "My real life," he told me, "begins after I return home in the evenings from work, bathe, change my clothes, and enter my meditation room." When he said that, I thought (though I didn't say), "What a pity not to bring a meditative spirit also into your daily work! In that way, you'd be able to live your 'real life' all day long."

There is another story. It may seem, superficially, to contradict what I've been saying, but when one understands it more deeply it shows the same truth, only from another angle.

A guru was teaching a young student. After a time he noticed that the boy's mind was not fully absorbed in his lesson.

"Where is your mind, child?"

"Oh, I'm sorry, Master. We have a new buffalo at home, and I've been thinking about it. Forgive me. I'll concentrate harder on what you're saying."

"Never mind," said the guru. "Just go to your room and think about your buffalo. That will be your lesson for the time being."

The boy went to his room obediently, and began to think about his buffalo.

After some time the Master returned, looked in the door, and asked, "What are you doing now, child?"

"I'm just thinking about my buffalo, Master. Shall I come out now?"

"No, remain where you are. Keep on thinking about your buffalo friend."

A little time later the Guru returned. He inquired, "What are you doing now?"

"Oh, I'm playing in the meadow with my buffalo. It's such fun! Shall I come now?"

"Not yet," was the reply. "Keep on playing with your pet."

The next day the teacher came back and asked, "What are you and your buffalo doing now?"

"What do you mean?" inquired the boy in a deep, gruff voice. "I *am* the buffalo!"

"That's good!" said the guru. "You may come out now."

"How can I?" the boy objected. "My horns are too big. They won't go through the door!"

The guru went into the room, touched the "buffalo" on the forehead, and his disciple went into *samadhi*, or divine ecstasy.

Concentration is important for every type of success. So also is meditation. Don't get so wrapped up in your work, however, that you lose your human identity! There are drawbacks to every story, as my Guru said. This is the drawback to that story. An example is only an example; were it perfect, it would *replace* the reality it exemplifies! What I am urging is the importance of one-pointed concentration; I am not saying, "Lose yourself completely in whatever you do." I have found when writing music, for example, that I do much better by deliberately not entering wholly, myself, into the mood of the piece.

I don't *become* sadness or joy: I am the Self, *observing* sadness or joy.

In business, to work from your inner center is necessary if you want to put *your* vibrations into your work. Moreover, it is those vibrations, even more than the work itself, that will truly determine the outcome.

That guru in the story was trying to teach his young disciple how, ultimately, to meditate on God: God *is* our true self; we must therefore become one with Him. The buffalo of course was not that boy's true identity. By shifting his developed concentration to the truth of his own being, he was able to merge effortlessly into the Self. Absolute concentration on money, on the other hand, would incapacitate a person for business, for it would reduce him to inactivity. He might come to believe, for example, that he actually *was* a pile of rupee notes! Still, to be so focused on anything you do that your energy flows one-pointedly toward that, and consciously outward from your own self, is the way to true success.

The more important an undertaking, the more essential it is to exercise *all* your faculties. By scattering them, you will deprive yourself of your latent power.

Interestingly, some of my Guru's most highly advanced disciples were successful businessmen. It was their ability to concentrate that gave them their success. They applied that same power of concentration to their spiritual search and achieved much greater success in this field than others managed by restlessness. Concentration on moneymaking, when that is the issue, need not at all prevent you from making progress spiritually also. Don't separate your duties to the world from your duty to God. See them as aspects of one and the same thing. God is in everything, including money.

"*Nishkam karma* (action without desire for its fruits)," the teaching of the Bhagavad Gita, is not a caution against action: It is a warning against acting with selfish *motive*.

Ego-motivation cannot be avoided so long as one is centered in the ego. And one cannot help being so centered until he is Self-realized, and his consciousness has become infinite. Ego-motivation must be generous, however, if one would grow spiritually. An outwardly expansive ego is self-liberating. *Selfishness* causes one to shrink in self-identity, as I have stated previously. Generosity, despite the fact that it, too, springs from the ego, *expands* our self-identity. When a person directs his interests toward a greater good, his self-awareness reaches out to embrace a broader reality than his own. The more expanded his self-identity becomes, the more successful he will be even in material undertakings.

It is important to understand also that, if one sincerely desires to achieve material success through yoga principles, he must also *live a balanced life*.

Paramhansa Yogananda once wrote an amusingly insightful article describing the imbalances that often develop in people's consciousness. Some people, he said, have huge biceps but tiny heads: they are, in other words, all muscle and no brain.

Other people have massive heads, but shrunken bodies. They are all intellect, but are stunted physically.

Still others sport monstrous bellies, which they push before them like wheelbarrows, but their chests are narrow and their quivering chins and thick lips all attest to their addiction to the pleasures of the "trough."

True happiness, my Guru was saying through those humorous examples, requires a balanced life.

It is important to keep your long-range desires at the back of your mind, at least, as you work hard to achieve success. Egoic fulfillment is no one's final goal. That goal, for everyone, is happiness. Happiness rises up from the soul. Its culmination lies in Bliss absolute.

One factor essential to inner peace is a clear conscience, born of facing every moral difficulty vigorously, from within. People too often allow their actions to be guided by social convention, or by others' opinions, or by the line of least resistance—even to the point of cutting corners ethically. ("Yes, I admit I should have been more firm in resisting that tempting offer, but with everyone urging me to accept it, what could I do?")

Learn to heed the quiet voice of your own conscience. Always keep in mind, whenever questions arise regarding what is truly in your *best* interest: *You owe this decision of conscience to no one but your own self.*

Right and wrong are often relative terms. Sometimes only higher guidance can settle which one really is right. Reason and emotion often speak both loudly and persuasively. What you decide intuitively, however, even if your inner voice only whispers to you, will be more true for you, if you will only listen to it. Intuition is the voice of wisdom.

Never do what others urge upon you unless your conscience endorses their advice. Remember the saying, "The majority is always wrong; the minority has only a possibility of being right." This isn't true, of course, if the people you select to help you were chosen for their discrimination as well as for their good attitude. Even so, people who are less affected by what you decide may not advise you on the strength of their discrimination even, but may be thinking only in terms of a general convenience. Seek assurance first of all, therefore, in your inner Self. If you fail to do so, you may feel, someday, that you've let yourself down in accepting the priorities of others. Let conscience tell you where your true duty lies, and don't hesitate to let it override the usual chorus of opinions. It is to your own higher Self, finally, that you are answerable.

Let me explain more carefully what I mean by inner peace, inner conscience, and duty to one's higher Self. I refer not to that sort of peace which comes, for example, by avoiding all difficulties, conflicts, and challenges. Peace cannot result from shirking one's duty, which is what the avoidance of conflict often entails. Peace must be won by inner *victories.*

"Do your duty, which is to fight!" was Krishna's advice to his disciple Arjuna. That advice was meant above all spiritually. Only in self-conquest can one find the peace of everlasting fulfillment. Self-conquest means victory especially over one's lower self. That, in the Bhagavad Gita, was the real issue. The battlefield of Kurukshetra was a symbol for the human body. Sri Krishna states this fact openly at the beginning of Chapter Thirteen.

Everyone wants peace. Even if people take occasional detours through the "fun house" of worldly excitement, they find, after the fun ends and all the lights are turned off, that their heart's desire has never really changed: What they really want is true, lasting happiness, calmness, and inner freedom. Usually, however, people make the mistake of equating peace with outer security. They delude themselves. Laboring with the obsession of madmen, they imagine that the more they pant after that "bottom line" of profit, the closer they'll be to achieving security and, as a result, to everything they've ever wanted. Their resulting restlessness robs them of inner peace: How, then, can they expect real fulfillment? "To the peaceless," says the Bhagavad Gita, "how is happiness possible?" That sentence is written as a question. It invites people to "test the waters" and form their own conclusions. That is what everyone on earth is busy doing: testing the waters. No one will ever find himself able, however, to state sincerely, "Aha! Here's an exception to that teaching: My life at present is very stimulating, and, man, you've no idea *how happy I am*!" Just wait. Soon your "wiring"—that is, your nervous system—will burn out from overstimulation! Many people equate happiness with excitement, but, as the Gita warns them, that way never works for anyone.

What everyone really wants is permanence: lasting security, lasting peace, lasting happiness. These three *desiderata* recede ever before them if they stretch out their hands to grasp them. Their dream-paradise remains ever beyond their trembling clutch where they themselves ever keep it: in the future.

Peace must be one's *present* reality. By straining to reach out to it, people only drive it before them like a bullock pulling a wagon. The *real* challenge they face is not, "How can I make more money?" or, "How can I afford to buy a new home?" or, "How can I put my son through college?" or, "How can I ever pay all these bills?"—challenges, in short, that are faced by everyone. One may be tempted to take moral shortcuts in an attempt to meet those challenges, but it is vitally important that he *never* do so. Going that route will cost you too much in terms of inner peace, self-respect, and happiness. Why sacrifice jewels like those for the price of a cup of coffee?

In more immediate terms, "cutting corners" will mean sacrificing even your material security, eventually. Moreover, to be constantly on the lookout for such shortcuts will make your mind restless, and your heart uneasy. Material success achieved at the cost of peace and happiness cannot be a guarantee of security, for peacelessness attracts failure and *is itself*, in a sense, a kind of failure. How, then, can an excess of money or power be even called success?

Certain yoga principles, listed as *yamas* in Patanjali's *Yoga Sutras*, are necessary to every kind of success. Harmlessness is one such principle. Never try to harm others in any way—not only because karmic law will inflict a painful retribution on you if you do so, especially if your act is deliberate. Karmic retribution is (let's face it!) not many people's foremost concern. Its demand for payment may—so many think—never come at all. Lo! they say, there are no clouds looming on my horizon.

Paramhansa Yogananda attributed that perfectly normal delay in facing the duns of karma to what he called, "The thwarting crosscurrents of ego." A common response to the scriptural warning, "You must eventually redress every evil you commit," is to scoff, "'*Eventually!*' Who cares about 'eventually'?" Many people see the karmic law as a kind of game of roulette. Success, they come to think, is determined more or less by accident. The ball of circumstance only *happens* to drop into the compartment with the right number.

All right then, let's forget for the moment that "dim" future. Let us, like Lydia in the movie, *Pride and Prejudice*, announce airily, "Oh, who *cares* what happens in five years!" Accepting what happens *today* as our "bottom line," let us see whether today, at least, anyone can really "cut corners" ethically and get off without being singed.

If one considers it a necessity, however regretfully, to harm anyone, or to *allow* harm to befall another in the hope of some immediate gain to himself, know this: A price must be exacted—not eventually only, but *today*. That price may seem to some degree nebulous, for the wrongdoer will probably have no clear idea of the benefits he is sacrificing. These lost benefits will include, to some extent at least, the magnetism to attract everything he wants: success; true friends; inner peace; and above all happiness. These prizes are coveted by everyone. They may, as I said, seem nebulous, but there will be another price, obvious and immediate: the loss of one's inner peace, happiness, the ability to function at peak efficiency, the respect and *sincere* (as opposed to superficial and meaningless) friendship of others.

If a person is willing to harm or to cause harm to come to anyone, he will create in himself a perception that others are equally willing, and perhaps eager, to harm *him*. Whether or not that perception is true matters little beside the fact that, merely by holding it as a perception, one develops tensions within himself. Peacelessness is the lot of anyone who concentrates on the thought that there are others in constant opposition to him. Even material success becomes, for such people, a mockery. *Ahimsa*, or harmlessness, is essential to the sense of inner security and peace everyone desires.

The same is true of each one of Patanjali's principles of *yama*, or control. It is true of his warning, for example, against untruthfulness. In the long run, to be truthful develops in oneself the power to manifest anything he wants by simply declaring that it is so. *Un*truthfulness, on the other hand, dilutes the power of speech, depriving one of the very power to succeed. The disintegration of such power usually takes time. A person may boast, "Behold! I told a lie and the only thing that happened was that I closed an important deal." Another one may scoff, "I've closed *many* deals in my life by telling lies, and not a single lightning bolt struck me. Just look: I'm still here!"

It has been said that for the first forty years of a person's life he has the face that God gave him; after forty, he must live with the face he has made for himself. His "new" face reflects the attitudes he has developed by his reactions to life. It takes time for our natures, as we've shaped them inwardly, to manifest themselves outwardly. It may take more than a lifetime for such changes to become blatant. Even at the time of death, wrongdoers may hurl bitter imprecations against the universe—never against themselves, of course!—for the way they've been "wronged."

It takes time also to mature. Were a child to say, "I haven't a thing to learn," wouldn't he seem merely silly? No one becomes suddenly and effortlessly wise merely by becoming an adult. Most people, spiritually speaking, are children no matter what their physical age is. Even though their bodies age, there remain many things for them still to learn. That is why wise sayings are transferred by tradition from generation to generation. People need those constant verbal reminders. If, on the other hand, they ignore those truths, or laugh at them as mere "truisms," they will pay the price, in time, of inner peacelessness.

Certain signs presage future disaster: it would do well to heed them. A man who thinks after telling a lie that he has "gotten away with it," will gradually find that others have begun to shun him as someone not worth listening to. It takes time, usually, to build a reputation, whether for good or evil. It may take less time, however, to develop that mental fuzziness which makes a person basically unsure of anything. A liar may be convincing for a time with his blustering, but gradually he will find himself becoming less and less effective at anything he tries to accomplish. Someone who always speaks the truth, on the other hand, develops the ability to bring his simple, strongly declared word to outward manifestation. This is called *vach siddhi*, the power to manifest one's mere word as a reality. Experience teaches one also, for that reason, to make only positive statements, and to entertain only wholesome desires!

It is easy enough to "cut corners," morally, but it is not so easy to pay the price they exact. Honesty, for reasons explained in the last lesson, is always "the best policy." Indeed, honesty should be much more than a policy. It should put down deep roots in a person's nature. One should develop a "straight-spined" determination to live by truth no matter how difficult he finds it to do so. The cost of being ever true to one's word—embarrassment occasionally, for example, and the alienation of false friends—will be light compared to the long-term suffering that dishonesty and untruthfulness bring. Sin—that is to say, moral error—appears at first to ask for only a "low, low down payment." Later, however, it demands pitilessly that one "pay, pay, and keep on paying until the last drop of blood is exacted!" And so shall you have to do, until you learn well that lesson.

In India, truthfulness was at one time the general practice. My Guru wrote, concerning that time, that an Indian would rather lose his home and everything he possessed than tell a lie in court. Jim Corbett, in his beautiful book *My India*, describes instances of heroic integrity among the simple folk he'd encountered in the Himalayan foothills.

Such, alas, is not always the case in India nowadays. I remember an incident in Long Beach, California, some fifty years ago. I had gone to the home of an Indian friend of mine to borrow a dhoti for a play that I'd written. One of his college friends, another Indian, happened to be visiting that apartment, and as I was leaving the house he assured me, "I will definitely be there." Why did he make that promise? He hadn't asked me where the play would be performed, nor when, nor what it was about. In fact, he hadn't asked anything. Nor, in fact, did he come; I'd been reasonably certain he wouldn't. Why, then, that assurance, including the word, "definitely"? To lie in such inconsequential matters seems to me absurd. I suppose he wanted to be pleasing, but wouldn't it have been more pleasing to be sincere? He could have parted from me with a smile. That might, at least, have suggested a true feeling.

For myself, I strongly feel that if I have once given my word, I must abide by it. I may sometimes give that word only to myself. It may even regard something quite trivial, like buying a newspaper. If later on, however, it becomes inconvenient for me to go out and get it, I will go buy it anyway just so as to keep my word to myself.

While we're on this subject, there is another, somewhat related, issue: Why bribe anyone, and why accept bribes? It is not honorable. I was astonished by something a newspaper reporter told me years ago. Our first Ananda community had been having difficulties with the county government. Certain officials were finding it difficult to fit our novel way of life into their established classifications. The reporter had come to me for an interview, and mentioned as if in confidence, "You know what works, don't you?" He proceeded to rub his thumb and forefinger together in the universal gesture suggestive of a bribe. Of course, I ignored the suggestion. (The article he wrote about us was not flattering. I wondered whether it might not have been mildly less so had I bribed him also!) I simply cannot function that way. Maybe I'd have avoided a number of trials in my life had I been willing to "contribute to others' delinquency," as a friend of mine once put it. The other side of that coin, however, is that I've achieved the success I dreamed of. Moreover, my spine remains straight.

Yes, it is possible to be dharmic *always*: to be kind, helpful, honest, truthful, and sincere with everyone—and in the process to succeed in one's life. Don't let worldly "wisdom"—which is another word for ignorance!—tell you any differently.

The Application

You have a faculty by which you can ascertain whether an action you are contemplating would be right or wrong. It is your own *intuition*.

Intuition is centered in the heart. It is not an emotion; in fact, people's emotions can, and often do, mislead them—sometimes seriously. Calm feeling in the heart is not to be confused with emotion. To achieve that feeling, one must be careful not to be prejudiced by likes or dislikes. Be calmly impersonal, yet kindly disposed. When you achieve that state of mind, intuition will become for you a reliable guide.

If, for instance, you've been wondering whether some newcomer is right for you and your business, concentrate at the point between the eyebrows. With a clear mind, then, recall his face, and especially his eyes, to your inward gaze. When he comes clearly into focus, offer his image to your heart's feeling, and see what that intuitive feeling tells you. Ask it whether this person is right for you.

If you detect, in your heart, the slightest tremor of uneasiness, drop the idea instantly of associating with that person; it would be risky to cultivate a serious relationship with him. If, on the other hand, you feel a calm, even a joyful, confirmation in your heart, take this reaction as a sign that he (or she) may have been sent to you for your good.

Again, if you are wondering whether a decision is right for you, form a clear concept of the issues at the point between the eyebrows. Ask your heart, then, whether or not the decision you are contemplating would be right for you.

Your intuition will develop toward increasing clarity, the more you ask it for help and respond to it calmly and impartially. This subject is so important that I'll discuss it further and more deeply later in these lessons.

Be clear as to your underlying purpose. In 1970, when our first Ananda Sangha community was still getting started, a young man came to me for advice. "I've received an inheritance," he said, "and I want to spend it wisely. I feel drawn to joining your community, but I also feel a draw to go to India. Which direction do you recommend that I follow?"

"How large is your inheritance?" I asked, simply to ascertain whether it would suffice for him to live in India for some time.

"Two hundred thousand dollars," he replied. This was, in those days especially, a great deal of money! It could have helped us greatly in building our community. But I wasn't even tempted. My concern was only for *his* welfare. On consulting my intuition, I realized that if he'd really felt to join us he would have done more than *ask* my advice: he'd have said, "I want to join your community." I therefore replied, "I feel you should go to India."

I built Ananda to help others. I would have been untrue to that purpose, in this case, had I placed our needs, which were very real, ahead of his own well-being.

Sometimes—I think naturally—I have not been able to live up to my own highest ideals. At such times, I have never lamented, "Oh, I'm a failure!" Instead, what I've done is simply acknowledge my mistake to myself, and have then told myself firmly, "I have *not yet* succeeded." My affirmation of eventual success has enabled me, in time, to honor my never-faltering resolution. Thus, every failure must be seen as only apparent, and can be turned to eventual success.

There was a wealthy businessman in America who attributed his success to a willingness to let his employees make their mistakes. "That," as he explained, "is the only way to learn."

Remember, in the search for perfection you have eternity before you! The essential thing, always, is to be completely sincere with yourself.

In practicing *ahimsa* (harmlessness), remember that the same divine Self is struggling in every ego to achieve final perfection. Some people's paths lie through dark shadows of rebellion and suffering. No matter how winding and tormented their way, however, the end of every soul's journey is eternal Bliss. How can it be otherwise? All of us were made from Bliss itself.

Love everyone, therefore: all are expressions of your own infinite Self. Love everyone with the sympathy one naturally feels for fellow strugglers on a hard journey. *All men are pilgrims on the path to Infinite Consciousness*, even if they are not aware of the fact. The worst criminal on earth wanders in delusion only temporarily. The plot he enacts, and the trail he walks, is no different essentially from the role you play and the trail you yourself follow to your goal in eternity. It is important to keep in mind also that it is not possible for unenlightened human beings to judge who is closer to or farther away from that goal of perfection.

Valmiki was a highway robber, yet his spiritual tendencies, or *samskaras*, had to have been highly developed in past lives for him to make such a sudden, complete reversal in his life as to renounce robbery and determine to become a saint.

When you come to love everyone with the genuine kindness of fellow feeling, you will find that others will even go out of their way to help you and to be fair to you.

MEDITATION

Do you ever feel like disobeying some spiritual principle? For example, do you ever feel like taking unfair advantage of someone, or striking others in self-defense, or telling an untruth, or "cutting a moral corner" for the sake of some entirely personal gain? If so, there probably lurks somewhere in your mind a certain measure of this fear: "What if I fail to close this deal? What if I *don't* strike out in self-defense? What if I fail to make known an inconvenient fact? What if I *don't* cheat just a little, to get what I want?" Fear is a major motivation in many people's lives. If it is your affliction, the following meditation may be of special help to you.

Remember: In your true Self you are eternal. Nothing can ever touch you, at your true center. In your eternal being, you are eternal *Satchidananda*: Bliss infinite and everlasting.

Try visualizing some situation of which you feel fearful: perhaps the loss of a deal that you'd like to close: or defeat by an enemy; or public disgrace; or failure in some overriding ambition. Visualize that fear as already fully realized in your life.

What happens next? *You are still you!* Nothing, in your deeper reality, has changed or ever *can* change! The little wave of your existence rises and falls constantly, yet belongs always to the great Ocean of Life, and is forever a part of it.

Meditate on your eternally changeless Self: the real You at the center of your ego dream. Remember, in your *true* Self, nothing can ever affect you.

AFFIRMATION

"Through all of life's changes, I am forever changeless at my true center, my deepest Self."

POINTS TO REMEMBER

1. Your "bottom line" should include both monetary profit and inner satisfaction. "What shall it profit a man if he gain the whole world, but lose his own soul?"
2. Tunnel vision deprives people of happiness and peace of mind, and may blind them to unusual opportunities for success that would enliven their very pursuit for money.
3. Keep inner peace as your first priority.
4. Never let yourself be drawn into other people's priorities, at the cost of your inner peace.
5. Help others to develop the executive skills needed to act on your behalf and represent the ideals of your organization. Look for those who seek the well-being of everyone and act with humility, cooperation, and intelligence. If you see this competence combined with kindness, devotion to truth and to God, and respect for others, give them your trust.
6. Devote all your energy and attention to everything you do, and refuse to worry over decisions needed in future.
7. Concentration is the key to success. If you make inner peace a priority, you will be able to concentrate more effectively on whatever you do. Meditation will help you to deepen your peace and therefore your concentration.
8. You, at the center of all your activities, need to be balanced as a human being. Be centered in yourself, always, and never fully identified with anything outward that you do.
9. Don't separate your duties to the world from your duty to God. See them as aspects of one and the same thing. *Nishkam karma* (action without desire for its fruits) is not a caution against action: It is a warning against acting with selfish *motive*.
10. Generosity *expands* your self-identity. The more expanded your self-identity becomes, the more successful you will be even in material undertakings.
11. One factor essential to inner peace is a clear conscience. Never do what others urge upon you unless your conscience endorses their advice. Seek assurance first of all in your inner Self.
12. True peace comes from victory over one's lower self. It must be one's *present* reality. By straining to reach out to it, people only drive it away.
13. It is vitally important that one *never* take moral shortcuts. Going that route will cost you your inner peace, self-respect, and happiness.
14. If a person is willing to harm or to cause harm to come to anyone, he will create in himself a perception that others are equally willing to harm *him*. *Ahimsa*, or harmlessness, is essential to the sense of inner security and peace everyone desires.

15. One should develop a "straight-spined" determination to live by truth no matter how difficult he finds it to do so.

16. To be guided by intuition, calm feeling in the heart is needed. To achieve that feeling, be calmly impersonal, yet kindly disposed. When you achieve that state of mind, intuition will become for you a reliable guide.

17. If you are wondering whether a decision is right for you, form a clear concept of the issues at the point between the eyebrows. Ask your heart, then, whether or not the decision you are contemplating would be right for you. If you detect, in your heart, the slightest tremor of uneasiness, drop the idea instantly. If, on the other hand, you feel a calm, even a joyful, confirmation in your heart, take this reaction as a positive sign.

18. Your intuition will develop toward increasing clarity, the more you ask it for help and respond to it calmly and impartially.

19. If you feel you have not been able to live up to your own highest ideals, acknowledge your mistake, and say firmly, "I have *not yet* succeeded." Thus failure becomes a steppingstone to success.

20. Love everyone as an expression of your own infinite Self. When you come to love everyone with the genuine kindness of fellow feeling, you will find that others will even go out of their way to help you and to be fair to you.

WORKBOOK IDEAS
by Joseph Bharat Cornell

Practice Truthfulness

Practicing truthfulness aligns us with what *is*. Seeing and honoring the truth in a given situation gives us clarity, and prevents mental vagueness and distortion. It's only by accepting things as they are that we can change them. Otherwise, our point of reference is based on fantasy rather than reality.

The willingness to adhere to the truth, no matter how inconvenient, expands one's reality beyond the ego and its self-absorption. Keeping a larger and more impersonal perspective invites cooperation and trust from others. Above all, truthfulness resonates with our higher Self, which sees all Life as its own, greater Reality.

ACTION ITEMS:

Practice truthfulness every day for a week. Reflect on your progress each day, preferably at set times, like at lunch, after work, and before sleep. Concentrate on the following aspects of truthfulness:

- Do what you say you'll do.

  Have fun with this and let it be a learning experience. If you decide to do something, and it later becomes inconvenient, do it anyway. We often make small, apparently inconsequential promises to ourselves and others and invest little thought or energy in fulfilling them. It's no wonder then that our words lack power.

  The benefit of making yourself follow through on your promises is that you'll become more careful in what you say. Your speech, then, will be more conscious and intentional, and yours words, therefore, will have more power.

  Do this:

  When you decide to do something, immediately write in a notebook what it is that you want to do. Near the end of each day check to make sure you've done it. If you haven't, do it!

- Avoid exaggerating.

  We all like to tell a good story or make a good point. Avoid, however, relying on stretching the truth to make it more interesting. To increase your story's magnetism, concentrate, rather, on sharing vibrations of goodwill and love as you speak.

- Be willing to be embarrassed.

  Paramhansa Yogananda said we should never reveal our weaknesses to others, since they might use them against us in the future. But when Life reveals our flaws to others, make an effort to remain impartial. Paramhansa Yogananda said that one of people's biggest problems is thinking that things affect them personally. If what happens to you is a wholesome source of amusement to others, try to join in on the fun!

- Think long-term, not short-term.

   If you are ever tempted to misrepresent the facts to gain an advantage, visualize yourself as the other party who will have to live with the consequences, for karma surely will place you in the same circumstances.

- Truth is always beneficial.

   Make a conscious effort to bless others as you speak, for truth includes the welfare of all, and encourages their highest potential.

   Avoid magnifying the importance of small issues. Try to see them in a larger context.

- Listen to your conscience.

   Listen to your conscience and *act* on its counsel. The more you do, the clearer your intuition will be. Our conscience is the higher Self calling us to attune to our divine potential.

Write down the following to remind you to practice truthfulness. Keep the list with you and refer to it often during the day

Do what I say	Think long-term, not short-term
Avoid exaggerating	Truth is always beneficial
Be willing to be embarrassed	Listen to my conscience

Reflecting on Your Experience

Answer the following questions after you have practiced this truthfulness exercise for one week:
- Did you notice any difference in the way people responded to you?
- Were you able to be more impartial and accepting of the truth?
- Did you ever want to ignore or misrepresent the truth? If so, what did you do?
- Did your will power become stronger from conscientiously doing what you said you were going to do?
- What was the most important thing you gained from your practice of truthfulness?

LESSON SEVEN

BALANCING WORK AND MEDITATION

Habit, in mankind, is a potent force. Subconscious drives keep us tied to a lower, non-discriminating perception of things. As human beings, however, . . . we have the ability to develop tendencies far outside the fixed patterns of instinctual behavior.

The Principles

For every person whose love of meditation is so deep he cannot easily squeeze in the time for a little work, there are thousands with quite the opposite problem. "How," they ask, "can I find the time for even a little meditation, when I have all this work to do?" People who meditate long and deeply haven't the same need for these lessons as those whose work is a priority. Both groups, however, *in the context of their own priorities*, have a need to balance outward activity and meditation, or—if they are unusually active—at least to balance their work with calm reflection.

Physical activity helps to keep one "grounded." Without it, a person tends to become lazy and absentminded. Mental activity is important for people also who are physically active: it keeps them from slipping into subconsciousness whenever they have nothing outward to do. The common expression nowadays, "couch potato," is as good a description as any of the person who is so mentally lazy that he spends all his free time sitting passively in front of the television screen.

There are, as I've said, two directions of development open to man: upward, or downward. Life below the human level is propelled upward automatically by Nature. Once it reaches the human level, free will enters the picture at least to some extent with ego-consciousness. The ego can hasten the evolutionary process toward divine enlightenment, but it can also delay it. Because lower life forms have only rudimentary self-awareness, even dogs and horses lack free will. Man's ego makes it possible for him to cooperate with the process if he so chooses, by aspiring toward the heights. Unfortunately, he usually chooses to pause at the human level, like a mountain climber after reaching a plateau, who may choose to rest a little before climbing higher. Man's ego can inspire him to continue upward with a will; usually, however, he opts for a long rest. Indeed, he fairly wallows in it—that is to say, in the desires the ego generates. The process of ongoing evolution is deferred indefinitely, as the ego weaves around itself a cocoon of millions of filaments of desire. Thus, the soul can take much longer to escape to higher-than-human stages of development than it took to reach the human level in the first place. Reasoning is rudimentary in the lower animals, which never even question how satisfied they are with their lot. Their sense of individuality is weak; thus, even when they suffer they are much less aware than we are that they themselves are suffering. Man, on the contrary, is not only aware of his individuality, but revels in it, and suffers also in consequence. His suffering is in equal proportion to any happiness he experiences, for such is the law of duality, which keeps him bouncing up and down with his emotions: happy one day, sad the next; overjoyed one day, miserable the next. Because he is able to experience happiness personally, he hopes that he will find complete happiness, someday. Bliss, or perfect joy is, indeed, his true destiny. It takes many incarnations, unfortunately, for him to develop the discrimination to recognize, in his suffering, the prods Nature gives him toward eventual escape from the prison of ego-consciousness.

A woman in Israel once told a friend of mine, "I've been reading about reincarnation, and guess what," she exulted enthusiastically: "We get to come back!"

The deeper-than-conscious memory of repeated disappointments and disillusionments—the "anguishing monotony," as my Guru called it, of bondage to this little "I"—is what sets us firmly on the path to soul-freedom at last.

In the *shastras* (the ancient scriptures of India) it is said that it takes five to eight million incarnations for the soul to evolve up to the human level. What a climb, merely to become a human being! Few people are aware of their great good fortune. They use their more developed intelligence to justify their delusions. Most people, having finally achieved the blessing of self-consciousness, take a long rest before resuming the climb to liberation. Their clearer awareness gives them a first-ever opportunity for hastening the process of upward evolution. Few take advantage of the blessing; instead, they wander for aeons in delusion, mesmerized by the limited, and self-limiting, rewards available to ego-consciousness.

Such is the power of *Maya*, known in some religions as Satan—Satanic delusion, in other words. *Maya* (Satan) is a relentless, conscious force, and by no means merely subjective. It works from within man's consciousness, and not only from without, through the principle of duality. Satan creates a balance to everything that is God-reminding and beautiful, by manifesting some other thing that is evil, goodness-obscuring, and ugly. *Maya* is the creative, outwardly projecting aspect of infinite consciousness, which brings all things into manifestation. That force is conscious, as I said, and tries to perpetuate everything in a state of manifestation. Satan works unceasingly, deliberately also to prevent ego-conscious beings from aspiring to a higher, more universal state of awareness.

Maya suggests to our minds, "Come on, old fellow (or old girl), things aren't so bad as they seem! Give them another try!" My Guru said, "I used to think that Satan was only a delusion in the mind, but now that I have found God I join my testimony to that of all who went before me: Satan is a reality. It is a conscious force, and works deliberately to keep mankind bound to the ever-turning wheel of delusion." That wheel takes one constantly up and down, alternating fulfillment with disappointment, and success with failure. The secret of a truly successful life is to be centered in the Self, not reacting outwardly with ego-incited emotions. Only to the extent that one is inwardly centered is his success assured permanence.

The true goal of life is to realize our identity with the source of life: *Satchidananda*. This definition of God, given to mankind by Adi (the first) Swami Shankaracharya, is the best, because truest, ever expressed. My Guru translated it for modern times from his state of oneness with God, as "ever-existing, ever-conscious, *ever-new* bliss."

What keeps people tied to the wheel of rebirth is their own energy-flow, which impels them outward even before they are born. Any glimpse they get of inner joy is projected outward onto the world, where they see dimly reflected through the senses the bliss-nature of the Self, like reflections of sunlight on slivers of broken glass. What makes those reflections attractive to us is our happy anticipation of happiness through them, when in fact each scintillating light is merely a projection onto the world around us of our inner joy.

The higher purpose of these lessons is to help you see that material success itself is only a steppingstone to perfection. From a yogic point of view, every kind of success is a good thing, for the qualities that bring material success bring also divine enlightenment. Qualities that produce material failure, on the other hand, produce also spiritual failure.

This course is important for another, more immediate, reason also. To "cut corners" ethically, with a view to increasing one's income, is a sure way to destroy one's very happiness. Apart from the obvious need for keeping body and soul together, the real reason people work or do anything is their desire for happiness.

Maya works "super-efficiently" through the restless mind! When our thoughts lack a clear focus, they are incapable of exercising discrimination. We should not blame Satan for every mistake we make! We ourselves invite *maya*'s power into our lives to begin with, by our *openness* to it. When Satan sees self-aware human beings trying to escape his net, he works urgently to prevent them. He can exert no force, however, except through our receptivity to him. People who have attained communion with God find it relatively easy to slough off Satanic temptation, for they are no longer securely locked in the prison of ego. Those, on the other hand, who are unable to meet life's trials with a sense of inner freedom suffer in consequence. Even during the severest tests that worldly people experience, however, joy runs like a river just beneath the surface of their consciousness. For no one can completely deny his soul-nature. If such people turned within, they would find joy on deeper layers of consciousness than the ego. Divine joy is their unchanging reality.

Ego—to change the metaphor—is the engine that pulls a trainload of desires, filled with passengers eagerly anticipating their journey's end and a shopping spree of pleasures and delights. What keeps stoking the engine's boiler with coal is the power of habit.

Habits, both good and bad, influence people more than they realize. A man may claim, "I'm free to do just what I please!" He doesn't see, in the very fact of being more "pleased" by one thing than another, proof already that he is not free at all. Habit conditions his mind to pleasures and displeasures. Habit is his slave master.

Habits can also help us, if they encourage us to rise toward truer understanding. Born in human form, however, as all of us are, we find that habit sides more often with our energy's natural predisposition to flow outward through the senses.

The way habit works is explained, allegorically, in the *Mahabharata*, which is really the story of the soul's long journey through *maya* to final liberation. My Guru explained that Dronacharya, preceptor of the youthful Kurus and Pandavas, represents the power of habit. The army representing soul qualities in that great epic is symbolized by the Pandavas. The army on the side of delusion is symbolized by their cousins, the Kurus. In any struggle between the two "armies"—light and dark tendencies in ourselves—Drona (Habit) sides with the worldly ones. Spiritual development is determined somewhat by habit also, but as one advances spiritually his progress becomes increasingly an act of free will. Thus, the closer we approach to spiritual transcendence, the less we are influenced by habit, and the more by the faculty of discrimination born of soul-consciousness. The more we are centered in the superconscious, therefore, the less we are conditioned by habit's mere mechanisms. Superconsciousness has nothing to do with such mechanisms. It is forever fresh, spontaneous, and creative.

Thus, the power of habit does not participate *actively* on the side of goodness. The best that a good habit can do is help to open one's consciousness to the descent of superconsciousness into it. Habit helps that process by not resisting it. It is the superconscious which actively guides the sincere devotee's life. Good habits, therefore, such as daily meditation, remembrance of God, and inwardly chanting His name, are beneficial primarily for the fact that they *invite* the superconscious to take part in our struggles. It is the superconscious that actively opposes, and eventually dissolves, our worldly tendencies. It is superconsciousness that banishes *maya*. Our good habits can only help by setting our feet on the upward path. Superconsciousness accomplishes the actual transformation.

Thus, Dronacharya's help in the *Mahabharata*, when it comes, is by default. Drona dies on the battlefield, after he is tricked into believing that his son, Ashwatthama, has been killed. At this news, Drona loses further interest in the war, and allows himself to be slain.

Paramhansa Yogananda explained the hidden meaning of this subtle teaching. Ashwatthama represents latent—that is, subconscious—desires. When we have uprooted every desire, even those of which we are not consciously aware, habit (until that point a strong influence in our lives) "gives up" the fight, and ceases to stand in the way of our progress toward enlightenment.

Although Drona sides with the Kurus, he is also the guru of the Pandavas. Habits in other words can—as we've seen—be good as well as bad. In the struggle between our higher and lower natures, we need good habits to begin with; habits can uplift as well as degrade us. In the inner war of Kurukshetra, however, bad habits, arising from the subconscious, tend to assert themselves in such a way as to oppose our aspirations. The reason for this self-assertiveness on their part is that they have been our constant companions for ages—indeed, for countless incarnations. Like burrs in a sheep's fleece, they are almost knitted into our thinking process.

Though God is Infinite Consciousness, in the cosmic dream He assumes the variegated appearance of His creation. Thus, although the rocks are unmoving, and apparently unaware, they are yet manifestations of His consciousness.

The same thing happens to us when we dream. We may dream the existence of rocks, which will seem completely lacking in consciousness. It is our awareness, however, that sustains them in that rocklike appearance. In some particularly bizarre dream, one of those "unconscious" rocks might stand up suddenly and do a lively dance!

As the lowest manifestations of God's consciousness bestir themselves gradually to wakefulness, the energy latent within them reaches upward to express lower life forms, doing so through trees, plants, and flowers; through microbes, amebas, paramecia and other motile creatures; through animals that are conscious enough to crawl gropingly on the sand; and through insects that fly about feeding on leaves and sipping nectar from flowers. Evolution is influenced by Nature herself to move upward. Diversity, though the focus of the biologist's interest, is not really what defines upward evolution. Nor does the mere "struggle for survival" tell us enough. Once consciousness itself is recognized as self-existent and not dependent for its existence on mere physical mechanisms, it becomes self-evident that evolution, rightly understood, is an upward progression from seeming unconsciousness to ever-clearer expressions of absolute consciousness.

Habit, in mankind, is a potent force. Subconscious drives keep us tied to a lower, non-discriminating perception of things. As human beings, however, being more conscious than the lower animals, we have the ability to develop tendencies far outside the fixed patterns of instinctual behavior. These become habits, which arise out of our relative freedom, but which, often, are detrimental to our further evolution. As a person's consciousness rises in the morning from sleep to wakefulness, so evolution is a process of *rising* from the sleep of delusion to perfect Soul-awareness.

Biologists have no criterion to go by of what constitutes evolution except the multiplicity of forms they know. Consequently, they have no basis for claiming that evolution is directional. As a psychologist, sold on their theories, once asked rhetorically, "Has man evolved more by producing a brain than the elephant has by producing a trunk?" (This, surely, is material suitable for another book of Alice's adventures in Wonderland!) Once it is realized, however, that consciousness is not produced by mere mechanisms, it is easy to recognize that evolution is no accident, as biologists claim, but a process of ever self-refining awareness. It is consciousness which *produces* mechanisms, as it was consciousness which produced matter itself through the medium of energy. A brain can only *facilitate* the manifestation of consciousness: It could never *produce* consciousness.

With life's upward evolution, instinctual impulses become more clearly defined until reason gives man the ability to suppress his natural instincts and develop patterns of behavior not always beneficial to his well-being—indeed, not always *reasonable*, even!

Man brings certain animal impulses over with him from lower levels of manifestation. These tendencies linger subconsciously, overlaid by more recently acquired human traits. Thus, the mind is burdened with "baggage," which weighs man's consciousness down and keeps him from rising in consciousness.

Most people do not labor creatively. Their work is automatic and uninspired. Such people's activities are directed mostly by what others have done before them. This is not the way to achieve notable success!

To achieve even material success through yoga principles, one must bring the higher aspects of awareness into play: intuition and superconscious inspiration. The ordinary laborer would be unlikely to benefit from these lessons, at least by reading them. Contact with others, however, who have studied them and have found them helpful can prove life-changing for him also. People who are farther down the ladder of human evolution can be helped by associating with love and respect with those who are higher up the ladder. Those higher up, on the other hand, can benefit if they help those of lower understanding. Once the student of these lessons develops true insight and becomes centered in himself and in high principles, his influence can filter down to others at every level of society. Such people can be uplifted only by the company they keep. One might explain to them the importance of including other people's happiness in their own, but experience itself, in the end, is their best teacher.

Even those whose intelligence is somewhat developed must be made to see that truthfulness and honesty are essential both for true personal fulfillment and for success.

It takes a certain amount of refinement to appreciate deeply the importance of dharmic living. These lessons are being written primarily for people of discrimination. I hope to persuade people in all walks of life, eventually, by clear exposition, that the path to material success is ultimately no different from the path to the highest spiritual triumph. You, who are studying these lessons, can exert a powerful influence on others, if only by a kind of osmosis, or magnetic influence. Even the common laborer can be transformed by silently addressing his soul, for in everyone the divine consciousness hides, underneath his mental darkness and delusions.

Material success through yoga principles may, to many people, seem a lost cause. How, they will ask, can a person live by high principles, considering how many people there are in this world who don't miss a chance to cheat others in the name of a personal advantage? Is it possible—they ask in effect—to be dharmic when dealing with pirates?

Well, why not? Ultimately, only dharma, not adharma, has power. "Ultimately" is the operative word here. What does it matter if we lose one or two battles so long as we win the war? Human beings are offspring of the same, one God—projections of His consciousness. All of them, therefore, have the germ of divinity within them. Most of them respond, moreover, to a higher spirit, when love and joy are projected toward them calmly.

Let me tell you a little story:

Many years ago—in May 1955, to be exact—I was visiting the east coast of America. I received an invitation from my parents while I was there. They were living in the south of France, where they hoped I would visit them; they offered to pay for my airplane ticket. I accepted gladly. In due course of time, at Idlewild Airport (since then renamed, John F. Kennedy Airport), I was standing in line in front of the check-in counter. The man in front of me, when he reached the counter, was informed that he would have to pay an extra fee for his overweight baggage. Furiously he pulled out every "stop" in his organ, shouting, "I've never faced this problem before! I've been patronizing this airline for many years! I'll never fly with you again!" Nothing worked. Finally he cried, "I demand to see the manager!" The supervisor came out, spoke to him as politely as possible, but explained that he wasn't in a position to change his company's policies. The passenger, fuming in rage, finally paid the required fee.

I, standing next in line, was a little anxious. My own luggage was in fact more bulky than his, and must surely have weighed considerably more. My parents hadn't offered to pay such extra expenses. My monastic allowance was $20 a month—hardly a maharajah's income! I wasn't even dressed in monastic garb, and couldn't hope for leniency on those grounds, therefore.

I decided simply to offer the problem to Divine Mother. Approaching the counter, I visualized Her as present in the man behind it—the same man as before—inspiring him. I smiled into his eyes, thinking of him, as I naturally do, as my friend in God. He returned my smile, then turned to my bags and said, "Well, what have we here?" Their weight was, in fact, over the limit. Without comment he handed me my baggage tags and boarding pass, and I was free to move on!

When one's aim in life is to serve others, and when one doesn't think of what he can get for himself, what happens, I think, is that he radiates a protective aura which shields him from usual, "business is business" attitudes. This sort of thing has happened in my life again and again. To emphasize my point, let me relate another—to me deeply inspiring—story:

I'll introduce it by saying that whenever I

finish a major literary work I like to celebrate with Divine Mother, whose inspiration, along with my Guru's, I always invoke while writing. I may celebrate by going out for a good dinner at a prominent restaurant, or I may take a vacation with a few friends. In any case, the celebration remains inward, primarily.

Thus it was that, many years ago, I completed one of my most important projects, a course of lessons on Raja Yoga. I was feeling that something special in the way of celebration was called for. The labor had been long and arduous. I went to the seaside town of Carmel, California—a favorite of mine. This was especially, however, a vacation with the Divine Mother.

I hadn't much money, as most of what I'd earned had gone toward the development of Ananda Village. On reaching Carmel, I learned to my dismay that there seemed to be no rooms available. (I hadn't taken into account that this was high summer, and Carmel was a popular tourist attraction.)

What should I do? Other "touristy" towns nearby didn't attract me, and I didn't want to go to nearby Salinas, a farming community. This celebration had to be "right"!

The central information service that the town provided told me of one room that, they said, was available, in a central location. I went hopefully to that hotel. Alas, the cost of the room was considerably more than I'd expected to pay.

"Divine Mother," I prayed silently, "what shall I do?" Feeling inner reassurance from Her, I told myself, "I've come three hundred miles here to celebrate with You. Surely You'll see to it that I have enough money to get home again!"

With that thought, I took out the money from my wallet for this room, and offered it to the man at the registration desk.

"No, don't pay me," he said.

"I'd rather pay in advance," I explained. I didn't state, further, that I was concerned I might not have the money to pay for my room the next morning.

"I don't want you to pay me at all!" was his answer.

"But—I don't understand. Why not?" I was nonplussed.

"I don't know," he replied. "I just like you."

Thus, Divine Mother let me know that She, too, was celebrating with me! Later, at dinner, the owner of the restaurant I'd selected came to my table and asked if he might sit down. Of course I said, "Please do."

"I heard you lecture last year," he announced, "at the University of Davis." We chatted a while. Later, he wouldn't let me pay for my meal.

Whenever I think of that weekend, my eyes brim with tears. How sweet is Divine Mother's love! To underscore the extraordinary nature of this experience, I should add that at no other time, in a life of extensive travel, can I recall a hotel desk clerk who, not knowing me and, to me, quite unknown, let me stay the night free of charge.

The point here is that people, and even animals, respond in kind to the energy we send toward them. Even people who make a practice of cheating others may not cheat *you*. And even if they try to do so, they may feel a sort of protective aura around you, and not want to penetrate it. Alternatively, you may find yourself simply steered away from them, and guided to others who are more on your "wavelength." Your magnetism will normally attract the right people, and the right circumstances.

The attitude you radiate should be of sincere, *impersonal* friendship for all in God.

Never think of yourself as exerting power over others. Once you've developed magnetism, you can use it also to gain power over others. If you misuse your power in that way, you yourself will be the loser in the end.

I remember one day at Twenty-Nine Palms, California. I was driving home, and had reached the outskirts of town when I saw an old man walking in the same direction. I stopped and offered him a ride.

"Where are you going?" I asked.

"There's a Mental Physics convention in the next town," he replied. "I'm headed there." Mental Physics was an organization that, as far as I knew, taught people how to influence people and events in their lives by mental force.

Soon we reached the grounds of the convention center; it wasn't a great distance. "Where," I asked, "would you like to get out?"

My guest, hardly bothering to reply, pointed sternly in the direction of the main hall. I had already tuned in to his thinking: it was that, by mental force, he had *made* me stop and give him that ride! Happily I went along with his fantasy. As we entered the convention grounds, he ordered me with a curt gesture to drive to the main building. On reaching it, he ordered me to stop. I smiled as I thought of him proudly telling everyone how, by mental power, he had forced me to obey his will. What a testimonial he had now! To me, it was all good fun. Why should I oppose his ego game with another one of my own? I drove off with a happy smile, wishing him joy in his little "triumph."

I should make it clear at this point, however, that the magnetism I hope you will develop, and project into the world around you, will be one of divine friendship for all, not of power over others. Yes, you can develop a magnetism of power if you like—I've even hinted at ways to do so—but ask yourself this simple question: Where is the bliss in it? Power will merely increase your bondage to ego. It will implant more bars in the prison of your ego-consciousness. Where, then, will be the gain?

One great benefit of meditation is that it helps one to become self-motivated. Thus one becomes—as I've said before—a cause in life, not an effect. No matter how people respond to you, you will preserve your inner peace. You may not even be aware that the attitudes of people around you are on a different "wavelength" from your own.

Several years ago I flew to Las Vegas, where I'd been invited to address a booksellers' convention. A friend of Ananda Sangha's lived in the city, and met me at the airport, drove me to my hotel, and, the next day, drove me back again to the airport. On the way to the airport he exclaimed in distress, "I didn't at all like that reception clerk's attitude toward you at the hotel!"

"Really?" I answered. "I didn't notice anything."

"She was intolerably rude!"

"Was she? Well, I'm sorry for her." Her attitude, as far as I was concerned, had been her own problem. I hadn't invited it by any attitude of my own, and wasn't even aware that she had an "attitude."

One of the benefits of living dharmically is that people usually treat you with kindness. If they don't, their behavior doesn't bother you.

I suggested earlier that *dharmic* behavior may seem a lost cause to many people, considering how many of them ignore it and even insist that spiritual values and material success have nothing in common. The opposite is true, however. Material success infallibly comes to those who know how to live calmly at their center. It would take a very strong "failure karma" to counteract the success vibration that is emanated by inner contentment.

People may still object that there is no hope in trying to improve society, or to bring about a substantial change in the business world. Is it not, in the last analysis (they ask), even selfish to concentrate on finding inner peace, oneself? They are mistaken. One who possesses inner peace naturally wants to help others to have it also. Moreover, he is not powerless to bring them such solace.

Inner peace and happiness are quite the opposite of selfishness. They emanate an influence which brings peace also to all who are capable of receiving it themselves. One symptom of extreme negativity is that it actually equates misery with virtue. As Jean-Paul Sartre, the French nihilist, (absurdly) wrote, "In this world that bleeds, all joy is obscene." What utter nonsense! Joy is *contagious*! So also is inner peace. As others respond to it positively, so they, in turn, have an uplifting effect on others. Thus, the ripples of positive, joyful influence spread outward into the world.

We may not be able to change the world, but we can certainly exert a beneficial impact on our own surroundings. The more God's grace, particularly, flows through us, the farther that influence spreads outward. As is stated in a poster that I have made of a rainbow in Hawaii, "Remember, whatever peace you bring on earth must begin on that piece of earth where you yourself live."

As higher, superconscious influences are activated in us, they percolate downward into the conscious mind, and create a powerful influence on those we meet, even on those with whom we have only casual dealings—and even on those who seem to resent or resist it!

Of the three aspects of mind—the subconscious, conscious, and superconscious—true success requires inspiration from the third: superconsciousness. Meditation is very important, therefore, to achieving the highest success, whether spiritual or material. Meditation brings well-being on every level of consciousness. Above all, what it brings is happiness.

Meditation is the way to perfect, conscious rest. Sleep is less refreshing, for it takes one down into subconsciousness. The rest we receive in subconsciousness is, therefore, passive: It is not dynamic.

All true scriptures teach the importance of living a balanced life—physically, mentally, and spiritually. Therefore, they say, we should eat right, keep the body fit by right exercise, and clear the mind by utter self-honesty, sincerity, and kindness to all, as well as by daily meditation. This teaching is essential for true well-being. As my Guru once put it in a letter to me: "Keep exercised and body fit *for God-realization*."

It is a mistake, then, to separate meditation from the effort to achieve material success. Rather, meditation is the most direct route to success of all kinds. I've mentioned before how Rajarshi Janakananda, Paramhansa Yogananda's most highly advanced disciple, devoted his morning hours to meditation. He was the chairman of several boards of directors, and had more responsibilities than most business people. I don't suggest you follow his example as to how you pass your mornings: That, for most people, would not be feasible! Everyone, however, can include at least a little meditation in his daily routine; it is a question of priorities. Think of it as a kind of hygiene—spiritual in this case, not physical! After all, you devote time daily to brushing your teeth, to bathing or showering, to shaving (perhaps), and to brushing your hair. You take time every morning to decide which clothes you want to wear that day. These activities are so natural, you hardly give them a thought. Why not add to them, then, a short "check-in" with your higher Self?

What keeps people from meditating a little every day? It is habit, primarily. They succumb to the tendency, born of habit, to rush about restlessly, repeating actions unnecessarily that, if they'd done them just once with concentration, would not have needed to be repeated. "The soul," my Guru said, "loves to meditate." What, apart from habitual restlessness, can hold at bay the thought of sitting still, for brief periods at least, and meditating? People who practice meditation regularly find in it a supreme attraction. Restlessness however, both physical and mental, is their obstacle in the beginning, militating against devoting any time to inner stillness and peace. Instead, restless habit reaches out almost hungrily for sense-stimulation, and for what my Guru called "fillers": picking up a magazine whenever you have a free moment, and leafing through it without really seeing anything; or turning on the radio or television without really paying attention to what you hear or see. Submit yourself to a little impartial analysis: You will see that the restless diversions in which you involve yourself—to avoid thinking about inner peace—leave you always with a yawning sense of emptiness inside.

To remove a thorn from the flesh, yogis say, use another thorn to dig it out. Once the imbedded thorn has been removed, both can be thrown away. Good habits, similarly, can be used to uproot bad ones. That is one of the benefits of daily meditation: it uplifts one's thoughts, and uproots any negative tendencies, empowered by habit. Considered only as a good habit, however, meditation will not, *itself*, provide superconscious inspiration. What regular meditation accomplishes is that it calms the mind, making it receptive to intuition.

Meditation enables one to become inwardly centered, and less subject to external influences. The less reactive we are to outer stimuli, the more we become masters of ourselves. Our reactions to circumstances are energized by the upward and downward movements of energy in the spine. By controlling those movements, we live less in our emotions, and are guided increasingly by intuitive feeling. People who allow their emotions to sway them become the slaves of circumstance. Pleasure/displeasure, attraction/aversion, excitement/depression: these are the supreme obstacles to wisdom. They create serious errors of judgment in life.

The reactive process is born of the movement of energy in the *ida* and *pingala nadis*, or nerve channels, in the spine. The energy in these *nadis* works together with the breath, and is, indeed, the subtle *cause* of the physical breath. As energy flows upward through *ida nadi*, one inhales. As energy flows downward through *pingala*, one exhales. Breathing is an outward effect of that upward and downward flow of energy in the spine. The body's physical need for air and oxygen is real, of course, but the rhythmic movement of breathing is caused by the flow of energy in the spine, a process that defines breathing in the astral body.

Whenever you encounter situations to which you react emotionally, pause a moment and consider: Emotions confuse the mind, interfering with clear, unbiased judgment. When an emotion seizes you therefore, try to control it by first controlling the flow of energy in the spine. Relax in the spine. Sit upright; inhale and exhale deeply; try to bring the flow of energy there under the control of your will. Then center the feelings, also, in the spine. Breathe deeply, until your feelings become calm, and you are aware of yourself as a cause, not an effect. That feeling of rising and falling excitement will relax inwardly, and will no longer be governed by agitation.

With daily meditation this inward control will become natural—indeed, it will become almost automatic. Try to live always in the awareness of your spine. (That is why many swamis carry a *danda*, or staff; it reminds them to live ever at their center, in the spine.) If you don't want to be swept helplessly down life's stream, never act only from peripheral awareness. The more balanced you are inwardly, the more likely you will be to make wise judgments regarding every problem and crisis that arises in your life. Inner poise will enable you to listen with an open heart to inner guidance.

With or without formal meditation, a meditative *attitude*, at least, is essential. When you are centered in yourself, try to *uplift* the energy in your spine. Whatever you may be doing, when you have a free moment concentrate briefly at the point between the eyebrows.

Why do certain people seem to exude an aura of success? One cannot easily imagine them failing at anything they try. They have the *magnetism* to attract what they want in life, whether answers to questions, solutions to problems, or opportunities they need for success. One feels a calmness in their presence suggestive of meditation and yoga practice—if not in this life, then in former incarnations. Without some kind of meditation, whether in this life or in some past one, that kind of magnetism is hardly to be found in anyone.

It would be a great aid to you, therefore, in your work and other activities to include meditation daily. If it seems difficult at first, don't give up: Before long, you'll find your life becoming increasingly happy.

The Application

To acquire a new habit, apply yourself to developing it with concentration. One day, when I was trying to break a certain habit, my Guru said to me, "Habits can be overcome in a day. They are nothing but concentration of the mind. You are concentrating one way. Concentrate another way, and that undesirable habit will cease to exist!"

Because prolonged concentration is difficult, especially in the beginning, try at first to meditate for relatively short periods.

It would be well sometimes however, in any case, to extend your time of meditation. Impurities never settle to the bottom of a glass of water immediately. Restless thoughts, too, require time to subside in the mind. Vary short periods of meditation, therefore, with longer ones one day a week. The ideal, for daily meditation, is at least fifteen minutes: enough time to give you a taste of inner peace. Gradually, as you develop a taste *for* meditation, sit longer. Meanwhile, don't incite your restless thought-population to rebellion! Let the desire to sit longer develop naturally.

The essential thing is that you make an earnest effort during whatever time you do sit, however briefly. Be a little stern with yourself. Don't let your thoughts wander like sheep without a shepherd. Intense but *relaxed* mental effort is the key. In time, your thoughts will come "to heel" effortlessly, and the practice of meditation will become increasingly attractive to you.

During activity, should you feel a need for inner guidance, draw it to you instantly by recalling to mind the peace of meditation. Withdraw—even for an instant—into that inner peace, or even simply into the memory of it. Then concentrate peacefully at the point between the eyebrows. Enlist your heart's energies, especially, and offer them up to the spiritual eye.

With your mind as focused as you can make it in that brief moment, offer a strong demand for guidance. My Guru described the right way of asking as a "loving demand." If you demand without the slightest hint of pride, but with a strong will to be given the guidance you need, the magnetism of that demand will attract the guidance you need.

Here are a few important rules to follow for daily meditation:

1. Try to create a place where you do nothing but meditate. This may be a room set aside for the purpose, or even a screened-off portion of your bedroom. As you meditate there regularly, vibrations will build up that will be conducive to deep meditation.

2. Sit facing the east, if possible. If for any reason that direction is inconvenient, north is the next best direction. Subtle currents emanate from these directions that help to raise the energy in the body, and to direct it to the point between the eyebrows.

3. Make it a point to meditate at the same times, if possible, every day. Gradually you'll develop a habit of actually *wanting* to meditate, when that hour arrives. (The same thing is true if you eat at the same times every day: you feel hungry when that hour approaches.)

4. The best times to meditate coincide with daily pauses in outer Nature when subtle shifts of energy occur in the earth with changes in the sun's movement. Dawn, noon, sundown, and midnight, or as near to those times as convenient for you, are normally the best times to meditate.

5. Place a woolen blanket over your *asan*, or meditation seat. Better still, cover the blanket with a silk cloth. If you can use a traditional *yoga asan* such as a deer skin or a tiger skin, that is best of all. According to tradition, the animal should have died of natural causes, but the truth is my Guru's deer skin *asan* had a small bullet hole in it! Suitable skins are not so easy to obtain. A tiger skin, I should add, is traditionally used only by yogis who are committed to a life of sexual abstinence.

For people who are unaccustomed to sitting on the floor, it is all right to sit on a straight-backed, armless chair. This seat is, admittedly, less desirable than the floor. If, however, you must choose between physical pain and calm concentration on God, a chair is definitely acceptable as a substitute. (Westerners, for instance, may find sitting on the floor difficult, for it may mean concentrating on their aching knees, not on God!) If you enjoy sitting cross-legged, select, if possible, one of the standard yoga positions: *siddhasana, vajrasana, padmasana*, or *ardha-padmasana*. Any of these is definitely preferable to the cross-legged "tailor" position, which makes it difficult to sit with a straight spine.

Place the hands palms upward on the thighs at the junction of the abdomen. Draw your shoulder blades slightly together to keep the back straight, and pull the chin gently inward, parallel with the ground.

6. Two rules are important for correct posture: Keep the spine straight, and keep

the body always relaxed and motionless. If you prefer sitting on a chair, position yourself slightly forward on the seat, away from the back. This way, it will be easier to keep your spine straight.

7. To relax completely, inhale and exhale deeply two or three times to free the body of any excess toxins. Then inhale again deeply; tense the whole body, and exhale forcibly, relaxing completely. Repeat this last exercise two or three times.

8. Now, hold the body perfectly still. Don't move a muscle. Concentrate on relaxing more deeply still by mentally checking the body for areas of tension; wherever you find tension, release it as if into space. It may help you to begin deep relaxation by relaxing the body *upward*, part by part, from the feet to the head.

9. Finally, meditate, concentrating on the breath. Watch it impartially as it flows of its own accord. Don't try to control it. *Enjoy* any brief pause between the breaths, especially after each exhalation: feel the freedom of breathlessness. Gradually the pauses between the breaths will become longer by natural degrees.

Don't worry if the pauses extend themselves for what seems to you an unnaturally long time. Breathlessness is normal for the body that is deeply calm and relaxed. It comes with complete centeredness and rest in the Self. The breathless state can be maintained indefinitely, but it can never be achieved forcefully. Don't worry if the breath stops of itself, for as soon as one needs to breathe, the body will do so. Even if you tried to stop the breath by forced *kumbhaka* (breath retention), you would be unable to do so, for you would eventually faint, at which point the breath would begin again automatically. Never force any yoga practice, as some people misguidedly do.

The technique of watching the breath is more effective when it is accompanied by a *bij*, or "seed," *mantra*. The mantra my Guru recommended was "*Hong-Sau.*" (The "Sau" is pronounced like the carpenter's saw.) The meaning of *Hong-Sau* is, "I am He." In Sanskrit the actual words are, *"Aham saha."* As a *bij* mantra, however, *Hong-Sau* vibrates with the astral breath, and helps to calm the process of physical breathing. Mentally say "*Hong*" with the incoming breath, following it all the way in. With "*Sau*," uttered mentally, follow the exhalation all the way out.

10. For at least the final third of your meditation period, sit quietly, simply enjoying the inner silence. Try, during this period, to deepen your enjoyment of inner peace. Pray to God mentally, in whatever form you find most appealing, and ask Him/Her: "Come to me! Fill me with Thy bliss!"

MEDITATION

While sitting still, visualize a candle flame burning without a flicker in your heart. Imagine darkness around it, and watch the light gradually spread outward in all directions, transforming that darkness into light.

Watch the light, now, filling your body then filling your mind. Body, mind, thoughts, and feelings: Bathe all in that calm light.

Visualize in those light rays, now, a vibration of joy. *You are that calm light*, that calm feeling, that calm awareness of inner joy. Delight, inwardly and outwardly, in your inner peace.

If you have time for longer practice, visualize the light expanding outward in all directions to infinity.

That light is your own Self. See it blessing your environment, blessing all those nearby, blessing every creature on this earth.

Lo! The very world has become radiantly joyful, the light of your own being!

AFFIRMATION

"I am light, ever calm, ever perfect. I am one with Thee!"

POINTS TO REMEMBER

1. Material success is only a steppingstone to perfection. From a yogic point of view, every kind of success is a good thing, for the qualities that bring material success bring also divine enlightenment.

2. The more we are centered in the superconscious, the less we are conditioned by habit. Superconsciousness is forever fresh, spontaneous, and creative.

3. Good habits, such as daily meditation, remembrance of God, and inwardly chanting His name, *invite* the superconscious to take part in our struggles. It is the superconscious that eventually dissolves our worldly tendencies.

4. When one's aim in life is to serve others, and when one doesn't think of what he can get for himself, he radiates a protective aura which shields him from usual, "business is business" attitudes.

5. People respond in kind to the energy we send toward them. Even people who make a practice of cheating others may not cheat *you*. Your magnetism will normally attract the right people, and the right circumstances.

6. The attitude you radiate should be of sincere, *impersonal* friendship for all in God. Never think of yourself as exerting power over others.

7. One great benefit of meditation is that it helps one to become self-motivated. One becomes a cause in life, not an effect. Thus, no matter how people respond to you, you will preserve your inner peace.

8. One of the benefits of living dharmically is that people usually treat you with kindness.

9. Material success infallibly comes to those who know how to live calmly at their center. It would take a very strong "failure karma" to counteract the success vibration that is emanated by inner contentment.

10. Joy is *contagious*! So also is inner peace.

11. True success requires inspiration from the superconsciousness.

12. Meditation is the most direct route to success of all kinds. Everyone can include at least a little meditation in his daily routine. Think of it as a kind of hygiene—spiritual in this case, not physical!

13. Daily meditation uplifts one's thoughts, and uproots any negative tendencies, empowered by habit. Regular meditation calms the mind, making it receptive to intuition.

14. Meditation enables one to become inwardly centered, and less subject to external influences. The less reactive we are to outer stimuli, the more we become masters of ourselves.

15. When an emotion seizes you, try to control it by first controlling the flow of energy in the spine. Relax in the spine. Sit upright; inhale and exhale deeply; try to bring the flow of energy there under the control of your will. Then center the feelings, also, in the spine. Breathe deeply, until your feelings become calm, and you are aware of yourself as a cause, not an effect.

16. Try to live always in the awareness of your spine. The more balanced you are inwardly, the more likely you will be to make wise judgments. Inner poise will enable you to listen with an open heart to inner guidance.

17. Whatever you may be doing, when you have a free moment concentrate briefly at the point between the eyebrows.

18. Some people have the *magnetism* to attract what they want in life, whether answers to questions, solutions to problems, or opportunities they need for success. One feels a calmness in their presence suggestive of meditation and yoga practice. Without some kind of meditation, whether in this life or in some past one, that kind of magnetism is hardly to be found in anyone.

WORKBOOK IDEAS
by Joseph Bharat Cornell

Meditation's Many Benefits

Creativity and concentration are crucial to success. Concentration brings all one's resources to the task at hand, and a creative mind sees fresh and transformative alternatives to traditional solutions. The best way to improve your concentration and intuition is to meditate. While creativity exercises that are popular in business today try to free you from habitual thinking, meditation takes you beyond thought altogether and attunes you directly to the source of inspiration, the superconscious.

Establish a Meditation Practice

ACTION ITEM:
1. If you haven't yet established a regular meditation practice, do so now. Begin by meditating fifteen minutes morning and evening. If you already have a practice, try to increase its frequency, intensity, and length.
2. After four weeks, ask yourself if you've noticed these changes:
   - I feel more centered and even-minded.
   - I have more energy and need less sleep.
   - I feel more peaceful.
   - Inspiration comes to me more often.
   - I feel more positive and loving.
   - I think more of God.

Change Your Destiny

The more centered you are, the more outer events adjust themselves to your inner control, because centered energy is stronger than dissipated, reactive energy. Meditation is the art of learning to live from one's center, because it dynamically brings your consciousness into the spine. If you want to control your destiny, relate to life from your center—not your periphery.

ACTION ITEM:
- Whenever you find yourself reacting emotionally to a situation, use the following exercise to calm and center yourself:

  Relax in the spine. Sit upright. Inhale and exhale deeply. Try to bring the flow of energy there under the control of your will. Then center the feelings, also, in the spine. Breathe deeply, until your feelings become calm, and you are aware of yourself as a cause, not an effect.

LESSON EIGHT

IMMEDIATE VERSUS LONG-RANGE GOALS

The secret of turning the truth of timelessness to best present advantage is to see change, and even evolution itself, as a process of unfolding awareness. Allow no fleeting concern to lead you away from that goal. At the same time, don't allow theoretical philosophy to blind you to present realities.

The Principles

The subject of this lesson is deeper than one might think from looking only at the title. The title seems to suggest a contrast between temporal satisfaction and eternal fulfillment. In fact, however, I intend to offer a new concept of time altogether, one which relates time to timelessness.

Of the classical Indian philosophies, three, as I say in the Introduction to these lessons, are especially important for Self-realization. Of these three—*Sankhya*, *Yoga*, and *Vedanta*—*Yoga* alone shows *how* to bridge the abyss separating *maya* from Absolute Consciousness. *Sankhya* explains *why* that abyss must be spanned, abandoning *maya* for the Absolute. *Vedanta* describes the Absolute Reality awaiting us on the other side. *Yoga* alone explains the method for crossing the bridge and attaining Brahman.

Yoga shows also how to make that traffic a two-way flow—how to relate present reality, in other words, to ultimate wisdom, and how to bring into practical life an intuition, at least, of higher truth.

Maya makes time and space seem real. *Yoga*, however, shows that present perceptions of reality can be related to timelessness and spacelessness. The concept of timelessness, which is our present concern, can actually be an aid in the quest for material as well as for spiritual success.

Time is, of course, essential to our perception of the things of this world. Nevertheless, great yogis and advaitins have all described time as a delusion. It certainly *seems* real, however, to all of us. Time is even logically sequential: we see past becoming present, and present reaching out to become the future. My Guru compared time to a movie film which, in the projection booth, can be turned at will quickly or slowly, forward or backward. The mind staggers under the weight of this concept. Fortunately, it won't be necessary in these lessons to dive into those swirling waters and attempt bravely to plumb their depths.

My Guru explained that the cosmic dream *is* real, at least *as a dream*. It is also, as a dream may be, self-consistent and coherent—but not altogether so, and sometimes not really so at all! I must, however, turn my back resolutely on such abstractions. They have nothing to do with the subject of material success.

What is important here is that it is possible to adjust our concept of time to our actual needs. We can narrow time, or expand it. Our concept of it may concern some problem of the moment, or it may flow freely toward solution-consciousness, carrying us lightly over the abyss of delusion.

Zeno, a philosopher in ancient Greece, proposed several "paradoxes" with a view to demonstrating the inadequacy of logic alone. One of his paradoxes was that, in order to cross a road, one must first go half the distance. Before going the second half, he must next go half that distance. No matter how minuscule the remaining distance, one must still go halfway before completing the distance. How then, demanded Zeno, can anyone cross a road at all?

Of course, we all know that crossing a road is a simple task that poses no problem even for the chicken in the well-known children's puzzler: "Why does a chicken cross the road?" ("To get to the other side.") The paradox is solved by introducing the element of motion.

Without motion, there would be no space. Without motion, time itself would not exist. Time *is* motion, creating the illusion of space.

Motion is not the series of static points that Zeno proposed. It is *vibration*. Vibration creates both time and space. Modern science has actually declared that matter is nothing but a vibration of energy. Still to be demonstrated, but universally declared by Self-realized masters, is something that many scientists themselves now suspect: that *all things in creation are only vibrations of consciousness*.

People who are wholly immersed in the delusion of time consider time necessary for every accomplishment. For them, often, the longer it takes to do a thing the more worthwhile must be the thing itself. The more the difficulties one faces in an undertaking, the greater his sense of accomplishment. People see time in terms of points along the way to completion. Most people, as they contemplate these separate points, see only problems needing to be solved. One with a consciousness of *flow*, however, ceases to concentrate on the separate, individual points, and in consequence may find the task perfectly simple.

If you want to transcend time, then concentrate on something motionless, like the ocean's horizon. If you want to be creative, concentrate on flowing motion rather than on all the points and problems along the way. If a thing needs to be done urgently, view the time you must spend on it against a background of eternity.

Some goals, indeed, may press upon us in terms of the time we have available for reaching them. If, however, we can keep in mind the truth that whatever happens is really happening *right now*, then the idea that time is a requirement for getting everything done is no longer a problem, for "right now" becomes the only time in which one can do the work at all.

Long ago, I faced a major problem that involved an insufficiency of time. The year was 1988; the month, May. On July the fourth, Ananda Village planned to celebrate its twentieth anniversary. The director of Crystal Clarity, Ananda's publishing house, asked me if I would consent to write a book in celebration of that event. I was just nearing the end of a month of seclusion, during which I had written several books. A week later, it would be necessary for me to adjust to new circumstances. What I really wanted just then was a rest from writing altogether. Besides, I said in reply, a week was an absurdly short amount of time for writing what she wanted: a book. I answered flatly, "I couldn't possibly."

"Twenty years," was her wistful response. "This is a *big* anniversary."

"I know, I know," was my answer, "but I really haven't the time I'd need for such a job."

Unfortunately for me, when I say No what I usually mean is, "Well, I'll think about it."

I thought about it. The celebration was scheduled in a little over a month. It did seem a good thing to offer something special for the occasion. But—a week? Firmly I repeated to myself, "Impossible!" The idea kept coming back to me, however: "It *would* be nice!" Suddenly I saw a solution. I couldn't possibly do it myself, but God could do *anything*!

Resolutely dismissing any thought of the difficulties involved—including the obvious question, "What on earth shall I write?"—I flung open my mental doors to higher inspiration. Mustering all my will power, I said, "*You* do it, Lord!" And He did! The chapters flowed smoothly and quickly, needing almost no rewriting at the end.

One day my resolution was severely tested. A man working on the electric wiring had, without realizing it, thrown the wrong switch.

That whole day's work was irretrievably lost from my computer. This setback was almost paralyzing. I'd been pouring all my energy into something that had seemed, even so, impossible. I simply couldn't face this blow, and could do no more work the rest of that day.

The next day, however, "girding up my loins," I went back to work again. Four days, not counting the day I lost, were all that the task required. I myself could hardly believe it. This book, titled *Cities of Light*, has been a popular favorite among my books.

Often in my life I have proved this simple formula: Though man can do little if anything on his own, God can do *anything*!

Success cannot come, of course, if one makes this teaching an excuse for drifting lazily down a river, telling himself, "Everything is in God's hands. Everything will be *all right*!" Nothing can be accomplished without will power.

The yogi doesn't deny the reality of time. He simply sees the fleeting events of life in relation to eternity. Obviously, he must "keep his feet on the ground," addressing life's events as they occur. To do otherwise would mean being merely a dreamer.

Some people, in the name of "philosophy," would deny the obvious. Imagine that someone gives you a dish of ice cream. Would you say, "Please leave it out on the table; I'll enjoy it tomorrow"? If you waited more than a few minutes, your "ice" cream would be a puddle of milk! Too "Vedantic" a view of things—like dismissing time airily with the exclamation, "There is no past or future"—might end in one's dying of starvation!

All of us have both immediate and long-range goals in life. In both of them, time is a consideration. We must decide, for example, when and what to eat. We must follow a sensible routine of life that permits us time daily for rest. If one wants to be married, he'd better find himself a spouse while he is still young and not wait until he is eighty-five. Time intrudes itself on our lives objectively, no matter what our subjective view of it is.

It is a mistake, however, to think that every serious decision demands a great deal of time and thought. As I pointed out earlier, far more important than the time we spend on a project is the *energy* we give it. Behind that energy, I said also, must be will power; and will power must in its turn be directed consciously. It is above all helpful for consciousness to be directed by *inspiration*, of which the source is beyond all vibration, in the eternal Now of Spirit.

Focused energy produces results quickly and effectively. Scattered energy might drag a project out indefinitely, producing few, if any, worthwhile results. Energy, moreover—more clearly so than any specific thing or event—has its roots in eternity. The more one focuses on a flow of energy, the less he needs to worry about the obstacles to getting what he wants, or even about the amount of time required in the getting. A flow of energy can cause one's consciousness of time itself to brush the hem of timelessness.

In 1925, Paramhansa Yogananda saw something he had beheld many times in superconscious visions: Mount Washington Estates, in Los Angeles, which was destined to become the international headquarters of his work.

The issue of prevision, albeit fascinating, is not my point here. I am telling this story for another reason: It shows how the Master shortened the time frame he was in, and thereby met his present needs.

The price of the property was $45,000: a princely sum in those days, before the dollar had become inflated many times over by overprinting. Students of the Master objected, "It would take us twenty years to raise that much money!"

"Twenty years," the Master replied, "for those who *think* twenty years. Twenty months for those who think twenty months. And *three months*, for those who think three months." Three months later, the property was his.

Time cannot be divorced from *maya* so long as one dwells in the realm of *maya*. Only in eternity is time nonexistent; otherwise, it is simply a reality. My Guru used to say, "If in your dream at night you strike your head on a brick wall, your dream head will hurt! Only on waking will you realize that both the blow to your head and the pain you felt afterward were imaginary."

Life's goals, whether immediate or long range, can be achieved more easily if we view them in relation to eternity. In the Spirit, goals don't exist. Progress and evolution are delusions. Paramhansa Yogananda said, in response to a question on evolution, "There is no end to it. You go on until you achieve endlessness." Whatever ambition you have, then, keep always in mind that your real goal is, and has always been, endless bliss. On the other hand, you must acknowledge and work with reality as it is in the *present*.

The secret of turning the truth of timelessness to best present advantage is to see change, and even evolution itself, as a process of unfolding awareness. Allow no fleeting concern to lead you away from that goal. At the same time, don't allow theoretical philosophy to blind you to present realities.

Every religion warns against being impatient in the quest for truth. "Haste makes waste" is a popular saying also, probably uttered similarly in every language. It was not haste that my Guru counseled in saying, "Three months, for those who think three months." Rather, he was urging his followers to step out of their normal time frame. Success of every kind should be sought calmly, in refusal to be ruled by time. Success itself is an unfolding—of awareness above all, not of events.

Success is inevitably followed, in time, by its opposite: failure. If, however, one can succeed in stepping outside the awareness of time, he can create alternate definitions of success, and thus have success of a kind always. He can be just as happy, then, in failure as in success. Moreover, he can actually complete in the shortest possible time whatever he attempts, with less difficulty than he'd normally face. Indeed, if one can remain inwardly unaffected in both success and failure, he will realize that failure itself can be a kind of success—not only spiritually, but materially. For while it is natural to rejoice in success, it is possible also to rejoice in failure. The secret is to remove one's inner joy from identification with anything outward.

No matter what happens, then, be always even-minded. Success and failure, joy and sorrow: these things are only states of mind. When calmness is not conditioned by anything that happens in time, one finds that the time it takes to accomplish a thing ceases to be a serious consideration: not because he becomes lazy, but because he can accomplish everything much faster. Patience, arising from non-attachment, can be the fastest path to success.

People find it difficult to combine patience with high energy. By living more in the consciousness that time is an illusion, however, they find themselves not bound by the usual restrictions of time.

I've often reflected on three lines of Paramhansa Yogananda's great poem, "*Samadhi*," from *Autobiography of a Yogi*:

> Thoughts of all men, past, present, to come, . . .
> I swallowed, transmuted all
> Into a vast ocean of blood of my own one being!

Past, present, and future: These three states arise, wavelike, on the surface of the Eternal Now. Time itself is but a product of vibratory movement, which produces the cosmic dream. Even the sequences of time are not absolute, being only ideas in the consciousness of the Absolute. Nothing that ever was, is, or shall be is a fixed reality; all things are only vibrations of thought and energy, set into motion by the vibrationless consciousness of Spirit. In omniscience alone are all vibrations known.

God's knowledge is not stored on bookshelves in some cosmic library. His way of knowing is very different from man's: He knows everything from its *center* outward. Awareness flows out from the heart of every atom. God already *is everything*! Divine perception was described by Paramhansa Yogananda as "center everywhere, circumference nowhere."

Since time is an illusion, it can be understood more easily by *calm*, clear awareness. Indeed, it is only in calmness that its reality is *experienced*. If, then, you have an urgent job to do and want guidance and inspiration for the accomplishment, pray for a new perception of the time involved. Include in the request the demand that time not impede you.

Here is an example of what I mean:

Several years ago, Warner Brothers, a well-known publishing house in America, asked me to write a book for them. (They'd already published another of my books, called *Secrets of Life*.) I suggested a title for this new book: *Meditation for Starters*. They gave me their approval.

My expectation at the time was that I'd have nearly a year to write it. In this happy confidence, I was disappointed. On a promotion tour for *Secrets of Life*, my pulse began racing at 160 beats a minute, staying there so long that, finally, I went to a cardiologist. After making a few tests, he informed me that one of my valves needed urgent replacement; otherwise, I might die at any moment. Two weeks later, I entered a hospital and underwent open heart surgery. This was December 18, 1994. After the operation, my three doctors insisted that I must take a whole year off, with complete rest.

Things developed rather differently, however, through no fault of my own. Signs inauspicious to rest began immediately. It was in the early evening that my operation ended. At three o'clock the next morning, the door of my room burst open and some prankster of an orderly charged in with a loud bellow, "Blood! I need blood!" I roused myself from my torpor to tell him in no uncertain terms that this was no way to treat someone who had just undergone major surgery.

That year was among the busiest and most stressful of my life. I survived it, though not altogether blithely. Not only was I forced for that whole year to engage in intense, mandatory work, but also that year was one of severe spiritual testing.

Two weeks before the operation, a summons had been handed me to appear before a court of law. This was an imperative, and could not be canceled or graciously postponed in the interests of my survival. My self-styled enemies would have been glad, indeed, to see me die. Their chief lawyer said to a friend of mine, "You can tell Mr. Walters I'm going to *destroy* him!" Fortunately (perhaps!) he didn't succeed.

As for the book I'd agreed to write, I might conceivably have begged off, or at least got Warner to let me postpone writing it. Unfortunately, I'd already spent my advance royalties on purchasing equipment for our sound studio, and was thus committed to finishing the work. I couldn't afford the chance of a refusal, and therefore wasn't able to return the money. Toward the end of April I received worse news in the form of a letter from Warner Brothers' editorial staff, informing me that what they'd decided they really wanted from me was a book titled, *Superconsciousness*. This posed a serious problem for me. There was no way I could "plaster" this new title onto the book I'd been planning. I would have to write another book altogether.

The subject they proposed was, as I saw it, one that would take prolonged preparation and more-than-usually precise writing. To do justice to it would, I believed, require at least two years. Even a relatively superficial job seemed impossible in less than a year.

I asked them how long they'd give me for this book. They replied, "Two months." The end of June, in other words. It was now nearly the end of April! Unfortunately, my schedule didn't even permit me that much time. I'd committed myself, before the operation, to doing a lecture tour during the first two weeks of June. The actual time available to me, then, for writing this book was hardly more than one month.

Other "unfriendly facts" stood in line to greet me that year with catcalls. I'd been told, even before the surgery, that an urgent job waited at the printer: a new book of mine that was ready for printing. The book's preface still needed my editing. The morning of surgery I edited the first half. The day after, clearing away clouds of anesthesia from my mind by will power, I forced myself to finish the second half, sinking back gratefully afterward onto my pillow.

Another literary project awaited my attention also, one to which I'd already given a firm commitment. This book was needed by the end of January. Again, I'd already spent the advance royalties on equipment for our sound studio. I therefore had no choice but to give this job my full concentration. I got it off barely before my deadline.

In fact, a continuous series of urgent demands were made of me that year. These included eighty hours of grueling deposition with that extremely hostile lawyer.

Well, I promised Warner I'd do my best. I then turned off my phone, accepted no visitors, didn't even look at my mail, and told God and Guru firmly, "You've *got to* help me! I simply cannot do this job alone."

Amazingly, the job did get finished on time! Once again, as I'd done with *Cities of Light*, I threw open the floodgates of my mind to the inflow of inspiration. Several times the thought came to me, "I've bitten off more than I can chew!" Each time, instead of giving up (as I was tempted to do), I simply turned up the volume on my inner flow of inspiration.

The manuscript was sent to New York on the next but last day of June, and reached there, as required, for the end of the month. I can only think of this entire episode as a miracle. Interestingly (in the light of this lesson on timelessness), even if I'd worked from normal inspiration I couldn't have finished the job when it was due, had I not made time itself part of my request for inspiration.

On several other occasions in my life, one of which I've related already in this lesson, I've had to include the factor of time in my prayers for inspiration. Strange as it must seem—to me even now, it seems *impossible*—I've never been let down. How was it possible for inspiration to come through repeatedly and so consistently?

The first and absolute necessity, I believe, is not to let the intellect interfere with one's flow of inspiration. This is true no matter what sort of inspiration you seek. It can be true even in perfectly mundane situations. In matters involving time, however, it becomes doubly true.

The intellect functions rationally only. It is, therefore, irrevocably tied to time. Repeatedly, when I haven't added time to my request for inspiration, problems have arisen and my mind, in protest, has rebelled, arguing, "I need more *time* to figure this all out. How can I produce deep insights at short notice?" As often, however, as I've answered my own objection by saying, "There just *isn't time* to *think* these things through. It's Your turn, Lord: Give me the insights I need," the answers have appeared instantly and with crystal clarity. Later, moreover, the clarity I received has stood up under the test of any logic that I could muster to challenge it.

Indeed, superconscious inspiration has met the tests of logic better than any process of reasoning could have done. The very act of reasoning things out would have shown psychic scars, later. Instead, the intuitions I received were like the facets of a diamond, each one reflecting light brilliantly no matter how I turned it to the light of my own actual experience.

The Lord tested me in other ways that year, as if with the deliberate purpose of keeping me from having twelve months, or even a week, of restful repose. In May, before my determined withdrawal from all society to write that book, I received a letter from Derek Bell, the well-known Celtic harpist from Ireland. Derek was a friend of mine, and wanted to record an album of my music during a visit he had planned to Ananda Village that August. I wrote back saying that I'd never written harp music, was unfamiliar with the demands of the instrument, and had no confidence of being able to meet his expectations. I pointed out in addition how little time there was before his arrival in August. (I made no reference to Warner's deadline.)

Derek replied, sternly insistent, "You can do it! Don't be fainthearted. You *must* do it!" It was a compliment to me, of course, and a great opportunity. By no means, however, did it further my doctors' order of complete rest.

Even after finishing the book, moreover, and before Derek's arrival in August, I'd already committed myself—again, long before the operation—to another two-week lecture tour in July. The time available to me, then, before departing on that tour, and after sending the manuscript to Warner, was three days. August, and Derek Bell's arrival, loomed over me already like a cloud.

So then, three days for writing all those melodies. Fortunately, I was still in a superconscious flow and was able to tune in on that level to the vibrations of Celtic music. I wrote all but three or four of the pieces (that I'd composed years earlier) in two days. This left me the luxury of a day for packing before I left on my tour. I gave the melodies to a gifted friend of mine, who had studied the technical aspects of orchestration.

When I returned two weeks later, I added words to several of the melodies. And then—Derek arrived. Fortunately, the resulting album, *The Mystic Harp*, was a success. So also was its sequel, *Mystic Harp Two*, which we did two years later. Several "cuts" from both albums have been played on national and international airlines, and in other public places like malls and restaurants.

I could not have accomplished any of these things had I allowed the delusion of time to control me. I simply *had* to think outside the normal time we all know.

It was a busy year! In fact, I've left out much of what was forced on me that year. Happily, I did eventually get to write that book I'd first proposed, *Meditation for Starters*. This one has been one of my most popular books, selling 11,000 copies in Holland alone in one year.

The day following Derek Bell's recording sessions, I set off for San Francisco and weeks of grueling legal depositions.

In what some people have described as a testing life, 1995 stands out in my mind as outstandingly difficult. (As a matter of interest, two years later, when that case finally went to trial, it proved to be in several important ways a great blessing for me. God tests us, but the darker the cloud (if we have faith), the more refreshing the rain that accompanies it.)

The point I am making here is simply this: Don't let considerations of time dissuade you from undertaking any project that seems to you important.

The Application

I have already given a few pointers on how to apply these teaching in what might be called "pragmatic timelessness." I also wrote earlier about the importance of living as much as possible at one's center. Time, of course, is not physically substantial. To live at one's center in time means to be centered not only in the moment, but in the timeless Now which ever hovers *behind* this moment. People usually define the present in terms of what is happening outwardly. Their concept of time concerns events, whether in quantity or in sequence.

Truly creative work, however, is often accomplished without reference to specific events. It manifests, rather, as a conscious flow. From one's center in space and time, one can simply *know* what needs to be done.

So often I've heard old people, especially, preface some remark of theirs by saying, "Under such and such circumstances, this is what I always say . . ." or, "What I always tell people is. . . ." Such people are "psychological antiques," to use a favorite expression of my Guru's! Everyone, whether young or old, should avoid the tendency to render everything commonplace by referring it to what is usual. Truly creative people see things both in reference to the totality of things, and also as unique. If you want really to succeed in life, never think in terms of what you "always" do. Every moment, both in time and beyond it, is *here and now*, and is in some way different from every other one. To do good work, address everything as if for the first time. Avoid the well-worn trails that, like old railway trains, take people rumbling down ancient tracks to ever-fixed destinations.

Suppose, for example, you work in an office where people make frequent and urgent demands on your time. Assuming that you are an employee and can't ignore the demands coming from "up top"—though leadership, far more than most people realize, is by no means a liberating position—the solution is to respond from your inner center. Here is the interesting thing: From your center, you will be able to shift directions quickly and thus be more efficient in everything you do. I do not counsel drifting through life, like a cloud, wrapped in some private dream. People who are never flustered are of two types: the inwardly calm, and those vague "exhibits" who drift along so languidly that they end up complete non-achievers.

My Guru sometimes spoke to us about Durga Mata, one of his women disciples who, though small physically, was intensely energetic. He told of how she and a few of the monks had repainted the main building at Mount Washington headquarters. "The men," he said, "worked slowly, waving their brushes in gentle, 'spiritual' movements as if in a graceful dance. Durga, on the other hand, plied her brush swiftly, as though she were fighting a battle. Single-handed she accomplished more than the others put together. At the end of the day," he continued, "she was full of energy, whereas the others were exhausted."

Durga also, at the end of the day, was calm. The reason for her high energy was partly that she was highly advanced spiritually, and was truly centered in herself. Her centeredness was not only physical, but a centeredness in the moment.

Whenever you find yourself "driven to the wall," as it were, by urgent demands whether by life or by other people, withdraw for an instant into your center within. Then tell yourself, "Countless millions of years have gone by in my own past! Many more may come in my future. I will not be ruled by time-consciousness. No matter how long my journey through *maya* in both time and space, I can only be right here, right now. I will live, therefore, in full awareness of the present."

There is a delightful story about Ramana Maharshi, a great saint of modern India. An English lady had come to visit him in his ashram in south India. At their meeting she said, "I've come here all the way from London just for this meeting."

"You haven't moved at all," was his reply. "You've been stationary. It was the world as you perceive it that moved around you."

Though you live through many incarnations, and on countless planets, you will remain forever centered in yourself. Wherever you are, and wherever your interests take you, you will always be right here, right now. Why not live wholly at the one spot you can never leave, no matter how earnestly you seek elsewhere: your own Self?

MEDITATION

Imagine yourself seated at the heart of eternity. On the outskirts of your vision, swirling away into the distance, are the mists of endless cycles of time. Those mists can never touch you. You, on the other hand, can control them, once you are fully, consciously centered in yourself!

From your center of inner calmness, radiate your energy outward in all directions. Behold: you alone are in control of all that happens to you. Visualize yourself as a king or queen, seated on the throne of consciousness. Everything that happens to you is an emanation of your true Self.

AFFIRMATION

"I am in control of my life. Time cannot control me, for I am timeless forever, right here, and right now."

POINTS TO REMEMBER

1. It is possible to adjust our concept of time to our actual needs.

2. If you want to be creative, concentrate on flowing motion rather than on all the points and problems along the way.

3. Keep in mind the truth that whatever happens is really happening *right now*, then the idea that time is a requirement for getting everything done is no longer a problem.

4. Though man can do little if anything on his own, God can do *anything*!

5. Far more important than the time we spend on a project is the *energy* we give it. Behind that energy must be will power; and will power must in its turn be directed consciously. It is above all helpful for consciousness to be directed by *inspiration*.

6. Focused energy produces results quickly and effectively. The more one focuses on a flow of energy, the less he needs to worry about the obstacles or the amount of time required to getting what he wants.

7. Whatever ambition you have, keep always in mind that your real goal is, and has always been, endless bliss. On the other hand, you must acknowledge and work with reality as it is in the *present*.

8. See change, and even evolution itself, as a process of unfolding awareness.

9. Success of every kind should be sought calmly, in refusal to be ruled by time.

10. If one can succeed in stepping outside the awareness of time, and removing one's inner joy from identification with anything outward, he can be just as happy in failure as in success, and discover that failure itself can be a kind of success—not only spiritually, but materially.

11. No matter what happens, be always even-minded. When calmness is not conditioned by anything that happens in time, you can accomplish everything much faster. Patience, arising from non-attachment, can be the fastest path to success.

12. If you have an urgent job to do and want guidance and inspiration for the accomplishment, pray for a new perception of the time involved. Include in the request the demand that time not impede you.

13. When faced with a challenging project, throw open the floodgates of your mind to the inflow of inspiration. If more difficulties arise, turn up the volume on your inner flow of inspiration.

14. Don't let the intellect interfere with your flow of inspiration. Instead ask God to give you the insights you need.

15. Don't let considerations of time dissuade you from undertaking any project that seems to you important.

16. To live at one's center in time means to be centered not only in the moment, but in the timeless Now which ever hovers *behind* this moment. From one's center, one can simply *know* what needs to be done.

17. If you want really to succeed in life, never think in terms of what you "always" do. To do good work, address everything as if for the first time.

18. Whenever urgent demands press on you, withdraw for an instant into your center within. Tell yourself, "I will not be ruled by time-consciousness. I can only be right here, right now. I will live in full awareness of the present."

WORKBOOK IDEAS
by Joseph Bharat Cornell

Live in the Present

John, a devotee of Sri Yogananda, once lost his way in the mountains. It was late spring, and snow still covered the high country. While hiking back to his car, John went down the wrong side of a ridge and into unfamiliar territory, going miles out of his way. When he realized his mistake, there wasn't enough daylight left to retrace his steps. John didn't have a coat, so it was imperative that he get to lower elevation and warmer, snow-free ground.

John knew that continuing his present course would *eventually* bring him to a road—if not that night, then certainly by tomorrow. Realizing that he might have some challenges ahead, John began consciously thinking of God and offering himself into His hands. And knowing that fear and imagination add fuel to worry and often cause unwise decisions, John was determined to remain calm and centered in the presence of God. As he did so, he found his walk becoming more and more joyful, even though the day was nearly done and the outcome uncertain.

Well after sundown John reached a large lake and began walking along its shore. When it was almost dark, he saw in the distance three men fishing. John wanted to ask them where he was but since yelling such a long way would disturb his inner peace, he kept on walking. God, John felt, had taken him this far, and God would surely see him home.

When John came to a small cove, he saw that the fishermen were still on the far bank. He was now able to ask them in a calm, normal voice the name of the lake. "Spaulding," replied one of the fisherman as his group walked away. John now knew his location. He was ten miles from his car.

Minutes later, as John cautiously made his way in the night, he heard one of the fisherman ask, "Why don't you know the name of the lake?" Curious about the hiker, the fisherman had waited to find out more. To his direct question, John calmly explained how he had come to the lake by mistake. The man exclaimed, "But your car is ten miles away, and it's nighttime! We'll drive you there."

While driving his own car home that night, John felt a great sense of victory and gratitude to God. Remaining content with his circumstances and not allowing time-consciousness to destroy his serenity was the secret to John's successful outing. Paramhansa Yogananda said, "Most people live in the past or future. When you can be truly happy in the present, then you have God."

When faced with a challenging situation at work, don't allow worry to drive your actions and scatter your energy. Remain calmly in the "here and now." A way to diffuse fear is to imagine the worst possible scenario, then say with determination, "If it happens, *I accept it*." The more you embrace the present, the more energy you'll have for making the most of any situation.

Work Without Tension

Whenever you feel pressure to meet an urgent deadline, use the following checklist to keep yourself calm and centered. Inner calmness will enable you to get things done much more easily and quickly. You also will be much more pleasant to be around!

Practice these principles all the time, and then when you face intense challenges, you'll know how to respond.

ACTION ITEMS:
1. Breathe deeply and center your energy in the spine.
2. Feel that God, not you, is the doer. Pray for His guidance.
3. Decide what needs to be done. Act from inner clarity; don't merely react to outer circumstances.
4. Stay centered in the moment. Ignore every thought that doesn't contribute to your goal.
5. Keep your energy focused. It is the secret to getting things done rapidly.
6. Do one thing at a time, even if you are overwhelmed by a multitude of projects. Doing one task with deep attention calms you.
7. If fears about the project plague you, imagine the worst that could happen, and then accept it. Worries, then, will cease to trouble you.
8. Keep your perspective. Ask yourself, "Three months from now, will I still feel worried about this?"
9. Pray that time not impede you. Consciously try to enter into the flow of God's presence in your life. In His consciousness, time doesn't exist.
10. Give everything to God.

Whenever urgent demands press on you, withdraw for an instant into your center within. Tell yourself, "I won't be ruled by time-consciousness. I can only be right here, right now."

LESSON NINE

THE IMPORTANCE OF HUMAN VALUES

Human and spiritual elements are essential to every aspect of life. You will never succeed, at least in terms of *your own need for happiness*, so long as you ignore the human factor.

The Principles

It is common to find people giving more importance to material success than to human values. In terms of what they themselves want from life, this is a serious error. They forget that what everyone really wants is happiness, not the "bottom line" as defined by most people. When we make ourselves displeasing to others, success itself may forsake us, for clients and customers will seek elsewhere for what we offer.

I remember a visit I made from California to Mexico in 1954. At the Tijuana airport just south of the border, some of my countrymen, finding themselves confronted by Mexico's "*mañana*" ("tomorrow") consciousness, complained loudly of the slow pace there. I said to one of them, "Why have you come here, if you want everything to be just as you have it back home?"

Slowness, in fact, has its charms—at least in its suggestion of a culture that doesn't put money ahead of human values. A change from the northern American hustle and bustle should be welcome to those who can be in tune with it.

In India, the contrast is strong not between one culture and another, but *within* the same culture. Some Indians show an eager, "get ahead" and "do it now!" attitude. Others appear satisfied to sleep in the sun. That willingness to absorb both attitudes is partly what I mean in naming this lesson, "The Importance of Human Values."

I think it shows a healthy society to be so variegated. A person might respond to the above example, "But *in*efficiency won't bring material success!" Granted, certainly. That isn't my point, however. I am saying that you *will* have greater success if you accept that you are a human being, first, and that your clients or customers, or whomever you look to for your success are human beings also, and not money-spewing machines!

Think back to the example I gave several lessons ago of the two bakers, William and Joe. Both men did the same work, and, for the purposes of this discussion, were equally skilled at it. Joe Crumpet also made friends, however, and it was he who really succeeded. The reason is quite simple: Joe *liked* people. William Baker may have been as dedicated to making bread as Joe was, but his dedication meant less to other people because he wasn't dedicated also to serving *them*.

Joe Crumpet's appeal was to more than the self-interest of others. They enjoyed him as a person. He appealed to their sense of *fitness*, also. If, for instance, they'd seen him being cruel to others, they'd have been almost as displeased with him, probably, as if he'd treated them cruelly, too.

Human values depend ultimately not on philosophical abstractions, but on human *feelings*. If you inflicted "punishment" on a rock by kicking it, people would probably not be outraged—at least, not for the rock's sake. If you kicked at it in anger, they might consider you childish, but any displeasure they felt would be due only to your wrath. As for the rock itself, however, they'd be sorry for it only if they had some reason to believe it could feel pain from being kicked.

Many people in their pursuit of material success are willing to treat others like rocks! They trample over people's feelings, or simply *ignore* their feelings altogether as though, where moneymaking was concerned, the human factor didn't enter into the picture. They are mistaken, which also is what these lessons are about: They are for helping people to see that the human and spiritual elements are essential to every aspect of life. You will never succeed, at least in terms of *your own need for happiness*, so long as you ignore the human factor.

Before I met my Guru, many people—students of acting in the theater where I was studying to become a playwright—tried to convince me that nothing mattered except "getting to the top." It didn't matter, they insisted, how many people I trampled down in the process. Nothing mattered except my own self. I alone had to be pleased; mine alone was the reality I needed to look out for; I alone counted. Those people had absorbed too much modern existential "philosophy," which had led them to believe that the only honest attitude in life is to be wholly subjective. It was this line of reasoning, among other things, that drove me almost headlong to the spiritual path.

For it was obvious to me even then that, if I trampled on others in my efforts to "get to the top," I would also be trampling on myself. The attitudes that I projected onto others would become imbedded in my own consciousness. If I was indifferent to the feelings of others, I would lose my own sensitivity to feeling itself, as a fundamentally important part of human nature. If I lost my sensitivity, I would cease to be a human being, and would become a mere automaton of flesh and blood rather than of metal. What I must do, I decided, was exactly the opposite: I must *deepen* my own ability to feel, my sensitivity to life and to everything and everybody around me. Some of those theater friends paid me a visit after my conversion to the spiritual path, and departed afterward with the same cynical smiles of inner emptiness.

A young man from India many years ago in America laughed as he told me how his grandmother, after listening to a spiritual talk on the radio, would place a flower on the radio—"as though," he chortled, "the radio itself were aware of what it was transmitting!" After we'd parted, I mulled over his words. His grandmother's sensitivity, I thought, was greater than his. Granted, the radio itself wasn't aware, but how else could she demonstrate her gratitude to God outwardly for the truths she'd been hearing? To her, the radio was simply a symbol, as was the flower she placed on it.

We live in a world of symbols. Behind everything we see—behind even other people, and behind our own thoughts—there exists a higher reality than the one revealed to us by the senses. Without a feeling for that reality, we will be unable fully to enjoy any success we achieve, and may become like Howard Hughes in the story I related earlier. Hughes, who at that time was probably the richest man in the world, was asked if he was happy, and responded, "Nah! I can't say that I've found happiness!"

An alternate approach to life is desperately needed nowadays. This approach may not help you to become a billionaire, but the subject of these lessons, remember, is not material *wealth*, but material *success*. Our lives are successful when we are happy. To equate success only with wealth misses the point altogether. These lessons *can* make you wealthy, certainly, if you practice their basic teachings with this end in mind. I hope that by this time in your study of them, however, you will have come to understand clearly that excessive wealth is, in a sense, a kind of failure. It will most certainly be that if it deprives you of happiness.

True success requires sensitive awareness of realities that are outside the narrow confines of your egoic existence. It wouldn't hurt even to ponder the fact that God's consciousness is everywhere, and in everything—even in the rocks. The rocks, of course, are not aware as you and I are. They give no evidence of conscious feeling when they are kicked, or even when they are blasted with bombs. However, J. C. Bose, the great Indian physicist, proved that rocks and metals definitely react to stimuli. It has been found since then that knives grow "tired" with overuse, and will keep their tone better if they are given a rest every now and then.

Plants—a rung or two up the evolutionary ladder—are more easily shown to have some kind of feelings. They haven't egos, but they demonstrate a certain amount of discomfort when they are treated harshly, particularly if the treatment is administered with anger or with other negative emotions.

One day, I and a few brother disciples were planting a heavy young tree on the hillside at my Guru's newly acquired property, the SRF Lake Shrine in Pacific Palisades, California. Evidently we were moving it too roughly, for our Guru called out to us from below, "Be careful! Can't you *feel*? It's alive!"

When an animal—several rungs further up the evolutionary ladder—is hurt, sensitive people may feel its suffering even more than the animal itself does. They are projecting their own emotions, of course, for animals themselves haven't strong egos to tell them, "It is I, myself, who am suffering!" The consciousness of human beings is more personally identified with their bodies; thus, they are more capable of feeling pleasure and pain.

We adjudge human *values* by the refinement of feelings in the heart. Goodness is called that because it brings us closer to the natural peace and harmony of our true being. We consider things evil if they disturb that inner harmony.

When we are kind to others, not only do we invoke their gratitude: We ourselves feel the better for it. This good feeling, moreover, is due to the fact that our consciousness of self expands to include those people's feelings: We become in our consciousness, almost literally, bigger people.

When we treat others harshly, on the other hand, we are instinctively aware that something is not quite right. People may try to relieve themselves of this uncomfortable feeling by treating others even more harshly! Their discomfort, however, comes not only from having offended against social norms, but even more importantly from the fact that in hurting others they've affirmed their own egos and, thereby, their littleness! Any egoic contraction is painful, even if one has not yet developed the sensitivity to understand why. On the other hand, any expansion of awareness, especially of *self*-awareness, puts us in harmony with what we and all people instinctively want: an expansion of self-identity. For this reason, self-expansion is gratifying, whereas self-contraction deprives us of inner peace and causes us to suffer.

We might compare ourselves to little pieces of glass in the sunlight. The more polished and clean those pieces, the better they will reflect the sunlight. Similarly with us, the clearer our consciousness, the more brightly we shine.

To express this thought more literally, all people feel an urge to know more, to possess more, to experience more, to *be more*. Expansion is a native hunger of the soul; it spills over into the ego, giving it thereby a desire for self-importance. The ego, however, is not real in itself: It is individualized Spirit, attached to the body by its outwardly directed energy. When the ego contracts upon itself, that contracting awareness squeezes like a band around the heart and deprives it of soul-nourishment. Selfish people alienate themselves from their true nature. Suffering ensues, for when people lose the ability to compare that starved sensation with more healthy feelings, they don't think of themselves as even suffering, inwardly. They imagine only that other people "bother" them!

Why is it necessary to include human values in your business or other gainful activities? Quite simply because you are a human being, not a machine! The hero in many a modern novel is described as lacking in sensitivity: as "efficient, ruthless, machinelike." Such fiction might as well add, "He was also dead." Dead, one suspects, is what the authors themselves are in their own hearts!

Why do you work? Is it only to earn a living? Surely there are other reasons for wanting to work besides the body's need to eat and be sheltered from the rain and cold. Marxian dogma claims that man will be satisfied if he only has enough food to eat and a roof over his head. This teaching may apply well enough to cattle, but with man, food and shelter are paramount issues only if he is grindingly poor. Otherwise, everyone obviously wants more out of life. He wants comforts and conveniences in addition to the basic necessities. Ultimately, what matters to people is how they *feel* about things: proud, or wanting recognition, or liking elegance, or—the true "ulterior motive" behind everything we do—desiring happiness.

Don't ignore human feelings. And don't make the serious mistake, where your own happiness is concerned, of thinking that how others feel is no concern of yours. Their feelings matter more to you than you may realize, for in treating others well your own happiness expands, and in treating them badly your happiness contracts and causes you to suffer.

Happiness and suffering are relative. A habitually selfish person isn't aware, except in his deeper self, that he is not really happy. He may imagine that happiness isn't even important to him—that all he wants is a "good time" occasionally. In this lack of awareness he may even be cruel to others, and believe he is finding pleasure in the cruelty even though his ego, unknown to himself, is causing him to suffer. In his insensitivity, indeed, unconscious of why he is suffering, he will only become more tense both physically and emotionally. He will imagine that the only way he can relieve his inner tension is to strike out at others ever more viciously. He is not aware of the fact that his consciousness is contracting. Thus, his innate desire for self-expansion may expresses itself in time in the form of an emotional explosion. He may become violent, or furious at the world and more determined than ever to hurt others as he considers that he himself has been hurt. Bitter at the way he thinks he has been treated, increasingly angry with the world, and as a result ever more tense inside, he blames everyone but himself.

Such people often end up jumping off a cliff, or shooting themselves in impotent rage. Many suicides are caused by a sense of hopelessness, derived from people's inability to escape their egos, under whose tyranny they feel suffocated. If the robot-like "heroes" of those novels I've mentioned neglect to commit suicide, it is only because they are dead already and no longer capable of feeling *anything*! Why be a living corpse? Your own nature will demand, finally, that you return to your infinite reality.

If you do business with others in disregard for their needs and feelings, you will deprive yourself even more than them of the happiness which is your basic reason for wanting to succeed in the first place.

Patanjali, in his *Yoga Sutras*, lists ten "commandments" for spiritual development. His well-known *yamas* and *niyamas* encompass the universal rules of behavior for aspiring yogis and for spiritual seekers everywhere. With certain modifications, however, those rules apply equally well to anyone who aspires to be happy. As a student of these lessons, you desire material success—obviously! Remember, however, that without happiness you will not feel that you've really succeeded even if you've amassed a huge bank account.

First among Patanjali's ten "commandments" come the *yamas*, or proscriptive rules: attitudes which demand self-restraint. The purpose of the *yamas* is to help the ego to find true, as opposed to false, fulfillment. The ego's impulse, if its attitudes are selfish, is to divert its own natural desire for self-expansion into ego-endorsing attitudes. Patanjali's *yamas* help to remove these blocks, enabling one's spiritual nature to flower as a matter of course.

The first *yama* is *ahimsa*, or "harmlessness." A woman student of mine many years ago met a young man from one of the seedier sections of New York City, who told her that he enjoyed the feeling of power it gave him to carry a loaded pistol in his pocket. It pleased him to think that he could shoot anyone who dared to threaten him. Such people usually don't live long. I'm sure that *your* nature, as a student of higher principles, harbors no such potential for violence, but you might, in your desire to succeed, be willing (I hope you are not) to take advantage of others for your own personal gain.

Everyone wants power of some kind. Power is an attribute of the soul. Ego-based power, however, is what many people mistakenly seek. Their dreams of self-importance are like soap bubbles: colorful, larger than the substance they contain, but empty and evanescent. The stimulating popular game of clever one-upmanship is attractive to the ego, and fun for a time, but it leads in the end to an empty heart. True power comes not from pitting oneself *against* others, but from *winning their support*. If one harms others, even mentally, he sets himself against them; consequently, he shrinks inward upon himself.

Patanjali states that persons who have attained perfect harmlessness, having overcome the desire of the immature ego to impose its will on others—ruthlessly, or cunningly, or competitively—manifest such a power of peace that even wild animals will become tame in their presence.

In support of this statement, on one occasion Paramhansa Yogananda confronted a tiger in the jungles of Bihar. It was well into the night, and the tiger was approaching to kill a cow that had been placed in a stall with the door open, left that way by an absentminded driver. In the morning, the cow was to pull the Master and a few of his school students out of that jungle in a cart. The Master issued forth into the darkness to close the stall door. The tiger continued his approach, but the Master gazed at it with love, beholding God Himself in that form. So magnetic was the love he emanated that the tiger, instead of springing, rolled onto its back and let the Master stroke it. Then it rose up and stalked away calmly into the jungle.

True power enlists the support of others as

well as of one's own higher Self. Egoic power, on the other hand, is as much a delusion as echoes in a canyon. A strong ego produces a feeling of increasing isolation from what seems to it an indifferent and hostile world.

A musical string instrument needs the support of a sounding board to amplify its sounds. Man, similarly, needs support from others if he wants to succeed in life. The hermit's "sounding board" is God, but a merchant would be foolish to set up shop in a desert! Our power to succeed in business increases to the extent that we are aware that a subtle connection exists between ourselves and the great web of life.

Harmlessness in business means never to take advantage of others. It means having the *goodwill* to serve them, to treat them and think of them as one's friends. It means recognizing that one's own welfare includes, in ways both subtle and overt, the well-being of all. Harmlessness flowers naturally as a sense of unity with all life. The joy that arises from this awareness is itself a kind of success. Complete material fulfillment comes from working with a spirit of selfless service.

The second of the *yamas* is "non-prevarication." Not to prevaricate means more than not to tell lies. It also means not wishing, ineffectually, that things were other than they are. If you really want to improve matters, do so by all means, but don't stand limply around, wringing your hands! Work within the frame of what *exists*, however, not of what you merely wish existed. Face the facts fearlessly and with honesty.

The positive meaning of non-prevarication, of course, is truthfulness. Patanjali phrases the concept negatively because the obstacle to truthfulness is man's tendency to distort the truth. Patanjali says that this quality, when perfected, confers the power of materializing one's words and of reaping the fruits of action without acting. In material affairs, the benefit of truthfulness is twofold: First, it carries conviction, for truthful people radiate complete integrity. Second, any words they utter with concentrated will can be materialized, simply because they spoke them.

People who misuse this power, having once developed it, simply lose it again. Krishna in the Bhagavad Gita speaks of people following either the upward or the downward path. One sometimes meets people who can lie very convincingly. They developed that ability in other lives. If, however, they lie in this life they will eventually lose that ability. No *siddhi*, or spiritual power, and no human ability is permanent until spiritual liberation has been attained. Thus, even if you have the charisma to convince others of untruths, they will "catch on" eventually, and will despise you the more because they once looked up to you. Make it a serious point, then, to be truthful always.

Asteya, non-stealing, is the third *yama*. If a person tries to attain material success by stealing he may end up in prison. This eventuality, however, is too obvious to require elaboration. Stealing means, in a spiritual sense, much more than merely obtaining things illicitly. Essentially, what Patanjali referred to was *non-covetousness*: that is to say, not desiring anything that belongs by right to another.

Non-covetousness has an even subtler meaning. It means not seeking to diminish others in their own eyes, or in the eyes of other people. It means not trying to diminish their reputation or credit. It means giving sincere respect to all, and graciously recognizing any success others achieve as though it were one's own. *Asteya* means viewing no one as a rival, but seeing others as *colleagues* and friends. In addition, it means never gossiping about others or belittling their achievements. It means not trying to draw credit to one's self.

The more you show appreciation for others, the more others—not even the same people, necessarily—will show appreciation for you, in return. The more support you give others, also, the more supported you will feel in yourself.

One who becomes firmly established in the quality of non-covetousness seeks nothing that is not his by right. Such a person develops the power to attract whatever he needs in life. As Patanjali puts it, "All jewels come to him." Indeed, by means that he himself may not be able to explain, he finds himself ever secure, financially.

All the *yamas* must be understood as states of mind, primarily. They should not be defined literally only. In *Autobiography of a Yogi*, Paramhansa Yogananda as a young man in his guru's ashram raised his hand one day to slap a mosquito. Reconsidering, he refrained from committing the act.

"Why didn't you finish the job?" his guru asked, sensitively aware of his disciple's thought-processes. Sri Yukteswar went on to explain, "Patanjali's meaning was the removal of the *desire* to kill."

The fourth of the *yamas* is *brahmacharya*, or self-control. This quality, again, refers to attitude above all. It is a state of mind. Outer self-control, unless it is balanced by a sincere attempt, at least, at inner self-control, serves little purpose. For the student of these lessons, *brahmacharya* is a useful concept in a broad sense, primarily. My purpose is not to make monks and nuns of the students of this course, but to help them to understand the importance of keeping a rein on their energies. Self-control, in this context, refers especially to words and thoughts. Self-control is, in fact, the essential meaning of *brahmacharya*. Self-control is self-*containment*, not self-suppression. The more your powers radiate outward from your inner being, instead of "fizzing" restlessly through the senses, the more you will have your energy under control and will therefore be able to direct it effectively, according to actual needs of the moment.

Excessive speech is a great drain on people's mental energy. This doesn't mean they should all be taciturn! The "strong, silent type" often exasperates everyone around him by his reluctance to communicate even the simplest thoughts. The "babbler," on the other hand, commands nobody's attention, and soon loses the respect of everyone.

Try to be circumspect in what you say. Take into consideration its possible negative consequences on others' feelings. Show *respect* for all, if you want them to respect you. The clearer your awareness is in these matters, the more easily you will penetrate through mists of uncertainty to the heart of all difficulties.

Non-greed, the fifth and last *yama*, is often taken to mean "the non-acceptance of gifts." The true meaning of this quality, however, is "non-attachment." Patanjali's *yamas* and *niyamas* must all be understood as *attitudes of mind*, not as rules of specific behavior. Where gifts are concerned, whether or not a person literally accepts them is a secondary issue; usually it depends on special and particular disciplines (monastic, usually). Our friends will be offended if we refuse to accept gifts from them, given as outward tokens of their affection. My Guru himself, indeed, accepted gifts; I never knew him to spurn them. The virtue he displayed in this regard was *non-attachment*, not "non-acceptance." He gave things away to others quite as freely, when he saw that they desired what he had. One time, as a young man, he gave away a motorcycle—instantly and gladly, though he had seemed to prize it greatly. On that occasion, he saw a perfect stranger eying the machine enviously, and said, "Take it! It's yours."

It is considered a pious act, moreover, to make offerings—that is to say, to give gifts—to the Lord Himself. Wouldn't it be deeply distressing to find that our gifts were somehow unacceptable to Him?

The issue of non-acceptance, then, must be understood also on a level of attitude as in the case of *ahimsa*. Non-attachment doesn't mean we must refuse to accept gifts. Rather, we should refuse to accept anything as really belonging to us, egoically speaking. This attitude may be understood in the context of Sri Krishna's advice in the Bhagavad Gita, to be non-attached at least to the fruits of action. This, for everyone, is a path to inner freedom.

Non-attachment differs from the third *yama*, non-covetousness, in an important respect: Non-covetousness means not to desire anything that is not one's own by right. "Non-attachment," on the other hand, means not to accept as one's own even that which *is* his by right.

An attitude of non-attachment is important for people who aspire to material success. It is far *more* likely to bring them success than an attitude of clutching feverishly at things. Attachment actually limits one's ability to succeed, for it prevents him from thinking beyond specific goals, and therefore from visualizing an even greater success. Indeed, attachment even limits one's understanding of the limitless potentials of success.

Success should be understood as signifying, above all, the feeling of satisfaction one derives from an accomplishment. As long as one lacks that feeling, he will not find true success in life even if he becomes a hundred times over a millionaire.

Attachment is a mind-set, binding one and preventing him from ever finding true happiness. To be happy, it is necessary to be inwardly free. Non-attachment, paradoxical as it may seem, actually *attracts* prosperity. Indeed, it already *is* a kind of prosperity!

Such, then, are the five rules of *yama*, or control. The rules for their opposite qualities, which again are five in number, are called *niyamas*, meaning non-control. They are:

1) Cleanliness
2) Contentment
3) *Tapasya* (Austerity)
4) *Swadhyaya* (Self-Study)
5) Devotion to the Supreme Lord

As in the case of the *yamas*, the *niyamas* need to be understood in a subtle as well as in an obvious sense.

Cleanliness, the first *niyama*, means purity of heart, above all. In the business world, purity of heart means not to entertain hidden, ulterior motives. Be clear about your true intentions. The more you view your work as a service to others, the more others will sense your generosity and have confidence in you. Ulterior motives unmask themselves, sooner or later. They are revealed sooner, moreover, in a person's eyes and general demeanor.

Consider a statement I've often heard made by shopkeepers in India. At the end of the day they've said to me, "Sir, if you will buy from my shop I will be lucky, for you will be my first customer today." I wonder how shopkeepers manage to make this plea with a straight face! A wiser merchant would show interest in the customer's luck, surely, not in his own! Much better would it be if he simply made people feel that he was glad to see *them*.

Contentment (*santosha*) is the second *niyama*. Scripture describes it as the supreme virtue. Contentment is akin to non-attachment. As I stated above, if you can be inwardly non-attached it will be easy for you also to be contented. Contentment, however, should also be practiced deliberately; it should not be sought in acquisitions. Joe Crumpet, in the example I gave earlier, was a contented man. As a result, he attracted more customers than William Baker, who was basically discontented. Contentment in the Self, even in the face of adversity, wins the respect and friendship of everyone, for it is a quality that everyone desires.

Tapasya, austerity (the third *niyama*), for the businessman means living an uncluttered life, in a consciousness of inner freedom. It means not casting about for unnecessary ways of keeping oneself busy. Austerity is necessary for the achievement of calmness and concentration. It is also necessary for achieving success, whatever one's field of activity. One who knows what he wants and directs his energies toward that achievement is far more likely to succeed than one who hopes vaguely to succeed, but isn't quite sure how to go about it. An uncluttered mind is a clear mind. It is essential for all forms of accomplishment.

Swadhyaya, the fourth *niyama*, may be understood simply, without a long explanation, as *Self-awareness*. *Swa* means the Self; *dhyaya* means study. More is meant here than introspection, however, and more, certainly, than "study of the scriptures," as this *niyama* is often translated. *Swadhyaya* means Self-awareness. This is a state of consciousness, which again should be developed deliberately. Even in the midst of a busy day at work, you can listen inwardly for higher guidance. Inspiration awaits you at the edge of your awareness, trying to guide you rightly. Inspiration, more than most people realize, is the highest secret of success.

"Devotion to the Supreme Lord" is the last *niyama*. This is something many modern businessmen brush away as being of no consequence to their work. Remember the story of Krishna, however, in the *Mahabharata*, when he offered a choice to the two generals of opposing armies in the war of Kurukshetra: either the support of his entire army, or himself, present during the struggle, but not taking active part in it. Duryodhana was happy to receive the support of Krishna's whole army. Arjuna was wiser, however. He told Krishna, "Lord, wherever You are, victory is ensured."

The Supreme Lord does not participate directly in His universe: He works through channels, inspiring them because of their openness to His inspiration. The materialist receives only occasional hints of the Lord's presence within—hints he grimly ignores! People who have faith, however, understand that without inner guidance and inspiration even the best undertaking is fated to crumble to dust at last. Without this final *niyama*, material success will forever recede from your grasp. Even if you succeed in grasping it momentarily, it will slip quickly away like water running through your fingers.

The *yamas* and *niyamas*, taken together, produce the ideal human being, with the highest sense of values. Human values are exalted not because society demands that we abide by them, but because they are what *we ourselves* want, if we have any discrimination. Armed with these ten principles, we must surely succeed at anything we attempt.

Human values help us to actuate the basic rule of success, which is simply this: Do what *works*, not only at the moment, but long-lastingly.

The Application

Much of what I have written in this lesson so far might have been placed under this heading, "The Application." For with human values, more than with most subjects, the principles spill over into their application. Really to understand a human value is to see it in relation to its highest potentials. Human values should be judged, moreover, by how well they work *in action*, and particularly by how well they work *in our own lives*.

A human *value* is anything that lifts us toward higher awareness and true happiness. We can apply this teaching by always asking ourselves, "Does what I am doing lead me *up* the ladder of awareness, or *down* it?"

To apply this teaching in your work, concentrate more on your inner *feelings*. Don't become so immersed in what you are doing that you become "thing-oriented." (That purely materialistic outlook makes one a mere robot.) Remember above all that you are a human being; what you achieve is secondary to what you *are*.

Practicing *swadhyaya* (self-awareness), observe the feelings of your heart. Direct them upward, and then outward: upward, toward your higher Self; and outward, to embrace all humanity. Particularize those feelings in the individuals receiving your services.

Whenever you have a decision to make, don't ask yourself whether such-and-such an idea is pleasing to your ego. Think upward, rather: Ask yourself whether *your higher Self* is pleased. Feel the response to that question in your heart, and see whether that feeling conveys a *calm sense of rightness*, or, on the contrary, conveys a restless uneasiness.

Next, visualize the people who will be affected by your decision. Don't merely take a poll of their opinions, for opinions, generally, are not reliable guides. Try, instead, to visualize how they feel in their *deeper* selves, not in their emotions. Do you sense happiness there? Think of them on a soul level: Are their souls, so to speak, smiling?

I've practiced these principles for many years, and am confident in sharing them with you. Whenever I've found that my heart says No to a proposition, if I've allowed myself to be persuaded to act contrary to that feeling I've found that things simply didn't turn out as any of us really wanted. When I've followed my deeper feelings, on the other hand, everything worked out well.

We cannot control the actions of others, but we can at least determine what *we* do. Often I find that people actually do smile when a decision I've made shows concern for their *higher* interests. The decision may come upon them quite unexpectedly, but what they usually say, in the end, is, "It feels *right*."

MEDITATION

Visualize light descending into the world from Infinity. Focus it on whatever you are doing. Don't mentally divorce what you are doing, in the effort to succeed, from the totality of what you hope to accomplish. Remember too, what you really aspire to is happiness. This means knowing who and what you *really* are, and what your true role is in the cosmic drama.

You will live in this body such a short time: only a few years. You must take seriously whatever happens in this ephemeral life. Nevertheless, keep your sights on changelessness. The best you can manifest is only a limited ray of the infinite light. Offer that best up to God, from whom all good things come. Ask His blessings on what you do. If you hold your most mundane actions up to His light, you will find everything in life becoming sanctified.

AFFIRMATION

"I am an actor in the drama of Infinity. I will do my best to fulfill the cosmic plan for my life."

POINTS TO REMEMBER

1. You will have greater success if you accept that you are a human being, first, and that your clients or customers are human beings also, and not money-spewing machines!

2. If we are indifferent to the feelings of others, we lose our own sensitivity to feeling itself. What we must do is *deepen* our sensitivity to everything and everybody around us.

3. Goodness is that which brings us closer to the natural peace and harmony of our true being.

4. In treating others well your own happiness expands, and in treating them badly your happiness contracts and causes you to suffer.

5. Patanjali's ten "commandments" for spiritual development, the *yamas* and *niyamas*, help the ego to find true, as opposed to false, fulfillment.

6. The first *yama* is *ahimsa*, or "harmlessness." True power comes not from pitting oneself *against* others, but from *winning their support*. Harmlessness in business means never to take advantage of others. It means recognizing that one's own welfare includes the well-being of all.

7. The second of the *yamas* is "non-prevarication," which means more than not to tell lies. It also means not wishing, ineffectually, that things were other than they are. Face the facts fearlessly and with honesty.

8. In material affairs, the benefit of truthfulness is twofold: First, truthful people radiate complete integrity. Second, any words they utter with concentrated will can be materialized, simply because they spoke them.

9. *Asteya*, non-stealing, refers to *non-covetousness*, not desiring anything that belongs by right to another. It also means giving sincere respect to all, and graciously recognizing any success others achieve. *Asteya* means viewing no one as a rival, but seeing others as *colleagues* and friends. The more support you give others, the more supported you will feel in yourself.

10. One who becomes firmly established in the quality of non-covetousness seeks nothing that is not his by right. Such a person develops the power to attract whatever he needs in life.

11. The fourth of the *yamas* is *brahmacharya*, or self-control. The more your powers radiate outward from your inner being, instead of "fizzing" restlessly through the senses, the more you will have your energy under control and will be able to direct it fully toward the actual needs of the moment.

12. Non-greed, the fifth and last *yama*, really signifies "non-attachment." It means not to accept as one's own even that which is his by right. Attachment prevents one from

13. Cleanliness, the first *niyama*, means purity of heart, above all. In the business world, purity of heart means not to entertain hidden, ulterior motives. The more you view your work as a service to others, the more others will sense your generosity and have confidence in you.

14. Contentment (*santosha*) should be practiced deliberately; it should not be sought in acquisitions. Contentment in the Self, even in the face of adversity, wins the respect and friendship of everyone, for it is a quality that everyone desires.

15. *Tapasya*, austerity, means living an uncluttered life, in a consciousness of inner freedom. Austerity is necessary for the achievement of calmness and concentration. One who knows what he wants and directs his energies toward that achievement is far more likely to succeed.

16. *Swadhyaya*, the fourth *niyama*, may be understood simply as *Self-awareness*. Even in the midst of a busy day at work, you can listen inwardly for higher guidance. Inspiration awaits you at the edge of your awareness, trying to guide you rightly.

17. "Devotion to the Supreme Lord" is the last *niyama*. The Supreme Lord works through channels, inspiring them because of their openness to His inspiration. People who have faith understand that without inner guidance and inspiration even the best undertaking is fated to crumble.

18. Concentrate more on your inner *feelings*. Direct the feelings of your heart upward, toward your higher Self; and outward, to embrace all humanity, especially to the individuals receiving your services.

19. Ask yourself whether *your higher Self* is pleased. Feel the response in your heart, and see whether you feel a restless uneasiness, or a *calm sense of rightness*.

thinking beyond specific goals, and therefore from visualizing an even greater success. Paradoxical as it may seem, non-attachment actually *attracts* prosperity.

WORKBOOK IDEAS
by Joseph Bharat Cornell

Embrace a Larger Reality

In the American Southwest a school teacher once asked his students to draw a picture of themselves. "Most of the children," he said, "completely covered the paper with a drawing of their body. My Navajo students, however, drew themselves quite differently. They made their bodies much smaller and included in their drawings the nearby mountains, canyon walls, and dry desert washes." To the Navajo, the environment is as much a part of who they are as are their own arms and legs.

Patanjali, the great exponent of yoga, said that when one no longer identifies with his little body, he experiences himself in all bodies. Swami Kriyananda tells of the time when Paramhansa Yogananda was having difficulty walking because he was in a deep state of consciousness. He said to Kriyananda, "I am in so many bodies, it is difficult for me to remember which body I am supposed to keep moving."

Practicing the following meditation will help you consciously affirm, and intuitively experience, your oneness with Life. While doing this exercise in the California Mountains, one woman said, "At first, I felt as though I were composing a picture; then, suddenly, I found I *was* the picture."

ACTION ITEM: EXPANDING CIRCLES MEDITATION
1. Find a pleasant place outdoors with a distant view and an interesting foreground. Look also, if possible, for natural movement of some kind—like a rippling lake or swaying trees.
2. Sit down, close your eyes, and become aware of your body.
3. Then open your eyes and extend your awareness beyond your body just a few feet to include the nearby grasses, rocks, and insects. Feel yourself moving and becoming alive in them. *Try to feel that you are in everything you see, as much as you are in your own body.*
4. Do this for a couple of minutes. When your mind wanders, gently bring it back to what's before you.
5. Now broaden your awareness to include the nearby shrubs and trees. Relax and allow your attention to flow spontaneously, from the closest grasses and pebbles to the nearest trees.
6. Continue expanding your visual awareness gradually in stages until it reaches the distant ridges and vast blue sky. Feel that everything you see is part of you. Finally, let your awareness flow freely to whatever interests it. Feel *inside yourself* the sky, the trees, the waving grasses.

7. End your meditation by repeating the following affirmation by Swami Kriyananda:

    I feel myself in the flowing brooks, in the flight of birds, in the raging wind upon the mountain, in the gentle dance of flowers in a breeze. Renouncing my little, egoic self, I expand with my great, soul-Self everywhere!

> If you live far from a city park or greenery, try this exercise in the early morning or evening hours when there is less human activity. Be conscious of the space around you. Feel yourself moving and living in everything you see and hear.

ACTION ITEM: CREATE A HARMONIOUS WORK ENVIRONMENT

Excessive self-involvement separates us from Life; practicing the *yamas* and *niyamas* affirms our unity with Life and makes us more expansive and empathetic.

Create a more harmonious atmosphere at work by practicing Ahimsa or Harmlessness:

1. Ask yourself, "Am I giving my full support to everyone at work?" If the answer is no, identify the individuals from whom you're withholding your energy.

2. Whatever your reasons for doing so, meditate on the harm you do to yourself, and others, by withholding your love and support.

3. Visualize these individuals as you imagine God views them. Think of how much God loves you, and that He loves everyone equally.

4. Throughout your day, see your colleagues as children of God.

5. Feel God inside of you, lovingly blessing His children through you.

LESSON TEN

HOW TO BE A GOOD LEADER

[The first] simple precept: "Do what *works*." . . .
There was a second rule . . . : "Do what is *right*."

The Principles

If you follow faithfully the principles outlined in the last lesson on human values, you will very likely find people coming to you for guidance even if you hold no leadership position.

In *Autobiography of a Yogi*, Paramhansa Yogananda tells of an episode in his guru's ashram when he was a young disciple there. Kumar, "a young villager from east Bengal," was accepted for training. After some time, Sri Yukteswar instructed Mukunda (later, Yogananda), his chief disciple, "Let Kumar assume your duties. Employ your own time in sweeping and cooking."

The account continues, "Exalted to leadership, Kumar exercised a petty household tyranny. In silent mutiny, the other disciples continued to seek me out for daily counsel." When Kumar complained of this fact to their guru, Sri Yukteswar replied, "That's why I assigned Mukunda to the kitchen and you to the parlor. . . . A worthy leader has the desire to serve, and not to dominate. . . . Return now to your earlier work as cook's assistant."

In every group enterprise, people will naturally seek advice from those who are *competent*, in preference to those even who hold leadership positions. Thus, this lesson on leadership is meant to help everyone, and not only people in positions of actual authority. Any competent person is, in a sense, already in that position. His ability, based on experience, confers on him a certain duty to share his knowledge with others. All can benefit from these principles. If they aren't managers in the workplace, they may have responsibilities in the home as parents, or at school as teachers, or even in buses as drivers. In simple daily contacts with people, there may be something they can give. Everyone has at least something to share with others.

This lesson will help all, therefore, to know how to share with others effectively and in the right spirit of humility, dignity, and kindness.

For the typical employer it would be unusual, to say the least, to impose ashram disciplines on his workers. His function is not to give them spiritual training, but simply to get the best work out of them. Even in that role, of course, he must train, supervise, and discipline. Though he is not their guru, his job is to guide them. In a sense, then, it is only the aims that differ.

One of the tasks that leaders in an organization face is to appoint others to act on their behalf. Thus, the delegation of authority becomes an important facet of good leadership. Selecting others for vital posts is important. In that selection, look for people to whom others turn instinctively for guidance, rather than persons who are primarily efficient, or who "talk big." An employer will save himself much grief, later on, if he considers as candidates those who respect human values and show consideration for the feelings of others.

I founded the first Ananda Sangha community in 1968. That was the peak of the hippie movement in America. The epicenter of that social eruption was San Francisco, California, where I myself happened to be living.

Few of the people who came to join Ananda Village during our beginnings had any interest in what I, as the founder, wanted to accomplish. Communes were the "in thing" in those days; young people were flocking to the countryside, hoping to create an alternative life style to the crass materialism of which they, with some justification, accused America. In those days, a saying popular among the young was, "Never trust anyone over thirty." I myself was a doddering forty-two. I had dreamed, however, of creating idealistic communities since the age of fifteen. My residence in San Francisco coincided, as I said, with the beginnings of the hippie movement. So also did the beginnings of Ananda Village. Perhaps both coincidences were significant, but that possibility, though interesting, has no immediate bearing on my subject.

My Guru, whose disciple I became in 1948 at the age of twenty-two, urged his audiences fervently and frequently to band together and build spiritual communities. He believed that communities created for such purposes were the solution for people who wanted to live a spiritual life in this busy age, and he pleaded with people to see the advantages of simple living in the country, surrounded by high-minded friends.

At a garden party in Beverly Hills, in the summer of 1949, he gave one of the most stirring speeches I have ever heard, urging his audience to embrace this idea. Speaking to nearly a thousand guests, he urged those especially who were young to go "north, south, east, and west" and spread his communitarian ideal. So inspiring was the address that I vowed to do everything in my power to make his dream a reality.

To return, then, to Ananda's beginnings in 1968: Yes, I had clear ideas as to what I wanted our community to become. I'd been pondering the subject since the age of fifteen: twenty-seven years. During all that time I had sought, in various ways, for methods of materializing an ideal community.

Few of the young people who were rushing to join the communitarian movement in the late sixties had more than a vague notion of what to do about it. Their one clear thought was to "get away." Few of them knew or even cared, moreover, about my Guru's vision. They didn't realize that the wave of energy which they were surfing was something he himself had launched that day in Beverly Hills, when he'd said, "I am sowing my thoughts in the ether, in the Spirit of God!" What they wanted was only to fulfill a personal fantasy of theirs. Many of them accepted in principle the concept of a spiritual life, but what that meant to them was a pleasant life of irresponsibility amid natural beauty. Responsibility of any kind held no appeal for them, and played no part in their dreams.

I wanted the members of Ananda to be students and followers of Paramhansa Yogananda. Indeed, the challenge of forming a new community was already formidable enough, without a medley of spiritual beliefs defining how we would live.

I soon realized that most of those coming were quite unfamiliar with my Guru's teachings, and had to be won over to them. It displeased them particularly that central elements in his teachings included the concepts of self-control and self-discipline. These concepts raised the specter of personal responsibility, and were an offense to them. What they believed in was absolute egoic freedom, which, to them, meant complete freedom of the ego to do as it pleased. From the start, therefore, I met indignant resistance. Most of those who came were unrealistic dreamers who, in fuzzy rejection of responsibility, needed simply to be weeded out from our garden before they succeeded in choking its development.

Yet it wasn't in me to drive people out. I had to get people to see for themselves that we were on diverging tracks. The "hippie way" would simply not define how Ananda was to grow; I was determined to win, but had to proceed in the right way, and that meant, *dharmically*. I had to be patient with them, therefore, and even to respect their freedom to believe as they chose.

The difficulties I faced were in some respects greater than those faced by the average employer in the business world, whose guidelines were established long ago by society. What our young "pioneers" wanted, however, was a new kind of society altogether, one that had no discipline of any kind. Though the circumstances were different from those facing an average employer, however, the solutions I found may be helpful for students of these lessons, for despite different circumstances human beings everywhere have much in common. Scientists, bankers, poets: These seem to exist almost on different planes of existence from one another, and to be incompatible in their interests. Yet, beneath the surface, the similarities are striking. One bond unites all humanity. Someone described that bond to Paramhansa Yogananda when he was a boy as, "the stalwart kinship of selfish motive."

In the hippie era, new "communes" began springing up all over the country like mushrooms after a heavy rain. Few such "utopias" lasted more than a year. Most of them disbanded after less than a month, and virtually none lasted as long, even, as a decade. Thousands were started, but mostly on entirely unrealistic grounds. Ananda, thirty-six years later, has been almost uniquely successful.

The greatest mistake made by the founders of intentional communities over the centuries has been to imagine that human perfection can be achieved through the "perfect system." Such perfection cannot be achieved by imperfect human beings, and must be achieved inwardly, by free will; it cannot be imposed on them from without. The universe itself was not created to make men perfect, but to give them an opportunity to *achieve* perfection, themselves. Earth is a school, merely, and those who are born here come to learn certain lessons: particularly, how to relate their natural ego-motivation to a much broader reality.

I countered people's abstract belief in human perfectibility with another, simple precept: "Do what *works*." This precept can be practiced and proved here on earth. It is as valid for scientists, businessmen, and housewives as for communities seeking better ways of life There is one thing that can never work anywhere: the creation of perfect conditions outside of Supreme Consciousness.

There was a second rule on which I insisted, one which is equally important for businessmen and for people everywhere as for intentional communities: "Do what is *right*."

Many people find both these precepts difficult to follow. As for the first one, what they want is to follow the call of personal desires. Those desires fly in the face of reality. Butting their heads repeatedly against a stone wall and refusing to make the necessary adjustments, they insist that what they want "*has* to work!"

One smiles. Why *should* it work? Facts are facts. Success is easier to accept, surely, than failure, once one accepts what *is*, simply, instead of chasing the will-o'-the-wisp of what one thinks ought to be. My father, a wholly practical man, mocked at what he called "the wonderful world of might-have-been."

It is often possible to bring the two together, however. Subjective ideals and objective reality are not necessarily hostile to one another. The very universe was produced by consciousness. To discover how to harmonize such apparent opposites, keep yourself open to what *is*, while remaining centered in high aspirations. Such is the simple difference between naiveté and common sense. Happy the person who can cling to his ideals while bringing them in line with reality. That is the secret of most great inventions.

The difficulty in working with people is that they have their own priorities, which must be treated as facts even if they are, in fact, mere delusions. Politically free people cannot be driven: they must be led. They must be *inspired* to do what is right. Sri Sathya Sai Baba expressed this fact to me in a letter he wrote me many years ago, in his own handwriting. He was encouraging me in my early attempts at building Ananda.

The second rule is even more important than the first: "Do what is *right*." Success that is attained by relinquishing high principles will end in failure, eventually. *Yato dharma, tato jaya*—"Where there is adherence to right principle, there is victory." This ancient dictum is important for success in anything. To do what is right, ethically and spiritually as well as pragmatically, wins the support of universal law.

In June of 1976, a forest fire destroyed most of Ananda Village: 450 out of our 650 acres, and twenty-one of the twenty-two homes we had in that area. None of the homes was insured. Many people, especially those far from us, expected us to fail after this devastating blow.

Shortly after that event, neighbors of ours who had also lost their homes telephoned us enthusiastically. The cause of the fire, they had learned, was a faulty spark arrester on a county vehicle. "We can sue them," they announced excitedly, "and get back the money to pay for everything we lost. We can rebuild!"

Our neighbors needed only to threaten a lawsuit. In a settlement, they collected. Ananda Village had been the biggest loser. Common sense dictated that we must sue also.

I don't want you to agree, necessarily, with what I did. Perhaps you won't even sympathize with it. Nevertheless, it may give you food for thought. I wrote to the county supervisors and assured them that we would not be suing. The officials themselves may have considered my decision an act of madness. To me, however, it would have been morally wrong to impose our hardship on others. Essentially, suing would have meant demanding that our fellow county residents bear our misfortune. I couldn't see us blaming anyone for our bad luck. It was, I thought, one thing to accept free-will donations from people who believed in us, but quite another thing to force "donations" out of people who had no desire to help us in our difficulty. A lawsuit was unacceptable to me.

Fortunately, many people across the country came to our rescue. Thus, we survived: moreover, from the beginning we did so in a joyful and uplifted spirit. Our neighbors got the money they wanted from the county. Yet, strange to relate, ten years later they were still grieving over what they had lost.

Am I suggesting that it is *never* right to sue? I won't go that far. Every situation must be judged on its own merits. Sometimes, dharma itself demands aggressive action. Consider the war of Kurukshetra, described in the *Mahabharata* as a righteous fight. Perhaps our neighbors were right to sue. I have no wish to pose as the voice of conscience. All I will say is, Before you act, consider the *rightness*, from a standpoint of dharma, of what you contemplate.

Karmic law works unobtrusively, but infallibly. Don't be drawn into anything for the hope of gain, merely. If you abide by true principles to the best of your ability, you will be always protected, and will be most likely to succeed in everything. Even if you fail, success *must* come to you at last. This is not a fairy story. I have seen this truth verified many times.

What I did from the beginning at Ananda Village—long before the ravages of that forest fire—was concentrate on possibilities, not impossibilities. ("Do what works.") Most of the people who were coming to us at that time looked on my Guru's ideals without great favor. My solution was to concentrate on those few who believed in him.

There remained the problem of how to bring those who resisted onto this path voluntarily. Most of them wanted, as I said, a life of bucolic ease. When I urged them to help support the community financially, they gazed at me, outraged. "Where is your faith in God?" they demanded. I stood revealed in their eyes as a gross "materialist." As for them—noble souls!—they had not come to Ananda to concern themselves with *money*: They had come for a *spiritual* life. This meant to them, as nearly as I could tell, going to the nearby Yuba River every day, and swimming.

It was particularly galling to me that they considered their faith justified by my very willingness to live outside the community to earn the money for our monthly mortgage fees. My sacrifice was proof, to them, that God did indeed intend to take care of them!

People kept coming: What was I to do? One afternoon there were seven cars parked in our driveway, filled with youngsters eager to join Ananda. Many of these, offended by my strict ban on hallucinogenic drugs, moved on. As for the others, I tried to be selective, but had also to admit enough people to justify, if only minimally, the large piece of property I had purchased with an eye to the future. A few of those who joined did express a willingness to do a little work in our vegetable garden. I'd been fortunate in attracting an elderly man as a gardener who'd had experience with organic farming. He described those "willing" workers in these words: "They make a few graceful gestures over the plants, and then take off to go swimming in the Yuba."

The swelling numbers of "members" insisted on "rule by consensus," a concept that had been popularized in literature of the day, touting it as the best way for small communities to function. Although the concept had its points, I at once realized that it was unworkable, for it would paralyze decision-making and hinder practical action. What was I to do? Consensus was a dogma among the "free-thinking" young of those days. To win them over, I realized I had to be flexible. It would have been pointless to oppose them on *everything*.

A fisherman, after hooking a fish, will "play" his line in order to tire it, lest it snap the line. I saw no reasonable alternative to employing a similar tactic. I allowed our members to hold regular meetings. Experience had taught me, in fact, that if meetings were completely free of direction, they would get nowhere. Discussions at Ananda meandered endlessly as every side of an issue was aired. Solid decisions were a rarity.

It took the community five years of its weekly meetings to agree, finally, that a dog named Blue must be taken far away and abandoned. Blue had wandered onto the land originally as a stray. No one had ever claimed him: he'd simply been given "squatters' rights." He chased the deer and barked at visitors, frightening many of them. With numerous points in his disfavor, and none to support him, it still took the community five years, by a process of consensus, to agree to his removal.

I was actually grateful for those meetings. I seldom attended them, but they helped by siphoning off the negative energy and leaving me free to concentrate on what was our true need: developing a right spirit among those who showed promise. I therefore let the all-community meetings go on and gave them as much free rein as seemed to me acceptable.

I also had no choice but to make concessions, some of which I didn't consider inconsequential, in order to protect my basic program. My greatest regret was having to relinquish an aspect of my dream that I'd always held dear, though it was not central to my Guru's teachings.

In Europe, where I'd grown up, I had been struck by the harmonious appearance of towns and villages. Their style of architecture was basically uniform, though pleasingly diverse also in the size and shape of the houses. Our members had grown up with the diversity of styles in the typical American suburb, and could only imagine a dreary sameness in the vision I presented to them. I decided it would cost me points unnecessarily to insist on this aspect of my dream, though I was sorry to have to make the sacrifice.

Later, as Ananda members began visiting Europe, they began telling me, "I see what you meant, now. What a pity that we didn't try to make a special contribution of that kind at Ananda to the concept of visual harmony!"

I had intuited, however, that leadership, if it is to be effective, must be played like a game in which points need to be conceded, sometimes, for the sake of long-term advantages. To win always is not possible, and may not even be good, for it means that people have probably been bullied into agreement. It must suffice for one's victories to be those which are the most meaningful.

Years later, a private inheritance made it possible for me to construct the present buildings and gardens of my residence, Crystal Hermitage, which I turned into a spiritual center for the community. Crystal Hermitage has achieved widespread fame for its beauty, based on the triple concept: space, light, harmony. This place of beauty has actually been instrumental in drawing people from far and near to live at Ananda.

Much of what I've been able to accomplish in my life, so far, may bear fruit long after I am gone. Leadership must be thought of in terms of the benefits it brings primarily to others, not to oneself. The rewards for oneself must ever be the satisfaction of having done something needed and useful.

As for those weekly community meetings, I answered their challenge to my authority by not letting them be a challenge. I simply let people talk. If they wanted to voice complaints, or to bring up problems, I insisted only that they suggest solutions, also. Otherwise, I said, "problem-consciousness" would paralyze everything. Meanwhile what I did was, as I've said, devote myself to uniting those who actually *wanted* positive answers, and especially those who wanted to follow my Guru's "solution-conscious" teachings.

Word reached me one day that certain "bigmouths" in the community were proclaiming a resolve to "call me on the carpet" for things which, they claimed, I wasn't doing for the community. They themselves were the sort of people who talk endlessly but seldom act. (Such people are always the first to complain!) As soon as news of their intention reached me, I myself called an all-community meeting, which I began by announcing, "There are certain matters requiring our attention as a community." I went on to enumerate the complaints, which had reached me. I then asked everyone, "What shall we do about them?" Thus, I succeeded in deflecting what had been intended as a challenge to my authority. In fact, those problems belonged on the shoulders of everyone. I asked people then to propose workable solutions. The meeting ended harmoniously, despite a little grumbling from the "bigmouths" who had failed to "call me on the carpet." These, of course, muttered that it had not been fair of me to snatch the carpet out from under them.

I was by now tired of the constant bickering. Feeling that this meeting had put the dissension "to bed" for a while, I went off for two months of spiritual recharging to India.

No useful end would be served by relating here in exhaustive detail all the difficulties I faced in those early years. For the purposes of this lesson, let it suffice to add this comment: If a leader hopes to win out over controversy, he must combine patience with astuteness.

The problem I faced from the beginning was how to *win* people. It would work against that effort to try to coerce them. Fortunately for myself, I never got angry—though in my dreams at night I did occasionally experience intense anger for reasons that I always forgot on awaking. Many leaders in my situation would have spluttered in helpless rage. To have done that, however, would have been worse than futile, and would have cost me many points in people's respect and support.

My first rule, as I've stated already, has always been, "Do what works." In those years, my solution to people's opposition was to concentrate on cementing the support of those members who showed willingness. I gave no more energy than I had to, to those who resented what I was doing. Their resentment was because my will conflicted with their desires.

As for the few who placed themselves in open rebellion against me, I ignored them as much as possible. Fortunately, as generally happens in such cases, although the negative ones resisted all positive action, they had no solution to propose. They found their satisfaction simply in complaining.

Gradually the opposition came to a head. I myself was the one who forced the showdown. I was already, of course, confident that the majority were on my side. To have acted prematurely would have revealed incompetence. I hadn't devoted so many years to this communitarian dream to toss it lightly aside just because a few people had different ideas. I was more than willing to give in on minor issues, but I certainly wouldn't throw up my hands in surrender on major ones. A leader must be strong in himself. He cannot afford to be ruled by people's emotions.

In choosing subordinate leaders in the community, I always sought those who wanted to serve, not to dominate. "Big shots" provide the worst kind of leadership. I've marveled at newspaper headlines in India that describe the "plums" of power as going to this politician or that one, as if high position were a reward instead of a serious responsibility. Power should be reserved for those who hold their country's, and not their own, interests at heart. Leadership is not important in itself. Service is the key word. Anyone who desires high political position in order to achieve self-importance is not fit to lead.

When I was twenty-three, my Guru placed me in charge of the other monks. This wasn't the first time anyone had been given this post. Others in that position before me, however—judging by the conditions that prevailed when I came—had not succeeded in creating a cohesive spirit among the monks.

Our Guru had stated, for example, that he wanted the monks to keep silence at meals. He himself never took his meals in our dining room, for his duties necessitated that he keep himself apart from our daily activities. Chaos, consequently, reigned supreme during mealtimes. I decided to ensure that the Master's wishes were obeyed.

Mere remonstrance, I found, had no effect. My admonitions could scarcely be heard over the hubbub. I decided to find a system that would work. First, I got those who were willing to cooperate to attend morning group meditations. (We'd been meditating in our rooms, on our own.) After meditation, it was relatively easy to get them to keep silence at breakfast. The monks who didn't come to these group meditations talked as merrily as ever at breakfast, but were embarrassed when others simply refused to answer them.

A few months passed. Then I proposed we hold group meditations in the evenings before supper. After meditation it was, again, relatively easy for people to eat in silence; they were accustomed already to keeping silence at breakfast.

I never needed to extend the rule of silence to lunchtime. By now, the monks were accustomed to keeping silence at the table, and liked it. Those who were uncooperative finally acquiesced, more or less.

Many of the monks were older than I in years, and also in the teachings. To some of them I seemed a mere upstart, despite the fact that our Guru had placed me in charge. My efforts, consequently, met a certain degree of hostility. This opposition was good training for me, many years later, in building Ananda.

I've always found, when dealing with negative energy, that it has little cohesion. Positive energy, on the other hand, even if expressed by only a minority, creates a vortex of energy and power.

It wasn't that I had to persuade *everyone* in the monastery to accept what I was trying to accomplish. Quite a number of the monks were on my side from the start. For the others, I decided to make only minimal efforts to enlist their support. The best that would have been accomplished, I could see, would be to bring a few of them from minus to zero. Once my energies were directed elsewhere, however, their own would slip to minus again. I therefore focused on the positive ones, with whom I sought positive solutions. I urged those of them who were worried about the naysayers not to pay too much attention to their negativity. Life had already taught me, and has often corroborated the lesson, that man needs to be "solution-conscious," not "problem-conscious."

The proof of my system was simply that it worked. Gradually, those of the monks who had been holding themselves aloof from my organizing efforts were obliged to recognize that a change was in the air. They either fell in with that change, or departed. My success was twofold. First, fewer monks left the monastery. Second, and much more important to me, our Guru expressed himself pleased with my efforts.

Interestingly, however, he hinted to me, later, that my position as head monk was not the role he saw as my destiny in serving him. He made it clear to me that I was to bring his message out to the world, through lectures and classes. In addition, he hinted that I was to spread his message in India.

I found, in time, that the principles of leadership that I'd learned in practice were also helpful in lecturing and giving public classes. Only the application is different.

Leadership means, among other things, persuading people to *want* what *you* want of them. Lecturing and teaching require a similar persuasion. It isn't enough, when lecturing, to talk *at* people merely, as if trying to air your own ideas. It isn't enough even to talk *to* them, to express your thoughts clearly. What is needed is to talk *with* them. One's words must, in other words, be directed at what people want and need to hear. A speaker must listen sensitively to unspoken thoughts and questions.

This method of inward listening works far more effectively than letting an audience ask questions openly, a process which often takes up too much time with secondary matters. When a speaker does reply to open questions, he should make it a point to generalize his replies so as to include the whole audience.

These leadership principles, as I've learned and applied them, will be helpful to business people everywhere, even in their dealings with the public.

In selling merchandise, for example, one must try to get people interested in what one has to sell. Think of your work as a service to them, and try sincerely to see if an item that you are selling meets their needs. If you can't see a way, suggest to them graciously some other place where they might get what they want. People will remember you for your helpfulness, and will be the more likely to return to you when they want something else. A satisfied customer will bring others to your shop. Concentrate above all, therefore, on *giving satisfaction*. It is an aspect of true leadership to focus on others' needs, not to concentrate only on what *you* want.

People in leadership positions often worry about "losing face," blustering in an attempt to prove themselves right. The worst thing a leader can do, when a mistake has been made, is to blame others. When he himself is actually at fault, any attempt to shift the blame onto others will be strategically weakening. People are seldom fooled by bluster. You will command their respect far more if you take the blame frankly, and without embarrassment, onto your own shoulders. This is true even if you are blameless.

People appreciate truthfulness, and, unless they are carpers, will not expect you to be infallible. Generally speaking it costs nothing to admit, simply, that you were wrong. People will have more confidence in you, and especially so if you then try to correct your mistake. Leaders who try to impress people with their inscrutable wisdom soon find that no one takes them seriously.

People will be more willing to follow you, in short, if you are sincere with them, and if you do only what works best. They will be even more impressed if they see that you want only what is right and true.

Should they ever realize, however, that what you care about most is being considered infallible, they will gradually withdraw their support from you, and will do so the more rapidly if they see you less concerned with being honest and truthful than with forcing people's acceptance.

If you don't realize this next point already, you will certainly do so in time. I suggest meanwhile, therefore, that you accept it on faith:

Those who work under you will enjoy working with you, if they respect and like you, and if you treat them well. If you make no effort to win their support, they will find ways of subtly undermining anything you attempt. Sometimes it may be better to give in to people's wishes and opinions, even if you consider your own ideas to be better than theirs. Most decisions are not crucial, after all, to the success of an enterprise. More important to its long-range goals is everyone's cooperation and harmony.

It is particularly important to *show* your support. I recall a time, during our school's first year at Ananda Village, when a student became upset with a particular teacher. This woman, though good at her job and loyal to our way of life, had a testing nature. She was opinionated and tactless. The headmaster, wanting to curry favor with the student, scolded the teacher severely in front of the other students. Later I told him, "The children will graduate and move on, but the teachers will still be with you. Be loyal to them first. Stand by them, even if they err. If they need to be corrected, administer the correction as tactfully as possible, in private. If all your efforts fail, replace the teacher, but never embarrass her in front of children who must learn from her."

I've tried to go along with others' wishes, when I felt I could do so without compromising my essential goals. I admit happily, moreover, that circumstances have sometimes vindicated their wishes. In no way do I want to claim infallibility. People learn faster with greater clarity when one encourages them not to fear making mistakes. They also learn better if the leader does not *impose* his will on them. Do your best, then, to win, but don't coerce others to your position. To draw the best out of them, support them as often as you can.

It will help leaders to think of themselves as skiers, in a sense. Though a skier's goal is to reach the bottom of the slope, he may have to veer left or right occasionally to avoid sudden bumps (moguls, they are called), or so as not to hit other skiers. To reach his destination, a skier must change directions as necessary.

Another good rule for a leader is, Be willing to take the blame, *even if you don't deserve it*. Our responsibility is to shoulder burdens, if others are not strong enough to carry them. This means, sometimes, shouldering responsibility for their mistakes. Always remember, it is you, the leader, who are answerable for what goes on under you. If others err, try not to blame them. Blame usually rests with the leader in any case, so be prepared to accept it even if you know you aren't to blame, personally. People will generally respect you, and will be all the more loyal to you.

Obviously, I am not saying that one should take the blame in matters of moral turpitude. If someone under you were to commit a serious fault, or even a crime, he himself, generally speaking, should shoulder the responsibility. I don't mean illegalities, therefore, or even immoral conduct. I'm referring to ordinary mistakes that people make during the course of their work.

To offer a specific example, let me describe a situation in which I myself was not in any way in charge, but was acting only to keep a deteriorating situation from becoming a disaster. It was in Charleston, South Carolina, several months before I met my Guru. I was studying stagecraft at the Dock Street Theater, intending to become a playwright. I was asked, for one of the plays we put on, to be part of a male quartet.

We were all amateurs, though I at least had had some musical training. The others quite naturally made mistakes. What surprised me was how consistently they blamed one another. Realizing that the only thing that mattered was "getting the show on the road," I took the blame each time onto my own shoulders. "It's my fault," I said, again and again. "It's okay. Let's forget it, and keep on going." The group finally managed to perform fairly well, though not brilliantly.

Later, a professional actor among us made a comment to the effect that so much time had been wasted by all of us in casting blame on one another. I said nothing to defend myself. To do so, I realized, would be to place the others in a bad light. I'd taken the blame on myself; now I must accept that it was mine.

This experience taught me how important it is, in getting a job done, not to cast blame. If people want to protect themselves, why not be tolerant of this very normal human weakness?

This principle is especially important for people in positions of authority. Much energy is often wasted in attempting to deflect blame from oneself. This is especially damaging in a leader.

Fortunately, as well as unfortunately, the human ego is a universal reality. Don't let self-interest blind you to the self-interest of others. Their wishes may easily be different from yours—and what a dull world it would be if everyone agreed on everything! To criticize others for being ego-centered is almost like criticizing them for breathing! What one's criticism implies, usually, is a desire to defend his own ego. Egoism is simply a symptom of immaturity. Almost every human being is, spiritually speaking, immature.

Be kind to others. Don't try to suppress them, but give them a chance, when feasible, to score their points. In ceding minor victories to others, you will win their long-term support in return. Like a skier, keep your destination—the bottom of the hill—firmly in mind. So long as high principles are not at stake, it won't hurt you to yield a few minor points. Be ready to swerve right or left, as necessary, with life's "slope."

Another good rule—though one all too often ignored—is this: Give credit wholeheartedly, where credit is due. Avoid, when possible, claiming credit for yourself even if the idea was your own, and especially if another person has done the actual work. Remember to give credit openly, in front of others. Don't be like a certain man in France about whom my father spoke with a chuckle. The man wrote the introduction to a book by somebody else, in which he stated, "We highly recommend this book, based as it was on our research, and written under our constant supervision."

A friend of mine founded a well-known community in Scotland. He was obliged to leave it, eventually, for he had made the mistake of thinking that he must always be in control—even to the point of deciding what flowers should be in the dining room, and exactly where they should be placed. He was a good man, and in many ways a good leader. One thing that impressed me about him was his willingness to learn from experience. He tended to express himself a bit forcefully, however. When others finally decided they could oppose him, they did so. In the end, he moved away to America.

He shared with me one interesting story, which has been helpful to me in my own work. He and several others had been pouring a cement walkway. The job had nearly reached completion when his wife came out of the house and invited them in for a cup of tea. They agreed to honor this ancient English custom of a "cuppa" at four o'clock. Afterward, just as they were ready to resume work, some other problem came up, causing them to delay the job temporarily.

"Do you know," he said, "it was several years before we were able to finish that job! Once the energy shifted, a great deal of time passed before we were able to get it back again. It would have been easy to complete the project at the time when we were working on it."

His story taught me something important: When one starts a project, he should finish it while the energy is still flowing. Of course, I can imagine this example being used to justify inflexibility. I've frequently found, in fact, that it takes an extra surge of will power to keep a project going, at least in my mind, in spite of interruptions. I suggest that you take his advice with a little "grain of salt," therefore, for I can't really imagine anyone—except a hermit, perhaps—being able to drive through to the end of very many projects without interruptions. Sometimes I've managed to do so, but never, I think, in my capacity of leader.

The English have left a legacy which it might be well to consider in light of its negative impact. Owing, possibly, to the fact that they live in partial isolation on an island, they've often had to live by their wits, rather than by force, and thus have developed a maxim that has stood them to some extent in good stead: "Divide, and conquer." This practice served them when dealing with larger countries on the European continent, and also in India. I believe, however, that leadership in the present age of energy will take a new direction. My hope is that people will depend more on sharing, and less on conquest and dominion. For what *wins* people is an all-accepting attitude.

Learn to take a back seat, when it seems right to you. I remember that many years ago I did exactly that—though, as it happened, there was no seat in the back anyway. Several monks were preparing to go by van from Encinitas to Los Angeles. I chose to sit in back, on the floor. Being young, it was in no way uncomfortable for me. Dr. Lewis, however, an older man who was in charge of the Encinitas colony, said to me, "You shouldn't be there. Your place is up front."

"Why?" I asked him, though I knew perfectly well what he meant.

"Because," he answered, "you're in charge."

"For that very reason," I replied, "my place is behind."

A leader who insists on always having a prominent position lowers his stature in the eyes of others. Leadership in the modern age, I hope and believe, will come increasingly to be seen as supporting others, not as lording it over them.

I don't say that such behavior would work in every situation. It would be inappropriate, for instance, in the army. Try always to be *appropriate* in your behavior. In many cases, however, the less you thrust yourself forward, the more others will boost you.

An important rule for leaders is never, with anyone under them, to put him at an unfair disadvantage. When starting Ananda, for instance, I might have claimed justifiably to possess inside and even unique knowledge of our Guru's will for the work. I was the only person at Ananda who had actually known him personally. (Today, thirty-six years later, only a handful of us are still living.) Certainly, my experience with him gave me an advantage over others—one that I might have claimed, had I wished to. If I'd done so, however, it would have shown a mean spirit. Why put others at a disadvantage? Instead, I've refrained, when possible, from alluding to this advantage when others have confronted me with ideas of their own. I've tried simply to let clear reason do the persuading. When that hasn't worked, I've let matters rest for a time so as to give others a chance to learn by their experience. Sometimes, indeed, I've been the one in the wrong. In such cases, I've readily ceded the point. After all, it would be foolish to claim I was right when I obviously wasn't! There are only two things that matter, moreover: what works, and what is right. It is perfectly possible that I've misunderstood my guru's meaning, sometimes.

Naturally, I do have inside knowledge in many matters. I am also willing to share my knowledge, when people want me to. I've never used that knowledge unfairly, by telling people, "You didn't know the Master personally. I did. Don't you think you should do as I say?" I've always tried to let reason prevail.

A leader should not concern himself excessively with his own comfort and convenience. Many people think that a leaders can do just as he pleases. The *good* leader, however, thinks first in terms of *giving* to others, not of *receiving* from them. Leadership, for those who accept that role sincerely, is a self-limiting position, not a self-indulgent one. A good leader must sacrifice his personal convenience for the sake of the work being done. On the other hand, he must include in his reality the wishes of others, among things to be considered. Moreover, he cannot expect others to be impersonal in such matters; therefore he must make up for any such deficiency in them.

Years ago in the monastery, lack of available space made it necessary for new monks to be housed in one, large room. In time, fifteen men were crowded into it. As newcomers, they had no experience of the monastic life, and were, besides, young and exuberant. They often stayed up late into the night, chatting instead of meditating. One evening, in a spirit of fun, they had a boisterous pillow fight—nothing wrong, of course; energetic youngsters need an outlet for their energies. Still, it wasn't for this purpose that they'd come. Their discussions, moreover, judging from what I heard, did not always soar to the heights of philosophy.

I lived in another building. My quarters were far from elegant, but at least they gave me privacy. Steps led down from my bedroom to a small basement, which I fondly called my meditation "cave." Here I spent several hours a day meditating.

Aware of the growing difficulty faced by those new monks, however, and anxious for their spiritual well-being, I hit on a solution: I must live in the same room with them. I remained there for a year and a half.

A good leader must surrender his own convenience, if he wants to be effective in his job. What some other leader does in similar situations is, of course, his own decision. No guiding rules can be written. I myself had no precedent to guide me to "sit in the back," for example. A leader must develop his own intuition in these things. Indeed, his duty will vary with circumstances. Sometimes it will be right and may even be important to be perceived clearly as the one in charge. Know your strengths, therefore; remember, you cannot afford to be perceived as weak under any circumstance.

It is important, on the other hand, not to be perceived as a bully. A good leader must *lead*, and cannot let himself be pushed about except in fun. If he is losing on any issue, however, it may be wise simply to give in gracefully, before others *perceive* him as the loser. Sometimes, on the other hand, he may have to insist even in trivial matters, calmly but firmly. This decision is one he must make. There can be no fixed rules in such matters.

I remember Dr. Lewis, to whom I referred above, telling me of a time when he and Mrs. Lewis were traveling by car with the Master. The Master opened the window by his side. Mrs. Lewis, saying nothing, reached over and closed it. The Master simply opened it again, without a word. A moment later she reached over and closed it firmly. Again without a word, he calmly opened it again. He knew it would not help her discipleship to be victorious in this silent struggle, petty though it was. (He might easily have gone breathless, had he so chosen! It was something he often did while traveling.) At last, Mrs. Lewis gave in. The Master could not, in his position of guru, permit her to win; it would have strengthened her ego. (The Master once told Dr. Lewis that Mrs. Lewis, in a former life, had been Queen Elizabeth I, of England!)

A leader cannot afford to let anyone *seize* the reins from him. I myself have sometimes found it necessary to tell people firmly, "I won't allow you to *tell* me what to do!" I don't like to speak that way, but if I must do so it would be shirking my responsibility for me to remain silent. The Master himself once told me, "I prefer to discipline people with love. I just wilt inside when I have to speak firmly."

After Ananda's first year, a young man of rather thrustful disposition announced, "A tradition exists in Japan that when the young people grow up, the old ones step aside and hand the reins of power over to them." His words were a blatant bid for power. He was twenty-four years old; I myself was forty-two—hardly an age for anyone to become dodderingly senile! I realized that I must be firm. "Dick," I said, "I did not start this community to turn it over to you!" He left soon afterward in search of a freer world. I wished him luck, mentally.

A leader must be firm in himself, even when he yields to necessity, or out of kindness. Never allow yourself, on the other hand, to feel threatened by actual ability in others. Don't belittle them, but do your best to *harness* their ability for the over-all good. A weak leader resents creativity in others. If he has no talent, himself, his resentment may be humanly understandable, but it will not make him a good leader, and will be tantamount to a confession of ineptitude.

It is incumbent upon leaders to be in some way creative. To be jealous or resentful of ability in others shows one to be undeserving of a leadership position. Any competent person knows that he cannot be outstanding at everything. He should therefore be grateful for genuine ability in others, and should try to find ways of putting that ability to best use. The worst thing he can do is scheme for such people's removal, or convenient sequestration in obscurity.

Andrew Carnegie attributed his business success to his willingness to gather people around him who—as he put it—knew more than he did. He kept the controlling reins in his hands, but he never insisted on being the horse!

Another successful businessman attributed his success to a willingness to let his subordinates make mistakes. As he pointed out, that is the only way to learn. Organizations that insist on everything being done right the first time condemn themselves to mediocrity. You cannot allow people to keep on making the same mistakes, of course! Nevertheless, give them a chance, if possible, to improve.

Another principle of good leadership is to avoid basing too many decisions on precedent. The fact that a solution worked well in the past does not mean necessarily that it will work this time. Consider each situation unique. It is a thing *in itself*, and unrelated to anything else. It is of course wise to consider different options before making certain decisions, but remember, *Habit is anathema to creativity*. No two snowflakes are exactly alike. Every atom, as my Guru stated, is "dowered with individuality." Every ego is, in a vital sense, different from every other. Even when the ego merges into the Infinite, so my Guru said, its memory of individuality is retained eternally, and can be remanifested at will.

Another rule is: Don't "type" people. I was corrected the other day for saying that. Someone said, "If you type others *positively*, however, they may feel encouraged." She was right, and I'd been wrong to overlook that aspect of the matter. Usually, however, it limits people to type them. It also demeans them, making it difficult for them to rise to their highest potential. Everyone deserves respect as a child of God.

Think of the simple words uttered by lovers since the beginning of time: "I love you." Somehow, whenever those words are spoken with deep feeling, they seem as though uttered for the first time. What makes them so special is the depth of feeling they contain; it makes an "old formula" fresh and alive.

What matters, therefore, is not so much what you do or say as your deep sincerity. That is, indeed, the true meaning of originality: something which issues from its point of origin in one's self.

Don't be like those weary people who, traveling to work every day on the subway or the metro, stare dully into space until they arrive at their destination, upon which they go marching like robots to work. Be "awake and ready" at every moment of your life!

Is yours a management position? In that case, you should feel to some extent responsible for the happiness and well-being of those under you. Keep in mind the importance, to your own success, of human values. *Feel* for others; nurture their growth, as you are able. Encourage them as their friend, and not as an office diplomat. Take the time to listen sympathetically to their problems. It will be worth your while to do so, for you could not succeed without their help.

Never become so involved in problems of the moment that you lose sight of your long-range goals. Keep those goals, rather, ever clearly before you. Many leaders allow themselves to be deflected by side issues. "Keep your eye on the road," as new drivers are told when they are learning to drive.

Keep a sense of humor, too, if only to help you to see things in a broad perspective. Nothing is worth holding a grim attitude for. It can destroy your happiness and have a negative impact on the happiness of others.

During the fire in 1976, which nearly destroyed Ananda, one of our founding couples lost their home and all that was in it. The wife had given birth ten days earlier to their first child. Understandably, the test was almost more than she could bear. Her husband remarked to her with a wry smile, in the hope of comforting her, "Well, at least we won't have to worry anymore about those leaks in the roof!"

Remember, your reality is *you*, not the passing scene before you. If you can keep that simple fact in mind, you will be able to smile under all circumstances. One who can come up smiling, after being beaten repeatedly to the ground, cannot fail to win in the end.

This is a thought I've touched on before, but it is worth repeating here: Don't try to be perceived as an authority on *every* subject! You'll only show yourself up as an ignoramus, and others will laugh at you behind your back.

Above all, be joyful inside. You can live in joy by deliberate choice. Nothing is so important to you as your own happiness. Isn't that the real reason you work at all? *Be happy this very moment!* Don't wait for an uncertain future to give you the happiness you crave.

The Application

In this lesson, as in the one before, I haven't found it possible to separate principle from practical application. In discussing specifically, here, how to apply my thoughts on leadership, I find I have little to add. The following are a few remaining suggestions:

Put first things first. Leadership itself is not a "first thing." After you die, God, or whatever angel or deva meets you "up there" won't ask you, "Were you a good leader?" You will be asked, if anything, "Do you love deeply?" What else really matters?

Never give supreme importance to passing issues. Things will change, but why change with them? In your true Self, indeed, you can never change. You will remain *You* for all eternity, a spark of the Infinite. There will never be a duplicate copy.

Keep in mind the transitory nature of success itself. If you always remember that fact, it will help you to move the sails on your boat left or right with every shifting wind. Flexibility will help you, in fact, not only to achieve success, but to *retain* that success through all of life's ups and downs.

Many years ago, the heads of several prominent corporations in America met for an important discussion. All of them were wealthy, respected, and powerful. What is especially interesting about that occasion is that *every single one of them*, not many years later, lost everything he valued: his position, his wealth, his power. He became, if not poor, then at least not wealthy and no longer socially prominent.

This sort of thing is happening constantly in life. It could happen to *you*. Never depend for your sense of self-worth on anything outside yourself. All you can ever be, forever, is your own self. At present you seem so finite, in your ego, but someday you will perceive yourself to be infinite. Live in the thought of your essential oneness with Brahman, the Supreme Spirit. Live in that thought through the many vagaries of life. Be happy *in yourself*. And bear in mind that, ultimately speaking, you yourself are, as I said, your *only* reality!

MEDITATION

Visualize a shining light radiating outward from the heart of infinity. Now, visualize that you *are* that light. Mentally send out light rays from your center to sustain the whole universe.

See leadership as a training ground for infinite consciousness. See yourself as *giving* light, not as receiving it. See all things—all creation—as needing what you have to give. Nourish all creatures in your light. Give to all of them your love.

See to it that your feeling for others remains impersonal, in the sense of asking nothing for yourself. Be concerned for the individual well-being of everyone.

You are free in yourself! You are the Lord of everything that exists. For all eternity, you are in complete possession of your own being!

AFFIRMATION

"I am self-contained. I need nothing. I live to serve all so that together we may grow into the highest success of all: God's joy!"

POINTS TO REMEMBER

1. Two important rules: "Do what *works*" and "Do what is *right*." Happy is the person who can cling to his ideals while bringing them in line with reality.

2. People cannot be driven: they must be *inspired* to do what is right.

3. To do what is right, ethically and spiritually as well as pragmatically, wins the support of universal law. If you abide by true principles to the best of your ability, you will be always protected, and will be most likely to succeed in everything.

4. Leadership, if it is to be effective, must be played like a game in which points must be conceded, sometimes, for the sake of long-term advantages. To win always is not possible, and may not even be good, for it means that people have probably been bullied into agreement.

5. Cement the support of those members who show willingness, who want positive answers, and especially those who share your fundamental goals. Give no more energy than you have to to those who resent what you're doing. Even a minority, if expressing positive energy, creates a vortex of energy and power.

6. A leader must be strong in himself. He cannot afford to be ruled by people's emotions.

7. In choosing subordinate leaders, look for those who want to *serve*, not to dominate. Look for people to act on your behalf to whom others turn instinctively for guidance, people who respect human values and show consideration for the feelings of others.

8. It is an aspect of true leadership to focus on others' needs, not to concentrate only on what *you* want.

9. People will be more willing to follow you if you are sincere with them, and if you do only what works best and what is right and true.

10. Those who work under you will enjoy working with you, if they respect and like you, and if you treat them well. *Show* your support for them as often as you can.

11. Try to go along with others' wishes, when you can do so without compromising your essential goals. People learn faster with greater clarity when one encourages them not to fear making mistakes.

12. Be willing to take the blame, *even if you don't deserve it*. It is you, the leader, who are answerable for what goes on under you. People will respect you, and will be all the more loyal to you.

13. Give credit wholeheartedly, where credit is due, openly, in front of others.

14. Never, with anyone under you, put him at an unfair disadvantage. Try to let clear reason do the persuading.

15. The *good* leader thinks first in terms of *giving* to others, not of *receiving* from them. A good leader must sacrifice his personal convenience for the sake of the work being done.

16. Never allow yourself to feel threatened by actual ability in others. Be grateful for genuine ability, and try to find ways of putting that ability to best use.

17. Avoid basing too many decisions on precedent. Consider each situation unique.

18. Don't "type" people. Everyone deserves respect as a child of God.

19. If you are in a management position, you should feel to some extent responsible for the happiness and well-being of those under you. Nurture their growth. Take the time to listen sympathetically to their problems. You could not succeed without their help.

20. Never become so involved in problems of the moment that you lose sight of your long-range goals. Keep those goals, rather, ever clearly before you.

21. Keep a sense of humor, if only to help you see things in a broad perspective. A grim attitude can destroy your happiness and have a negative impact on the happiness of others.

22. Above all, be joyful inside. *Be happy this very moment!* Don't wait for an uncertain future to give you the happiness you crave.

23. Flexibility will help you, not only to achieve success, but to *retain* that success through all of life's ups and downs.

24. See leadership as a training ground for infinite consciousness. See yourself as *giving* light, not as receiving it. See all things—all creation—as needing what you have to give. Give to all of them your love.

WORKBOOK IDEAS
by Joseph Bharat Cornell

During World War II, an American infantry unit was hunkered down in foxholes as German shells fell. Their commander, a second lieutenant, was seen moving among his men to ensure their safety. When someone asked the officer where his foxhole was, he replied, "If I had one, I'd be in it."

Like all good leaders, the lieutenant understood the importance of staying aware of the larger picture. By sacrificing his personal safety, he also won his men's loyalty. People are intelligent. If they see their leader selflessly serving them and their cause, they are more willing to follow.

Even the universe supports us when we act nobly. In the early 1900s, after his ship was trapped and sunk by pack ice in the Antarctic, Sir Ernest Shackleton and five of his companions took a small boat on an eight-hundred-mile journey across the Southern Atlantic, one of the roughest seas in the world, to summon help for his stranded crew.

After landing on the island of South Georgia, Shackleton and two others traversed seventeen rugged miles across sheer glaciers and mountains to reach a whaling station for aid. During their epic journey, the three weary travelers tangibly felt a benevolent presence guiding them. They lovingly referred to this presence as the "unseen One" and their "Fourth Companion."

Expand Yourself Through Many

Practicing good leadership affirms your infinite consciousness. Bringing out the best in others, and channeling goodness into the world, expands your self-identity toward infinity.

ACTION ITEMS:

It is part of human nature to want to influence others, but we should always be respectful. An enlightened leader allows people the freedom to come to his position in their own time.

- Before offering a suggestion, ask yourself if the person can understand your idea enough to generate his own enthusiasm for it. Honor as a sacred trust his native enthusiasm, for it is his greatest asset and what moves him forward.
- Observe how your words affect others. Are they energizing and empowering?

Be Aware of Your Magnetism

The dictionary defines magnetism as it manifests in human relations as "the power to attract, fascinate, or influence." We can listen to some people talk forever, while with others, we may want to leave the room!

ACTION ITEMS:

1. Observe how people respond to you and your ideas. Observe also how others react to your colleagues. Are there co-workers that everyone listens to? If the answer is yes, ask yourself, "What is it that makes them so appealing?"

2.   To increase your magnetism and ability to work with others, practice the following suggestions by Swami Kriyananda:

- Harmonize your emotions by deep meditation. Emotions, especially, weaken your magnetism.
- Say "Yes to Life." Unwillingness diminishes your energy-flow, while willingness increases it.
- Eliminate inner conflicts within yourself. This greatly increases your flow of energy.
- Infuse everything you do with positive thoughts and energy. The more joyful and loving your consciousness, the more uplifting will be your magnetism.

LESSON ELEVEN

PRACTICALITY IN INVESTMENTS

By glancing even briefly at the innumerable signs all around us, you may realize even now that the most practical investment you can make is simply . . . to adjust your expectations. *Learn to think in new ways.*

The Principles

There are two aspects to this subject. The first is investment for financial gain or security. The other is one's investment of time and energy. Where the second aspect is concerned, material success is less tied to money than to the effort and energy one puts forth.

The first kind of investment seeks to profit from *other people's* time and energy. This might be called modern absentee landlordism—a practice which got the French aristocracy hated by the peasants, and ended in the social explosion that was the French Revolution. When an individual invests money in stocks, although he is helping others to succeed in their business, he is also hoping they'll devote their time and energy to making him rich. Rarely do people invest in the stock market as a service to others. Their usual motive is self-service: greed, in other words.

That is how most people see their investments. They want to become rich with as little effort on their part as possible, and hope to see all their investments grow magically in value without continuing effort on their part. A disadvantage to this way of making money is that it is, of course, risky. In a rising market, every investor may seem a financial genius, but when the bottom falls out of the market even those who may have been brilliant often end up bankrupt. The main danger, however, in karmic terms, is that stock market investments are made from a desire to gain without effort. For business to be in harmony with karmic law, it should have also, as an important motive, service to others. Business nowadays, unfortunately, is becoming motivated instead by increasing greed.

My purpose in writing this lesson is not to teach businessmen the principles of money investment. Those principles are adequately taught in business colleges. The imponderables in such investments, moreover, are many, and have little or nothing to do with our present subject: material success through yoga principles. Too often, the main reason behind people's investments is in conflict with yoga principles.

I shall begin this lesson by discussing a probable event in the near future of which every student of this course ought, I believe, to be aware. It concerns a financial crash that Paramhansa Yogananda predicted frequently toward the end of his life, speaking with great fervor and conviction. He said it would be disastrous for humanity, and would come as a simple result of man's greed. Greed, in fact, has been people's principal motive for investing in the stock market. Because this prediction was made by a great spiritual master, and was seen in visions in a state of divine consciousness, it deserves consideration primarily for that fact, and only secondarily as a logically possible outcome of the present situation. He said it often: "A great depression is coming." It would be well for people everywhere to take this warning very seriously.

Often I heard him speak of these things in public. "The next depression," he warned, "will be far worse than that of the 1930s." A senior disciple of his told me she had heard him say, "The dollar won't be worth the paper it is printed on." I never personally heard him make this statement, but it is perfectly in consonance with everything I did hear him say.

India's suffering will, I suspect, be less than America's. He was speaking in America, which has been profligate in its spending. In

India, I believe people are traditionally more careful to save their money, and to invest it safely, if at all, instead of taking foolish risks to achieve wealth without effort. Americans have been too long accustomed to over-all prosperity, and are to some extent intoxicated with the expectation that their prosperity will never end. Thus, instead of saving their money they spend it "like water," going far beyond their actual income by using credit cards and going into debt. At present, American personal indebtedness amounts to an average of $20,000 for every man, woman, and child in the country.

There is another reason why I believe that India will suffer less in a global depression. A person who falls to the ground from a low ledge may suffer only light bruises. One who falls to the ground from three storeys up, however, may be killed. Americans generally speaking have farther to fall, economically, than Indians, who are also more accustomed to the sight of poverty. Thus, Indians may find it easier to adjust to a serious depression.

Yogananda did not predict destitution for America. Rather, he said that Americans would lose half their wealth. So spoiled have Americans become by wealth, however, that they will see even a lesser loss as devastating.

There is a positive side to this picture also, however. My Guru added, "But they will be more spiritual."

On one occasion when he was uttering these warnings publicly, I was startled to hear him say after a brief pause, speaking with great force, "You don't know what a *terrible cataclysm* is coming!"

Perhaps he was only emphasizing his general theme of depression. It seemed to me, however, that these words were an insertion into his theme. The word, *cataclysm*, usually refers to some massive *natural* catastrophe, perhaps threatening the entire planet. I've not known it to refer to a man-made disaster. In any case, his words were dire enough, whatever their actual intent. If he meant them only to emphasize what he was saying about preparing for economic hard times, it is certain that he meant at least, "Take my warning *very* seriously!"

He explained repeatedly that the reason for the coming depression was *greed*. Would it not be fitting, indeed, for such a depression to begin with a stock market crash? The stock market is an exact expression of people's growing greed, and their hope of attaining wealth without actual effort.

Money earned by the sweat of one's brow, or by straining one's intellect, is honorably earned. When people try, however, to gain wealth by other people's efforts, they are treading on "thin ice," for the attempt goes counter to karmic law. If one seeks gain without giving anything in return, he gains bad karma. Nowadays, more and more of the wealth of America is being produced in other countries, where labor is relatively cheap. Can Americans afford indefinitely to sit back and let others do their work for them? In what way can this attitude be considered honorable?

The Indian people, perhaps because of their long habituation to at least *seeing* poverty, may prove more generous than the French peasants, for they will probably not cast blame on others. I have not observed in India an envious attitude toward America, for example. I believe they are only determined to "come up" economically, also. I imagine they'll think, "Well, we don't want the Americans to suffer." In any case, they may feel that America's problems are its own; they may even imagine they won't be affected by them. The trouble is, the whole world's economy is inextricably intertwined. That economy, fortunately or unfortunately, is also tied to the American dollar. As Brazil has been endangering the planet by clear-cutting vast tracts in the Amazon jungle, so America is endangering the whole world by its fiscal irresponsibility.

Will everything work out for the best in the end? Of course it will! Everything does, for duality swings back and forth. Good times will always turn bad again, in the end! That phrase, "in the end," however, can cover a long period of time. My Guru stated that the coming upheavals will eventually produce an era of worldwide peace and prosperity. It is even a good thing for America, in the long run, that so much of her wealth is presently being produced in other, relatively poor countries. Thus, international production is equalizing the prosperity of all peoples, even if Americans fail to realize that non-productivity at home will be, in the long run, to their economic detriment.

Prosperity will eventually become relatively equal all over the world. Obviously, such an outcome is desirable. The process, however, will be initially painful for everyone—for Americans, because they will wake up to the fact that, in actually producing less, they have less *real* wealth; and for poor countries, because they are much too dependent at present on the strength or weakness of the dollar.

No one country deserves to be singled out for sole blame. What is really happening is that the leading disease of modern times, greed, is infecting the whole planet. Until things balance themselves out, the worldwide upheaval will cause pain everywhere.

Anyone, moreover, who believes that world wars are a thing of the past is closing his eyes to the obvious. Again and again one hears the comforting words, declared with firm conviction: "A nuclear war is impossible: No one would accept something so horrible!" Everywhere, however, hatred seems to be on the increase; fear is on the increase; envy, jealousy, and anger are on the increase. People are willing—indeed, they seem eager—to blame everyone but themselves! How can peace come to a planet that seethes with such negative emotions? If you accept the dictum I proposed in the last lesson, "Do what *works*," you cannot ignore its obvious corollary: "Avoid doing what *doesn't* work"!

Understandably, no one wants to hear predictions of doom and disaster. Most people, perhaps, would rather stop their ears than listen to such words.

I myself, as a boy in the 1930s, lived in Europe. I knew at first hand the fear Jews held of persecution. I also saw them react in two ways to that fear. One group emigrated abroad to safety. The other group kept on affirming that fear was groundless. "Germany needs our prosperity," they frequently insisted. Someone explained to me years later that the Jews believed in keeping their money in gold, in addition to using the official paper currency.

Meanwhile, everyone in Europe saw Adolph Hitler on newsreels, inflaming his countrymen with hatred of the Jews. The motivation for that hatred was envy. Those Jews who decided it would be wise to leave Europe while there was still time were the pragmatic ones. The wishful thinkers dismissed fear as "negative thinking." The realists asked, in reply, "What is so negative about facing facts?"

I was on a train once, traveling across Germany on my way to school in England. When the train reached the Dutch border, a man in my brother's sleeping compartment was arrested by the German Gestapo. What could we assume but that he ended in a concentration camp, where, as we were to learn in time, millions died?

Terrible things have happened in our times. Think of the mass slayings, after the partition, of Hindus by Moslems, and of Moslems by Hindus. Is it "negative thinking" to face the possibility that these things may happen again?

I don't insist that you accept this view of the future. I do consider it my duty, however, to share with you what I consider to be a *more than likely* event. Why not make a few preparations, at least, for that eventuality? It is evident that there is a danger of hard times ahead. If I am wrong, you will anyway have made a sensible investment. If a global depression does arrive, and perhaps even a global war of terrible proportions, you may be able with a little preparation not only to help yourself and your family, but also to save many friends as well as others. These are difficult possibilities to face, but surely it would be unwise to do nothing to prepare for them. There are at present too many signs pointing in the direction of disaster. On the other hand, if no disaster occurs, at least you will have the satisfaction of knowing that you took sensible precautions. Wishful thinking cannot change the world's karma. *Positive* thinking may help to *mitigate* that karma, but even mitigation will require a far greater change in mass consciousness than we are seeing today. As long as greed rules the mass consciousness, it must be accepted there are serious lessons needing to be learned. Since what I am speaking of concerns mass consciousness, humanity *en masse* will have to learn the same lesson, whatever other lessons they need also.

Were everybody to turn to God, the trials would certainly be mitigated. Karma, however, which is simply energy in action, cannot be destroyed: It can only be minimized, by an equal and differently directed energy. How likely is it that mass greed will be dissolved by mass love? Not likely at all! Too many people have turned *away* mentally from God. Foolishly, they blame Him for their suffering when it is something they've brought on themselves. Meanwhile, a consciousness of greed, hatred, and increasing violence is festering in too many hearts.

"After the coming disasters," Paramhansa Yogananda prophesied, "humanity will have grown so tired of violence that it will live in peace for three hundred years." It will be, he said, a new and wonderful world. Meanwhile, the question forces itself upon us: "Have they suffered enough yet?" In answer to that question, one cannot help observing that the main causes of man's present suffering—hatred and greed—are on the increase. They are not diminishing.

"Someday," the Master predicted, "America and India will join hands and lead the world to a right balance between spiritual and material practicality."

A vitally important question is sure to be asked: How soon will these dire predictions be fulfilled? And the truth, surely, is obvious: their fulfillment has begun already! Never has the world's economy been so unstable, despite everything that politicians and newspaper editorials declare in an attempt to reassure everyone. I don't mean that everything is getting worse all over the world. India, for example, still seems to be on an economic upswing. The American economy still looks fairly strong, but it is much weaker than the propagandists insist.

Please be very careful from now on about how you invest your money, as well as your time and energy. Don't live in a dream world of wishful thinking. Numerous investment newsletters, which are free from the influence of political considerations, foresee imminent disaster. Even they, however, try to keep their readership by promising the possibility of emerging from hard times more wealthy than ever. I challenge that promise. The world, instead, is speeding rapidly toward bitter disillusionment. Even those newsletters, which are more truthful than the newspapers, still fan the flames of greed. Humanity must learn its lesson. Only then will it rediscover the only thing that, forever, has really worked: Doing what is *right*.

Meanwhile, why join the lemmings crowding forward to leap into the ocean of self-destruction? The surface of the water shimmers, the radiance seeming to suggest wealth, but that superficial appearance is destined to end, with the eternal impersonality of karma, in the financial drowning of millions. Follow what my Guru's guru, Swami Sri Yukteswar, counseled, "Learn to be comfortable within your purse."

In my own life, there have been times when I've had to live on very little. By the standards of India's villagers I was not poor, but by the standards of my own country, I was well below the accepted poverty line. For three months I lived on only $10 a month—bare subsistence, Americans would call it. Nevertheless, I found that I could actually enjoy my poverty! It challenged my ingenuity to shop around for foods that cost little but that were nonetheless nourishing.

Instead of bread I made chapatis. Instead of fresh milk I mixed powdered milk with water at a third of the price. Instead of a bowlful of dessert I made a single bowlful last me a whole week by eating only a teaspoonful after each meal. Well, I don't suppose Indians need lessons from me on how to live economically! Still, I'd like to add this thought: I found the experience not only acceptable, but enjoyable. All I did was *adjust my expectations*. I did lose a little weight, but not drastically.

People will need to adjust their expectations to a lower yield. They will find it not so difficult to accomplish. Think of it as a challenge, not as a disastrous deprivation. By glancing even briefly at the innumerable signs all around us, you may realize even now that the most practical investment you can make is simply that: to adjust your expectations. *Learn to think in new ways.*

Practical Steps

From today onward, make it a principle to avoid debt. If for any reason you need to borrow, make a serious attempt to pay off that debt as soon as possible. It simply won't be worth the cost, in terms of your peace of mind, to have debt of any kind hanging over your head like the sword of Damocles.

Try—every week, if possible—to put a little money aside. Don't place too much faith in banks. During depressions of the past, many banks had to close their doors, leaving their depositors without recourse.

Above all, don't place too much faith in paper currency. The way in which governments the world over are printing money these days in attempts to meet their national commitments, all the currencies of the world may well lose all their value in time.

In 1958, when I first came to India, I seem to recall that the exchange rate was about eight rupees to the dollar. At present, it is about forty-five-and-a-half rupees. And what of the dollar? I have read that America is currently printing *one and a half trillion dollars* a year!

Where do you think all that printing will take us? A nation awash in paper cannot in reality be considered prosperous.

If possible, keep a certain amount of money in solid assets. Don't rely too heavily on your government's promises. Democratic governments everywhere try to be responsive to the will of the people, but that will is guided almost entirely by self-interest. It is a recipe for disaster. The question people generally ask, when voting, is, "What's in it for me?" It is this consciousness which elects their representatives to government posts. The persons most likely to be elected over and over again are those who make outrageous promises, each one of them targeted toward satisfying people's greed. Will those promises ever be fulfilled? *All* of them? Impossible! Already people's mind-set is to get much more than any sane government can possibly supply. The governments keep on trying, but they know there is a limit to how much they get by taxes. The solution they hit upon, inevitably, is to print truckloads of paper currency. This is monetary inflation. It is also called "hidden taxation." The way governments everywhere manage to have more money than they dare to demand in taxes is by way of the printing press.

In Germany, during its time of hyperinflation (in 1923), the father of a friend of mine went into a shop and left outside it a wheelbarrow full to overflowing with his earnings for the day. The money, being worthless, seemed safe enough; who, after all, would steal it? When he came out later, his money was blowing about in the street: Someone had stolen his wheelbarrow, first emptying it of its contents!

Gold and silver are better understood in India than in America, where people have been conditioned by government propaganda to view gold as a "barbarous relic." It isn't that those who own gold are less likely to be spoiled by greed, but at least gold can't be printed like paper money. Its relative scarcity makes it a protection against hyperinflation. Should the dollar no longer be "worth the paper it is printed on," don't expect other currencies in the world to fare any better. Place your trust in God first; then invest some of your money in things of solid worth. Tomorrow, paper money may be "gone with the wind." Gold and silver are safer investments, and are likely to increase in value astronomically relative to the value of paper currency.

I myself have never been interested in money for money's sake. As the founder of several communities, however, which have been dependent on my practical and not only my spiritual guidance, I've considered it important to keep abreast of the broader economic picture. I've reflected deeply, therefore, on my guru's predictions regarding the world economy. He, too, was concerned for others' welfare. In trying to keep abreast of these matters, I've made a study of things that would otherwise have been of little interest to me.

From what I have studied, it seems clear to me that the safest investments, monetarily, are silver and gold. These investments are the ones most highly recommended by people whose counsel I incline to believe.

Of other investments I am more doubtful, even though these, too, are highly recommended. I consider the sustained value of such collectibles as paintings, for example, to be less reliable. Large items, moreover, are more susceptible to damage or theft. Gems, though small and easy to transport, undergo wide fluctuations in their market value.

Land

What my Guru particularly urged people to invest in was land. He wasn't thinking of its monetary yield; in other words, he wasn't counseling people how to be greedy with safety! Rather, he urged them to think in terms of having life's basics, so as to be free to concentrate on higher things, and of course especially on the search for God.

Peasants and others who sometimes live in desperate poverty have no spare time or energy for seeking God. It is no accident that most of the residents of ashrams in India come from well-to-do homes. One who lacks food for his stomach is too hungry to think of higher matters!

I want to emphasize that the Master wasn't recommending investment in income-producing property such as apartment houses. Certainly he wasn't trying to make zamindars (landlords) of people. His recommendation was to purchase only enough land as one needs in order to supply one's self and a few others with the basic needs. With land, they could grow their own food, have a sufficient water supply, and if they buy with discrimination, not burden themselves with heavy mortgage payments.

During economic hard times, the definition of material success is not money, but security. Whatever assets you have, invest as much money as you can in things that you can control. You cannot control the stock market. The "get rich quick" schemes of stock investors are as foolish today as would be investments in sandy wastes with the rationale that there is oil beneath the sands of Arabia! Put whatever money you can spare into buying land with arable soil. Plan to grow your own food. Buy property in a low-tax area, and preferably where there is a minimal danger of social unrest.

There is a supposedly true story about a man who, in the aftermath of World War I, realized that there was likely to be a World War II. In an effort to avoid it, he traveled throughout the world in search of some place that would, he hoped, be trouble free. Finally he bought land and settled on the island of Guam. That was in the mid-1930s. As many still remember, in only a few years Guam was the epicenter of the Pacific war theater in World War II!

Place your faith in God above all. He expects you to use common sense also, but don't concern yourself too fearfully with finding a place of perfect safety. Your very fear might *attract* danger like a magnet. Human life will never be perfectly secure. Do what seems reasonable to you, then leave the results in God's hands. Remember, sooner or later you will have to leave this world anyway; it is not your true home. Do what seems reasonable, therefore, but be free of attachment to the results of your actions.

If you hold that attitude, you will certainly find it in keeping with yoga principles to be sensible also. Don't imagine that God will be more pleased with you if you face life passively with the thought, "Whatever comes is my karma. I can't control anything in my life." The purpose of karmic law is to teach us, through punishment and reward, to *act always for the best*. Don't expect to be protected by faith alone—unless, indeed, your faith is so strong, and focused so one-pointedly, that *all* your energy flows toward God.

Buy land within your means. If you can't buy it outright, get property that you can pay off in a reasonably short time. Try to settle in the general vicinity of a small town, where others can help you in times of need. Don't get land too near a large city, where violence might easily erupt during general social upheaval. If that land should contain a house, all the better, but if it doesn't and you can afford to build, or if you have the skill to build a home for yourself, it may be to your advantage to build exactly according to your own tastes and needs.

Food, clothing, shelter: these are life's basic necessities. If possible, store basic food supplies: foods that will retain their freshness a long time. Make sure that whatever food you buy for future use is tightly sealed, in an air-proof container, safe from mice, insects, and other pests, and safe also from excessive heat and humidity.

In this modern age, many people are accustomed to such amenities as electricity. In times of emergency, however, electricity can be dispensed with relatively easily. At Ananda Village it was years before most of us could install electricity in our homes. We were perfectly comfortable with bottled gas for cooking, and, for lighting, kerosene, candles, or oil lamps. Interestingly, our homes were more peaceful *before* we introduced electricity into them. My impression has long been that the magnetism generated by electric wiring in the walls makes a house less peaceful even if electricity enhances a home's efficiency.

One thing that will help your home very much during extremes of cold and heat will be insulation in the walls—particularly in the ceilings. That insulation needn't be expensive. Even newspapers, wadded up and crammed into the walls, can be very effective. Books are available on this subject. Study them, and see what kind of construction will be the most cost-effective, efficient, and practical in your area.

If you can't live immediately on your property, try to get away to it for weekends, and also for longer periods occasionally. Even if there has to be someone on the property to take care of it, you may be able to supervise from a distance the creation of a small vegetable garden.

Energy: Your Most Essential Investment

The most important investment to keep at your command is your own energy, mental as well as physical. All human energy is mental primarily. I've quoted my Guru heretofore as saying, "The greater the will power, the greater the flow of energy."

Some of the wealthiest families in the world have been reduced to penury as a result of relying too much, and too passively, on their handed-down inheritance. India won her freedom not only because of her moral vigor under the leadership of Mahatma Gandhi, but also because England had begun to lose its moral vigor—the consequence of centuries of taking from others without compensating them generously in return. Your energy can be expanded, quite literally, to infinity. Alternatively, it can contract to virtual nonexistence. Some of the greatest fortunes on earth have been made by people who started with almost no money, but with great zeal.

Money is one of mankind's three great delusions, the other two being sex and "wine" (that is to say, intoxication of all kinds, including hallucinogenic drugs). Money is listed with these three for several reasons. One is the expectation it gives of happiness. The second is the expectation of security. And the third is the false belief that, with money, one becomes powerful, important, and superior to anyone with less money.

With the sense of superiority money very often gives a further delusion: the thought that people without money are worthless. Wealthy people often succeed in imposing this delusion on the poor, making them, by contempt for them, actually *feel* worthless.

What makes these three delusions supreme is the fact that they strengthen the ego, alienating people thereby from their eternal reality: soul-identity with Infinite Consciousness.

The delusion that money can bring happiness evaporates not long after its acquisition. Wealthy people are seldom happy. If they are newly rich, they may delight for a time in the thought of being able to buy whatever they want. That delight soon palls, however, for the very desire for things is itself an affirmation of lack, which in turn is a kind of poverty. Though they can remove that lack with money, their very consciousness that they lack anything becomes, in time, a habit! The more constant they are in seeking fulfillment outwardly, the more difficult they find it to be happy. It is not possible to fulfill every desire; thus it happens that wealthy people are often less happy than those who have relatively little.

In poverty, a person is obliged to limit his desires to the essentials: food, clothing, and shelter. The rich, however, want far more. Their desires are never ending. They want utterly unnecessary "necessities," necessary, to them, only because they imagine they need them. In fact, these things can become suffocating luxuries; they create an inner emptiness, which people excavate with the shovel of ceaseless desires. Their emptiness of heart may not show outwardly, but it cries to them from within.

The proof that money doesn't bring happiness is underscored by the sad fact that statistics show suicide to be more prevalent among the rich than among the poor.

Money, ultimately, brings happiness only if it is shared. When it is used generously to help others, one feels happy in himself and finds his happiness expanding to include others' well-being. Money, in this case, can be a real blessing, not a misfortune. Rich people who center their attention on themselves, and on their own needs and interests, find the initial sense of self-expansion which comes with the acquisition of wealth shrinking in an ever-tightening vice.

The thought that money makes one powerful, important, and worthy of admiration seems again, at first, expansive by its swelling affirmation of the ego. As one basks in the sense of personal power and of others' admiration, however, the heart's feeling shrinks. And it is in the heart that happiness resides. Thus, it becomes increasingly difficult to regard others with sympathy for their needs. The more one separates himself, in sympathy, from the needs and interests of other people, the more constricted his consciousness becomes. That ensuing narrowness causes him to suffer. This is the very opposite of fulfillment.

The belief, finally, that with wealth one is now secure causes some people to relax their energy output, and others to turn the energy into a whirlpool of fear. At first, of course, the acquisition of wealth increases one's energy-flow as he realizes he can accomplish so much more than before. This realization is embraced with enthusiasm. New wealth, therefore. conveys the illusion of increased happiness. This is an illusion, however, and lasts only temporarily. The expansive sense of self-importance makes one imagine himself fulfilled. Gradually, however, he begins to feel the limitations of too many possessions, as it dawns on him that his sense of self-importance comes from others, and that the fulfillment it gives him is entirely vicarious. Those things which brought satisfaction at first fade like autumn leaves, then become brittle, and one realizes that no amount of material security is a sure protection from personal disasters like disease, betrayal, and natural calamities. At such times especially, one is made aware that material security is an illusion. Misfortune, when it falls, is the more disappointing for the fact that delusions of power, self-importance, and self-assurance have been so fondly nourished.

None of this is to say that wealth is, in itself, a misfortune. Everything can be enjoyed, provided certain basic conditions are met:

First, one must enjoy money—indeed, all things—in moderation. One must rigidly exclude the temptation to *define* himself by them. Second, he must employ his gifts to be of help to others also, and not only for selfish ends. Third, he must develop non-attachment, realizing that nothing possessed can be permanently one's own.

Finally, one must understand that the source of all happiness lies *in oneself*, never in outside things. One must develop an inner life—particularly by meditation, and by offering himself to God.

Years ago I prepared a slideshow called *Different Worlds*. It showed the many different worlds men live in, and made it clear that those worlds depend not on a person's nationality, race, age, or status in society, but on states of mind. In photographs that I'd taken around the world—from exotic places to the most familiar—people are shown trying to eke happiness out of life for their own ends, and finding, instead of fulfillment, only dryness, bitterness, and pain. Then I showed people in many countries who obviously felt concern for others, instead, and for their well-being. The faces of these people all radiated inner peace and happiness. This lesson-in-pictures carries conviction. The different worlds we live in are not outside ourselves. No society, no scenes of natural beauty, and no amount of wealth can give people what all are seeking. Only one's own state of consciousness defines the world he lives in.

The Application

Include Others in Your Investments

Sharing with others is particularly important when it comes to simplifying your lifestyle. Simplicity will probably be more natural to country living.

Do you, personally, know how to grow food? how to build a home? how to maintain a home? If you want to live alone, or with only your intimate family, you may find country living more difficult than you thought.

One of the advantages of living in community with others is that the larger the group, the greater the chance that someone among you will have at least one special skill needed by the community to maintain itself.

I am aware that in India, especially, social restrictions exist on doing work that is considered beneath one. I myself grew up under similar restrictions, and have a better understanding of it than most Americans would. When I was a child, and our family went on vacations to America, we stayed with relatives. At the home of an aunt and uncle of mine in Tulsa, Oklahoma, it shocked me to be served meals in the kitchen, where the cook and the other servants ate. It took me time to recognize this attitude for what it was, and to reject it.

I remember working, years later, at my Guru's desert retreat. We were shoveling sand when, one day, he paused from his writing, came out of doors, and shoveled sand alongside us for a while. I noticed him panting slightly from the exertion, and remarked lightly, "It's hot work, isn't it?"

He looked at me a bit sternly, and commented, "It is *good* work!"

He very much appreciated the spirit he'd encountered in America, where every type of wholesome work is considered dignified and is given respect. Once I'd learned this lesson myself, after my family moved to America in 1939, I discovered that it was a joy to do hard manual labor, provided I balanced that work with other interests. Sometimes, during a heavy snowfall, cars found it difficult to move. I saw it as a privilege to help them out of snowdrifts with a shovel. Often they offered to pay me, but I refused; it was a joy to be able to serve in this capacity.

Yes, I overcame the foolish class prejudices of my childhood. I am aware that I had them, however, and I realize that prejudices of this sort cannot be dismissed lightly. Let me only say, then: Try to look upon *all labor* as honorable that is done in a spirit of joyful freedom.

Thus, if you need to hire someone to farm for you or to build your home, give him respect, and the honor and dignity every human being deserves as a child of God. Affirm your kinship with everyone, in God, including especially those who serve you. Consider no one beneath you, and no one above you. All men equally are born of the same Father, God.

My Guruji said, "Every nation has its own misery-making karma." The caste system, to which he referred particularly in that statement, is India's "misery-making karma"—not because the system itself is wrong—indeed, it is rooted in divine law—but because people, in their egotism, have misunderstood it. In a future lesson I will address that misunderstanding, for the subject is of vital importance. Above all, what is needed is to understand that what one is derives not from race, nation, system of beliefs, or place in society: It derives *entirely* from who and what one is in himself.

One should respect all men equally as God's creations. That respect should include also respect for *their* realities. One who has been accustomed to owning very little may preen himself, to his own detriment, if, on finding himself thrust suddenly into company with people who are accustomed to plenty, he is *treated* by them as an equal. They would be wise in his presence to behave toward one another, even, with a certain circumspection—not by a display of arrogance, but by calmness and a little reserve.

Let me explain something here about our Ananda Villages which, as an international network of autonomous communities, are sufficiently numerous for their membership to demonstrate a variety of skills. Indeed, among our members *someone*, usually, has some skill in anything that is required. Such variety would be difficult to find in smaller groups, who may not find it easy even to be minimally self-sufficient. Ananda Sangha's communities exist in a variety of locations, some of them miles from any town. Others are close to the center of cities. All follow the same spiritual path. There is a great advantage, spiritually, in satsang, or spiritual fellowship with fellow seekers. It strengthens everyone's commitment to the spiritual life.

The homes in each community may be widely separate from one another, or they may be clustered together. The concept of community living doesn't at all require crowding everyone together in one building, or even onto a small space of land. Economic self-sufficiency may require hiring outside help. A community may earn money to buy some of life's necessities outside the community.

A large community also has certain disadvantages. It can increase the problems of human interaction. I wrote in the last lesson about how I faced some of these problems when I was founding Ananda Village. Today, those problems have for the most part been resolved. It took years, however, and many trials, for us to achieve our present level of harmony, which now is considerable. Without the strength and inspiration that come from affiliating with an already-functioning network of communities, the wisest thing may well be to "think small."

Paramhansa Yogananda himself recommended to most people that they pool their resources with a few friends. If you can find a few in your circle of friends who would like to join you in this venture, get them to join you also in investing a certain sum of money. My Guru suggested $10,000 each. Today, that sum would be considerably more. In India, however, the problem must be reconsidered in light of India's economic realities. Even the present rupee equivalent of ten thousand U.S. dollars might be too much to ask of people. This I don't know. Try, then, when holding meetings with friends, to agree on a sum that all of you can afford. Help them to understand that this investment is vitally important for their own future safety and well-being.

Let me repeat, Paramhansa Yogananda's advice to people was to "get land." This was among the most urgent things I ever heard him say in public talks.

It is important for those joining you to invest at least *some* of their own funds in this project. Without that commitment, you may find it difficult, later on, to get their help in other vital matters also, when that help is really needed.

If you join hands with others, you will probably want to set up some kind of legal society. I strongly suggest that the basic sum of money people invest be non-refundable. Otherwise, even one person dropping out might cause the whole venture to collapse. At Ananda Village we insisted on the non-refundability of the basic membership fee.

In future lessons, we shall have several opportunities to explore this subject further and from a variety of angles. For now, I suggest that each of you take on a special assignment: Study one particular aspect of the project. Hold regular meetings to discuss these matters further. It may be wise, initially, to get no more than ten families involved. This figure is not absolute, of course. The main point I want to make is, Don't admit too many members at first. At the same time, don't have too few, for too small a number may severely hamper your beginning efforts. The number you envision must be flexible enough, of course, to accommodate actual realities.

Much more might be said on this subject. Some of it will be covered in future lessons. I suggest here, in addition, that before actually moving on such a project, and after all of you feel sincerely committed to this idea, a few of you visit me in India, or visit the people directing our communities in Italy or in America. Try, if possible, to spend some time in one of our Ananda communities; live among us for at least a week. This is a matter in which understanding must come largely by osmosis. It cannot come only through the written or spoken word.

MEDITATION

Greed is in the process, at present, of attracting global poverty. It is also alienating mankind at present from divine blessings. The universe functions on certain clear principles, which are emphasized in the yoga teachings: loving energy, conscious harmony, mutuality of sharing. It has been said that subtle forces are consciously responsible for plant life on this planet, and that these forces are, at the present time, withdrawing their energy. In ancient times, the Vedas taught that one should give energy to the *devas*, who create and sustain plant life. By giving them energy, we can live in reciprocal harmony with them, through nature.

People nowadays scoff at this as "superstition." My Guru said it is a mistake to do so. It is, he said, important not only to draw what we can from nature, but also to give back to it, by praying to God through those subtle entities, and by loving and showing them gratitude. It is an error to treat them as though they had no existence. In seizing what we can only for ourselves, we withdraw ourselves from nature's abundance. When we do that, nature, in return, withdraws her abundance.

Famines, earthquakes, volcanic eruptions, and other natural disasters are on the increase these days. My Guru said it is because of the growing disharmony in people's hearts. Everything in the universe is conscious. Man, being more conscious than the lower forms of life, has a powerful influence on his environment and, in the aggregate, on the planet. When people live in harmony with one another and with nature, all good things flourish. When people live in disharmony, however, they starve themselves of divine energy. Our planet then reacts with outrage.

In meditation, picture to yourself a large garden in the springtime. Flowers abound everywhere. Alas, they feel the coldness of human selfishness and greed. Even though the weather has been growing warmer, the flowers keep their buds tightly closed.

Now, pass mentally among them. Instead of demanding that they open their buds, so that you may enjoy their beauty, smile at them with warm sympathy. Mentally breathe on each of them, offering them your kindness and love. Watch now: See how, wherever you pass, the petals open in gratitude for your love and goodwill.

Develop an attitude of generous giving. Don't take from life, selfishly. All nature, now, is responding to your love. Feel love for everything, and feel your love expanding like a roseate cloud, blessing and bringing everything joyfully to life.

You and all life are one. You and infinite life forever share together, dancing in rhythms of perpetual laughter and love.

AFFIRMATION

"I am one with all life! I am one with all Nature. We are all dancing together in God's joy."

POINTS TO REMEMBER

1. Toward the end of his life Paramhansa Yogananda frequently predicted a financial crash. Speaking with great fervor and conviction, he said it would be disastrous for humanity, and would come as a simple result of man's greed. Because this prediction was made by a great spiritual master, and was seen in visions in a state of divine consciousness, it would be well for people to take this warning very seriously.

2. "The next depression," he warned, "will be far worse than that of the 1930s." My Guru added, "But people will be more spiritual." My Guru also stated that the coming upheavals will eventually produce an era of worldwide peace and prosperity.

3. When people try to gain wealth by other people's efforts (investing in the stock market, for example), they are treading on "thin ice," for the attempt goes counter to karmic law. If one seeks gain without giving anything in return, he gains bad karma.

4. The world's economy is inextricably intertwined. If a crash happens in America, the whole world will be affected.

5. It is not "negative thinking" to face the possibility that depression, cataclysm, and war may happen. Why not make a few preparations, at least, for that eventuality?

6. Please be very careful about how you invest your money, as well as your time and energy.

7. The most practical investment you can make is to adjust your expectations. *Learn to think in new ways.*

8. Make it a principle to avoid debt. Make a serious attempt to pay off any debt as soon as possible.

9. Try—every week, if possible—to put a little money aside. Don't place too much faith in banks.

10. Place your trust in God first; then invest some of your money in things of solid worth, such as gold and silver.

Land

11. Paramhansa Yogananda's advice to people was to "get land." This was among the most urgent things I ever heard him say in public talks.

12. He recommended purchasing only enough land as one needs to supply one's self and a few others with the basic needs: food and water. Buy land with arable soil. Plan to grow your own food. Buy property in a low-tax area, and preferably where there is a minimal danger of social unrest.

13. Place your faith in God above all. Use common sense also, but don't concern yourself too fearfully with finding a place of perfect safety. At the same time, don't expect to be protected by faith alone.

14. Try to settle in the general vicinity of a small town, where others can help you in times of need. Don't get land too near a large city.

15. If possible, store basic food supplies: foods that will retain their freshness a long time.

16. Make sure your home is well insulated, and that you are prepared to live without electricity.

17. If you can't live immediately on your property, try to get away to it for weekends, and see to the creation of a small vegetable garden.

Include Others in Your Investments

18. Wealth can be enjoyed, provided certain basic conditions are met: First, one must enjoy everything in moderation. Second, he must employ his gifts to be of help to others also. Third, he must develop non-attachment, realizing that nothing possessed can be permanently one's own. Finally, one must develop an inner life—particularly by meditation, and by offering himself to God.

19. One of the advantages of living in community is that the larger the group, the greater the chance that someone among you will have at least one special skill needed by the community to maintain itself.

20. Try to look upon *all labor* as honorable that is done in a spirit of joyful freedom.

21. Paramhansa Yogananda himself recommended to most people that they pool their resources with a few friends. Try to agree on a sum that all of you can afford. It may be wise, initially, to get no more than ten families involved.

22. I suggest that before actually moving on such a project, a few of you visit me in India, or spend some time in one of our Ananda communities in America or Italy. This is a matter in which understanding must come largely by osmosis.

23. Develop an attitude of generous giving. Feel love for everything, and feel your love expanding like a roseate cloud, blessing everything.

WORKBOOK IDEAS
by Joseph Bharat Cornell

Akio Shoji, President of Aleph, Ltd., started his food services business in a tiny four-by-six-foot stall. Today Mr. Shoji operates over four hundred restaurants in Japan. He attributes his success to heeding the words of his mentor: "A businessman should be like the Buddha and educate and enlighten people."

Instead of focusing on profit, Mr. Shoji concentrates on offering an uplifting dining experience and serving his customers wholesome food, much of it organically grown on his farms. By not thinking, "What can I get from people?" but, rather, "What can I give them?" Mr. Shoji has attracted a tremendous flow of abundance in his life, which he shares by supporting noble causes throughout the world.

Akio Shoji's generosity and expansive business practices have attracted hundreds of like-minded employees who enthusiastically share his vision and ideals.

Expansive Energy Audit

Generosity attracts abundance. Living expansively and thinking of others opens a channel in ourselves for energy to flow freely.

ACTION ITEM:
Accepting the rewards of good karma, without giving back in return, dissipates any karmic blessing.

1. Ask yourself this question: Am I expressing dynamic love and generosity in the following areas of my life?

   - Financial
   - Career
   - Relationships with others
   - Relationship with God

2. If you've seen areas where you could become more expansive, what concrete actions can you take to be more sympathetic and supportive to others?

> The most important investment . . . is your own energy. . . .

> **For business to be in harmony with karmic law, it should have also, as an important motive, service to others.**

LESSON TWELVE

WHAT *KIND* OF COMPROMISES?

Often it is only by hindsight that we can know whether a course of action was right or wrong, wise or foolish, informed or ignorant. These things are revealed finally in their results. Experience in such cases is the best teacher. Determine *by your experience* what works best, and what doesn't work if only because it has deprived you of happiness. By our mistakes, wisdom is achieved.

The Principles

Compromise is of several kinds. A compromise of principles is always reprehensible, whether it be from moral weakness or from motives of gain. Always, however, it is our *inner motive* that counts most, whether karmically or for profit.

There are of course many sorts of compromise. Diplomatic compromise usually means merely sacrificing one advantage for another. That is not the kind of compromise that concerns me here. There is mercantile bargaining, engaged in for greater profit. This, too, is not the kind of compromise I intend. There are compromises of love and friendship, which people make to reassure one another of their goodwill; this comes closer to what I mean. And there are the kinds of compromises made in the name of peace when, between conflicting principles, peace seems the more important.

Compromise, in other words, is sometimes right and desirable, and sometimes wrong even if it has a desirable end.

Decisions that people claim to base on "principle" too often equate principle with mere convenience. In business as in government, compromise is often merely a question of agreeing on what is acceptable to all persons concerned. It is in the matter, however, of what is right ethically and spiritually that the question becomes serious. Unfortunately, this may be the most difficult question of all to resolve.

Again, fortunately, these difficult questions of high principle concern us here only rarely. Usually, where business or political or even familial situations are involved, the principles are not spiritual, but only human. Such situations sometimes cry out for compromise, but the issues involved are not absolute; they indicate, rather, a need for harmony, or for expanded sympathy.

Supposing a decision in business concerns an acquisition of wealth on the part of some, but a loss to others of freedom and dignity: to decide in favor of the few at a cost to the many would be unprincipled. A decision, again, that is based on self-interest but is likely to create enemies is almost always unprincipled. A decision that seems perfectly reasonable from an organizational standpoint, therefore, but that is sure to do harm, should be rejected as contrary to right principle. Often, making a right decision is fraught with difficulties.

Sometimes a purely human consideration is at stake. Years ago there was a member at Ananda Village who decided to leave the community. He requested a higher recompense for his home than the rest felt was reasonable. In this case, the majority were clearly in the right: This man had, admittedly, devoted many hours to building his home as he claimed, but the time he'd spent was not commensurate with the quality of his workmanship. Why, the rest of the community asked, should they bear the cost of his ineptitude? Our accountant especially argued that the value of the building should be set according to some exact standard, and of course he was right. However, no standards had been set so far. The accountant concluded his argument by saying, "It's a matter of principle." True indeed. The principle to which our accountant referred was that to give in might establish a dangerous precedent.

I took another line, however. Admitting that his line of reasoning was both right and reasonable, I said, "But isn't it an important principle also to be *compassionate*?"

This introduced a different, though unbusinesslike, dimension into the discussion. For reasons I won't go into here, compassion *was* important in this case. Everyone accepted my opinion, and eventually realized that the decision had, for a spiritual family, been right. As a precedent, moreover, that decision did us no harm at all. Rather, it helped to show those who came that our way was to do our best to follow one of our basic principles: "People are more important than things." Our decision in his case underscored the basic fact that Ananda is run on human, and not on only monetary, principles.

Sometimes there are considerations in business, also, that should be kept in mind apart from the usual "bottom line" of profit. I urge all students of these lessons to keep the importance of human values in mind. If someone insists that business has no other purpose than to make money, he overlooks the vital fact that concentration on money alone causes one's humanity to shrivel up. What is money, indeed, without happiness?

Often it is only by hindsight that we can know whether a course of action was right or wrong, wise or foolish, informed or ignorant. These things are revealed finally in their results. Experience in such cases is the best teacher. Determine *by your experience* what works best, and what doesn't work if only because it has deprived you of happiness. By our mistakes, wisdom is achieved.

Another point worthy of consideration is the character of those on whose decisions people depend. The American Revolution was an example. What justified it in the end was the high character of its leaders.

Loyalty is a virtue, of course. Should the American colonists, then, have remained loyal to the king of England? Many thought this was their duty. The revolution, however, was justified not only by its results, inasmuch as it paved the way for the birth of a great nation, no longer a subsidiary colony of the British Empire. The American revolution was justified above all by the character of its principals. George Washington, John Adams, Thomas Jefferson: these and other great men and women sufficed by their own shining integrity to validate the revolution.

The English king, on his side, was not loyal to his subjects. His very lack rendered null and void, surely, his claim on their loyalty. He should have been the first to show loyalty to his subjects. Instead, he repeatedly expressed contempt for them and for their eminently reasonable demands. When a ruler denies to his subjects their human dignity, he relinquishes the right to rule them.

The question of principles arose in my own life also in my dismissal from my Guru's organization, for reasons which I knew were untrue and unjust. Had I tried subsequently to foment rebellion, the results would have shown me in the wrong, for they would have produced disharmony. Had I insisted that I alone was right, and everyone else, wrong; or had those over me pleaded in vain that I reconsider my position: in every such case the probabilities would have mounted that they were in the right and my own position, therefore, untenable. Instead, as soon as I was informed that my work didn't have their support, I gave up all my plans, in the name of harmony. Later, they summoned me from India to New York, where two of them met me to inform me that I had been categorically dismissed. I pleaded, "Please, put it in writing that I will do nothing for the rest of my life but wash dishes. I'll sign that paper immediately. I came to this organization for no other purpose than to find God through service to my Guru."

"*Never!*" was the reply. Later on during our talk they told me, "From now on we want to forget that you ever lived!" What could I do? My life, so it seemed to me, had just been destroyed.

In retrospect, what do I see? It has become clear that they did me a signal favor! For they released me to serve my Guru in ways that he himself had told me to do. I believe that for me it was right to offer them every possible compromise, not out of weakness, but out of a desire to establish harmony in the family of our Guru. For, of course, I wasn't *their* disciple. It was to him that I had sworn my loyalty. My repeated offers of compromise, however, were rejected out of hand: an outcome that turned out the best for me, at last.

To offer compromise in good faith is, I think, right and, often, necessary. It clears the path ahead. With a clear conscience, one can devote all his energy to his next step, for he has been released from any possible doubt as to the correctness of his course.

What about my erstwhile companions? Did their rejection of my offers of compromise help them in the end? That is for them, not for me, to say. In the end, what must concern everyone is his own clarity. I was, and remain still, their friend; that, as far as I personally am concerned, ends the story. "My spine is straight," as an Indian friend of mine used to put it. In my own work, however, I am still convinced that I owe it to those who work with me to give loyalty to them, first.

India, which consisted not of colonists but of a people conquered, was doubly right in its non-violent revolution. Indians were right also in their so-called "Sepoy Mutiny," though not necessarily in all of the acts they committed during that mutiny. India's independence was karmically speaking, in fact, a foregone conclusion. And England's fall, which is in the process of happening, was also a foregone karmic conclusion.

There are human and spiritual laws ruling in these matters. Businessmen, and not only spiritual people, need to learn those laws and to live by them.

Legend has it that when Martin Luther broke away from the Roman Catholic Church, he posted a challenge on the church door at the castle of Wittenberg listing ninety-five Church dogmas and practices that, in his consideration, conflicted with Scripture. "Here I stand," he declared. "I cannot do otherwise. God help me. Amen."

Luther was convinced that his stand was principled, for he showed that certain Church practices opposed the actual teachings of Jesus Christ. Luther failed to understand, however, that mere words, even when appearing in scripture, can never be absolute. Words are too susceptible of misinterpretation. Scriptural truths must be discerned in their *spirit*, not in their terminology. Scripture cannot be written as a legal document, in which lawyers try to close every possible loophole. Even legal documents, moreover, are fallible. For this reason, scriptural statements can actually be used to support unjust, and not only just, causes. As the saying has it, "Even the devil quotes scripture."

Luther himself had a fundamental disagreement in later years with Zwingli, another Protestant leader. At the famous Marburg Colloquy, the two of them, basing their arguments wholly on scripture, disagreed as to one of its fundamental meanings. The truth depends at last, then, on *wise interpretation*. The very teaching in the Bible, "Love thy neighbor," is open to diverse interpretations, depending on whether, for instance, the interpretation is made by a saint or by a libertine! The truth is, one can judge only by experience—one's own experience, or someone else's.

I lived for several years with my Guru. It astonished me to see how often his words, which he enunciated clearly and forcefully, were understood variously by different disciples. Always, I realized, it depended on how wise they were, themselves.

Religious wars have been a blight on the tree of history. They have been fought by protagonists who had, one supposes, equally sincere convictions.

The outcome of an action is the most certain test of its validity. It takes action, of course, for results to be obtained. And that is why people need the freedom to make their own mistakes. Fortunately, that experience doesn't always have to be one's own. From studying the lives of others, many lessons can be learned.

Luther's uncompromising challenge to the established order was the key event in the Protestant Reformation. It took moral courage on his part, certainly. Yet I wonder how much of it was courage, and how much, sheer stubbornness. Usually, an adamant stand like that demonstrates refusal even to listen to reason. To decide whether a person who stands firmly by his beliefs is really only being rigid, and whether or not compromise would be the wiser path, requires an open mind.

On one of several ocean voyages that my family made to America during my childhood, my younger brother Bob invented a private game of his own. He would run headlong down the deck, keeping his eyes tightly shut and bumping blithely into anything or anyone in his way. He was only a child, after all, and people therefore thought him cute. Indeed, by means of his game he made many friends.

For an adult to rush through life similarly, however, keeping his eyes closed to all danger, would be madness. And that may be the correct diagnosis for adults who refuse to listen to reason. Religionists make that mistake constantly when they declare that their values are absolute. Martin Luther's claim was absolutist. The Roman Catholic Church, in its dogmas, was even more absolutist. Indeed, dogmatism increases in direct proportion to one's inability to prove his point.

Ananda Moyi Ma, a great woman saint of modern India, and as non-dogmatic a person as I have ever known, had a favorite way of describing God: "It (the Spirit) is, and It isn't, and neither is It, nor is It not." A conundrum? Certainly! Her meaning was simply that God is beyond all rational explanation.

Atheism, by contrast, can be justified only by opposing it logically to reasoned definitions of God. It cannot be justified by opposing it to higher states of consciousness, for those states transcend reason and must be *experienced*. It would be absurd even for an atheist, moreover, to challenge the obvious fact that he exists, though some have tried to do so. The French philosopher René Descartes tried to prove that we exist by stating, "I think, therefore I am." His so-called "proof" is deeply flawed, for we are actually more conscious when we don't think, but are deeply aware: for example, during deep spiritual experiences.

Atheists who advance rational arguments to prove the nonexistence of God depend on a long line of reasoning, piling premise upon premise as if building a wall of bricks. Looking down from above, the base of that structure is often so far down as to be invisible and lost, to one's befuddlement.

There is a story from the life of William James, the philosopher and psychologist. An old woman had listened to his discourse on the nature of the universe. She corrected him sternly. "Mr. James," she said, "you're quite wrong. The world doesn't spin through space, as you claim. It sits on the back of a turtle."

"Thank you for the information," replied the famous man, humoring her. "Now then, tell me: What does that turtle stand on?"

"Why," she replied, as if stating the obvious, "on the back of another turtle."

"I see," said the famous sage with a twinkle. "Please tell me, then: What does that second turtle stand on?"

The woman was prepared for this challenge. Seeing the direction of his reasoning, she raised an admonitory finger. "It's no use, Mr. James," she scolded. "It's turtles all the way down!"

At that point I imagine he only smiled, letting her feel that she'd won the argument. There is no other way to reply to ignorance. A mistake often made is to try to drive the nail of logic into a metal rod. The attempt is useless for both victor and vanquished. Compromise, in certain matters, is impossible.

Indeed, the woman's reasoning was not wholly unlike many people's arguments for atheism. Premise rests upon premise, like that "totem pole" of turtles, until the base of that pillar of reasoning is lost to sight altogether.

James Crowe, a psychologist, once demanded of his students rhetorically, "Has man evolved more by evolving a brain than the elephant by evolving a trunk?" Just think how many "turtles" had to stand one on the other in his line of reasoning!

His first premise stood on the presumption (perfectly normal in modern biology, actually) that evolution is purely accidental. That premise totters upon another: that the brain, which is a physical organ, is the *producer* of thought.

The third "turtle-premise" is that consciousness is the product of that thinking.

The fourth is that the elephant's trunk functions separately from its guiding brain. (Crowe cannot have taken this point into consideration, however; the objection, once seen, is too telling to ignore.)

The fifth premise is that awareness is no more significant to the elephant than is its trunk, which it uses for grasping leaves and raising them to its mouth.

And so the logic goes on, plunging to ever-more-murky depths, but never so far down as to reach two fundamental questions: first, If the elephant is not conscious of what it eats, what motive has it for eating at all? And second, If the human brain is no more functional than a feeder, how can one account for man's curiosity in even asking such a question? It isn't that a physical organ, the brain, is more "useful" to him than his nose. What makes the brain such a wonder is man's very capacity to wonder.

A man once challenged me following a lecture I'd given, "I'm an atheist. Can you define God in such a way as to help me accept what you say about Him?"

I paused in reflection a moment, then suggested, "Why not try thinking of God as the highest potential you can imagine for yourself?"

He was momentarily taken aback. Then he replied in a tone of astonishment, "Well, yeah, I can live with that!"

It is foolish to argue on such abstract subjects as absolute truth. As Paramhansa Yogananda put it, "Fools argue: wise men discuss." Often only a very faint dividing line exists between what appears as moral courage and what is, in fact, pigheadedness.

It is not usual, of course, for business people to concern themselves with absolute truths—at least, not in their discussions on work. Those interchanges concern relativities. In such discussions, it is easier to accept the need for compromise. What hinders agreement among businesspeople is not bigotry, but conflicting desires. Once a businessman has recognized that selfishness is self-limiting, he will incline, more naturally than most theologians, to be fair-minded. It is even to his advantage to see other points of view than his own, for it helps him to make his points more convincingly.

To refuse absolutely to compromise is like taking up arms in battle. It is a confrontational attitude, reminiscent of a line in *Autobiography of a Yogi*: "Reason had forsaken him, but he could still shout."

Many years ago, I had an instructive lesson in my own need for open-mindedness without sacrificing my basic beliefs. It was when I was doing the research for my book, *Crises in Modern Thought* (since then renamed, *Out of the Labyrinth*). I had lived for fourteen years in a monastery where, for all of us, certain beliefs were self-evident and in no way controversial.

A time came in my life, with the crisis I referred to above, when I realized that I was free to follow my Guru's instructions to me to write books. Just before my dismissal, in fact, I came upon an article in *Span*, the United States Information Service magazine in India, written by the head of the philosophy department at MIT (Massachusetts Institute of Technology). The article explained certain major trends in modern philosophical thinking.

My training had been altogether different from that widely accepted line of reasoning. My Guru had schooled us in the subtle teachings of ancient India. In light of that training, I could see clearly that modern philosophy was fatally flawed, even in its own terms. Some of its errors, indeed, were so blatant that the article astonished me.

It would make a wonderful contribution to the history of philosophy, I thought, were *someone* to write a book exposing the fallacies of modern materialistic philosophy. Present-day insistence that everything is "meaningless" rests on modern scientific biases.

Researching this subject was, for me, a highly uncongenial task. To finish that book required all of sixteen years—squeezed in among other activities. My difficulty lay in confronting my own narrowness of thought. It was natural for me to ridicule points of view that were, to my mind, patently absurd. I had no choice but to acknowledge, however, that many thinkers whose ideas I wanted to confront were brilliant, even if they had succumbed in their thinking to certain false assumptions of modern times. I was sure that many of the supposedly proved "facts" on which their thinking was based would someday be discarded—as many have, indeed, gone out of fashion in the past. Scientific claims, and even "proofs," are by no means infallible. Every insufficiently tested premise can create a spreading web of error. Meanwhile, however, I had to accept those concepts provisionally, at face value. Otherwise, my arguments would fail to convince those whom I wanted to reach. I had then to analyze their data to see if they necessarily dictated the conclusions that had been reached on the basis of them. I had to pay close attention to other arguments and show them respect, for most of them (not all) were persons of integrity.

To do all this was, for me, a great challenge. I had to go into the camp of the "enemy," so to speak, listen *with an open mind* to his arguments, and then—not by offering alternate facts, but working *from the same set of facts*—challenge his conclusions. Needless to say, the task was by no means enjoyable for me. All my sympathies lay in the diametrically opposite direction.

Fortunately for me, I emerged unscathed. Indeed, I came out at the other end of that dark tunnel armed with new insights that I could never have gained in any other way.

One thing I learned as I deeply pondered those points was how important it is to keep an open mind, and therefore to be willing to compromise, if necessary—not by sacrificing one's principles, but by questioning the structure of ideas that has been raised on those principles. I had forced myself to *listen* to opinions that were utterly incompatible with my own, expressed often with a superior sneer for people's faith in God. I had even to consider sincerely whether those people might be right. And I found, in the end, that my understanding of the teachings of *Vedanta* and *Yoga* was deeper than ever. I had, moreover, managed to avoid the temptation—which, in thinking, is a pitfall—to reject out of hand points of view which I was certain were wrong. Should any reader pounce on me with the cry, "Aha! In other words, you, too, were biased in your thinking!" I would reply with calm conviction, "No, I was not. And it cost me a great deal not to be."

I fully realized that the people I was opposing were widely accepted in the world as being some of the most brilliant thinkers of our times. No matter how brilliant a thinker, however, he cannot *invent* truth. It dismayed me to realize that most studious people would dismiss my conclusions anyway, and not give them a second thought, for they themselves were biased in their thinking. They would consider it a mere presumption on my part to have taken on all those famous people. I reminded myself, on the other hand, that the truth simply *is*: It cannot be arrived at by presumption. One must never, if he seeks the truth sincerely, leave the last word to any so-called "authority." He must gaze at the facts clearly, and keep an unprejudiced mind. What matters is not *who* speaks, but simply *what* is being said.

Throughout history, I reminded myself, some of the brightest minds had been shown, in the end, to have been wrong. And though I myself accepted completely the authority of my Guru and India's great sages, I had to set aside even that faith, at least provisionally. It was a solace to me that those great sages have always been in agreement with one another, and have shown a wisdom far beyond the brilliance of any modern skeptic. I had, however, to judge *for myself* the supposed "facts" proclaimed by modern science.

My faith, I am happy to say, is now stronger than it ever was, and I am in a position to champion with clear modern logic the wisdom of great saints and masters, who are far wiser than I, but who have not taken the trouble to wrestle with this particular set of follies. My own integrity has increased owing to the fact that, for a time, I used my reasoning mind, as others have, to work through what they've presented to the world as conclusions based on facts.

Later, when I founded Ananda Village, I realized that I had trained myself to listen with an open mind to others' points of view; to compromise with these points of view when necessary, without sacrificing my principles, and even to change certain directions in my own thinking, if anyone succeeded in showing me wrong on any point. For what counts in the end, after all, is only the truth.

Human nature does not find it easy to accept compromise, particularly when one is in the stronger position. Compromise, in such cases, must come not from weakness, but from self-honesty.

Applying these considerations to business situations and to the issue of material success, I understand more deeply than most people, perhaps, the need for frequent compromise. Especially when what is at stake is not a high principle—and even when principles do seem to be at stake—the mind must be held open to every possibility.

To return to my example of Martin Luther: Both he and his Church superiors thought their disagreement was based on principle. The main principle, in the Church's view, was obedience. Ought someone who is committed to a religious path *always* to obey his superiors, even if he considers them wrong? And ought a worker in a business organization always to comply with his boss, even if he thinks the boss wrong?

I would answer that it is important to comply, in certain matters at least, simply in the name of harmony. In other matters, however, and particularly in matters of conscience, to compromise might be a mistake.

I have read of young novices in Catholic monasteries who were told to plant seedlings *upside down* in the ground as a test of their obedience. Common sense rebels against complying with such unreasonable demands. Integrity, moreover, rebels against surrendering one's own will to someone who, one has reason to believe, lacks wisdom.

I cannot imagine that I am unusual in having had, in my life, to deal with what seemed to me unreasonable demands from others—not only bosses and superiors, but many who tried to get me to conform to what they wanted.

What I've always tried to do—and I think my experience might be helpful to others—is affirm an inward sense of freedom, so that my reactions would proceed from my own integrity, and not be influenced by others' opinions. I've then considered all aspects of the matter, impartially. If the demands seemed reasonable to me, I've followed them. If I considered them unreasonable, it wasn't that I necessarily rejected them. Sometimes, I decided it was good to submit, at least for the sake of my own spiritual development, as an exercise in humility perhaps, or to help someone else, and in the interests of harmony. (Few decisions, after all, are matters of life and death!) I've never given anyone reason to believe that he'd "beaten me down," however. When I've compromised, it was always because such was my free decision, not because I'd been driven to it.

My own Guru's recommendation on obedience was that it should be given unconditionally only to someone of true wisdom—specifically, to a true guru whose guidance one has accepted. Otherwise, he said, blind or forced obedience can weaken one's will power.

Monastic discipline is often imposed intentionally, indeed, for the very purpose of weakening the will. Religious orders often teach that any manifestation of will power indicates *self*-will. Nonsense! Spineless people will never find God. The real reason religious superiors don't like disagreement from those under them is that they cannot give reasonable answers!

I urge everyone who wants material success to live by three principles above all: First, work always with a sense of inner freedom. Second, work for over-all peace and harmony, even if doing so entails making difficult, though acceptable, compromises. Third, offer up to God the fruits of everything you do.

Sri Krishna in the Bhagavad Gita counseled action without desire for the fruits of action. His counsel should serve as a guideline not only for devotees, but for people seeking success in the world. By non-attachment, one is much more likely to succeed, if only because he will then be free to change his direction at a moment's notice.

Many years of experimenting with these truths have convinced me that, when one follows them, everything turns out eventually for the best.

The early American "rebels" (as they were considered by the English) also offered their actions up to God, from a desire to please Him. Early in this course of lessons I quoted a friend of mine from South America saying to me, "The difference between your country and our countries in South America is that yours was settled by people who were motivated by their desire for freedom of worship. Settlers in our countries, on the other hand, came in quest of gold. Just see the consequences. Your land has flourished, whereas ours have been in constant turmoil."

India's freedom, also, was won by spiritual means. Therefore her prosperity is assured. My Guru declared several times that India and the United States of America would someday unite to lead the world toward progress, prosperity, and happiness, inwardly and outwardly.

The Application

In seeking to know whether a course of action that you contemplate is right or wrong, consult, among other things, the pages of history. Compromise has been effective only when it has been offered from a position of strength, not of weakness. One's strength may be moral as it was in Gandhi's case, or it may be military. In any case, it *must* be strength, not cowardly weakness.

A study was sponsored by a certain group in Congress in America who wanted support for their claim that disarmament was the best way to persuade all countries to disarm. Several hundred thousands of dollars were spent on this research, but the results proved embarrassing. *In every single case*, countries in the historic past that had laid down their arms were later conquered by others that were militarily strong.

This discovery was, as I said, far from welcome to those who believed in peace and harmony maintained by a sacrifice of military strength. One cannot argue with the facts, however. Perhaps, in some more spiritual age in the future, the way to peace will be paved by general disarmament. If so, that age is still distant from us. As Paramhansa Yogananda said, "The reason India won her independence by non-violent means was that the English are gentlemen. Had the struggle been against Russian communism, however, it would have failed. If you try practicing non-violence on a tiger—unless your power of love is very strong—you'll finish practicing it in the tiger's stomach!"

Be realistic! As my Guru once put it to me, "Be practical in your idealism." Do what works. Also, within that framework, do also what comes as close as possible to dharma. Compromise is sometimes necessary, but, as I have said, never compromise from a position of weakness.

I may seem to have committed that mistake myself in my life, but that was a perception by others. It was, in fact, in strength that I offered the ultimate compromise of which I was capable. For I offered to *give* Ananda to my gurubhais in his organization. They thought this was a plea for help, and I didn't mind their misconception. I was simply holding firmly to the truth as I myself understood it. After several years they actually tried to destroy me by legal means. That attempt ended in failure, and I and those with me became, in the end, all the stronger.

MEDITATION

In any action you contemplate, try to ascertain the rightness of your principles. Remember always, when doing so, that firm conviction is not proof in itself that your principles are right. Offer your proposed course of action mentally, therefore, to the spiritual eye in the forehead. Ask God and your own superconscious, "Is this action justified? Is it *dharmic*? Is it fair to everyone concerned?"

Then listen to the feeling response in your heart. Seek there your answer. Is that feeling one of calmness? Does it suggest peaceful confirmation? Or does it suggest a certain restless uneasiness? If your heart is receptive, you will learn more and more to trust its response in everything.

AFFIRMATION

"My will, Lord, is to do Thy will alone, for actions alone that are in harmony with Thee can lead to true success."

POINTS TO REMEMBER

1. Compromise is sometimes right and desirable, and sometimes wrong even if it has a desirable end. A compromise of principles is always reprehensible.

2. A decision that seems perfectly reasonable from an organizational standpoint, but that is sure to do harm, should be rejected as contrary to right principle. Always keep in mind the importance of human values.

3. Often it is only by hindsight that we know whether a course of action was right or wrong. Determine *by your experience* what works best, and what doesn't work. By our mistakes, wisdom is achieved.

4. To offer compromise in good faith often clears the path ahead. One can then devote all his energy to his next step, for he has been released from any possible doubt as to the correctness of his course.

5. As Paramhansa Yogananda put it, "Fools argue: wise men discuss." Often only a very faint dividing line exists between what appears as moral courage and what is, in fact, pigheadedness.

6. Selfishness is self-limiting. Seeing other points of view than one's own helps one to make his points more convincingly.

7. One must gaze at the facts clearly, and keep an unprejudiced mind. What matters is not *who* speaks, but simply *what* is being said.

8. Compromise must come not from weakness, but from self-honesty.

9. In business situations, frequent compromise is necessary. The mind must be held open to every possibility.

10. Obedience should be given unconditionally only to someone of true wisdom. Otherwise, my guru said, blind or forced obedience can weaken one's will power.

11. Three important principles for material success: First, work always with a sense of inner freedom. Second, work for over-all peace and harmony, even if doing so entails making difficult, though acceptable, compromises. Third, offer up to God the fruits of everything you do.

12. By non-attachment, or action without desire for the fruits of action, one is much more likely to succeed, if only because he will then be free to change his direction at a moment's notice.

13. Firm conviction is not proof in itself that your principles are right. Offer your proposed course of action mentally to the spiritual eye in the forehead. Ask God and your own superconscious, "Is this action *dharmic*? Is it fair to everyone concerned?" Then listen to the feeling response in your heart. Does it suggest peaceful confirmation? Or does it suggest a certain restless uneasiness? If your heart is receptive, you will learn more and more to trust its response in everything.

WORKBOOK IDEAS
by Joseph Bharat Cornell

Centeredness—Key to Inner Strength

Last year while I was in New Jersey on a lecture tour, Thomas, my host, told how centering his energy helped him calm a potentially dangerous situation. Thomas is the superintendent of a small, rural school district. He had recently suspended the high school wrestling coach for verbally abusing his players. The suspension had enraged the coach and his large, extended family—so much so, that some of them had physically threatened Thomas.

One Sunday Thomas was working alone in the district office when four cars came to a screeching halt in front of his building. Out came a furious mob of the coach's relatives. As they charged into the building, Thomas called his daughter to notify school security.

In the seconds remaining, Thomas centered himself, and waited for the approaching storm. His "guests" barged into his office and began yelling, trying to intimidate him. Calmly, and without fear, Thomas listened to their tirade about why he was wrong to suspend the coach, and then quietly explained why he had made that decision.

The coach's relatives were very physical people, who respected strength. Thomas's demonstration of courage and centeredness won them over. Soon afterwards, they not only accepted his explanation, but also helped to resolve the situation with the coach.

In this particular case, Thomas didn't to compromise. His clarity and calmness resolved the controversy. We all want to influence others positively. The clearer and more centered we are, the more we can do so, because centered energy is more magnetic than dissipated, reactive energy.

The Secret of Winning People

The difference between self-centeredness and Self-centeredness is one of direction. A contractive ego refers everything back to itself, while one who is centered in the Self is broad in his sympathies. A person whose consciousness is expansive feels himself in others. This feeling of being united with Life makes him extremely effective in working with others. When Mahatma Gandhi lived in South Africa, the British administrators told newly arrived officials from England, "Don't go near Gandhi; he'll get to you." Gandhi treated everyone as a friend, even his opponents. His love and fair-mindedness caused the British officials—if they weren't careful—to appreciate his point of view, too.

ACTION ITEMS:
1. How we think is predicated on how we *feel*, since feeling influences reason. When you negotiate with others, use the suggestions below to foster communication and trust:

   - Pray that the truth prevail.
   - See yourself as the other person's friend.

- Appeal to that person's altruism.
- Concentrate on presenting solutions.
- Look for points of agreement.
- Forge lasting bonds.

2. If you anticipate any disharmony during your meeting, pray beforehand, using these guidelines:

   a. Ask God to guide you and open your heart and mind to His will.

   b. Visualize your upcoming discussion and surround everyone with divine light and love.

   c. Remove from your heart any criticism or fear of others. Feel only harmony flowing from you to them.

   d. Clearly sense every participant's willingness to accept the highest good.

   e. If you have a controversial topic to discuss, introduce it during your visualization. Feel everyone calmly considering it without resistance.

This way of praying attunes you to the superconscious and its unitive view of life.

LESSON THIRTEEN

KEEP YOUR FEET ON THE GROUND

Material success through yoga principles means, among other things, probing *beneath* the ordinary to subtler levels of insight.

The Principles

In the last lesson I quoted some advice my Guru once gave me: "Be practical in your idealism." Those words were in fact a reprimand, though he couched them, as usual, tactfully. He had recently finished writing his commentary on the Bhagavad Gita, and in May of 1950 he told me he expected the book to be out before Christmas in December of that year.

Later in the day I was asked to take Laurie Pratt's mail over to her. Laurie was the Master's chief editor, and at this time was editing his new book. She lived in a small house not far from the Master's retreat. When I saw her, I happily mentioned his words to her. "Why," she protested, "I couldn't *possibly* get the book out so soon!"

Later that day, I again saw the Master and told him her response, my thought being that he might want to adjust his expectations accordingly. His reply surprised me. "Delays! Always delays!" His tone of voice held an eloquence beyond his words. After a pause, he added, "I will write to her. You take the letter over to her."

I hadn't realized how anxious he was to get the book out that year. Decades later, I saw that he'd known that if the book failed to come out that year, it wouldn't come out during his lifetime. I think, in fact, that his main concern was that in that case it might be over-edited—always a danger when editors labor too long on a book. As things turned out, fifty years passed before that book finally saw the light of day.

At that time I knew only that Laurie's reply distressed him. It had been my mistake, I felt, to report her words to him. As I handed her the letter, I remarked apologetically, "I'm sorry. It's my fault."

Later I learned that he hadn't even touched on this subject in his letter! Perhaps he wrote only to encourage her, by reiterating how important it was that she get the book finished and keep focused on her editing work. Laurie, of course, the moment she heard my callow apology, understood what the letter really intended, and that he was displeased with her. She too, of course, was distressed, especially so because in Master's letter he must have expressed himself very supportively. Thus I became, quite innocently, the cause of friction between them.

Reflecting on that episode over the many years since it happened, I have wondered whether more might not have been involved than I realized, after the scolding he gave me subsequently. I had evidently blundered insensitively into a situation where care was needed. Any karma I incurred by that rash act was paid off in great pain for me, years later, when disharmony shattered my friendship with Laurie. She it was who drove me out of the work for reasons that only projected her displeasure with me, and were not related to any objective reality. Perhaps Master was distressed because he foresaw that future, and realized it was now inevitable. (Who can fathom the subtle understanding of a master?)

It was after that episode of the letter that Master said to me, "You must be practical in your idealism." He said it with so much force that I might have taken it as a hint, had I been more aware, that there would be karmic consequences for myself. Today, fifty-four years later, I realize that the reason he scolded me was also, as he had already said to me, because he wanted me to serve others as a teacher and spiritual guide. It was important that I learn to be more sensitively aware of people's deeper realities. "Do what works," I remarked earlier. This advice means also to be conscious of the possible consequences of one's actions.

There was much I still needed to learn, and my Guru did his best to help me in the process. Evidently, one thing I needed was to learn more tact. For though I was young and inexperienced at the time, I was certainly old enough to be aware of what I was doing. My Guru was saying to me sternly, "Grow up!"

It often amazed me to observe how subtle his insight was into human nature. What is particularly interesting in this thirteenth lesson is the need to "tune in" sensitively to subtle realities. Keeping oneself grounded means much more than the advice one so often hears, "Don't live with your head in the clouds." Indeed, some people *need* to be more aware of clouds than of the land's contours. An airplane pilot's first concern, for example, must be less with the ground than with the air. In this age of growing energy-awareness, material success often depends more on nonmaterial realities than on earthly ones.

A farmer who earns his livelihood by growing vegetables may scoff if he sees someone sifting the soil for minerals. A bird, listening for the call of its mate, may not even notice beautiful music if it is played by a string quartet. If, to you, keeping your feet on the ground means only to remain focused on what is familiar, you may succeed in earning a living, or in supporting a family, but your success will never be outstanding.

The yoga science helps people to probe beneath familiar realities. It makes them more conscious of their breathing, for instance. It helps them also to deepen their awareness of subtle realities of the body such as energy and consciousness. Material success through yoga principles means, among other things, probing *beneath* the ordinary to subtler levels of insight.

One purpose I have had in writing this lesson, then, is to probe beneath the commonplace. In past centuries, when people thought of matter as immutable, keeping one's feet on the ground meant no more than learning to accept reality as we see it. In business, that advice meant not to sit dreaming up airy schemes for moneymaking when the means of doing so were already well-known and obvious. Nowadays, people, recognizing their need to be practical, are aware that realism includes an awareness that seemingly "airy nothings" may contain important realities.

People are increasingly aware that energy is the very basis of matter. Thus, the reality of energy demands consideration in the merchandising world also—indeed, in almost anything that one does. A customer is more likely to buy, for example, if his *energy* is stimulated. Lively music is often played in stores and malls because of this realization. In time, I hope this dawning awareness will someday be lifted to higher levels, for I cannot but suspect that many customers find the present-day blaring, restless music more of an irritant than a stimulus. Such restless music is, I believe, more likely to bounce people out the door. At least, that is how many people I know react to it! To stimulate people's energy without jarring on their nerves seems to me far more sensible, for it will encourage customers to linger—fondly, perhaps—over items that attract them, and to decide more carefully what they will buy. Often, people who linger longer buy more. Music, in other words, that is universally pleasing, instead of tearing at the nerves with jagged rhythms and anguished harmonies, is more likely to result in satisfied customers who will leave the shop smiling.

In the malls of Gurgaon, south of New Delhi, music is sometimes played that is melodic and soothing to listen to.* The fact that better music is now being played with greater frequency makes me think that a few shopkeepers, at least, are beginning to appreciate the logic of what I have suggested here. In other words, it "works" to play music over loudspeakers in the stores, but it works better if the music isn't so loud and invasive that it distracts people from their shopping. Americans, at least, will appreciate it if I say that Coney Island makes different demands of one than a bookstore.

As recently as a century ago, shops kept their merchandise out of reach behind counters, where the customers couldn't touch it and, perhaps, slip it into their pockets or purses. Even today, many pharmacies in Italy wrap purchases carefully by hand, instead of simply placing them in a bag. In America, where these things were first studied carefully to find what works best, it was learned long ago that wrapping purchases took an unnecessarily long time, and made the customer more impatient than grateful. (After all, when they get home they'll only strip off that wrapping paper anyway!)

The American supermarket concept, which was new when I moved there as a boy, must have met initial resistance, representing as it did a radical departure from traditional merchandising. I can imagine the scenes in board rooms across America where directors, accustomed to seeing products kept safely out of reach of the customers, expressed concern at this revolutionary concept. Some "graybeards" must have objected, "If the customers are allowed to touch a few things before they select them, they may also appropriate some of them surreptitiously!" One visualizes them wrangling back and forth in board rooms, and imagines the protest, "Just think how much of our merchandise will be stolen!"

"Well," must have been the reply, "there may be losses, but think of the huge increase in sales!" That, partly, is what I mean by urging businessmen to think in terms of energy, even more than of the specific items they are selling. This idea was tested until merchants across the country were finally convinced that it was a clever way of stimulating customers to buy things that they hadn't even thought they wanted.

Most people, on entering a shop, have specific needs in mind. The modern shopkeeper tries to interest them enough in what they see around them to get them to pause a little, gaze, and then (perhaps) buy more. At the same time it is better, surely, that they not be stimulated to the point of restlessness, for a restless person is likely to pass on hurriedly from one item to another, and will seldom give any item enough attention to think seriously about buying it. People mustn't be encouraged to resemble those persons in a poem I wrote when I first moved to America at the age of thirteen. The poem describes my early impressions: "They never more than glance at things, / for fear of missing one."

The people in India are rapidly moving to embrace these concepts as well as other features of modern merchandising such as a multitude of attractive displays. The shopkeeper wants to *invite* people's interest. What he sells, therefore, should not be packaged in such a way as merely to inform customers of a product's nature. Bright, pleasing, and colorful

---

* My own music has been played at the Sahara and Metropolitan malls in Gurgaon, and also at the nearby Bristol Hotel.

containers, and an attractive arrangement of merchandise also, are factors that definitely enhance sales. Everyone knows that what really matters is only the contents of a package; still, if you are given a choice between a book with an unattractive cover and one that is colorful and well designed, even though the contents are the same, won't you buy the attractive one? And while nobody thinks of eating the cereal box, if the cereal is pleasingly packaged customers are more likely to buy it.

So many factors are involved in salesmanship nowadays! Those factors are so well known by now that I'm sure I need only mention the fact that these things, too, belong with the advice, "Keep your feet on the ground." The simple reason is that they work.

In past centuries, that advice didn't include being energetically creative. Rather, what it suggested was a dull, colorless, and plodding outlook on life. Matter, in those days, was thought to be solid and substantial, and not awhirl with atoms and virtually flowing in rivers of energy.

As a writer, I've found that sound, rhythm, and verbal "coloring" are as important as the merchandising ideas I've recommended. Nowadays, a writer using a computer can let his ideas flow out onto a page as freely as a brook. I myself used to write laboriously with a pen. The sheer laboriousness of the process, of getting my thoughts onto a page, of thinking them through carefully in advance so as not to have too much rewriting to do afterward, and of being forced to watch helplessly as good ideas flew out the window before I could capture them and put them to good use, forced on me a painful deliberation. The invention of typewriters was a step upward from the days when people could only use quill pens, then fountain pens and pencils. Nothing, however, could compare to the laptop. Before typewriters, sentences tended to be longer than normal speech or than thought. Consequently, people tended to speak ponderously also.

Meanwhile, much more is involved in good writing than sound sentence structure. In this age of energy, especially, writers would be wise to pay more attention to the vibrations of their writing.

When an idea is expressed not only simply and clearly, but *attractively*, readers will give it more attention. I've found that "keeping my feet on the ground" as a writer means visualizing the reader as someone seated across the desk from me. The more real I can make that image in my mind—even to the point of imagining us actually conversing together—the more interesting my writing can become. One problem with writing is that, because writers express only what is in their heads, they may feel out of touch with their readers' actual realities and labor their points endlessly. That is what senile people, or those who've grown deaf, often do who aren't really trying to communicate, but are only rolling out tedious monologues, like rugs.

I usually go over a piece of writing many times—sometimes thirty or even fifty times before I am satisfied not only that I have said what I wanted, but also *communicated* my ideas. Much of that labor is simply a matter of getting the rhythms right. For by its rhythms a sentence can either enliven or deaden a reader's interest. There was a time when I used to read out loud what I had written. Nowadays I no longer feel that need, but the sounds and word sequences remain very important to me, even though I read them silently.

A change in one part of a sentence often requires a compensating change elsewhere—perhaps for no other reason than to maintain the rhythm. It is important also to vary that rhythm, so as to hold the reader's interest. The easiest way of doing that is to change the rhythm unexpectedly. Writers should avoid long sequences of graceful cadences, which lull readers to sleep with their rhythmic monotony.

"But," one may object, "what has writing to do with material success?" Surely it has a great deal to do with it—at least, for those who write for a living! It is vitally important also when writing advertising copy, and for choosing the right wording for a box of merchandise. It is even important in signs announcing a place or a product, which must be brief and succinct even at a cost to good grammar.

"Winston tastes good like a cigarette should" is a famous example of what I mean here. "*As* a cigarette . . ." would be better grammar, but it would not be nearly so forceful. "Good" rhymes aptly with "should." The copy is altogether perfect for what it was designed to do.

An example of deplorable writing, on the other hand, appeared years ago on a sign in a shop in Lugano, Switzerland, located on the elegant via Nassa. I could hardly believe my eyes when I first saw it posted: "The customer is advised that the objects in this shop are for sale. Please don't handle them unnecessarily. If you see something that interests you, don't touch it, but ask one of our salespeople about it. Please, moreover, don't bother them with idle questions. They are not here to gossip." I've paraphrased, but I'm exaggerating very little. The actual sign may have been even ruder. (I was pleased, a year or two later, to see that this offensive announcement had been removed.)

Speaking personally, I'm grateful for the fact that I don't have to write books or music for a living. My books and compositions help to keep afloat the organizations I have founded, but I am under no pressure to write for profit. Thus, when a project holds no personal interest for me, I've been free to reject it and concentrate on writing mostly what I actually wanted to do. I've also been free to devote time to learning how best to express the "music" of my heart. The result has "paid off," evidently, since over three million of my books and recordings have been sold so far.

In anything you do, to keep your feet on the ground means to be sensitive also to the subtle realities of your work. Don't merely "keep your nose to the grindstone." Take the time out to think about what it is you are doing, and *why* you are doing it—as well as about *how* to do your very best in everything that you undertake.

Another important thing to remember is that whatever you do is always, and uniquely, itself. Don't try to make it a carbon copy of anything else, not even of something you yourself have done. To keep your feet on the ground means, among other things, to live in the present. Even when making plans for the future, project your consciousness into that future time as though it were right now.

Keeping your feet on the ground, then, means much more than placing your feet on the earth itself. Bear in mind, in fact, that even the earth is insubstantial, composed of whirling atoms and, relatively speaking, of as much space as exists between the stars in outer space. Above all, remember that the very ground *is energy*.

The more aware you become of these seemingly insubstantial realities, the more you will feel mentally free to contemplate further possibilities for your continued success. Remember, in an age of countless inventions, the most profitable ideas often come from contemplating hidden possibilities in what, heretofore, have seemed mundane realities.

Who could have imagined, a mere one hundred years ago, the things that virtually define our civilization today? As late as 1949, a major science magazine in America predicted that, at the rate computers were shrinking in size, they might someday weigh as little as one ton! Laptops today hold more information than computers once did which required whole rooms to house them. The defining feature of our present world is no longer *what* has been invented—amazing enough as it is—but the realization that there seem to be no limits to the further possibilities of invention.

Keeping your feet on the ground means also, of course, not being absentminded. Whatever you are doing, be focused on it one-pointedly. Don't, on the other hand, let anyone tell you that it is impractical to ponder possibilities that lie beyond the known. To keep your mind on the ground means, as I've said before, to be solution-oriented, not problem-oriented. In a world where matter itself is known to be a manifestation of energy, people are coming to accept that the ground they walk on hasn't the solidity it seems to, to their senses: that even the air we breathe is not the "nothing" that Aristotle claimed, for it is substantial enough to carry huge "air ships," even as the ocean carries huge passenger liners.

People generally, these days, are becoming more and more aware of energy. A flow of electricity generates a magnetic field. Many people are learning also that, as Yogananda taught, will power generates a flow of energy in the body, and solution-consciousness can generate the necessary energy to *attract* success. Solution-consciousness can *attract* ideas, inspirations, and solutions. Problem-consciousness, on the other hand, actually attracts the problems one dreads.

I have been trying, through these lessons, to help you to stimulate your subconscious toward success-consciousness, and—more even than that—toward being solution-oriented. The very rhythms of these sentences are intended to help you toward success. How, you ask? By keeping that thought of success vibrant and alive in mind as I write.

India's great teachers claimed long ago that all things material are composed of vibrations of energy. Those vibrations were, they said, expressed as the contrasting, and therefore self-canceling, movements of *dwaita*, or duality. A way to understand this fact is to compare duality to the movements of ocean waves. Every rising wave is, as I said earlier, balanced out by a corresponding trough. The over-all ocean level remains unaffected by the height of its waves. No storm could alter that level. All creation obeys the principle of duality; everything has its balancing opposite: heat and cold, pleasure and pain, joy and sorrow.

The more you identify yourself with either outward success or with outward failure, the more susceptible you will be to *maya*'s oppositional fluctuation. The more, however, you concentrate not on things, but on mental *attitude*, the sooner you will discover that failure can be transformed to success by a steadily positive attitude toward anything that happens—as a steady wind may gradually uncover a house that lies buried under sand. The opposite is true also: success itself can prove to be a kind of failure if one anticipates the worst.

Many years ago I accepted an offer to teach Indian culture to a hundred young Peace Corps volunteers. I really wanted them to have a deep appreciation for the greatness of that culture, so that they might go as cultural ambassadors and not limit their services to teaching matters such as modern farming techniques. After devoting myself for weeks to this effort, I was forced at last to acknowledge defeat. To the students, this India assignment seemed a gay adventure. The highlight of the week, for them, was Saturday evening when they could go out and carouse.

Failure was a new thing for me. I say this despite the disaster of my dismissal from my Guru's organization, which at least didn't close the door on my heart's dedication to God and Guru. Once I was able to see that apparent defeat in a new light, I realized that I could still follow my Guru's instructions to me. This time, however, I had to face the simple fact of complete failure, and to look about for other teachers to replace me who had the kind of knowledge these lads wanted: five year plans, and the like.

This self-admitted failure had an interesting sequel, however. Once I'd accepted it as a fact—in other words, once I'd "put my feet firmly on the ground" again—I found, much to my surprise, that several students in the class *were* eager for what I could give them. First came one, then two; soon twenty young men were coming regularly to my room every evening, eager for discussion.

Thus, by accepting reality as it was—the reality in this case being my failure—my energy became wholly positive, and I attracted success!

Success depends, in other words, to a great extent on one's willingness to accept reality as it is: as a thing to be faced, if he hasn't the ability to control it.

The worst thing about "keeping one's feet on the ground" is that people usually take that advice to mean placing supreme importance on things, while overlooking human needs and human sentiments. They become, consequently, selfish and self-centered. Human considerations are, however, an important part of most realities with which human beings have to deal.

Long ago I worked under someone whose idea of keeping one's feet on the ground was to squelch any suggestion I made that hadn't been endorsed by years of experience. More and more frequently, my suggestions were met with exasperation: "It just isn't *practical!*" What that meant, I discovered in time, was only, "This idea hasn't been tried before. We must follow custom and tradition, and not take chances that might turn out to have been foolish!" What was being said, in effect, was, "Keep your feet on the ground." The problem we faced was that we each had very different ideas as to the meaning of that word, "ground."

Perhaps what I am introducing here is a revolutionary concept. Nevertheless, I give it as the fruit of experience. If you want to achieve notable success in your life, and don't want merely to "make a living," have the courage to break new trails. We live in an age of energy. People cannot afford to be too rigidly matter-conscious. It is amazing, for example, that a whole library of information today can be condensed onto one hard disk in a computer! Times *have* changed, clearly.

The Application

People often confuse a positive attitude with wishful thinking. They associate negative attitudes, on the other hand, with being realistic. Thus, they incline more to view things negatively than positively. Realism, however, needn't at all be a wet sponge!

What I have tried to do in this lesson is point out that positive thinking, if it is directed wisely, can become a kind of magnet, actually *attracting* success. Negative thinking, on the other hand, attracts failure. Since success and failure are both part of the total reality of life, failure itself is no more a demonstration of reality than success is. Failure at anything may, indeed, be turned to success if one will only change his attitude, and therefore his magnetism.

The difference between positive attitudes and wishful thinking is wisdom, born of experience. It is wise to test new concepts so as to make sure they work. To set foot too confidently onto boggy ground would be foolish. When you have reason to doubt the firmness of what you walk on, tread cautiously. Don't, however, have a prior expectation of unsafety. To do so would be negative thinking.

If your place is to advise people, tell them not to place their feet on the ground unless they know the ground to be safe. Too often, people in the past gave that advice because walking, to them, was the only way to travel. It didn't mean what the expression means today, when it conveys a suggestion of challenge to new ideas.

If no one had ever tried riding a horse, everyone might still be going by foot. Going back farther in time, cave men might still be trudging about looking for something or someone to clobber. Farmers might still be lumbering about in bullock carts. Railway travelers, proud of their modernity, might still be bouncing along on rails. And automobile associations might greet the suggestion of air travel as a pipe dream. Nowadays, interplanetary travel is still confined to science fiction, but few people anymore would scoff at the thought that it might be possible in the future, at least, to travel to other planets.

Who today would consider it literally wise to say, "Keep your feet on the ground"? The knowledgeable answer to that advice might be, "What ground?" What the advice really means today is, in the modern vernacular: "Get real!"

Modern science is looking more and more like a page out of the *Vedanta* teachings. To the physicist, nothing is substantial, for nothing is solid: The true substance of matter is energy. And the true substance of energy is the will power and ideas that brought energy into manifestation. The true substance of those ideas, finally, is the vibrant power of divine Consciousness.

What all this means is that, in the effort to achieve material success, it would be wise to project *energy* into everything material that one does. One is even wiser if he takes the concept still further and tries to harmonize energy with ideas and awareness that bring him calmness and inner *joy*.

I have mentioned bringing more energy into your shop through *appropriate* colors, sound, symmetry of placement, and variety—all of which can energize your customers' expectations. The next thing is to stimulate them in a way that is compatible with the sort of things you want them to buy. Don't consider only energy itself, but also the *concepts* behind that energy: not just sound, for example, but the right kinds of sound.

What *kind* of energy does your place of work represent? To specify more clearly, would you, in a shop connected to a planetarium, offer music that is reminiscent of a nightclub? Of course not! And surely, if you think about it at all, you'd play music suggestive of calmness, expansion, and the vastness of space. In a shop by the beach, it would be ridiculous to play sitar music, or a ponderous Beethoven symphony. You'd do far better to play music suggestive of fun, or of the lulling effect of rolling waves. You might even play recordings of waves breaking onto a shore. There are recordings available of natural sounds like waves, light rainfall in the forest (nice to listen to when the weather is hot and dry!), birds singing or wind sighing in the trees.

Often, shop owners leave it to their salespeople to decide what music they like to hear. To do so is sheer folly. Young salespeople, especially, are usually more insistent on what they like than people of more mature years, and like to listen to music that is "in" at the moment even if it is completely unrelated to the customers' tastes. Devote serious attention yourself, then, to the question of what music is *appropriate* for your workplace.

There is another important consideration: Try to help raise the energy level also of your employees. Don't surrender to their unpremeditated choice on such matters as sound and color. For public places, give primary attention to your customers' tastes, but in an office, especially if it is less frequented by the public, choose music that is conducive to concentrated work.

I remember once asking the waitress in a restaurant to play more soothing music, and not the pounding beat she evidently preferred. She replied dismissively, "I happen to *like* this kind of music!" as if that settled the matter. I wrote to the owner that, although the waitress should be free to play any music she liked at home, the restaurant, in consequence of that answer, had just lost a customer. The owner was outraged enough to write back saying that he would never permit such a mistake to occur again.

In ways that don't affect your customers adversely, however, do your best to please your employees. Consider also, of course, the fact that tastes vary. Try to choose what will have a more or less universal appeal. Otherwise, young employees may inflict their tastes on others who suffer from their decisions.

In offices in India, too little thought, usually, is given to creating harmony in the workplace. Perhaps customers never come there; I don't know. Even in the boss's office, the atmosphere is often drab and uninviting. Considering the fact that others—what to speak of yourself!—must spend a great part of the day there, surely it is not a waste of money to make your office, and those of your employees, simple, neat, and attractive rather than haphazard and chaotic. Almost certainly they will do better work.

"Keep your feet on the ground" not by making everything cloddish, uninspired, and brown, but by making it more alive. Remind yourself that the very ground you walk on is energy. The realities you deal with daily should stimulate you not only to be energetic, but to have *the right kind* of energy. Thus, you and everyone around you will probably turn out optimum work.

To offer advice on these matters might make a very good profession. Many business places, I suspect, would appreciate suggestions on how they might stimulate people in a way that is compatible with the work they do.

MEDITATION

Don't depend wholly in such matters, however, on professional advice. I've been surprised at how many supposed "experts" in their fields are mediocre in the work they do. You'd do well to make sure that you are satisfied also personally. After all, everything in your work environment should be compatible with what you want to accomplish. Otherwise, even a very good interior decorator or sound expert might fail to tune in to what is appropriate for *you*.

I used, before giving lectures, to sit near the lecture hall and meditate on what each particular group of people wanted and needed to hear. Because what I would say had also to be something that inspired me, I would offer both these thoughts up to God and to my own superconscious, and try to *feel* what to say. This, usually, was all I did to prepare for a lecture. Thus, I learned to be responsive to people's actual needs, rather than giving them thoughts I had plotted out in advance. Though I've given many thousands of lectures in my life, no two of them have ever been quite the same.

In the same way, sit daily for meditation, and try to attune yourself to what you must do, to what you want to give, and to what you think other people want, need, and can receive from you. Realize that these factors will never be exactly the same. Try always, in your mind, to be *fresh and expectant*. It is good, if your budget allows it, to adapt outward conditions also to your changing needs.

You may complain, "But that isn't meditation!" Well, why not? Everything can be spiritualized if it is produced in the right spirit. The greatest thing you can do through your work is help people to tune in to their own highest reality, the divine Self.

AFFIRMATION

"Let everything I do, Lord, reflect my attunement with Thee!"

POINTS TO REMEMBER

1. "You must be practical in your idealism." This advice means also to be conscious of the possible consequences of your actions.

2. In anything you do, be sensitive to the subtle realities of your work. Take time to think about what you are doing, and *why* you are doing it—as well as about *how* to do your very best.

3. Live in the present. Even when making plans for the future, project your consciousness into that future time as though it were right now.

4. Remember, the most profitable ideas often come from contemplating hidden possibilities in what, heretofore, have seemed mundane realities.

5. Whatever you are doing, be focused on it one-pointedly. Don't let anyone tell you that it is impractical to ponder possibilities that lie beyond the known.

6. Will power generates a flow of energy in the body, and solution-consciousness can generate the necessary energy to *attract* success. Solution-consciousness can *attract* ideas, inspirations, and solutions.

7. Don't identify yourself with either outward success or outward failure. The more you concentrate not on things, but on mental *attitude*, the sooner you will discover that failure can be transformed to success by a steadily positive attitude toward anything that happens.

8. Success depends to a great extent on one's willingness to accept reality as it is.

9. If you want to achieve notable success in your life, have the courage to break new trails.

10. Positive thinking, if it is directed wisely, can become a kind of magnet, actually *attracting* success. Negative thinking, on the other hand, attracts failure.

11. The difference between positive attitudes and wishful thinking is wisdom, born of experience. When you have reason to doubt the firmness of the ground, tread cautiously.

12. Project *energy* into everything material that you do. Try to harmonize energy with ideas and awareness that bring you calmness and inner *joy*.

13. Bring more energy into your shop through *appropriate* colors, sound, symmetry of placement, and variety—in a way that is compatible with the sort of things you want customers to buy.

14. Devote serious attention to the question of what music is *appropriate* for your workplace.

15. Try to help raise the energy level of your employees. Choose music that is conducive to concentrated work.

16. Make your office, and those of your employees, simple, neat, and attractive rather than haphazard and chaotic. Almost certainly they will do better work.

17. Sit daily for meditation, and try to attune yourself to what you must do, to what you want to give, and to what you think other people want, need, and can receive from you. Try always, in your mind, to be *fresh and expectant.*

WORKBOOK IDEAS
by Joseph Bharat Cornell

Be Innovative

In his five revolutionary scientific papers of 1905, Albert Einstein didn't include one footnote or citation. Einstein's discoveries were intuitive and therefore fresh. A modern physicist confessed that if Einstein submitted a paper today, it would be thrown away because of his usual lack of references!

Paramhansa Yogananda said intuition comes from within, thought from without. To make an original contribution in your field of expertise, it is important to understand your subject intuitively. According to Yogananda, man's senses and reasoning have discovered only "a millionth part of the nature of matter and all things."

To develop your intuitive ability, calm reasoning and feeling are essential. Yogananda recommended the following practices for increasing one's intuition: common sense, daily introspection, depth of thought, continued activity in one direction, and meditation.

ACTION ITEM:
Select a problem you have been working on. Magnetize a superconscious solution to your problem by doing the following:
1. Begin by concentrating at the spiritual eye. Focusing here quiets your emotions. Do this until you feel calm.
2. Reflect on and analyze your problem.
3. Practice deep thinking. Don't let your mind hop from one idea to another.

4. Make a sustained effort. Putting forth strong, continuous energy is magnetic, and attracts a solution.

5. Meditate deeply. During this time, don't think about your problem. Let your mind and breath become calm. Then ask your Higher Self to guide you.

6. If you don't receive an answer, keep practicing steps one through four for several days. Then meditate again and ask for superconscious insight.

7. Use common sense to evaluate your answer. Ask yourself, "Is my guidance in harmony with higher truth?"

LESSON FOURTEEN

WORKING *WITH* OTHERS

> Goodness is simply a clearer reflection [than evil of the] Supreme Will; it triumphs in the end because, for Absolute Perfection to be realized, the gift of discrimination is required, and discrimination is acquired only by goodness.

The Principles

An old Western folk tale tells of an old man who, as he lay dying, called his six stalwart sons around him to give them final words of advice.

"My sons," he said, "fetch me seven thin sticks, about three feet long."

When they did so, he took one of the sticks and, weak as he was, broke it easily in half. He then asked them to tie the remaining six together. "Now," he told them, "each of you see if he can break that bundle." One by one they all tried; none of them could do so.

"My sons," the old man said, "let this be my parting counsel to you. If you remain loyally united together, no one will be able to break you. But if each of you goes his own way, you may meet some people who, wanting to break you, will succeed in doing so."

Success at anything seldom comes easily. Even people who work alone—artists, writers, or the way-finders in science—usually, to be successful, meet many obstacles on their way. I have frequently quoted in these lessons the ancient Sanskrit saying, "*Yato dharma, tato jaya*": "Where there is adherence to right action, there is victory." The path of dharma is in no way compatible with merely passive righteousness.

A few months ago I watched a movie based on Tolkien's *Trilogy*. It tells a great story, as does the literary work it is based on. The author pitted the mighty forces of evil and darkness against human goodness. I was dissatisfied by this one-sided evaluation, however. The story depicts persuasively a single, overarching power of darkness, but it portrays goodness as merely human and relatively weak. The good people in the story strike one as average, well-meaning Englishmen, best exemplified in good old Frodo, the hobbit hero, honest and kindly, who manages almost by chance to stumble into heroism, and *deserves* to win because he is a fine fellow and wishes no one harm. Frodo is virtuous almost by default. His glory is entirely his own. The goodness he demonstrates is something of which most of us might at least feel capable. Tolkien offers no suggestion that any greater power supports Frodo or might support us. He seems to have wanted to show that human goodness, frail reed though it is, presents the best antidote there is to the world's evil. Goodness, he implies, is not powerful, and good people shun the idea of exerting power over anyone and of controlling others by power, even as they reject the idea of being controlled by others in return. This concept displays the sweet innocence of a fairy tale. Tolkien failed to understand the potential grandeur of his own theme. Indeed, Frodo, too, represented a greater force than he himself knew. The issues involved here, which Tolkien himself missed, relate to the very nature of free will.

The war between good and evil is, for one thing, cosmic in nature; it is far subtler than people usually suppose, and than anything Tolkien suggested. True freedom can be won only by heroic effort; it grows, however, in nourishing soil that has been plowed and fertilized in that perennial struggle.

There can be no stirring plot in any play, novel, or other work of fiction that doesn't contain at least a suggestion of the two cosmic forces, forever pitted together. The beauty of Tolkien's epic is its semi-grandeur: the great sweep of the dark forces on earth. It depicts life as few ever trouble to see it, yet in part as, behind the scenes, it really is: a war between cosmic forces of good and evil. If the story fails, ultimately, as a true epic it is because the understanding it reveals isn't of two well-matched forces in the universe, but only of the Will to Evil, reduced to temporary impotence by blind luck, or by sheer pluck.

Valmiki's *Ramayana*—one of the great epics of ancient India—describes goodness, by contrast, in a vast and more balanced struggle against evil. Rama wins the war against Ravana after a heroic struggle, but does so not because he is a "good fellow" merely, but because he, together with his supporting army, express the cosmic power of goodness. Frodo wins also, smiling gamely to the end, but only because he is a "first class" fellow, and not because of any alliance with a greater power of Goodness. He is not a human (that is to say, a Hobbit-like) expression of infinite Kindness, Truth, and Love. He is simply well-meaning, and *deserves* to win for that reason alone. A vast power of conscious evil and darkness lurks behind the evildoers in Tolkien's story. They influence, and perhaps even direct the actions of the villains. No greater consciousness, however, animates Frodo and his friends.

Tolkien was, as I have indicated, not able to understand the nature of free will and cosmic freedom. The truth is, no one could even think a single thought unless some greater consciousness were moving within him. Scientists have predicted that computers will someday become sophisticated enough to be conscious. That is a baseless dream. What could be *less* conscious than a worm? Yet the worm is obviously conscious enough to squirm away if it is pricked. Consciousness is *the cause*, not the effect, of everything in existence.

The human ego expresses, however minutely, the infinite, eternally conscious Self. Man's will can be free only to the extent that he is able to attune himself to the divine consciousness. God alone is free, for he is not compelled to be or to do anything.

The story of Rama shows goodness as a force ultimately greater than evil. In human life, indeed, not only is the potential for goodness ever-present as an influence for self-awakening: Goodness is a higher truth which the law of karma forces us in the end to accept. We learn, in the process of erring, suffering, and correcting our errors that right action puts down roots in a greater good, whereas wrong action roots us in a greater evil. Everything we do expresses realities greater than those we know consciously. Whether the expression is of light and truth, or of darkness and untruth, is consequent upon the degree to which our will is actually free. Free will is the ability to act for our own highest happiness. Man's lack of freedom lies in his bondage to delusion.

The mighty consciousness that created the universe is even above good and evil. Goodness is simply a clearer reflection of that Supreme Will; it triumphs in the end because, for Absolute Perfection to be realized, the gift of discrimination is required, and discrimination is acquired only by goodness.

Two notable qualities of cosmic *maya*-delusion are the will *and also the power* to divide the underlying truth of conscious oneness into innumerable appearances of separate "realities." *Maya* fragments the one Infinite Spirit ever-increasingly—in appearance only, to be sure. It separates cosmic manifestation into seeming opposites. The more specifically it seems to divide, the more toweringly do these oppositions appear—even as tall ocean waves seem more distinct from one another than little ripples, although they have, in common with all waves and ripples, the fact that they are made of the same ocean water.

In the business world, as in everything we do to achieve success, competitiveness is commonly considered necessary to achievement. The president of a large corporation many years ago made a practice of telling the executives under him, "I expect you to try to outdo one another in your struggle to get ahead. The plum of promotion will always go to him who shows the most competitive spirit." Essentially, his philosophy was, "Survival of the Fittest," a teaching which, as I firmly believe, must lead eventually to self-destruction, *not* to victory.

I have not made a deep study of the history of modern corporations. Yet I have done some reading on the subject that has been, for me, enlightening, though some of it for the disastrous results it produced! According to another story, the president of a large firm—it might for all I know have been the same man I just mentioned—made it a practice every year to invite the senior class of a prominent business college to visit him in his office. His purpose was to give them a brief glimpse of his "view from the top." Every year he proposed to them the same hypothetical question:

"Suppose your business has a supplier who has served you loyally for twenty years. You know that his business depends wholly on yours—to such an extent, in fact, that without your firm's orders you know he would go bankrupt.

"Now then, suppose another supplier someday offers you the same product at a better price. What should you do?"

I was appalled by his own answer to that question: "*Of course* you should go with the lower price. Business is business. As a businessman, you must never let sentiment rule you."

Well, I assume that this self-serving "amoralist" would at least give his loyal supporter of many years a chance to counter that newly competitive price. From the way he formed his question, however, it appears to me that he'd have shunned even that solution as too "sentimental." Let us then look at the matter from another angle altogether. Isn't it highly probable that this "new kid on the block," with his lower price, would in fact have lowered that price on one item simply to lure your business away from your longtime supplier? In this case, isn't it also probable that, once your friend had declared bankruptcy, your new provider would *raise* his price again to reflect the product's actual market value?

This sort of thing happens all the time in the business world, and people's heads, in the process, are constantly being lopped off. I would call that president's hypothetical "solution" naive in the extreme!

For assuming that he continued—always in the name of "hardheaded realism"—to get the best prices, make the shrewdest deals, and beat out all his competitors so that he became at last—oh, wow!—a *millionaire*: What then? Leaving aside all the enemies he'd acquire like fleas in the process, wouldn't he also reap another, and increasingly bitter, harvest: self-hatred? How could it be otherwise?

Anyone who sets himself against others must inevitably steel himself to receive their opposition in return. Joseph Stalin (that self-assumed surname meant, "Steel"; thus it was that he deliberately presented himself to the world) was a classic example of my point. Inwardly he lived in a hell of constant tension, heightened by his awareness of the animosity he'd awakened in others. Those who knew him have described him as paranoid. Tension was his constant companion. It would have been the inevitable inner reflection of his own cruelty. From what one reads, paranoia destroyed Stalin's peace of mind, and, along with it, any chance he might have had for happiness.

Similar attitudes will do the same to anyone who lives a "dog-eat-dog" philosophy.

The purpose of these lessons is to help you to achieve success in life *at every level*. Let us for present purposes, however, accept the common definition of worldly success as achievable only through competition. In fact, let us assume that, up to a point, competition actually works.

To begin with, I must emphasize that competition is not necessarily, in itself, a bad thing. Business monopolies have shown repeatedly over the years that their goods diminish in quality when monopoly permitted them to become complacent. They've been able to foist onto their customers the claim that their way was the only right way of doing things. The customers themselves had no option if they wanted those goods but to accept what that company made.

The best kind of competition, however, is a striving for improvement over *one's own* norms. The drive toward excellence reflects, in fact, a constant desire to improve *oneself*. A truly creative spirit is self-rejuvenating. Even outward competition, if it inspires outward self-improvement rather than driving one to attempt to defeat his opponents, is a good thing. For few people are creative by inclination. Most of them follow the lines of least resistance. In the marketplace, however, too much reliance on habit produces mediocrity. Most people who work for a living, unless they are constantly inspired by others to improve, slip quietly into a rut of habit.

On the other hand, in a company where the employees are competitively at one another's throats—or, as is more often the case, where greedy ambition is the ruling passion—the over-all focus becomes obscured by dust-clouds of infighting. I have seen groups that were so intent on winning their little office disputes that the company's larger aims were all but forgotten.

Whatever your work is, never lose sight of its true goals. Ask yourself always, "Will what I do serve those goals?" Every business should aim higher than mere wealth. Indeed, when profit is the sole motive, customers end up seeking their goods elsewhere. How many people, after all, really care about *other people's* profits? What they want is anything that will serve their own needs. Infighting is the very worst way, surely, for any company to fulfill its very reason for existence!

I have often thought that these simple—indeed, obvious—facts reveal a major weakness in modern democracy also. How can any president or national leader accomplish alone everything his position demands of him? Society is far too complex these days, with international questions looming ever larger on all fronts, for any one person to decide everything that needs deciding at an executive level. A national leader cannot govern effectively without an efficient team. Under the present system, however, he himself is elected for his own abilities, strictly. Throughout much of his tenure he must work with a cabinet selected on personal merit, but not as a group. Few of its members have ever worked together before. They may view one another as rivals. They may even dislike one another. Under such conditions, how much constructive work is possible? Wouldn't it be better for a whole team to be elected to the highest office together—a group of people with proven ability, from years of harmonious cooperation, to work together? This scheme would, I admit, need more—in fact, considerable—clarification. It is a novel concept, and certainly not one for elaborate discussion in this lesson. Still, it suggests a principle that applies to businesses also. For the more that people learn to work *together*, the more productive they will be.

Working *with* others is a vital necessity for almost every kind of success. The concept of cooperation does come with a caveat, however: The people you work with must be united creatively in a good cause. I do not at all mean to say, then, that togetherness itself is necessarily a good thing. Drinking buddies may, in their "togetherness," commit acts of great folly. Unity in error can be dangerous. Such unity is, moreover, more difficult to penetrate with the shafts of common sense than a veritable free-for-all of conflicting opinions.

Ultimately, what determines the effectiveness of any group effort is the *creative support* it receives from the person in charge. This person must himself be creative; it is not enough for him to support the creativity of others.

I have emphasized repeatedly the importance of dharma (right action). What concerns me most here is the fact that, where issues of deeper right and wrong are concerned, group thinking can sometimes obscure them.

When working with others, be aware always that the decisions reached must be supported sincerely by every individual in the group. Each should consult his own understanding, and not let himself be swept away by group fervor. Each should consider calmly within himself every subject that is proposed to or by the group. For there usually exists in such groups a certain pressure toward conformity.

Realistically speaking, what the need for consensus usually means, especially in important matters, is that teamwork functions best under the guidance of a good leader. Seldom is it true that many heads are better than one—folk "wisdom" to the contrary notwithstanding. In creative endeavors especially, what usually happens is that teamwork can empower an idea and carry it through to completion, but the idea itself begins with an individual. That person need not necessarily be the leader, but certainly the idea must have the leader's endorsement; otherwise, dissension may be the result.

What I suggest for committees and for any group working together is that only those be invited to serve on them who have specific areas of responsibility. Otherwise, what I've observed is that members without such responsibilities tend to talk excessively, if only to show that they, too, are carrying their weight. Responsible solutions, in such cases, are difficult to reach.

In committees where every member has a specific responsibility, a subject can first, before it is introduced, be given to the concerned member. He can offer his informed opinion, or study the matter further and knowledgeably, then return to the committee with a carefully thought-out proposal based on considered opinion. No problem should be simply dumped in the committee's collective lap. It should first be considered carefully by someone who is already, if possible, informed on the subject. Endless hours may otherwise be wasted as each member tries to speak authoritatively simply because he thinks opinions are expected of him. A committee's time is best spent, usually, in appraising solutions that have already been considered.

The role of a leader is important to effective group action. His leadership, however, should be supportive, respectful, and impersonally friendly to all. Only such leadership will draw out the best in others. I should repeat that, in my experience, creative ideas almost always come from individuals: It is in the implementation of the ideas that group effort may be required. Group discussion serves best as a means of *evaluating* an idea that has been already worked out carefully.

The Application

People in groups are always rushing heedlessly, like lemmings, over a cliff to disaster because no one dared to raise a warning finger and declare, "Let's be sure this is a wise decision and not a mistake!"

Group effort can be a wonderful thing, when everyone works with a joint purpose, understands what needs to be done, and is committed to achieving something worthwhile for all concerned. In most of the situations one faces in life, people find it necessary to work at least part of the time with other people. Individuals who work alone—creative artists, for example, and inventors—may also find it helpful to keep in mind the benefits they envision for others through what they do. In my own writing, for instance, even though I work alone, I find it helpful to visualize my reader—many readers, that is to say, condensed into a single person—seated before me, listening to my words and discussing silently with me whatever I am committing to paper.

The first thing to do is, if possible, to gather around you people who you believe will work well together in creative harmony. Such a combination is not always easy to find. When you cannot do so, and when you find you have little in common with your co-workers, take this fact as an opportunity provided by your own karma to work on self-development. You may even decide to leave that workplace and seek a job elsewhere. That solution, however, may not always be so easy or felicitous as it seems. A friend of mine afforded me a glimpse, many years ago, into this aspect of karmic law. It was something I have never forgotten.

"Do you remember," he said, "how I used to hate J——? [He named someone we both knew—not an easy man to get along with.] I couldn't stand working with him. It was owing partly to him, in fact, that I left this work. Well, where I work now there are *six* men exactly like him, all grating on my nerves in the same way!"

I've never forgotten this story. It is an excellent example of a very simple truth: Karma cannot be simply avoided. Often, indeed, it is simply wiser to square off bravely and accept it, while concentrating on developing whatever attitude is needed to keep one's own peace of mind.

Troublesome people cannot always be worked *with*: they may have to be worked *around*. It is indeed laudable to try to win them over, but usually the demands life makes of one necessitate working with people with whom it is relatively easy to get along. People whose negativity is ingrained will slip back, more often than not, from whatever plus you hold out to them into their habitual minus zone, as soon as the positive energy you've pumped into them is exhausted. Everyone has his own specific center of gravity. To rise to a higher level, one must *himself want* to change. It may be possible to motivate him to rise, but to do so necessitates, first of all, a focus more on people than on projects. If the important thing, for you, is outer accomplishment, then you will have to make that your primary concern. In that case try first, if possible, to work with those with whom you already feel a certain harmony.

The important thing, always, is to be harmonious first in yourself. Working *with* others, especially if your place is *over* them, demands that you give more of yourself to the job than you ask of anyone else. Give others support before you demand support of them. Express a cooperative attitude toward them before demanding cooperation from them. In all likelihood, they will then be happy to cooperate with you. Don't expect the world to change for you; it never will. You can always do your best, however, to change yourself.

MEDITATION

Imagine a field of tall wheat grass. You are the breeze bending the grass one way and the other. Reflect: What it takes to make the grass lean as you would like: not a dominating force so much as an *influence*.

People can't forever be driven. They must be influenced *from within*—in your case, from your own inner self to theirs. Only thus will they bend willingly to your wishes. The grass they represent will stand tall again once that influence ceases. Let your influence in this world be one of kindness and support, not of driving force or coercion. Leave to everyone his free will. When you try thus to help others, they will always be with you.

AFFIRMATION

"I am one with all. I work with all toward our common goal: success and happiness."

POINTS TO REMEMBER

1. Success in work rarely comes without effort. The path of dharma doesn't indicate a merely passive righteousness.

2. Right action puts roots down into a greater good, whereas wrong action puts roots down into a greater evil. Goodness triumphs in the end because it takes discrimination, acquired by goodness, to reach Absolute Perfection.

3. Anyone who sets himself against others must inevitably steel himself to receive their opposition in return.

4. The best kind of competition is a striving *for*, not *against*. The drive toward excellence reflects a constant desire to improve oneself, as well as what one offers.

5. Most people, unless they are inspired constantly to improve, tend to slip unobtrusively into the muddy ruts of habit. On the other hand, where greedy ambition is the ruling passion, the over-all focus becomes obscured by dust-clouds of infighting.

6. Ask yourself always, "Will my work serve an over-all purpose?" The true aim of every business should consist of something loftier than moneymaking.

7. Working *with* others is a vital necessity for almost every kind of success *if* the people you work with are *creatively* united in a good cause.

8. Ultimately, what determines the effectiveness of any group effort is the *creative support* received by the group from the person in charge. This person must himself be creative; it is not enough for him to support others in their creativity.

9. When working with others, individuals should calmly consult their *own inner* understanding on every issue, and not let themselves be swept away by group fervor.

10. Creative ideas almost always originate in one individual. That individual need not be the leader, but certainly he must have the leader's full endorsement.

11. For committees, invite only those people to serve on them who have specific areas of responsibility. Any subject that requires further study can be given to the responsible individual, who then returns to the rest with a carefully thought-out proposal. The committee's time is best spent in appraising solutions that have been considered already.

12. The leader should be supportive, respectful, and impersonally friendly to all. Only such an attitude will draw out the best from others.

13. Group effort can be a wonderful thing, when everyone works with a joint purpose, understands what has to be done, and is committed to achieving benefits for all concerned.

14. The first thing to do, if possible, is to gather around you people who you believe will work well together, in creative harmony.

15. Troublesome people usually can't be worked *with*: they must be worked *around*.

16. The important thing, always, is to be harmonious first within yourself. Working *with* others demands giving more of yourself to the job than you ask of anyone else. Give them support before demanding it of them.

17. You must influence people as it were *from within*—from your inner self to their inner self. Let your influence be one of kindness and support. If you try in this way to help others, they will always be with you.

WORKBOOK IDEAS
by Joseph Bharat Cornell

Cooperation vs. Competition

Some Navajo children once taught a school teacher a valuable lesson in human relations. During his first week at their school, the teacher asked one of his Navajo students to answer a simple question. The young boy couldn't answer correctly, so the teacher asked if anyone else knew the answer. The other Navajo children, however, stared straight ahead and wouldn't respond.

The teacher was puzzled by their silence because he felt that most of them knew the answer. Later, the teacher learned why: The young Navajos didn't want their classmate to lose face. Their friend's self-confidence and well-being was far more important to them than impressing the teacher.

In eastern Siberia, the nineteenth-century Russian scientist Peter Kropotkin eagerly sought proof of evolution's "survival of the fittest" premise. To his surprise, the young scientist discovered that the most successful animals weren't the most competitive ones, but those that coped with the harsh environment primarily through cooperative behavior. Applying his Siberian experience to humans, Kropotkin asked rhetorically, "Who are the fittest, those who are continually at war with one another, or those who support one another?"

The benefits of cooperation are shown by the success of Japanese car manufacturers. In Japan, automakers and suppliers are true partners. Companies like Honda and Toyota have long-term relationships with their suppliers, and go to great lengths to ensure their survival.

Meanwhile, U.S. automakers often have an adversarial and short-term relationship with suppliers, who are often forced to sacrifice quality and their own bottom line to meet automakers' demand for rock-bottom prices. Working *with* their suppliers has helped Japanese car companies thrive; American brands have struggled to maintain market share.

According to Alfie Kohn, author of *No Contest: The Case Against Competition*, competitive environments increase anxiety and inefficiency, and shift one's focus to victory over others, and away from intrinsic motivators such as curiosity, interest, and excellence. Cooperative environments encourage sharing resources and knowledge, and become more important when tasks are more complex, creative, or challenging.

ACTION ITEMS:

The ego, like the sun's gravitational pull, draws everything back to itself. Contractive, me-first attitudes expressed in the workplace undermine group harmony and purpose.

Create more unity at work by thinking of the needs and perspective of your colleagues or employees. Choose a time each day this week to practice one of the following:

- **Listen to others.** Practice not dominating the conversation; concentrate more on drawing out others.
- Take the time to **learn from others**. Find out their concerns and insights.
- Deepen your sense of gratitude and appreciation for others by reflecting on how each colleague contributes to the over-all health and dynamism of your organization.
- Let other people shine. Give credit to others whenever possible. See your colleagues as part of your Greater Self. Enjoy their victories as you would your own!
- When you are with another person, ask yourself, "How can I help him do his job better?"
- When a colleague is experiencing work-related or other challenges, ask, "Is there something I can do or say that will lift his spirits? free his energy?"

LESSON FIFTEEN

EFFECTIVENESS AS AN EMPLOYER

You will be more successful in your work if you surround yourself with creative, intelligent people — co-workers and, in that sense, equals to you. A good employer thinks not only of the usefulness of others to himself or to the firm. He thinks also of his usefulness to them.

The Principles

I am writing these lessons for people who live in a new and, I believe, more enlightened age, and especially for those, the children of this age, who recognize the importance of energy in the universe, and therefore in the workplace. Leadership that focuses on increasing the energy-flow and inspires others to direct their energy creatively toward achieving positive results is becoming increasingly recognized these days as a new paradigm in business.

The employer who fits this paradigm views his work in terms of energy-output rather than of his own position and importance. He may not be familiar with the principles of yoga, but in fact he is, in a sense, practicing them already. His unitive view is basic to the principles of yoga, and is also basic to creative and constructive activity in general. In these times people have passed beyond the iconoclasm that was popular a hundred years ago, when protests were hurled against the outmoded and constricting social patterns of the so-called "Victorian era." In those days men like Nietzsche, George Bernard Shaw, Sartre, Karl Marx, D.H. Lawrence, and numerous others raised shouts—whether in humor or outrage—that this, that, and the other thing was all that was wrong with the world. Many of them favored various kinds of social amputation, so to speak, before things could improve.

Nowadays, progressive people are interested in finding ways to build, not to destroy: ways to unite disparate concepts into a complete and more rounded understanding; to unite people in a greater power of accomplishment; to unite their efforts for more positive results. Increasingly there is a tendency today to stop tearing down the old edifices and to work cooperatively, instead, to erect useful ones. There is a growing spirit, now, of working together to create a harmonious world.

I am aware that the obstacles to this realization are great in both size and number. Ere a better world emerges we may expect great upheavals and, possibly, widespread destruction. Beneath the storm-tossed surface, however, there is a current moving powerfully toward eventual worldwide brotherhood, progress, and peace.

This course of lessons is designed to help that ideal to become manifested.

"Unity in diversity" has been a slogan in India since ancient times. Because I believe that those who read these lessons are people who believe in unity and progress—a goal shared by the yoga teachings—I am writing for progressive people who are unlikely to remain satisfied with long-held but increasingly outmoded traditions. Still less are students of this course likely to endorse practices that are still commonly held in society today, which deprive whole classes of citizens of their essential dignity as human beings.

The view of leadership that is, in fact, increasingly being accepted in the commercial world no longer supports worn-out usages that affirm a sharp dividing line between physical and intellectual labor.

I've already mentioned how my Guru came out one day to help a small group of us who were digging in the garden. I observed him panting slightly from exertion, and commented lightly, "It's hot work!" He replied somewhat sternly: "It is *good* work!"

When I lived in India, from the late 1950s to the early 1960s, things were in many ways different from what I've experienced since my return to live here in 2003. I know I haven't seen much of the country yet, this time; for one thing, an aging body reduces my motility. I do sense, however, that there is a new spirit in the air.

The employees in many places do, no doubt, still rise to their feet when the boss arrives at the office. And "defilement" is still, I imagine, an issue in many parts of India. If coffee gets spilled on the office floor, moreover, it may still be left there, perhaps all day, until the right person comes to clean it up.

In this respect America is, possibly, on the cutting edge of the sweeping changes in social awareness that are needed everywhere. In most American offices, the boss wouldn't hesitate to wipe up his own coffee spills; nor would he consider it undignified to do so. Typically, the sons even of wealthy American families think nothing of taking summer jobs at a gas (the American word for petrol) station, or of mowing lawns in the neighborhood. I myself used to mow lawns as a teenager, and to do similarly menial jobs like washing people's cars. Naturally, one finds "stuffed shirts" in America: people bent on impressing others by looking important. Such people however, generally speaking, make themselves objects of fun—at least behind their backs!

To accept social inequalities as proof of the superiority of small groups of people in society and the inferiority of other groups demeans the true nature of man. Even ego-inflated business tycoons or emperors actually denigrate their true worth as sons of God. Self-importance causes them to preen themselves with foolish pride. They don't reflect on how brief life is, with its short seasonal glories. In one's present life, he may play the role of ruler and in his next—more probably so if he has ruled badly—he may be a beggar, or at any rate live in a hovel! (I mentioned earlier having seen a girl begging outside Howrah station many years ago. She looked as if she might once have been a queen.) To emphasize one's own superiority over others goes against a basic principle of yoga: namely, that all beings are manifestations of the one, Supreme Self.

India, where I live now and where I am writing these lessons, is the seat of the most ancient and spiritual civilization on earth. This is a country rich in inspiration, where the sensitive person feels spiritual power welling up out of the ground. This is a supernal blessing, which has enabled India since time immemorial to rise above the disintegrating influences of time that have caused other ancient civilizations to crumble to dust. Certain age-old prejudices remain—unfortunately but inevitably. Some of them do so because, when rightly understood, they are valid and true.

One such prejudice, based in fact on a truth, is the caste system. As this system is understood and practiced today, it acts as an obstruction to progress and to India's efforts to claim her rightful place among nations in the present age. Let me therefore discuss that system in the light of its pros and cons.

To begin with, the concept of caste is, as I said, valid and true, and based on a simple recognition of reality. For mankind, too, needs to evolve. Darwin's theory of evolution is incomplete, and succeeds only as an explanation for the variety of life on earth. It doesn't explain, however, the deeper truth: namely, that all that variety displays an innate urge on the part of consciousness itself to break out of the cocoon of partial consciousness. Man is the highest of the animals not because he has crowned himself as such, but because, in mankind, self-awareness has come to a focus. Mankind's evolutional duty is to expand that awareness of self beyond his ego to infinity. The human body is capable, as the lower life forms are not, of aspiring to the heights of pure consciousness.

This is not to say that all men are created equal. That is a mistake made by modern democracy which may eventually prove its undoing. Human equality consists only in the truth that all men equally are children of the One God, and have an equal right before Him to aspire to their own highest potential, and to achieve it by their own effort.

The caste system was originated to help men to understand in which direction to point their evolution: from duller to ever clearer perception; from self-involvement, ultimately, to divine, absolute awareness. As the system has evolved over countless centuries, however, it has become a rationale for keeping whole classes of society suppressed. The needs of our times no longer support suppression on the part of the elite classes over human beings who are lower on the social scale. That is a mind-set belonging to the past; it was never the system intended by Manu, the originator of the caste system. In the future, humanity will develop a keener sense of the underlying oneness of all mankind. That consciousness cannot evolve, however, out of insisting, "I'm just as good as anyone else!" The only reasonable answer to that claim is, "As good at *what*?"

In the modern business world, the relationship of employers to employees needs to be lifted above both misconceptions. No one, obviously, is the same as anyone else at doing anything. Everyone can *and should*, however, rise above his present limitations to an ever-clearer understanding of life and of his place in the great scheme of things. That place may be for now only that of a street sweeper; if it is so, others should respect it. People higher up the hill ought, for their own growth, to try to help those lower down to climb also. *Everyone's* duty as well as destiny is, sooner or later, to reach the top. To devote energy to keeping others from climbing is not honorable, and hinders oneself from climbing toward his own spiritual destiny.

The ancient caste system was given to humanity as a thing noble. It was meant to inspire. Instead, today, it has become an instrument of oppression. What debased it was the desire of certain members of the higher castes to ensure that their offspring received the same respect as themselves. Caste (so my Guru explained) was not hereditary. Although there is a greater likelihood that people's offspring will resemble them physically than otherwise, everyone knows that great differences do exist—indeed, fairly frequently. The child of a brahmin may be born with the nature of a *vaisya*, or he may display the characteristics of an even lower caste. Such people are not, in themselves, brahmins, and should not bear that mark.

Today we live in a new age. Whatever sentiments some have on this score, the discoveries of modern science have certainly opened the eyes of all men to an entirely different class of realities. We must all adjust to them if we are to cope with them effectively.

In 1959, I made a suggestion to a young man in India for some method I thought might help him in his business. Interestingly, his reply was addressed not to the merits of my suggestion, if any, but rather to tradition. He said, "But you see, Sir, this is how my father did it."

Since then, so many changes have occurred that it is obvious we are now living in different times—almost in a different world. Sweeping changes are occurring in India, also, owing partly to computer technology, partly to biotechnology, and also to many other modern developments. Nowadays the question, "How did my father do it?" is becoming irrelevant for growing numbers of young people—not because they have lost respect for their elders, but because no one, today, can ask people of an older generation how to work a computer or work with biotechnology. When I lived in India before, that technology didn't exist. New ground these days is being broken on countless fronts. It seems almost incredible to one who lived here forty-five years ago to find that people in America can telephone what they think is a local number, and someone in India answers!

My father was a geologist for Esso (Standard Oil of New Jersey), which, during his lifetime, was the largest company in the world. The goal of every oil company is of course to find and develop oil as a source of energy. Energy is rapidly becoming the key to progress. My own birth took place in Romania, where oil was first found seeping up out of the ground. My father became in time Esso's chief geologist for Europe, and was made a *chevalier* of the Legion of Honor in France for his discoveries in that country. He was, in other words, at the forefront of the search for energy sources. His own views, moreover, were compatible with the expansive perceptions that are developing everywhere, which embrace mankind's ever-growing need for energy. His comment on the honor he'd received from the French government, and the only thing I ever heard him say on the subject, was, "The credit belonged not to me alone, but to our entire office team."

Employers of the future will, I believe, come to view their employees as teams, and not as people whom they merely pay to obey them. This new spirit, which was the subject of my own last lesson, is already developing out of man's growing *energy*-awareness. Success will depend no longer on how many people do a job but on how much energy they generate—in human, mechanical, and electronic terms.

In India especially, I think the great weight of tradition, which has in many ways obstructed progress, must be and is being removed. "Every country," my Guru stated, "has its own misery-making karma." The degradation of India's lower castes is an example of this kind of karma; indeed, I believe it was specifically in reference to the caste system that my Guru made that remark. Originally, as I've said, the caste system was created to offer people a spiritual direction. For isn't it self-evidently fallacious to insist that all men are created equal? There are vast differences in human intelligence, ability, and understanding.

The caste system was conceived originally as a way of helping people to understand that everyone's destiny is, eventually, upward, from lower to ever higher states of conscious awareness until divine perfection is attained. The modern democratic insistence that all men are equal should rightfully be understood to mean equal in opportunity only; obviously it is not actual reality. Men are equal only in the sense that all human beings should have the equal right to develop to their own highest potentialities.

India's "misery-making karma," then, is not the caste system itself, but the degradation of that system into a social mechanism for the suppression of lower levels of society. A "magic" circle was long ago drawn about the higher castes, to the detriment of social elasticity.

Today, some elasticity is returning to India. I have seen places of business where people work together as a team, in friendly cooperation. It is this spirit which will transform the country, and make her once again a shining example for all the world. First, however, India will have to transcend the disintegrating influences of caste, which, generally speaking, has lost its true meaning.

In this lesson I want to convince employers that a cooperative attitude toward those working under them can bring greater benefits to everyone, including themselves. I am addressing the kind of employer, then, who is more interested in doing good work than in *being* important, personally. Such a person *wants* to work *with* others. He doesn't want others to treat him with servility, for he views those working under him as valuable assets to his firm who deserve to be treated with respect.

Analyze yourself. Determine what kind of employer you yourself are or would like to be. Do you insist on making every important decision yourself? Do you want personal credit for everything that goes well in your establishment? Do you view those working under you as "underlings" rather than as co-workers?

Think how much more you might accomplish by *including* them in your creative energy! Think, too, how much a sense of inner freedom might contribute to your sense of accomplishment. The more credit a person claims for himself, the more he encloses himself within walls of ego-limitation.

You will be more successful in your work if you surround yourself with creative, intelligent people—co-workers and, in that sense, equals to you. A good employer thinks not only of the usefulness of others to himself or to the firm. He thinks also of his usefulness to them. He wants not only obedience from them, but their creative input and willing energy. Success, to him, means expansion both in his business and in the prosperity and happiness of everyone who works there.

We are studying these matters from a standpoint of yoga principles. Yoga *means* "union." Success sought through yoga principles must be achieved through an awareness that truth is one, and that the Spirit of Truth is present equally in everything. Whenever I think of this vision of oneness, I think of how my Guru demonstrated it in all that he did. He never commanded anyone. And though he requested obedience of us, his disciples, what he meant by obedience was revealed, in practice, to be simply an apprenticeship in wisdom. It meant cooperating with him in his guidance of our attempts to achieve perfection. He never demanded anything for himself. He asked only our cooperation with him in achieving our own spiritual enlightenment. What I myself found in that obedience, indeed, was that the more I attuned myself to his consciousness, the more clearly the whole world around me took on a new and deeper meaning. I found myself not only doing things differently, but doing them much better. I learned, for example, to view and behave towards other people in an ever more kindly, supportive spirit. I began to look for ways in which to help them more. The consequence of this growing attitude in myself was that those who worked with me did better work also.

Can my Guru's way be of benefit to others in less spiritual activities? Indeed, yes! Even those with a less spiritual motivation can emanate supportive thoughts toward others and thereby inspire and encourage them to *enjoy* their work.

Your duty, as an employer or executive, is to get people moving in the same general direction as your own. When they've begun, they will add to the atmosphere of creativity you are trying to develop without becoming, in the process, mere "carbon copies" of yourself.

Other principles, for those who employ others or direct their activities, are important also. One such principle is effective communication. So many people seem interested only in expressing their own ideas, without *listening* for others' reactions. Moreover, they don't consider the need to *communicate* what is in their minds. It is not enough merely to *state* one's ideas. He must communicate them in such a way that others will understand and appreciate them.

I visited Harvard University many years ago to give a lecture. I'd never been on the campus, and asked a passing professor where the hall was located.

"It's in that direction," he replied, waving vaguely to his left.

"Are you referring to that gray stone building on the corner?" I inquired.

"Yes, *yes*, YES!!!" he shouted irascibly as if he'd been addressing some particularly irritating student in a classroom of idiots. Obviously this was his normal way of communicating with others. The episode, brief though it was, has remained with me as an example of the resentment many feel at having to communicate at all.

When dealing with others, try to understand and appreciate their point of view. Place yourself mentally in their shoes. Let them see that you *desire* to communicate with them.

Be patient. Consider that it may have taken *you* years to reach your present conclusions. Other people may also need some time, at least, to grow into concepts with which they are as yet unfamiliar.

Respect those who work under you. See them as human beings like yourself. Don't expect them all to live at any one level of intelligence, talent, or capability. My Guru used to tell us, "You are all like the fingers of my hand; each serves his own function, has his own strengths, and is capable of serving in some special way. All of you, moreover, are equally precious before God." Look for the special strengths of each person working under you. Don't dwell on anyone's weaknesses or inadequacies. Assume that all of them have both strengths and weaknesses, as you have, yourself.

Never belittle the contributions of even the least of those who work under you. A boss must, above all, control his own emotions. Even if he loses his temper at times, he should never be ruled or rule others by it, and would be wise never even to *show* it. View with alarm, rather, any temptation you feel toward becoming angry. Anger is a fault to be overcome, rather than an emotion to be enjoyed. It obstructs the expression of truth.

Do you want to blame others? Then search out something blameworthy in yourself. You might try, when explaining a thought to others, to put it this way: "Perhaps I didn't explain myself clearly. Let me try to put it better." I remember one occasion many years ago, by contrast, when I wrote to a superior in my editing department and asked her to clarify something she'd written me.

Her peremptory reply was a stunner: "I never leave the reader in doubt as to my meaning," she wrote. Was I not, after all, one such "reader"? And wasn't I at least intelligent enough to be working in her department? The person you address may in fact be aware that the fault is really his. Still, he will appreciate your gesture if you try to help him to save face. The more you express yourself both sincerely and kindly, the better. Be *kind*. Be *interested*—especially in those working under you. Your *manner* of self-expression may be more effective than any specific *words* you employ.

When communicating with others, don't look off to the side, or away from them. Look at them openly and sincerely. You may even find it helpful to gaze at the point in their foreheads between the eyebrows. This can help to raise both their consciousness and yours. Another common tendency people have is to gaze constantly back and forth between one eye and the other when speaking with someone. To my mind, this practice suggests uncertainty. You might try, instead, to look at them, again, between their eyes—perhaps even at the bridge of their noses or (again) between the eyebrows. (This will be a way also of not getting drawn into their magnetism.) If you look downward you may lower the level of communication between you. Looking off to one side, however, may give the impression that you aren't really interested in the conversation. (Looking off to the side is natural, however, when one ponders a point deeply. It shows that he is taking the matter seriously.)

When speaking, convey *energy* through your eyes as well as through the tone of your voice. Think of other people as human beings, not as mere points of contact.

When I recorded a series of India-wide television talks in 2004, I looked *through* the camera lens *at* the people, as I imagined my listeners behind it.

I still remember an occasion when, as a young man, I was having my eyes examined. The examiner was an attractive young woman, and perhaps for that very reason I was particularly aware that, even though she gazed deeply into my eyes, she did so quite disinterestedly. To her I was not a man. She was gazing into my eyes in a purely clinical manner. I asked myself how I could be so certain. It was that she was projecting no energy to me. She merely noted what she saw there.

When you communicate with others, don't merely look at them as that young lady did. Make it a conscious point to project energy toward them, as fellow human beings.

At this point, some of my students may wonder, "Is this energy something one can actually *feel*?" Indeed, yes! You yourself can develop an awareness of that energy-flow by learning and practicing Yogananda's energization exercises regularly. Everyone would do well to learn and practice them daily. He will find himself developing an awareness of the body's energy. If you do them, you will be able after a time to send energy out consciously to others through your eyes, through your voice, and through your very facial expressions. You'll even be able to project a force-field around you, one that people will actually feel in your presence.

I have found that whether I am lecturing to ten people or to thousands, this energy flows out to all of them. People often remark afterward that they could feel that energy.

I have learned many things from lecturing. One of them is never to speak *at* people. I find it isn't enough even to speak *to* them. Rather, I've learned to speak *with* them. That is to say, I share with them with full sincerity.

When you try to communicate with others, go beyond speech itself. Embrace them mentally, rather, in your energy field. Radiate energy toward them. When you do so, you will find more and more that you can *inspire* people with your ideas, as you yourself are inspired.

Never "pontificate." Never "talk down." Never make statements like, "When you've had my experience, you'll know what I'm talking about." Never lump people into a personal abstraction of your own, by telling them, "What I always tell people is. . . ." Try to make your comments relevant to the individual or particular group of persons. Try always, in doing so, to address their own level of understanding.

Try also to emanate kindness and goodwill. Above all, show respect. Never condescend, even mentally. View your humblest employee as your equal in everything but, perhaps, experience. As a matter of fact, you may be (and probably are) wiser, more talented, and even, perhaps, more intelligent than most of them, at least. Still, never "talk down," or condescend. Show respect and courtesy to everyone, and never think of yourself as anyone's owner merely because you pay his wages. See those under you, rather, as favoring *you* by working for you. These attitudes will inspire in others a sense of respect toward you and your ideas. Make your hold on people be the magnetism of your kindness toward them, and never by instilling fear into them. If others see that you respect them, they will return that respect manyfold.

Another vitally important point, especially if many people are in your employ, is this: *Learn to delegate authority*. It is foolish for any leader, especially if his responsibilities are far-flung, to insist on making every decision himself. If you don't delegate, very little work will actually get done. The larger the vehicle, the wider its wheel-base must be. Just as your brain delegates authority to the fingers, so your employees are, in a sense, extensions of your energy. A pianist cannot think of his fingers specifically while playing. He must let the fingers flow, as he has trained them to do, expressing in their own way his inspiration. You will succeed, especially in a large enterprise, only if you recognize that it simply is not possible for you to make every decision.

When I was developing the first Ananda communities, in all of which, now, about a thousand people live, I learned certain principles that I think every employer—indeed, everyone conducting a group enterprise—would find worthwhile to know. Let me list a few of them.

1) Some of those you attract as employees will understand your ideals, and will share in them. Others, however, may have priorities that are very different. If you want your enterprise to be successful, concentrate on those employees who are with you *in spirit*; work especially with them. It doesn't matter if their own solutions to problems differ, sometimes, from those you might have reached. There are, after all, many ways of approaching almost any problem. The vital thing is that those who work under you share your *basic ideals and spirit*. Over the thirty-seven years to date of Ananda's existence, it has been the above policy more than any other that has developed a team of leaders whose decisions all spring from a central vision. Though our communities are spread in the world, we all of us are, even today, a single, harmonious unit.

Best of all at Ananda is the unity of friendship, kindness, and goodwill. Arguments are virtually nonexistent. Indeed, I recall none to mind, and certainly don't remember any basic disagreements over more than twenty years that haven't ended amicably. (In the early days, when Ananda Sangha still needed definition, things were somewhat different.) Harmony prevails now because the leaders rule benignly, and because everyone shares the same basic vision and understands that the spirit behind the work is more important than the work itself.

2) It is important, when working with people, to realize that each of them may also have a personal agenda, and is working out his own karma. Everyone, after all, is centered in and functions from his own ego. This fact may in the abstract seem unfortunate, but it should not be deplored any more than we regret the fact that night follows day. What *is*, simply *is*. Man's ego is a gift to him from God—one not granted in equal measure to any other species. The ego helps man eventually, as it prompts him to refine his consciousness of self, to an understanding that his true Self is infinite. One ought not to equate ego-consciousness with pride. What it signifies, rather, is self-awareness, which leads to an expansion of awareness to infinity.

Pride, on the other hand, is the greatest barrier to spiritual growth, for it affirms a delusive self-importance, and impedes one from climbing further up the ladder of awareness. As my Guru put it, one must avoid both superiority and inferiority complexes, for they prevent one from expanding into a greater reality.

The way to reach people is to understand them *from within*—from your own center to their center. You must inspire them to *want* whatever you ask them to do. Remember, at the same time, you'll never be able, and should not even want, to undo all the complexity that has gone into making people who and what they are. Some will support you; others, and for many reasons, may not only withhold their support but even betray you. "Loyalty," my Guru often used to say, "is the first law of God." This quality is a precious ornament. Never *presume* of anyone that he is adorned by it. Simply be grateful, when you find people who are loyal. At the same time, keep in mind that some people wear cheap imitation jewelry. They may hide their lack of concern for your priorities behind a mask of merely pretended enthusiasm.

3) Don't be afraid to test people—especially before you give them a position of importance. Give them a chance to show their true mettle. Test their sincerity. Test their honesty. Test their truthfulness. Never withdraw your friendship from anyone, even if he turns against you, but keep your eyes open to the simple fact that few will be, to you, as you would like them to be. Keep a calm center in your heart from which you look out impartially upon the world, things, and other people. Never judge, but at the same time don't be a simpleton. Don't encourage in anyone the thought that he can easily fool you. To be conscious of human fallibility is not to develop a suspicious nature: It is simply to be aware of human realities. The consequence of this awareness is, perhaps surprisingly, a *greater* trust in everyone for the simple reason that, recognizing man's infinite possibilities for error, you place your trust fully in God.

4) A leader cannot afford to be too easily influenced by emotions, whether his own or those of other people. If you hold a position of authority, you may feel a need to have a few confidants, with whom you can air your frustrations and disappointments. Don't, however, let yourself be drawn into other people's emotions. The boss who can control his own feelings, or at least his display of them, will find it relatively easy to minimize the politics in the workplace that so often disturb the general peace.

5) Before you employ anyone, consider his attitude more even than his capabilities. People with wrong attitudes, even those who

are very skillful, will in time become thorns in your side.

6) Because human nature carries no guarantee that it will follow a single track, if someone you've hired proves to be unwilling or unable to tune in to the group spirit you're trying to develop, he should simply not be given too much energy, Don't waste time in excessive effort to win him over. Let others who insist on doing so take on that job. In my experience, any such attempt proves almost always a simple waste of time and effort. Concentrate, rather, on working with those who are willing, supportive, cheerful, and loyal.

7) It is always painful when people turn against you, misunderstand your good intentions, or betray the friendship you've given them. If (or perhaps I should say, *when*) this happens, don't let anger poison your heart. Continue to be their friend—in your heart, at least. Not only will such an attitude protect your peace of mind, but it will help you thereby to develop gradually a team of loyal co-workers whose support and friendship is yours outside the workplace, also. The love all of you share together will have a greater value for you than any amount of jewels.

8) There was a slogan where I once worked: "The individual is not important: all that matters is the work itself." I disagreed with that slogan at the time, and disagree with it even more strongly now. Any work, especially one that is intended to be of service to others, must be defined in terms of the people it is intended to serve! If they are not given first consideration, the crop will be barren! Your co-workers must be given first consideration, then.

When the roots of a tree receive no water, what matters it subsequently, once the tree dies, if the land around it all becomes flooded? The people you serve—that is to say your customers—are the final test of whatever you produce, but your first loyalty should be to your staff. *After them* in importance come those who want the products you offer. I don't mean to heed too literally the famous slogan of Macy's department store, "The customer is always right." The important thing is that your customers' wishes be *respected*. Even when you disagree with them, give their wishes kindly and respectful attention and consideration. And give the same—indeed, even more so—to the wishes of your co-workers.

9) Not a few times in my life I have gone along with ideas that I expected to prove impractical, simply in order to let their proponents learn from their own experience. (Sometimes, they have been able to show they were right.) Once, by contrast, I had a boss who used to dismiss my ideas scornfully. If your job is to lead others, try this simple principle: *Lead*; never *drive*.

10) An important part of your job is to encourage creativity in others. Don't mind it if someone under you outshines you. A boss who tries to outshine others at everything becomes, in the end, outstandingly inept.

11) Give as much credit to others as possible. Don't try to "hog" the credit all for yourself. My father once chuckled over the introduction to a scientific book he'd read in French. The fact that it was in that language may account for the quaintness of the phrasing in the English translation. The introduction, after praising the book, added, "The author has carried out his task ably, in accordance with our directions, and under our constant supervision." (!) Even if an idea was your own, ideas themselves are impersonal: They cannot be owned by anyone.

12) The same may of course be said for any direction you give to others. I've often smiled

at the memory of a family I accompanied to Disneyland, in southern California, many years ago. A little lake on that property contained boats which ran on underwater tracks, and were "decorated" with fake steering wheels to give passengers the illusion of being in control of the movements. We rented several craft. From where I was floating I saw two of my guests, an elderly couple, a little distance across the water from me. I hailed them, and the wife in answer called out cheerfully, then turned to her husband and said, "Look, Dear, wave back!"

"Don't interrupt!" he cried tensely. "Can't you see I'm trying to steer clear of those rocks just ahead!" What fun we had, teasing him afterward when the "danger" had passed, and we'd returned "safely" to land.

13) A further point: Don't begin a staff meeting by asking for ideas. Have an agenda, and make sure everyone follows it. Make a proposal, and then invite suggestions, but never let the discussion degenerate into a conversational free-for-all. Hold the reins in your hands. If people stray from the point—a very common tendency in group discussions—bring them back gently, but firmly, to the issue at hand.

14) The extent to which you need to make clear the fact that you are the boss, as opposed to being everyone's friend, cannot be written into any system of rules. Many issues must be resolved intuitively. Moreover, there may be many factors involved, including differences of personality and situation, and varying degrees of emotional intensity.

15) It is important that you be perceived clearly as the one in charge, whenever the need for that perception arises. It is also important, however, that fair-minded people not perceive you as being a dictator. (There are disgruntled persons whom no amount of concession will appease. These individuals ought to be simply ignored.) The choice between discipline and permissiveness will often be subtle. If others do not clearly perceive you as the one in charge, the work force itself may lack any real discipline. On the other hand, if you rule with too heavy a hand, especially in petty matters, people will cease to respect you and will look for ways to get around any directive they don't like. On this issue you will have to feel your way sensitively. No one rule applies to every situation.

16) The most important rule for you, as the leader, is to be always centered in yourself—in the spine, as the yoga philosophy teaches. From that inner center you will be able most effectively to influence others—each of them at *his* own center. Visualize yourself as relating to others from your center to their center. Even janitors and others in your work force whose position is relatively menial will respond supportively if you treat them, equally with everyone else, as expressions of God. In their inner Self, indeed, they always shine with His light.

The Application

Try always to discriminate between your egoic and your spiritual self. Not only will you be happier and more fulfilled when you do so, but you will succeed better in the work you do. Maintain a certain impersonality even toward yourself. If you follow Krishna's advice, in the Bhagavad Gita, regarding non-attachment to the fruits of action, you will find it relatively easy not to let anyone's emotions affect you and will think rather in terms of what actions lead to success.

In any serious enterprise, desires and emotions have no place. I do not at all mean to eliminate *feelings*, as such: enthusiasm, for example, for a worthwhile project. Feelings, however, cannot be constructive unless they are directed calmly towards worthwhile goals. They become disruptive if they are agitated, or are fanned to flames of desire and emotions.

In any situation, be clear, always, concerning what is right and true. Never do what *you* merely desire. Above all, if ever you feel yourself getting angry, and especially if you feel like expressing that emotion outwardly, do your best not to express it as a *personal* emotion. Truth and rightness must always be your first concern. Righteous indignation can sometimes, in fact, even be a good thing, but it should always be expressed with concern and respect for other people's feelings. You yourself, in your leadership position, cannot afford the pettiness of personal emotions, and must always at least try to remain calmly centered within. It is also important to respect the emotions of others, for, whether you approve of their actions or not, these are realities with which you must deal. Never scoff at or ignore anyone.

Being a boss or leader is a very good discipline in the art of yoga. Learn, if circumstances place you in that role, to play it with wisdom!

MEDITATION

Think, while working, that you are sending waves of light and energy out into the world. These are not conquering waves. Try, rather, to *inspire* in receptive souls a kindred light and energy. Mentally invite them to join you. Visualize yourself, and all of those with whom you work, as diffusing light and energy to the world. Inspire others to be more aware *at their own inner center*. See all that you do—whether administrative, selling, or creative work—as *projections of your energy*. Imagine that the quality of that energy is uplifting everyone who needs peace and happiness.

AFFIRMATION

"I serve others through the work I do. Let my energy ever be a channel of Thy love and joy to all."

POINTS TO REMEMBER

1. Leadership that focuses on increasing the energy-flow and inspires others to direct their energy creatively toward achieving positive results is becoming recognized these days as a new paradigm in business.

2. To emphasize one's own superiority over others goes against a basic principle of yoga: namely, that all beings are manifestations of the one, Supreme Self.

3. A cooperative attitude toward those working under you can bring greater benefits to everyone, including yourself.

4. Success, to a good employer, means expansion both in his business and in the prosperity and happiness of everyone who works there.

5. Emanate supportive thoughts toward others and thereby inspire and encourage them to *enjoy* their work.

6. Your duty, as an employer or executive, is to get people moving in the same general direction as your own.

7. A leader must *communicate* his ideas in such a way that others will understand and appreciate them. Try to understand and appreciate others' point of view.

8. Be patient. Consider that it may have taken *you* years to reach your present conclusions.

9. Look for the special strengths of each person working under you. Don't dwell on anyone's weaknesses.

10. Never belittle the contributions of even the least of those who work under you.

11. The more you express yourself both sincerely and kindly, the better. Be *interested*—especially in those working under you.

12. When communicating with others, look at them openly and sincerely. You may even find it helpful to gaze at the point in their foreheads between the eyebrows. When speaking, convey *energy* through your eyes as well as through the tone of your voice.

13. Yogananda's energization exercises will help you develop an awareness of the body's energy, which you can send out consciously to others.

14. Speak *with* people. Embrace them mentally in your energy field. You will find that you can *inspire* people with your ideas, as you yourself are inspired.

15. Above all, show respect. Never condescend, even mentally. Make your hold on people be the magnetism of your kindness toward them.

16. *Learn to delegate authority*.

17. The vital thing is that those who work under you share your *basic ideals and spirit*. Concentrate on working with those who are willing, supportive, cheerful, and loyal.

18. Realize and accept that each person may also have a personal agenda, and is working out his own karma.

19. Avoid both superiority and inferiority complexes, for they prevent one from expanding into a greater reality.

20. Don't be afraid to test people—especially before you give them a position of importance.

21. Keep a calm center in your heart from which you look out impartially upon the world and other people. Never judge, but don't encourage in anyone the thought that he can easily fool you.

22. A leader cannot afford to be too easily influenced by emotions, whether his own or those of other people.

23. Before you employ anyone, consider his attitude more even than his capabilities.

24. The people you serve—that is to say your customers—are the final test of whatever you produce, but your first loyalty should be to your staff.

25. An important part of your job is to encourage creativity in others. Give as much credit to others as possible.

26. Have an agenda for your staff meeting, and make sure everyone follows it. Make a proposal, and then invite suggestions.

27. If others do not clearly perceive you as the one in charge, the work force itself may lack any real discipline. On the other hand, if you rule with too heavy a hand, people will cease to respect you.

28. The most important rule for you is to be always centered in yourself—in the spine. Visualize yourself as relating to others from your center to their center. Treat everyone equally, as expressions of God.

29. Try always to discriminate between your egoic and your spiritual self. Maintain a certain impersonality even toward yourself.

30. Be clear, always, concerning what is right and true. You cannot afford the pettiness of personal emotions. It is, however, important to respect the emotions of others.

31. Visualize yourself, and all of those with whom you work, as diffusing light and energy to the world. Imagine that the quality of that energy is uplifting everyone who needs peace and happiness.

WORKBOOK IDEAS
by Joseph Bharat Cornell

Radiate Goodwill

The Indian scriptures say that in higher ages all things live in joyful harmony. People and animals, and even trees, support one another and take delight in the well-being of all. As an employer, you have a wonderful opportunity—and responsibility—to create an atmosphere of harmony and support for your employees. Paramhansa Yogananda said, "The instrument is blessed by that which flows through it." The more you support the higher needs and well-being of your employees, the more you and your business will prosper.

Employees usually treat each other the way their employer treats them. Being kind and respectful to one's staff inspires them to be considerate in return. A happy, harmonious work force is crucial to the magnetism and success of any endeavor.

You can create a more supportive work environment by consciously projecting thoughts of goodwill to your staff. Conversing with others is a dynamic way of sharing your vibration and consciousness. The more you relate on a soul level with your employees, the more your work relationships will be exalted, and the more your staff's motivation for working for you will be selfless and idealistic.

ACTION ITEMS:

1. Even if you are a skilled communicator, applying the following principles will take your skill to a higher level. Take time beforehand, if possible, to prepare yourself for conversing with others by doing the following:

- Calm your feelings. Make sure they are directed toward a productive goal.
- Be impartial. Ask what is right and true for this situation, these people.
- Meditate to feel the divine presence.

2. While speaking with people focus on the following:

- Visualize yourself relating to others from your center to their center.
- Mentally embrace them by radiating your energy outward to them.
- Concentrate on projecting energy through your eyes, as well as the tone of your voice. Gaze at the spiritual eye, or point between the eyebrows, of those you are conversing with; this will raise both their consciousness and yours.
- Don't just state an idea. Communicate it creatively. Ask yourself, "What can I say that will help this person embrace this idea more fully?"
- Never speak *at* people or even *to* them, but *with* them.

- Appreciate their point of view. Listen for their reactions to what you say. Doing so will allow you to anticipate and answer their unspoken questions or concerns.
- Be patient. Work *with* people's realities, not *against* them.
- As you interact with others, keep the following guidelines uppermost in your mind: Be kind. Be interested. Be gracious.

Feel Yourself as Energy

The more aware you are of energy flowing in your body, the more you can direct it toward anything you do. Practice the following technique from Paramhansa Yogananda's energization exercises.

Do this three times before conversing with others. Then concentrate on radiating the energy you feel outward to them.

- Stand upright. Inhale slowly, and gradually tense the whole body (with low, medium, and then high tension) to the point where it vibrates. Gaze upward at the point between the eyebrows; with concentration, feel energy flowing into the body. Hold the tension for a few moments and consciously fill the whole body with energy. Then exhale and slowly relax, *feeling* the energy as it withdraws from the body parts. Always tense with will, then relax and *feel*.

LESSON SIXTEEN

BEING A SUCCESSFUL EMPLOYEE

This is, indeed, the greatest secret of material success: keep an *uplifted consciousness*. Success radiates outward from uplifted awareness, whatever outward mechanics are involved.

The Principles

To be a successful employee means more than to be successful *as an employee*—more, in other words, than to be an employee who receives a decent salary and has an adequate position. To be a *successful* employee in the sense of bringing success to one's firm, and a *feeling of success* to oneself, is to be the kind of person who is a real asset to the company for which he works. This he can be only if he takes an intelligent and supportive interest in the company and in its over-all aims.

In large companies it is common for an executive to have people both above and below him. He must therefore filter the fundamental aims of the company *from* anyone immediately above him down *to* those immediately beneath him. The ability to honor high principles while remaining obedient to directives, and to further the policies of the firm itself, depends on several factors:

The first consideration is whether the firm's policies themselves are principled. The second is whether the people running things are doing their best to honor those principles. Third, does everyone in the chain of command abide by those principles?

An employee has little control over such matters—diminishingly so, the farther down he is in the chain of command. Not even the majority of executives can really "call the shots," except in matters of minor importance. Indeed, if the company is owned by shareholders the president himself may not be free to do everything he'd really like to do.

For this last reason when, many years ago, I founded Ananda, I rejected the temptation to speed our development with the help of outside investors. My thought was, What if some of them should decide someday to take Ananda Sangha in a different direction from the purpose for which I founded it? The success of a large project requires help from many people, but what most investors want, generally speaking, is simply a financial return on their investment. Even in a spiritual work, where those returns, if they exist, are secondary, the investors may have their own ideas as to what they want the work to accomplish. I decided I'd rather fail than be controlled by people who, potentially, didn't share my ideal of promoting my Guru's teachings, and my insights into them. I didn't want dissension.

It was difficult to go it alone. I had limited funds, and knew of only one way I could earn it: by teaching yoga classes. This I did tirelessly in many cities! Fortunately, I was in demand. With God's help, and after several years of hard work, I finally succeeded. Probably what helped me to do so was the truth expressed in the well-known maxim, "Where there's a will, there's a way." Even more, what sustained me was my faith in, and the subtle help and guidance from, my Guru.

If one must accept employment under another person, however, his options are even more limited, for decision-making will not be his responsibility. In a large company, you may find yourself transferred from department to department and working under one boss after another. What should you do if even one of those bosses is not so supportive as he might be of the firm's principles?

Such a situation is ripe for office intrigues. A supervisor who doesn't wholeheartedly agree with the aims of his firm may be able to mask his lack of support for many years, especially if he supports most of them. Such a person will want everyone under him to agree with him. Thus, he will try to get transferred, or perhaps even fired, subordinates who don't seem in his eyes to be giving him the backing he wants. Gradually he will gather around him people who are, if anything, even *less* supportive of the company's policies than he is himself. From such a team, an infection of negativity sometimes spreads throughout the company. Wisdom dictates that disaffection like this be excised completely—if possible, by eliminating the supervisor himself, but, if not possible, by getting him transferred to a place and a position where he can do no harm. (He will of course try to hide himself carefully, meanwhile, behind smoke screens of protested loyalty.)

Corporations can become hotbeds of office intrigue, politics, gossip, and dissension. I say this although the company my own father worked for and in which he was an executive—Esso or Exxon as it has been renamed in America, both of which are short for Standard Oil of New Jersey, at that time the largest company in the world—was, as nearly as I could tell, stable enough not to be undermined by any negative currents that appeared. I assume, however, from my knowledge of human nature, that such currents existed there also. (I got whiffs of it from time to time, but evidently any such currents were reabsorbed into the mainstream. At any rate, they seemed to be of little concern to my father.)

The truth is, human nature often seethes with ambition and self-interest. These ego-boosters intrude especially where large groups of people work together, and certainly when the main stakes are money and power. Unfortunately, employees are more obliged even than executives to compromise. This being the case, it may help them to reflect that all life is a compromise! We must all accept some need for it in this work-a-day world. The important thing is not to betray our conscience in important matters.

The compromises begin with the simple fact that we have human bodies! We cannot fly like the birds, even if our spirit soars. We cannot swim under water for long distances, like fish, without material assistance. We cannot leap like monkeys, fight like tigers, or lift weights like elephants, no matter how strong we consider ourselves. We must adapt to numerous inconveniences such as the need to eat, breathe, sleep—whatever our private fantasies.

The rule for living a sane life is that one must work with *what is*, while remaining faithful to higher ideals. If one is not in a position in his firm to make executive decisions, his options in that regard are slim to nonexistent. If he has a family, he may have to accept more compromises. Ideally, he should seek work in a place that has high principles. Life, however, is not always so conveniently arranged. Sometimes one finds himself working among people who only *seem* principled at first, but who in time disappoint those expectations. What can he do?

A friend of mine wrote recently that she was finding herself repeatedly in that predicament. What could I say? She is still looking for work that matches her insistence on truth and honesty. What if she fails? Shall she seek honorable work that is beneath her actual abilities? That, of course, is for her to decide. Is she courageous enough to start a new organization on her own? That, again, is for her to decide.

I must say truthfully, and not boastfully, that I believe I would rather have starved than go counter to my ideals. Still, I am not so naive as to imagine that every student of these lessons will be free to be so firm, even if he wants to be. For one thing, speaking personally, I am not married. I have no family to support. Even the people who depend on me for guidance know that I would never sacrifice a valid ideal for more security—my own or anyone else's. Indeed, several times in the past I have risked everything for truth. Yet I am fair enough to realize that not everyone is free to risk *everything* for his ideals. I cannot, therefore, and I will not presume to tell anyone what he must do. In matters of this sort, all must decide for themselves. Even so, you can seek employment in some place that is at least known to have high principles. That can be your priority. You don't have to "throw in the towel" and resign yourself to the belief that such places don't exist. They *do* exist. Good employers also *do exist*. The more all of us try to create vortices of positive, *good* energy, the more that energy will expand outward. Perhaps, in time, it will cover the world.

If the place where you work doesn't meet your expectations, scout around in your free time for alternatives. You needn't quit your job immediately. You must be practical, of course. Even so, while working in one position you can always look elsewhere. Don't leap off the diving board before checking to see whether the pool contains water.

Above all, pray to God for help and guidance. As countless people have found, prayer really *works*!

There is an alternative to intense involvement in the work you do, if high principles seem too demanding to you. Seek work that is moral, of course, but don't become too involved in it emotionally. Employers need competent workers, but it would be unrealistic for anyone to expect that everyone who works for him will be fully *committed* to the work. From an employer's point of view, it is always wonderful to have people who share his vision, but he surely understands that, realistically, the number of such people cannot be vast.

I myself, by patience and forbearance, have been fortunate in attracting more supporters than most who fully share my vision. But then, what I've called them to has been not only challenging, but inspiring. Had I started something very different—a plumbing company, for instance—how many would I have attracted whose eyes shone at the thought of creating functioning bathrooms and kitchens? The best I could have hoped for would have been one or two men who, perhaps, really *enjoyed* their work. It would have been virtually a certainty that most of my employees worked with me primarily, if not entirely, for the salary.

During Ananda Sangha's beginnings, not many came who understood what I wanted to accomplish. I had to accept some in the hope of attracting the kind of people, eventually, that I really wanted. They did come, gradually. Reflecting on those who came first, I see clearly that they needed first to be convinced.

Thus, if you yourself need to work under someone else, and cannot devote yourself wholeheartedly to the job you get, be at least honest, truthful, and honorable. Work sincerely for your pay. Don't be a "clock watcher"— one who puts in the necessary hours while he waits anxiously for the day to end. Man's duty in life is to become, above all, increasingly *aware*. This path all must follow toward their final destiny, cosmic consciousness. Be the sort of worker, then, who applies himself intelligently, conscientiously, and *supportively* to the tasks he is given. You don't have, in other words, to become emotionally involved in the goals of your firm or of your employer to do your work well. Indeed, let Sri Krishna's advice to Arjuna be your guide: *Act without desire for (or attachment to) the fruits of your action.*

I once met a Kriya Yogi in Calcutta who was employed, I imagine, in a more-or-less minor capacity; otherwise, I would expect him to have been more emotionally involved in his work than he seemed to indicate. He commuted to work by train every day. While traveling, he would practice a few Kriya breaths, and go breathless. He remained in that superconscious state until his destination was reached, at which point he resumed breathing, returning to outwardness, and descended from the train. This he did going in both directions, morning and evening. I imagine he was inwardly reflective, practicing the presence of God, even while working. Yet he kept his job, and must have been good enough at it to satisfy his employer.

Would such a man be a loss to firm and family? More likely, his presence was a blessing to both.

An elderly sister disciple of our Guru once told me of a stroll she had taken with him one afternoon on the grounds of his seaside hermitage in Encinitas. As they were walking they came upon Rajarshi Janakananda, his most highly advanced disciple, seated on the ground in meditation. The Master whispered, "Let's walk very quietly here so as not to disturb him." The sister's recollections continued: "When we'd gone a little distance further, Master turned to me and said, 'You've no idea what blessings are attracted to this work when even one member of it can meditate as deeply as he does!'"

A place of business is blessed to have a true yogi on its staff, even if his outward contribution is very minor. The magnetism he emanates will attract success at every level to the organization itself. This is, indeed, the greatest secret of material success: keep an *uplifted consciousness.*

Success radiates outward from uplifted awareness, whatever outward mechanics are involved. It is entirely possible for a firm to do everything right, and still fail. And it is also possible to do something completely unorthodox which no one has ever succeeded in doing before, and—if one's consciousness is uplifted—to achieve stunning results. Karma also is involved, of course, but even so one can draw the best from karmic law itself if his consciousness is inspired.

As Patanjali wrote in his *Yoga Sutras*, when non-avarice is entrenched in a person's nature "All jewels are attracted to him." This was a poetic way of saying that material success of all kinds is drawn to one. (Again, this attitude embraces the principle I've quoted often from the Bhagavad Gita: action should be performed with inner freedom—that is, without attachment to the results of action: *nishkam karma*.)

To the worldly mind, material success seems attainable only by "blood, sweat, and tears" (quoting Winston Churchill as he exhorted England to stand firm during World War II). In reality, divine assistance also was involved—something that very few people realized. Karma and Divine Consciousness worked together for England, using the courage of her people as their instrument. Great yogis in India later stated, and my Guru corroborated, that they had been working subtly through Hitler's and Germany's karma to ensure their defeat. This is not merely a pious belief. Sri Aurobindo stated that he himself was one of those yogis. My Guru, Paramhansa Yogananda, was another. Although the influence of karma is supreme, great masters often do work *within* that law to hasten its effects, whether nationally or personally. They involve themselves especially when the issues concern the eternal struggle between darkness and light.

A mere employee, especially in a large company, will not usually see himself as being able to influence his company's policies and directions. Don't underestimate the power, however, of consciousness itself. Often when a situation seems objectively speaking to be hopeless, a change of consciousness in even one corner of an enterprise may have far-reaching results. Because everyone seeks happiness, though some seek it misguidedly, even one person may, for example if he is radiantly happy, influence others for the better by simply *being* happy, himself.

One who gives positive, willing, and cheerful *support* through his work may, even in a minor position, influence everyone around him for the better. It is a simple fact, often stated by Yogananda, that the darkness, although it cannot be driven from a room with a stick, is dispelled at once by simply turning on the light!

An example was told me of a shop, the large parking lot of which had become a teen-age "hangout." The youngsters played heavy rhythm music loudly all day on their radios. The shop owner did not like the music, and felt that it interfered with his business. He was not in a position, however, to tell the youngsters to lower the volume. He brought a positive solution to bear on the problem: He played Mozart and other soothing classical music through a loudspeaker into the parking lot. The teenagers soon took their fun elsewhere!

Even if the position you hold is subordinate, there is much that you can do to create good vibrations around you by simply emanating a cheerful attitude. You don't have to express disapproval of certain policies and attitudes, if they need to be changed. You can do much to change the surrounding *vibrations* by simply expressing a positive energy.

Very few people can be like that Calcutta Kriya Yogi. Even so, you can help to uplift the general consciousness at work by projecting positive vibrations, yourself. Realize, however, that a mere lack of interest is usually negative. To be successful at *anything* requires one to take active interest in *something*. Never be apathetic. Look upon your work as an opportunity above all for lifting your own consciousness.

Try to find a job that will help your own spiritual advancement. You can do this, to begin with, by analyzing your own deep-seated tendencies. Reflect especially on the nature with which you were born. The tendencies a child expresses during the first six years of its life are a good indication to the nature it developed in its last life. Present life experiences may gradually overlay those tendencies, but were you drawn as a child, for instance, to beauty? If so, was it to any particular kind of beauty: to color, form, texture, or to any other aspect?

Were you interested in mechanics? If so, was it toward design, creating, or operating machinery?

Did money interest you? If so, was your interest in buying and selling, or in simply handling money?

Did sports come naturally to you as something you understood as if *from inside*?

Did you have a native flair (as many children have nowadays) for electronics?

The field of inquiry is endless. I propose the above possibilities simply in order to interest you in probing the question. To have a flair for anything may be an indication to the kind of work you might do successfully in the present life.

Next, ask yourself this question: What line of activity do I think might *expand* my sympathies and understanding? In what line do I think I might *serve* others best? Does any line for which I might have a natural aptitude—public speaking, for example, or acting—awaken images of self-glory, rather than of helping and uplifting others? Activity that leads to personal glory, even though it is successful, could have the spiritual disadvantage of increasing the ego's grip and leading, thereby, to an increase of inner bondage, not of inner freedom. Normally, any activity that increases the hold of ego is contrary to yoga principles, even if it results in worldly glory. It is important to realize, however, that all desires must be fulfilled. If the dream of glory is deep-seated, it may need in any case to be realized. In this case, try to direct it expansively toward uplifting others, also. The more prominent one's position in the world, certainly, the broader the good he can do.

A common way to find one's own natural bent is to ponder not only the strengths, but also the weaknesses of one's own heredity. For heredity does play a role, albeit a secondary one, in determining a person's nature. How much we actually inherit from our parents is less actual than may seem to be the case, but to study our forebears may help us toward self-understanding. We inherit some of our physical characteristics, certainly. These are our biological legacy. Each of us comes into this life also, however, with many characteristics that reflect not so much our biological heritage as our former incarnations.

One example, albeit a minor one, may suffice. I personally have always had a somewhat delicate digestion. My Guru once asked me about it. To my reply in the affirmative, he commented, "That's because you had that trouble before." This weakness derived, in other words, not from my parents, and wasn't a genetic transfer from any ancestor. Biologists would say, "Well, it had to be in your genes somewhere." Maybe, but the mind is stronger than material influences. In the case of human beings, the physical tendencies implanted in the subconscious by past experiences may be stronger than anything inherited biologically.

My Guru stated that the consciousness of a couple during sexual union sends out vibrations into the astral world which express their state of mind at the time. Souls that are ready for rebirth, and that are compatible with that vibration, are attracted to it. Often, what a soul (that is to say, of course, a disincarnate ego) in the astral world shares with the couple is only one particularly strong characteristic. Thus, explained Yogananda, a saintly person may sometimes even be born into a criminal home, if he shares with them a strong attraction for example to peace. Of course, the selection also depends on the number of opportunities that are available at the time a soul is reborn.

From these facts it must be understood that the caste system in India, and the racial or class prejudices elsewhere on earth, are all born of misunderstanding of the way these things work. A brother disciple of mine once asked our Guru, "Are not white people with a strong prejudice against blacks likely to be reborn black in their next incarnations?"

"Of course!" replied the Master, chuckling slightly. That simple fact may explain why many "black people" in America nowadays have a strong prejudice against whites: their prejudice carried over in reverse manner from the past!

The caste system must, then, be understood very differently from the way it evolved in India. So also must the class and race distinctions in other countries. We come into life, as the poet Wordsworth said, "trailing clouds of glory [or of inglory!] from afar." Originally, as I have explained, the caste system was an enlightened method for guiding people on the path toward their own liberation.

In lower forms of life, an entity evolves upward by natural degrees. Nature herself draws them upward. According to the Indian scriptures, it takes from five to eight million lifetimes for the Spirit, individualized in material form, to reach the human level. At this point, it acquires a nervous system and brain that are refined enough to continue the process of evolution by its own free will.

It takes time also as a human being to develop in consciousness. Sensitivity develops, over incarnations, into a longing for spiritual enlightenment. So-called "young souls" as human beings have more animalistic urges. The ego requires time to realize that it can use its brain for intelligent thought, and not seek only sense gratification. People on this lowest level of awareness were named *sudras*. Such people think only of their physical needs.

The ancient Indian teachings identified *sudras* with peasants—workers of the soil, in other words. That label was symbolic, however. There have, to be sure, been highly intelligent peasants who were obliged by circumstance to till the soil, or to do other manual labor. They were not necessarily true *sudras*: Some of them may actually have been saints. Society in ancient India was itself far more complex than implied by the simple labels of the caste system. Nowadays, *sudra* types can be found on all levels of society.

Once the ego comes to realize that it can use its intelligence for furthering its self-interest, it acquires cunning; that is to say, it uses its intelligence for selfish ends. The caste system labels such a person a *vaisya*: symbolically, a merchant. (Obviously, again, the leap from peasant to merchant was simplistic in the extreme.) The term refers to all who see human intelligence as a means only to selfish ends.

When, after further incarnations, the ego begins to feel a concern for others' needs and sufferings, it acquires a sensitive desire to help others and to improve their well-being. At this level, a person develops sympathy, and wants to help and uplift others. This class of people, anciently, were labeled, *kshatriyas*. This name generally was applied to soldiers and aristocrats. The soldier best symbolizes this level of refinement, perhaps, for duty calls him to lay down life itself, if need be, to defend others.

As the ego grows further in refinement, it understands that the best way to help others is to show them how they themselves can attain happiness. At this stage, the ego realizes that other benefits are only means to that higher end. What everyone wants, basically, is true joy. Indeed, happiness has its roots in God, *Satchidananda*: ever-existing, ever-conscious, ever-new bliss. Happiness cannot be found through physical acquisition or sense-gratification. The service one renders who has reached this level of refinement, therefore, is primarily spiritual, not material. Such a one is a true *brahmin*, a label identified with the priestly caste.

There is, indeed, a higher level still: *triguna rahitam*, a state transcendent above all caste distinctions and human characteristics. It is the state of the *true brahmin*, the knower of Brahman, or God. From such a person alone emanate those subtle insights which enable souls to escape the prison of ego, and to realize oneness with the Infinite. Philosophical thought alone cannot grant such insight. It can be granted only by a true guru, who himself has attained those heights. The *Sat* Guru alone can transfer Self-realization upon the disciple who is ready for it.

This teaching, of course, takes us far above the level of lessons on material success. I can only indicate it, here, as the *direction* in which everyone must develop if he follows yoga principles to the end.

If you desire to be a good employee *and at the same time* to grow in consciousness, seek work that will somehow uplift your consciousness! Labor that is done automatically and mindlessly with the mind fixed only on the income received takes one downward in consciousness again, toward the *sudra* state.

How many ascents and descents are experienced before the ego finally determines that it must and *will* lift its consciousness to infinity! The fluctuations of fortune are uncountable; they depend entirely on the individual's free choice.

Seek work above all therefore that is compatible with your own needs for spiritual development: work that will assist you in releasing the hold your ego has upon you and deepen your understanding and empathy with others. Keep those ends consciously in mind while you work. Try to please your employer, but never by flattering him. Please him by taking an interest in whatever work he gives you to do. Mental acceptance of whatever must be done is uplifting to one's consciousness. Mental rejection has a lowering effect.

If you work in a large company, and feel you'd rather work under some other company executive, show an intelligent interest in what that person does. Everyone who has others working under him is pleased when they show an active interest in the activities of his department. It will therefore be reasonable for you to hope that, when an opening occurs in that department, the boss may ask that you be reassigned to him. Meanwhile, do as well as you can in whatever department you are now in.

The Application

Keys to Relating to the Boss

1.

Be neither too formal nor too familiar toward him. The customs that govern relationships between employer and employee differ from country to country, but certain modes of behavior apply more or less universally. If custom requires a relationship of strict formality, there may be little communication between you and, therefore, little feeling of cooperation. Even in such a case, however, a supportive attitude accompanied by an occasional smile can go far toward developing mutual appreciation.

In modern times, especially in America, familiarity is often encouraged in order to facilitate easy communication. Many bosses want their subordinates to address them by their first names. Although this may be good, it can also become tricky. Over-familiarity encourages employees to take undue advantage of their bosses' goodwill—blinding them to the fact that they must still do as they are told. Excessive familiarity can also impair the boss's ability to express himself firmly when necessary.

Even friends who find themselves in that relationship need to draw a line between the friendship they enjoy outside the office and the more formal relationship required at work. Since these things depend so much, not only on custom, but on the personalities involved, no rule can be made. Nonetheless, it will help everyone to realize that familiarity can impair the boss's judgment also, while detracting from a high sense of purpose in the employee.

2.

Never be a sycophant, or "yes-man": one whose priority is to please the boss, rather than to do his job well and conscientiously. Some employers foolishly encourage this spirit in their subordinates, favoring those who curry favor with them. The resulting spirit can harm the whole firm.

3.

Relate to your boss from your own inner center to his. Doing so will help to keep your interrelationship on a high, creative level.

4.

Try always to relate to the best that you can see in your employer. Human nature being what it is, you may feel there is not a natural affinity between you. Look, then, for his good points (reflecting that he must have some!), and concentrate on them.

5.

Frequent contact between employer and employee can often create emotional tension—perhaps especially in the subordinate. A superior of mine once remarked to me, "Let's face it: You have no taste!" I was outraged. I think this was the only time I actually wept in frustration over our relationship. The truth is, I felt that, of the two of us, it was I who had good taste and *she* who lacked it! In any case, to have to submit to her judgment on matters unrelated to our work, merely because she was the boss, was an excellent lesson for me in even-mindedness—a lesson which, I'm afraid, I failed that time to pass. Might I have done better? Yes, by remaining centered in myself; by directing my heart's feelings upward; by concentrating on her good points; by *nishkam karma*—giving our relationship to God; and by enjoying the humor of the situation—which in fact I did inwardly, despite my tears!

6.

Develop a supportive attitude. Remember, it isn't likely that your boss will actually enjoy bullying you; probably he wants simply to do as well as he can at his job. If in fact, however, he gives you a hard time, what better "revenge" than to support him quietly, with a friendly smile?

7.

How can you change your boss's mind if ever you think he is mistaken? One way is to agree with him *in principle*, but then to add, "On the other hand, what would you say to this suggestion? . . ." Or perhaps, "What would you say, were I to try it this way? . . ." If the friendship between you exists on firm ground, be completely honest with him. Say, "I suggest we do. . . ." A good boss, even if the two of you are not close friends, will listen to you with respect. Don't insult a person of such honesty by implying, through excessive tact, that you think his ego needs pampering. Tact is a virtue, but with truthful people it should not be wrapped carefully in cotton wool! That very effort may offend them.

8.

Concentrate impersonally on *what* is being done, not on *who* is doing it.

9.

Familiarize yourself with your boss's nature and work with it realistically. Most people have their ups and downs. Understand when to express your personal feelings, and when not to. This doesn't mean you should wheedle, ever. Rather, it indicates a sensitive regard for who and what kind of person your boss is.

10.

Be completely true to your word. Never promise to do a thing and then forget to do it. Let your simple word be your bond. The boss who knows he can rely on you will place his full confidence in you. You will be one of the greatest assets any firm can have.

11.

When your boss assigns you something, try to *go beyond* his expectations. The truly conscientious employee is the one most likely to receive promotion.

12.

Be loyal to your boss. Never speak against him. Answer firmly and supportively of him any criticism others make against him.

I remember once many years ago an announcer in a radio station who, after playing a recorded song of mine, made what I thought was a ridiculous suggestion regarding it. I casually mentioned what he'd said to the receptionist in the front office. She replied, "Oh, that man has no taste." I agreed, and mentioned to my father later on what had happened. I was surprised, and gratified, by his reaction.

"She had no right to say that!" he stated indignantly. "As long as that firm pays her, she should support it and say nothing to its discredit."

He was right. It had been a mistake to chuckle at her words.

13.

Be completely sincere. Don't pretend reactions you don't really feel, simply in order to please your boss. At the same time, respect the fact that he, like most people, probably has foibles of his own. If, for example, he tells what you consider a bad joke, smile kindly even if you don't laugh. To "smile *kindly*" means not cynically or sarcastically, but pleasantly! To be sincere doesn't mean to show disapproval. Be supportive in spirit, above all.

Keys to Relating to Your Fellow Employees

1.

Never try to give the impression that you are "in" with the boss in ways that others are not. This is, universally, a good principle to follow. I could have resolved many a conflict during the founding of Ananda by telling dissenters simply, "I knew our Guru. You did not. Don't you think you should listen to what I say?" I've never once held that club over anyone's head. Instead, what I've always done is let "sweet reason" persuade for me. If I've failed, I've simply let it go at that. Your co-workers will accept you better if you never try to "pull rank" on them.

2.

If you disagree with the boss in anything, never voice the fact generally. If you do speak of your disagreement to a few friends, let it be outside of office hours, on your own time.

3.

Try never to compete with your co-workers. Allow each his "place in the sun." Try, rather, to win by merit, and never by attempting to show up anyone or by displaying yourself as better than others. Such generosity is compatible with yoga principles. It is true that one may sometimes win by scheming. To do so will, however, make you fail in other ways, eventually. The truer you are to the truth itself, the more likely you will be to attract the success you need and deserve.

4.

Be kind to your fellow workers. Help them whenever they need it, and when the opportunity presents itself. If you act thus, they will respond to you in kind. A pleasant atmosphere in the workplace will bring blessings to everyone there.

5.

Go out of your way to show an interest in your co-workers, in their lives, in their problems. Do everything you can to offset a spirit of competitiveness, if it exists, even if it is encouraged from above. If that atmosphere exists, it may even be wiser for you to seek employment elsewhere. For when such a spirit emanates downward from above, there may be nothing you can do about it—though it might be a fascinating challenge for you to try!

6.

Never share information with others that you've been given in confidence. On the other hand, remember always the scriptural dictum: "If a duty conflicts with a higher duty, it ceases to be a duty." If the confidential information concerns a harm that is being plotted against anyone, don't feel in this case that your lips are sealed by the word you gave. To do so would be to compound one mistake with another, even greater!

7.

Make a point to look consciously for good qualities in your co-workers. In disagreements, try to see also their point of view. When you win a point, never beat them down by saying, "I told you so!" Give them a graceful way out.

8.

Greet your fellow workers in a friendly manner at the beginning of each day. At the day's end, again, wish them well. Little courtesies like these do much to keep the machinery of our relationships running smoothly.

9.

Keep to yourself any sad mood you feel. It isn't fair to dump your private worries onto others, like a bucket of cold water.

10.

Politeness is something people often reserve for strangers or for people they meet seldom. It will help to keep the "machinery" of your daily relationships running smoothly if you are polite and considerate also to those you work with daily.

11.

The patterns of speech you use toward your co-workers can have an uplifting or a depressing effect on the entire work force. Be clean-minded, courteous, and never coarse. Be just as much so in your relaxed speech.

12.

During the humorous banter that naturally occurs among co-workers, laugh *with* them kindly. Never laugh *at* them.

General Suggestions

Depend on no specific *thing* to get you interested. Develop a habit of just *being interested*. Interest depends not on the energy you receive, but on what you give out to your work, to others, and to the world. Thus, referring back to that Kriya Yogi in Calcutta, although he was probably not deeply involved in his work, yet he must have given it willing energy and shown an interest in the sense that his work commanded his full and concentrated attention. God is in everything, after all. To know Him, one must seek Him either in everything or in nothing! One can adopt an attitude of "Not this, not that" (*neti, neti*), thereby eliminating gradually from his heart every desire for anything external to himself. This is not a useful attitude, however, for employees in a workplace.

The other attitude is to see the Lord everywhere, and in that spirit to enjoy everything one does.

A beautiful book by Corrie ten Boom, *The Hiding Place*, describes a Nazi concentration camp, to which the author and her sister were sent after they'd been discovered helping Jews in Holland to escape. Corrie's sister, especially, was an extraordinary woman. At one point she said to Corrie, "We must thank God for everything."

Corrie balked. "Even for the fleas infesting our barracks?" she protested.

"Even for them!" retorted her sister.

Some time later, the two sisters were in their barracks holding a forbidden prayer meeting with a few other prisoners. All of a sudden the guard of their barracks arrived at the door with a group of military visitors whom she was showing around. Had they entered and discovered that group, all of them would have been summarily shot. The guard, however, on reaching the door, turned to her companions and said, "Let's not enter here. This place is infested with fleas!"

Corrie's sister died in that camp. After death, her face was radiant with divine bliss.

Whatever motives you have for gratitude, remember something Paramhansa Yogananda said: "Conditions are always neutral. They seem either sad or happy depending on the sad or happy attitudes of the mind."

To be a good employee, then—satisfying to your employer and even more satisfied within yourself—remember: Whether you enjoy your work and do well at it depends less on the work itself than on the *attitude* you hold toward it.

MEDITATION

Visualize yourself as a traveler in a foreign land. Carry a bright light, like a torch, in your heart, shining forth energy and joy onto everything. Whatever pleasure you derive from the sights around you depends on how you react to them.

Shed light everywhere around you. Smile with confidence in the fact that, as you are within, so will this foreign land be for you. *Be* joyful inwardly first, then. With that joy, observe everything around you. What you bring to the world will determine what you gain from it.

AFFIRMATION

"I *enjoy* life; I enjoy *myself*, no matter what is bestowed on me!"

POINTS TO REMEMBER

1. To be a successful employee means to be the kind of person who takes an intelligent and supportive interest in the company and in its over-all aims.

2. One must work with *what is*, while remaining faithful to higher ideals. Ideally, he should seek work in a place that has high principles.

3. If you need to work under someone else, and cannot devote yourself wholeheartedly to the job you get, be at least honest, truthful, and honorable. Be the sort of worker who applies himself intelligently, conscientiously, and *supportively* to the tasks he is given.

4. The greatest secret of material success is to keep an *uplifted consciousness*. A change of consciousness in even one corner of an enterprise may have far-reaching results.

5. One who gives positive, willing, and cheerful *support* through his work may influence everyone around him for the better.

6. Never be apathetic. Look upon your work as an opportunity above all for lifting your own consciousness.

7. Try to find a job that will help your own spiritual advancement. You can do this, to begin with, by analyzing your own deep-seated tendencies. Next, ask yourself this question: What line of activity do I think might *expand* my sympathies?

8. Seek work that will assist you in releasing the hold your ego has upon you and deepen your understanding and empathy with others.

9. Take an interest in whatever work your employer gives you to do. Mental acceptance of whatever must be done is uplifting to one's consciousness. Mental rejection has a lowering effect.

Keys to Relating to the Boss

10. Be neither too formal nor too familiar toward him. Relate to your boss from your own inner center to his. Doing so will help to keep your interrelationship on a high, creative level.

11. Develop a supportive attitude. Familiarize yourself with your boss's nature and work with it realistically. Never speak against your boss.

12. Be completely true to your word. Never promise to do a thing and then forget to do it.

13. When your boss assigns you something, try to *go beyond* his expectations.

Keys to Relating to Your Fellow Employees

14. Be kind to your fellow workers. Help them when the opportunity presents itself. Do everything you can to offset a spirit of competitiveness.

15. Never share information with others that you've been given in confidence.
16. Make a point to look consciously for good qualities in your co-workers.
17. Keep to yourself any sad mood you feel.
18. It will help to keep the "machinery" of your daily relationships running smoothly if you are polite and considerate to those you work with daily.
19. The patterns of speech you use toward your co-workers can have an uplifting or a depressing effect on the entire work force. Be clean-minded, courteous, and never coarse.

General Suggestions

20. Depend on no specific *thing* to get you interested. Develop a habit of just *being interested*. Interest depends not on the energy you receive, but on what you give out to your work, to others, and to the world.
21. Whether you enjoy your work and do well at it depends less on the work itself than on the *attitude* you hold toward it.
22. Shed light everywhere around you. What you bring to the world will determine what you gain from it.

WORKBOOK IDEAS
by Joseph Bharat Cornell

Where Would I Go?

In snow country, sled dogs are noted for their tremendous enthusiasm for running and pulling heavy loads. Yet, as with humans, not all sled dogs are alike. The secret of a successful sled dog team is taking advantage of the strengths of each dog. Some dogs are strong, but they don't listen very well. These dogs are placed close to the sled, where they can do good hard work, and follow the other dogs.

The dogs in front of them are "team dogs." They, too, do best following other dogs, and they provide the "horsepower" to move the sled. Some dogs enjoy the mental challenge of being the lead dog. These dogs have the energy to run very fast, but they must, in addition, be good listeners. The musher, or driver, depends on them to listen for and follow his commands. Lead dogs also keep the sled's "towline" taut to prevent his team from tangling up.

The lead dogs, however, would be unable to turn the rest of the team without the help of the "swing dogs." These dogs run immediately behind the leader; they help him keep the fast pace and aid him in getting the team to turn when necessary.

Another ingredient in a successful team is that each dog participates fully. Occasionally a dog will run with the team but not pull any of the weight—he is betrayed by his slack tug line, which ties him to the main tow line.

The parallels to humans in the workplace are obvious. The goal is that each person be able to use his strengths to the utmost, and that in doing so he fully pull his weight for the organization. Not every employee can be a leader. But every employee can be energetically supportive. Remember, what you bring to the world will determine what you gain from it.

ACTION ITEM:
Reflect on your attitudes at work and ask:
1. If I were a sled dog, where would my strengths and temperament place me?
2. How can I apply myself more intelligently, conscientiously, and supportively at work?
3. What two things would I like to implement this week? Write them below:

ACTION ITEM:
Yogananda said: "Conditions are always neutral. They seem either sad or happy depending on the sad or happy attitudes of the mind." How much you enjoy your job depends less on its tasks than on your attitude.
- This next week, vow that you will greet each part of your job with enthusiasm. Experiment by welcoming each challenge and putting your best energy into it. Pay attention, and see if doing so brings you not only more enthusiasm but more energy and creativity as well.

The people in an organization should count more with you than the work they are doing. *"People are more important than things."* If you make your co-workers your priority, you will inspire them to do far better in their work.

—Swami Kriyananda, *The Art of Supportive Leadership*

LESSON SEVENTEEN

THE IMPORTANCE OF A HARMONIOUS ENVIRONMENT

A harmonious decor will assist toward developing a harmonious consciousness. Although it is *consciousness*, actually, that produces the vibrations, a harmonious decor, and harmony also in the other features I've described, will encourage an uplifted consciousness.

The Principles

During my first or second year at Haverford College I had the bright idea that it might help me, while studying for an exam, to take a job baby-sitting for an evening in a neighbor's home, removed from campus distractions. After the parents went out, I spent a half hour or so romping with their two boisterous children, and then I had the house silently to myself.

To my surprise, something kept me from concentrating on my studies. The atmosphere seemed to discourage any serious focus. I looked around me. The home was pleasant enough; I noticed, however, no serious reading matter in the living room: only a few popular magazines scattered on the coffee table, but no bookshelves or books anywhere, and no indication that the couple thought seriously about anything. The vibrations seemed superficial. I'd come there with a purpose, but found it necessary to exert unusual will power in order to concentrate at all. I did manage to study, but only with difficulty.

I use this illustration to call attention to something I consider important in the workplace. Perhaps everyone has experienced it at times: namely, places may possess vibrations, which reveal the consciousness of the people who have lived in or frequented them. The strength of those vibrations depends on the intensity and duration of the awareness that was focused there. The vibrations, even of holy shrines, may have become overlaid in time by other vibrational layers: worldliness perhaps, or tourism.

Centuries of focused devotion produce powerful vibrations, particularly if the feeling expressed has been deep and sincere. It is possible to "excavate" intuitively in such places by a kind of spiritual archaeology, and thus to descend through centuries of other vibrational layers that have accumulated there. I remember doing just that at Capernaum, on Lake Galilee in Israel. Meditating there, I felt all at once the living presence, two thousand years ago, of Jesus Christ and his disciples' youthful enthusiasm.

At Delphi, in Greece, which was for many centuries the primary place of spiritual pilgrimage in the West, I was thrilled by the ancient spiritual vibrations that still permeate that holy place long since the days of pilgrims who came from afar. I was amused also to pass a group of American tourists as they exited a shrine just as I was entering it. Strangers, evidently, to silent awe, they were chatting volubly together about trivial matters back home.

It is quite understandable, for this reason, why certain holy temples in India forbid entry to non-Hindus. They do so not to preserve any secrets, but rather to preserve the sacred vibrations of devotion. In certain temples—at the Vishnupad Temple in Gaya, for instance—the vibrations are so strong they override the worldliness even of worshipers who go there to pray for earthly boons. (At least they do pray there!) Wherever great saints and yogis have deeply meditated, their power remains embedded, so to speak, in the very stones.

The vibrational aspect of different places I've visited has become, for me, the most fascinating aspect of traveling. I make it a point wherever I go to "feel" the vibrations, instead of merely gazing at the tourist attractions. Indeed, as places of tourist interest those places are, for me, less of a draw now than as places to be *felt*. Often, the places are deeply imbued with the vibrations they've gathered over centuries, owing to the consciousness of the people who lived, worked, played, or worshiped there.

Here are a few more examples of a phenomenon that will, I hope, help to convince you of a feature of your own workplace that deserves serious attention:

I've noticed more than once when traveling from California to Mexico a change in the vibrations as I crossed the border in either direction. In Mexico, I was immediately impressed by the slower, more relaxed vibration of what Mexicans themselves describe as "*mañana* (tomorrow)" consciousness.

When crossing the border from the state of Nevada into California, I've noticed a certain "lift" in the atmosphere. Nevada gains much of its wealth by gambling, and has, in consequence, developed something of a *taking* consciousness, not one of giving or of wealth earned by hard work. Entering California from that state, I've been repeatedly aware of a higher, more creative energy even as I crossed the state line.

Again, going north from California into Oregon I've noticed even while crossing the border a diminishing tension in the air, a feeling that people wanted more to live in harmony with Nature than to conquer her.

The vibrations in India are highly spiritual—a fact on which many Westerners have commented. Even in Calcutta (or Kolkata), one of the noisiest, dirtiest, and most crowded cities in the world, I am thrilled by the deeply devotional vibrations in the air. It is the city I love best in all the world.

I remember also arriving at the airport in Delhi. I've had the same feeling there repeatedly, but this time it was many years ago, late at night. I took an airport bus to Connaught Place, at the center of the city. Around me in that rattling conveyance were Western travelers, but no Indians. The darkness outside prevented me from seeing anything of the countryside. Thus, there was nothing, visually speaking, but the bus itself to remind me that I was in India. Yet, as I closed my eyes, I actually felt a joy welling up out of the ground—the enduring legacy of thousands of years in that land of great yogis and rishis who, in deep meditation, left their blessings in the soil. This legacy will never be destroyed by any amount of modernizing.

America, too, despite the karmic wrongs it has committed (as have all nations), has basically good karma, which will see it through the hard times that, my Guru often said, would soon come upon the world. In fact he told us that America and India will lead the world, in future, toward a more balanced material and spiritual way of life. Students of this course will add their positive energy, I hope, to that wave of good karma.

Let me finish these few prefatory remarks with two more brief but relevant stories:

One day while I lived at Mt. Washington (the international headquarters of the organization my Guru founded), a group of us monks went in a pickup truck to the mountains for a day of skiing. When we returned, I lay in the bed of the truck with my eyes closed, meditating. Suddenly I sat up and exclaimed, "How peaceful it feels!" I opened my eyes and saw that we had just driven in the gates of the grounds on Mt. Washington.

Another time, many years later, at Ananda Village I had a similar experience. I had just come back from a trip overseas, and was strolling with a friend down the dirt road below the property on which my home is located. On our return, I was paying little heed to where we were. Suddenly I exclaimed, "How peaceful it feels!" Looking around, I saw that we had just crossed the boundary onto Ananda land.

I've devoted quite a lot of space till now describing things that may not seem relevant to this lesson, but that will, I hope, help to clarify points I want to make here. My purpose has been to convince you of a point few people may think about: namely, that places develop vibrations according to the consciousness of the people living, working, or worshiping there. This fact leads me to emphasize the importance of the vibrations you infuse into your workplace, which can either contribute to your success, or obstruct it. Those vibrations deserve to be taken quite seriously, and not ignored as they usually are.

If the over-all "feeling" where you work is harmonious—and harmony is assisted by neatness and cheerfulness—it will encourage everyone who works there to concentrate on his job. If, however, the feeling is one of disorder, restlessness, or gloom, the vibrations will discourage efficiency and will dampen people's enthusiasm. Success thoughts should be objectified in the very decor, which can help to uplift or depress the workers' spirit, and can thus aid in creating good vibrations. The vibrations will be enhanced by appropriate sounds, colors, shapes, and designs. If all these factors suggest a sense of dullness and confusion, they can produce vibrations of failure. It is possible to aid deliberately in the creation of good vibrations even if the space you've inherited comes with disharmonious vibrations infused in it by its previous occupants. A harmonious decor will assist toward developing a harmonious consciousness. Although it is *consciousness*, actually, that produces the vibrations, a harmonious decor, and harmony also in the other features I've described, will encourage an uplifted consciousness.

Several of the Ananda communities in America were run-down housing developments purchased because that was all we could afford at the time. They were rebuilt, and today they are, in fact, model communities. Though the vibrations of those places were low, our vibrant, positive energy soon drove out the slovenly energies.

Rebuilding with positive energy places that have become decrepit will reduce the initial expenses, especially if you have people who are able to do that work, or if you can get it done cheaply. If you can afford a new place, however, this may well—in terms of developing the vibrations you want—be the best solution.

Harmony in the workplace depends first of all on the consciousness infused into it. A harmonious consciousness objectifies itself naturally as outward harmony. Pleasant sounds and colors actually help to induce a more dynamic, energetic state of mind. Success depends to a great extent on clear thinking, which is enhanced by outer harmony.

Most important, of course, is, as I've said, the predominant *consciousness* in the workplace. It is this which becomes reflected in such things as outward appearance. That consciousness can, however, be deliberately enhanced by outward appearances. Thus, to promote a general atmosphere of efficiency, important for promoting success at every level, there is much that can be done not only by admonition, but through improving the decor, the arrangement of the furnishings, the level of noise, and by a number of other factors that we'll present in this chapter. It is important to understand also that non-attention to these factors can create an opposite sort of atmosphere: negativity, arguments, laziness, anger, and other emotions which cannot but impact negatively the very work flow.

When I was a schoolboy in England, fighting was kept under control by a simple rule: A boy's impulse to strike someone had to be deferred until a formal match could be arranged in the gym, complete with boxing gloves and seconds. Thus, the bellicose energy of young boys wasn't suppressed, but the cooling-off period (encouraged, though not always with success!) between the challenge and the actual moment of battle was sufficiently often long enough to cool off angry tempers.

I am not suggesting that a similar solution be adopted in your workplace. That rule in an English school was designed for rambunctious boys. In offices, physical fighting is rare to nonexistent. *Arguments* and harsh words, however, are fairly common. What I suggest is that, wherever possible, a separate room be set aside for activities unrelated to the actual work. If an argument seems to be brewing, people could be required to go to this room and "talk it out." The room could also be a place where people go for their "coffee breaks" or moments of relaxation and simply chatting. The important thing is not to disturb the vibrations where work is done. The workers themselves can be encouraged to limit their activities at work to more serious matters. By "serious" I hope you understand that I don't mean *grim*! Cheerfulness is important to enthusiasm, and enthusiasm is essential for real creativity.

The above suggestion depends also, of course, on the kind of work that is done. If your business is manufacturing, and if it employs many workers, the situation may not permit having a special room set aside for any separate purpose.

In the case of a manufacturing plant, you may want to think also about infusing your products with uplifting vibrations. Modern mass-production is efficient, but from a vibrational point of view it is hardly ideal. Things will not change, of course, so long as they facilitate the production of cheaper goods. Realistically, then, the assembly-line method will be with us at least for the present, despite the fact that it tends to dull the workers' consciousness as they sit there all day, doing a single movement, like tightening a screw, as the conveyer belt passes by. This system works, a fact which will be its supreme rationale until some better and *workable* system is found. Someday, perhaps, the general level of affluence will induce people to buy things that have been produced also with loving care, and not only with the mind-numbing motions that are required on the assembly-line. I sincerely hope so.

Even now, however, such care can be infused into *designing* a product. Shapes and colors can still be mass produced that are pleasing to eye and heart, and not merely functional. Such products are attractive, even on display in mass-appeal department stores. I'll buy such things only if I need them, of course, but it is always good to find beautiful things at low prices. Love needn't be missing altogether from any workplace, even if such feeling is expressed only in the design department, behind the scenes.

There are many people—let's face it—who will work mechanically in any case. They'll at least be more cheerful if their take-home pay pleases them. And this kind of pleasure is the most likely result of modern manufacturing methods. Better this, usually, than old-fashioned, inefficient, but for all that still-plodding labor. Mass production methods, moreover, please also the customers in their correspondingly lower prices.

The consciousness with which a person works is, as I said, the most important ingredient of success. Not all work demands *creative* consciousness in the actual doing, but even uncreative work can be done with focus and efficiency. Offices where disharmony and disorder prevail are the opposite of efficient. How can success-consciousness be the rule, where people must spend minutes in finding the things they use daily, which ought to be at their fingertips? How can they concentrate, where distractions are constant? And how can they work with calm attention in places where the very colors are restless and even depressing?

Sound also exerts a very important influence on the mind. Music in the workplace has proved helpful in many situations. It can help even by obscuring the disruptive effect produced by people talking on the telephone, or discussing business matters with one another — sounds that are necessary to most workplaces, but that distract others who are trying to concentrate on their own work.

Shop owners often delegate to their salespeople the decision of what music to play for the customers. This form of delegation can be a serious mistake. Often the sales force consists of restless youngsters, hopefully committed to their work, whose taste in music reflects a general disinterest in anything serious. The music recordings they play are often loud and annoying to customers whose preference, usually, is a calmer atmosphere. Personally speaking, I should add that restless music has actually driven me out of a shop. When people are shopping they may want to take time in making their selections. When eating in restaurants, too, they enjoy and digest their food better in a calm atmosphere. When selecting books in a bookstore, they need not only a thoughtful, but perhaps even an uplifting atmosphere. The music played in all these places should be selected with other considerations in mind than the frequently restless tastes of the salespeople.

There are places, of course, where restless music can help in energizing people. A carnival atmosphere is suitable for places where people like excitement. The thing is to understand that the sound selected for a store ought to help in creating vibrations that will promote whatever activity is to be encouraged.

Returning to the subject of decor, I have been in offices — especially in India — where files are stacked up to the ceiling, conveying a "fuddy-duddy" impression. In such a place the workers, when confronting any problem, must tend to think, "Now let me see — it seems to me this problem came up years ago. When was it? Oh yes, back in '76. How *did* we handle it then? Ye-e-es, yes, we must have gone at it in something like this way." And so, hemming and hawing, they proceed with abstracted eyes and minds. Tradition rules supreme in such places, and fresh ideas are almost studiously shunned.

If many people work together in your workplace, it might save the firm money to hire an efficiency expert, to suggest ways of improving the work flow. If that person is really good at his job, he may be able to take into consideration such things as sound, color, and lighting. Considerations like these, however, will probably not be specialties of his.

As regards lighting, keep in mind that it isn't easy to work with energy in poor lighting. A wise employer will spend the necessary money to provide good lighting.

Tungsten lighting has been found to be tiring on the eyes after a time, and therefore to have a dulling and even sleep-inducing effect on the mind. Full spectrum lighting can be a good investment; do at least consider it. A friend of mine, on the other hand, has made a long study of this particular subject for his work, and has offered me the following suggestions. He recommends using *new* fluorescent lighting. Ideal, he said, is a combination of two tubes, one of them with "cool white" light; the other with "warm white." Halogen lights are excellent also, as a supplement. He recommended 75-watt spotlights for detailed work, and 150-watt floodlights for work requiring manual skill in assembling things.

Color can be very important. Some colors are soothing, some, energizing; still others have a depressing effect. It has been found in hospital rooms, for example, that a soothing shade of green can have a healing influence, and is certainly an improvement over the usual, antiseptic white. Pure, bright colors energize the mind, whereas muddy colors tend to dull it.

A bright cherry red is cheering, whereas certain darker reds can have an aggravating effect, and may even upset some people emotionally, especially if they themselves have a tendency to get angry or emotional. There are quiet red shades which, when balanced harmoniously against other colors such as a golden yellow, can help to influence the mind to be wakeful and relaxed. In my home in India there is a room on a mezzanine where a darkish hue of red mixed with a little blue on the arms of the chairs and a sofa is offset against a golden hue for the backs. This color scheme helps to energize and also to relax the mind.

A bright orange should be used with care, for it is the color of fire. A pure orange can uplift the mind, but a more violent shade will draw attention—excessively, usually—to itself. The colors in the workplace need to help in energizing people, but should not be distracting.

A soft yellow helps to stimulate mental activity. Usually, yellow is best in a golden shade rather than in a lemony hue.

Green is, as I've suggested, a healing color. It is also relaxing, and therefore a good color, possibly, for restaurants. It will be less helpful in shops where one wants to encourage customers to pull out their money and *buy*! And although green may be good in real estate offices, it may be excessively calming in places where the staff itself needs stimulation.

Blue—you may have noticed that I am going through the colors of the rainbow—is calming and expansive to the mind. Blue, therefore, is a good color for intellectual work. Lighter shades of blue are more activating in their effect than darker hues.

Indigo is a dark blue, and may be good for spiritual work, for psychological or philosophical counseling, and for inspirational activity. Indigo is less helpful, however, where outgoing energy is required.

Violet, finally, is excellent for reading or writing poetry, and for studying or writing works of spiritual inspiration. It offers less support to outward activities, however, for it tempts the mind inward.

A soothing off-white, not too glaring, is an excellent basic color, and goes well on ceilings especially, where it reflects light clearly.

Neatness is a "must" in business offices—except, possibly, where newspaper work is done. In newspaper offices, a certain amount of excitement, accompanied even by a little disorder, may help in reporting the jumble necessary for producing exciting, last-minute news items.

It helps for the furniture in a workplace to be pleasant and uplifting to the spirit. Solid colors are more soothing than patterned fabrics. Avoid especially any patterns that are jarring. Tiger, zebra, and leopard designs spring to mind. A friend of mine in America had a cat for a pet. She bought herself a dress with a leopard pattern. The moment her cat saw it folded up and laid over the back of a chair, it froze in terror, then backed carefully away out of the room as if fearful of being attacked! A strange reaction, surely, considering that it had never seen a leopard! Perhaps what distressed it was a suggestion of emotional disturbance in the pattern. "Busy" patterns of any kind can induce a certain uneasiness in the mind.

The work in a large office is helped by dividers separating different areas of activity. The dividers should be of a uniform, neutral color. An off-white beige may be effective as a means of promoting calmness and concentration. I have never tried another color, but green might work well also; certainly not blue, nor any of the cooler colors at the other end of the spectrum from red. And red, orange, or yellow will have the effect of intruding too much excitement into a workplace when calmness is required.

The carpets selected are important for their color scheme. Since they'll mostly be hidden by desks and other furniture, however, solid colors may be best except in areas where they are fully visible: in rooms, for example, where visitors sit, or where staff members relax together.

Pictures should be placed in wall areas where people can look up for a moment and enjoy them as a means of relaxing their minds. Tranquil landscapes have a much more soothing effect than jarring "moderns"—though abstract color designs, if well selected, can also be soothing. It is important, in the case of abstractions, that they not be so bland as to be no longer interesting, in time.

Space is an important consideration in most offices. The attempt to economize by crowding the desks together, with uncomfortably narrow aisles to walk through, may in time be counterproductive.

The ancient oriental feng shui and Vastu methods are no doubt excellent; it would be well to give them serious consideration. Those systems are outside the scope of the present lesson, however, because I myself haven't studied them. The one fault I find with them—which accounts for a certain resistance I feel toward them—is the fanaticism of some of their votaries, who seem almost religious in their dedication! As with many fads, these systems can become emotional issues that obscure common sense.

Finally, the clothing people wear in the workplace is important both for their own morale and for the general look. Where some sort of dress code is required, of course I make no demur. Where factory work is being done, again, how workers dress is less important. Their clothes are more or less hidden by machinery, in any case. In offices, however, and in retail shops and other similar places, if no uniform dress code is required it matters very much that everyone dress neatly and in good taste—not for purposes of showing off, but simply to be pleasing to the eye. Whether the people to be pleased are one's fellow workers or the customers, do try—out of respect for others, not out of vanity—to dress pleasingly.

The Application

Expense is a major consideration when designing any workplace. Most employers would rather concentrate on what is being produced than on the labor involved in production. To ignore the production end, however, can be counterproductive. Even to concentrate only on efficiency, while forgetting the workers' morale and energy level, is to cut their output significantly.

Harmony in the workplace certainly affects people's attitude. Because it is the mind which rules the body, so also positive energy ultimately ensures the success of any enterprise. Deprive the workplace of this feature, and you put your entire work at risk of failure.

I mentioned one or two lessons ago the need for the boss to keep the controlling reins in his own hands. I once had a boss who justified her unwillingness to let other people make decisions by stating, "I have to keep the reins in my hands!" Sometimes the thought occurred to me to reply, "Yes, but that doesn't mean you must be the horse!" Sometimes it is necessary to let the horse have its head.

Recognize the workers' importance in any group endeavor. Devote kindly and respectful attention to their needs. Understand that money spent on their behalf may bring you significant returns. If you cannot afford immediately to make every change you'd like, create an agenda. Make a few changes at a time, when and as you can afford them. But do let people see that you are moving in the right direction.

I've suggested consulting an efficiency expert to improve your work flow. My suggestion, when I made it, "bled over" into an area that might be considered more properly the domain of an interior decorator. There can be a problem, however, with any expert, for experts often want to draw attention to their own expertise rather than focus on the real needs. I am inclined, in fact, to suggest that you not seek help from such people unless really necessary. Instead, you might ask a friend, or one on whose taste you rely. You could even depend on your own taste if you have the self-confidence to make decisions as to which colors, patterns, and color balances to choose. A word of caution: Don't let the choosing be a team effort. For many people, even if their taste is individually good, contradict one another to such a degree that the over-all effect is merely to disrupt the harmony.

There was a practice in Japan many years ago. Maybe it is still in use; I don't know. The idea was that all the employees gathered at the start of the day to sing the company song. This practice smacks, perhaps too much, of flag waving; I confess I myself would be embarrassed to sing a company-boosting anthem. To sing songs, however, that energize people, and that have meaningful words, may be a good idea for you.

I myself have written over 400 pieces of music, about 250 of which are songs, most of which are meant to inspire. I'm thinking now of one of them which the members of Ananda often sing, which might be good for any group of workers at the start of the day. Let me write out the words. You could get the melody—and the parts for choral singing—by writing to the publisher.

> Many hands make a miracle:
> Let's all join hands together!

Life on earth is so wonderful
When people laugh and dance and struggle as friends,
Then all their dreams achieve their ends!

Many hands make a miracle:
People climbing together!
Soon we reach to the pinnacle
Of every mountain peak we hazard as one,
We'll lift our hands to welcome the sun!
    We lift our hands to welcome the sun!

We've found in our Ananda communities that singing this, and also other songs, together—I don't like to call them *mine*, for they were received in divine inspiration—does more to bring people together in unity than any other single thing at Ananda. Choirs from the Ananda Sangha communities often travel, even abroad, and have often performed to standing ovations.

Singing is, of course, merely a suggestion. You may think it a trivial one. Still, you might find it more helpful than you imagine. Moreover, it won't cost you anything!

MEDITATION

Visualize a clear night sky full of stars—as many stars as might be seen together through a powerful telescope. Then imagine melodies of joy accompanied by rich harmonies, filling the universe with divine joy and aspiration toward perfection. Sing with the stars! Sing till you feel your oneness with existence itself!

AFFIRMATION

"I will work with the universe to achieve every worthwhile end in my life. My efforts and Thy joy are *one*!"

POINTS TO REMEMBER

1. If the over-all "feeling" where you work is harmonious—and harmony is assisted by neatness and cheerfulness—it will encourage everyone who works there to concentrate on his job.

2. Pleasant sounds and colors actually help to induce a more dynamic, energetic state of mind. Success depends to a great extent on clear thinking, which is enhanced by outer harmony.

3. Wherever possible, set aside a separate room for activities unrelated to the actual work.

4. Love needn't be missing altogether from any workplace, even if such feeling is expressed only in the design department, behind the scenes.

5. The consciousness with which a person works is the most important ingredient of success. Not all work demands *creative* consciousness in the actual doing, but even uncreative work can be done with focus and efficiency.

6. Sound exerts a very important influence on the mind. The sound selected for a store ought to help in creating vibrations that will promote whatever activity is to be encouraged.

7. If many people work together in your workplace, it might save the firm money to hire an efficiency expert, to suggest ways of improving the work flow.

8. Keep in mind that it isn't easy to work with energy in poor lighting. A wise employer will spend the necessary money to provide good lighting.

9. Color can be very important. Some colors are soothing, some, energizing; still others have a depressing effect. Pure, bright colors energize the mind, whereas muddy colors tend to dull it.

10. Neatness is a "must" in business offices.

11. It helps for the furniture in a workplace to be pleasant and uplifting to the spirit. Solid colors are more soothing than patterned fabrics.

12. The work in a large office is helped by dividers separating different areas of activity. The dividers should be of a uniform, neutral color.

13. Pictures should be placed in wall areas where people can look up for a moment and enjoy them as a means of relaxing their minds.

14. Space is an important consideration in most offices. The attempt to economize by crowding the desks together may in time be counterproductive.

15. In offices and in retail shops, and other similar places, it matters very much that everyone dress neatly and in good taste—not for purposes of showing off, but simply to be pleasing to the eye.

16. Devote kindly and respectful attention to the needs of the workers. Understand that money spent on their behalf may bring you significant returns. Make a few changes at a time, when and as you can afford them. But do let people see that you are moving in the right direction.

17. To sing songs that energize people, and that have meaningful words, may be a good idea for you.

WORKBOOK IDEAS
by Joseph Bharat Cornell

Examine your workplace—as if seeing it for the first time. What do you feel when you walk in the door? Do you feel a rise of energy or a lowering of energy? A sense of joy or discouragement?

Look more closely: Do you see a place that encourages focused and creative work? If you are serving customers, does your business welcome them with appealing colors, decorations, sounds, smells, and friendly staff?

ACTION ITEMS:
1. Use this simple survey to assess your work environment to see where you might make some improvements:

   Is Your Workplace:

   1 2 3 4 5 6 7 8 9 10
   CLUTTERED   CLEAN AND TIDY

   1 2 3 4 5 6 7 8 9 10
   DISORGANIZED AND CHAOTIC   WELL-ORDERED AND EFFICIENT

   1 2 3 4 5 6 7 8 9 10
   NOISY AND IRRITATING   CALM AND HARMONIOUS

Are a) the colors, b) lighting, and c) furnishings:

1	2	3	4	5	6	7	8	9	10
DREARY									CHEERFUL

2. Is the over-all energy:

1	2	3	4	5	6	7	8	9	10
LOW AND DEADENING				ENERGIZING			OVERSTIMULATING AND NERVOUS		

3. How does your environment affect the attitudes of the staff? Of the customers?
4. Is the environment aiding the success of your business or hampering it?
5. Look at the following list of changes and see which you can do:

    a. Immediately

    b. In the coming month

    c. As a long-range goal

    - Clear the clutter. Cleaning and organizing can make a profound difference.
    - Open the closets and drawers and clean them out. Clear the surfaces.
    - Clean. Wash windows, clean dust and cobwebs.
    - Simplify. Get rid of duplicate items and things you're no longer using. Each item should have a specific and current reason to be there.
    - Consider changing or adding colors, using paint or fabrics.
    - Consider adding more light.
    - Add uplifting imagery—art or prints appropriate to the over-all energy desired in your space.
    - Play uplifting music that is appropriate for your work environment.

You may not be able to accomplish some of these changes during normal work hours. Plan an all-staff workday on a day when the business is closed. Have everyone wear casual clothing, and serve a picnic—create a fun experience that will help raise the spirits and closeness of the staff and involve everyone in taking responsibility for a better working environment.

LESSON EIGHTEEN

SECRETS OF EFFECTIVE ADVERTISING

Advertising can help to affirm the perfection towards which you yourself should always aspire. Advertising can help you to clarify in your own mind what your goals are.

The Principles

Advertising has become so sophisticated nowadays that it might almost be described as a science. I don't suppose much remains to be said on the subject, so much is well known, and has been fully explained in numerous, excellent books. I may be able to add a few thoughts here, however, as they relate to yoga principles. Effective *yogic* advertising, moreover, will have a deeper and more long-range impact than most salesmanship has nowadays, some of which reminds me of the merchant who is said to have addressed a customer, "Oh, you want a *green* suit! Please in that case, sir, step over here under the green light."

Advertising can tend to be like a comment made by a character in a play of mine, who asks whether a particular endorsement would not seem "rather like a purveyor of wonder medicines beginning his presentation with the word, 'frankly.'" Peddlers of "wonder medicines" do well, generally, to get out of town fast before their products get tested and are found to consist of furniture polish!

Many of the claims one sees show little concern for the real merits of the items being sold. All the advertisers seem to care about is that people buy, *buy*, BUY!

Two recollections of questionable salesmanship have brought a smile to my lips. The first was an announcement that appeared many years ago in a college newspaper: "RAPE! MURDER! MAYHEM!" Underneath that "scare" headline appeared the message: "Now that we've got your attention, there will be a meeting of the French club next Wednesday at 8:00 p.m."

The other recollection is of something that appeared—again, many years ago—in a general newspaper: an advertisement which read, "Your last chance to send your dollar to Box 213!!!" No reason was offered for sending that money. I was told that this little piece of nonsense reaped sizable rewards!

Most advertising is designed, in fact, with not much more scrupulosity, even if it does manage to be clearer as to its true intentions. Still, I do get the impression that people are more conscious these days of the importance of truth in advertising. Granted, most advertisers would still like to get more returns for less worth, and sometimes even the most for the least: the most sales for the least effort; the most rewards for the least value; the most popularity for the least concern for the customers' actual needs.

I'd like to propose a new approach: one that is in keeping with yoga principles and also effective in terms of the benefits reaped, not only by the buyer, but by the seller as well. What I propose should, indeed, bring benefits to you in terms of greater success. I'm assuming, of course, that you want your business to be long-lasting, not a "fly-by-night" venture. This course is designed for people who want to carve a stable and meaningful niche for themselves in the world. It is not for purveyors of medicine made of furniture polish! The broader your base, especially in people's goodwill, the more stable will your own work be.

There is a commonly expressed thought that business cannot be mixed with spirituality. I hope these lessons have, so far, proved to you that it not only can but *should* be so balanced. Allied to that false concept that spirituality should be excluded from the business world is some people's insistence that spiritual truths ought not to be advertised—that, in fact, the higher an ideal, the less one should "stoop" to promoting it. My Guru's answer to these attitudes was, "If Wrigleys can advertise chewing gum, why shouldn't one print ads that encourage people to chew good ideas?!"

Any hesitation I myself might have felt on this subject was answered for me very convincingly many years ago (in 1959) in Simla, India. It was the last day of a week of daily yoga meditation classes that I was giving. On that day, several people came to me in tears. "If only we'd known one week ago that you were here!" they lamented. "Now you are leaving, and it may be a long time before we'll get another chance of receiving these teachings!"

I realized then how important advertising can be—not for self-promotion, but with the purpose of letting people know what *they themselves* want to know. Advertising can, in other words, offer to others an important service.

People often think of advertising as only self-serving. It can be that, of course, but aren't there many times also when you yourself have needed to know how and where to locate something? And haven't you also been drawn to those ads which presented the solution to your needs in a way that was interesting and attractive?

Advertising your own products or services can also encourage *you* to do better. In fact, the main benefit—as far as you yourself are concerned—may be *increased personal energy*! Advertising can be helpful also to *you*.

The first rule in advertising should be, "The truth above all." This motto doesn't have to mean that the truth needs to be stated in a lackluster and grey manner!

In 1965 I made the first record album of my songs. I called them, generically, "Philosophy in Song," and named the album, *Say "YES" to Life!* An acquaintance of mine recommended to me the name of a promoter in Los Angeles whose specialty, he said, was working with spiritual groups. I decided to give the firm a try. The choice, however, was not a happy marriage! The promoter kept insisting on making exaggerated claims about me: that I was a "great master," a "world-renowned composer and singer," and (in God knows how many fields) "a glittering international success"! I refused every one of his suggestions. After he'd suggested a little more grandiose hyperbole, all of which I rejected, he cried out exasperatedly, "How do you expect us to promote you? You aren't letting us say *anything*!"

Well, I decided that the best solution was not to use him at all. Better that, than having nonsense shouted about me! Truth was my "bottom line." Some people might say, "Well, but if it gets people to buy a good thing, where's the harm in a few grandiose claims to promote it?" No actual harm, perhaps—except to one's own integrity. If you promise people wealth, but give them only a copper coin, they may settle for what they get but in the process you, yourself, will have lost your greatest wealth, which, always, is your integrity. The consideration, What does the promotion do for you personally? doesn't always occur to people who are overeager to sell.

If you want to achieve material success through yoga principles, the first thing to consider is *your sincerity—above all, before Infinite Consciousness*—that is to say, before God, who ever dwells in your own heart.

Oddly enough, most people equate truthfulness with bland mediocrity. This was something that drove me almost to despair before I met my Guru: the tendency so many people had of meeting strong statements with, "Well, now, I don't know"—and then, in their attempt to be "fair-minded," to qualify everything said until there was nothing left but a grey puddle.

Truth is *God*! And isn't God the most glorious truth in existence? His glory far outshines the greatest earthly splendor! Oneness with Him, as my Guru wrote in his poem "*Samadhi*," is "beyond imagination of expectancy."

Obviously, what you're selling isn't that splendid! But unless you are trying to represent at least some part of His creation that, to you, is eminently worthwhile, you should be in another line of work! Even if you sell only doughnuts, you can have fun doing so! Moreover, that sense of fun can be communicated to your intended customers. Fun is an expression of energy, and energy is an expression of God! *Certainly* it is possible to be truthful and say something more interesting than, "Our doughnuts are all right. We think you might like them, or, at least, you won't gag on them."

Promotion with a sense of fun is one way of raising your own energy level, as well as that of those you are trying to reach. Is this, then—one might ask—what is meant by "truth in advertising"? Well, at least it is not *un*true. Moreover, if it increases your own energy level, any rise in energy will lift you *toward* a more expansive vision of truth!

Paramhansa Yogananda used, in America as a young man, to come running out onto the lecture platform with "his long black hair streaming behind him," as Louise Royston, an older disciple, once described him to me. He would begin his addresses with a challenge to his audience: "How is everybody?" then lead them in the shout, "*Awake and ready!*" Next came the demand, "How *feels* everybody?" Again the same response: "*Awake and ready!*" He wanted everyone who heard him to rise to his own level of dynamic energy.

Years later he continued this practice in his church services in California. He would have everybody, again, respond enthusiastically: "*Awake and ready!*"

In his San Diego church, where he gave the service every second Sunday, the alternate minister was a medical doctor—a good man, but, as physicians tend to be, carefully measured in his every statement. Before introducing me at the first service I gave there, he explained to me, "I do things a little differently here." He proceeded to "launch" my service by declaring matter-of-factly, "I trust everyone here today is awake and ready." He called for no response. Then he explained who I was—again, in carefully modulated tones, and allowed me to speak. Truth, for him as for so many others, needed to be washed clean of all color, in the name of sincerity.

Another cautious friend of mine—a good friend, but one with a similar temperament—was described thus to me once: "If he were writing a poem, he'd say, 'The trees are green. The grass too is green. And the sky is blue.'" Wouldn't a genuine poet express himself with more feeling than that? Certainly, if he felt genuinely stirred.

Truth is more than a catalogue of dry facts. *Feelings* are a normal part of human perception; they belong to our reality. Between lurid advertising and modest understatement, there is a possibility of many shades of expression. Some advertisements avoid garish excess, but manage also to express lofty truths and noble sentiments with verve.

Don't let your advertising plod along in mere stock phrases. Each time you describe a product, try to say something new about it. Try, a least in this sense, to imitate God, who in His cosmic creation *never* repeats Himself. Every snowflake is, in some way, unique. Try to view with a fresh mind everything you do! Do think, of course, of the impact your advertising will have on others, but make that impact secondary to your own feelings about your products. If your job is to advertise other people's products, *familiarize* yourself with them. It may seem almost too obvious to give such advice, yet many advertisers don't seem to have familiarized themselves properly with the products they are supposed to promote.

When advertising a product, there are two things especially on which to concentrate: what you yourself like about it, and what you think the customers will like. You can be sincere, even colorful, without resorting to hyperbole. Any attempt to "make a sow's ear into a silk purse" will be quickly evident to sensitive people. Others may at least subliminally perceive the falsity. "Phony" advertising generally puts people off. Exaggerated claims soon lose the power to convince.

This happened once when a Hollywood producer stated, regarding a screenwriter's script, "It's stupendous! It's colossal!" The writer replied dejectedly, "You mean—you don't like it?" Years of conditioning had shown him the falsity in that kind of praise; he recognized it as mere "puffery."

The blurb on the back of a novel I once read announced that the hero in the story went to Germany, where the main action took place. In fact, somebody from Germany did enter the story, somewhere, but all of the action took place in another country entirely. Whoever wrote that blurb obviously hadn't even read the novel!

If you can't promote a product sincerely, it would surely be better to refuse the account. Indeed, it would not be even honest to accept it. In losing that income by your refusal, you'd gradually build up a reputation for integrity. The right people, then, would seek you out for that very reason, in time.

As for advertising your own products, give a little further thought to the difference between truth and fact. Facts may indeed be drab and uninteresting, but truth itself can *and should be glorious*! Truth should inspire. The higher the truth, the more noble, beautiful, helpful, dignified, inspiring it is. What follows in the wake of truth is inner *joy*.

One aspect of joy, on a human level, is its capacity to stimulate in people a sense of fun. If you can plumb deeper than the mere facts, why not describe a product in terms of the *most* that it can supply? And why not do it joyfully? Be sincere, but why be grim?

One good reason for advertising is that it can hold out goals *for yourself* in producing the product. Advertising can help to affirm the perfection towards which you yourself should always aspire. Advertising can help you to clarify in your own mind what your goals are.

If, for example, your product is outstandingly beautiful, you will naturally want to advertise the fact. In this case, doing so will inspire you to work all the harder also to *make* it as beautiful as possible. Advertising can, in other words, help *you* to achieve greater clarity regarding your own products.

Repetition is often helpful in advertising. Repetition must, however be done carefully; never let a formula that works reach the point of dullness in reiterating it. "Marlborough country" is a good example of a theme in cigarette advertising that, so far, has worked well. It would not continue to work, however, were not the photographs depicting that country varied constantly. Variety around a single theme, however, can be very effective.

That is another matter of importance also: Test your advertisements. If you have several, test them in several places to see how well they work, and which of them works best, and where.

The little bit of doggerel, again, that has somehow caught on—"Winston tastes good like a cigarette should"—would not have worked for so many years had it not been constantly varied in its presentation. It pays to emphasize a good formula repeatedly—but never to the point of becoming "tired." Each time you present it, it must be done afresh, with fresh *energy*, especially.

Is it moral to advertise? If your product is worthwhile, why not? In this case, is it moral to advertise cigarettes? That's another story. Smoking is bad for the health. Were I an advertiser I wouldn't accept an account with any cigarette company; I would advertise only products in which I myself sincerely believed. Even so, one cannot help admiring the skill in those advertisements which successfully promote their products.

What was it, then—returning to the story of my first record album—that I really wanted from that Los Angeles promoter? Above all, certainly, I hoped he would listen to my music before going on to tout it. Of course, I hoped he would also *appreciate* the music. Otherwise, what would he possibly gain by promoting it? His stock phrases were like the hole in a doughnut! Of course I'd wanted him to be *creative*, but I also wanted his words to be genuine. Otherwise, what could he have done for me? Anything he said would be a disservice.

I've been active in a number of fields: music composition, song writing, singing, lecturing, teaching, writing "how-to-live" books, trying in a variety of ways to inspire people, founding and leading communities. Many people in these various fields have achieved greater success than I. How long-lasting has their success been? In some cases, it has endured hardly a season. As for others, the future remains to be seen. I myself seem to be an "old war-horse"; that is to say, I've got on fairly well over many years. My successes have not been "flash in the pan." And because I haven't allowed anyone to promote me with "hype," whatever success I've achieved has been won on merit rather than on empty promises. Some people in these fields, who have allowed others to promote their efforts bombastically, have had more sales than my three million. I don't think that "hyping" will wear well in the long run, however. Moreover I don't see in the faces of those "hypees" (excuse the word-coinage!) the kind of satisfaction which comes from a clear conscience, and from an experience of inner peace and joy.

Advertising should be a means of bringing joy—and also fantasy—not only to others, but above all to oneself. The results of anything one does seriously should be greater than the somewhat grim satisfaction of a large bank account. It should be the joy of offering to others something worthwhile, something to improve the quality of their lives, something which does so in ways which they themselves desire.

In terms of yoga principles, I grant you that the more non-attached and desireless one becomes, the higher he will rise spiritually. Non-attachment and desirelessness, however, come not by self-suppression and self-denial. Material fulfillment, albeit fleeting, is at least positive in itself, however disappointing in its aftermath. Through fulfillment one is drawn toward the joy which lies beyond everything material. This is not to say that people should seek to fulfill all their material desires before they seek God. Think of the haggard faces of people who follow only *that* path! Then think of the happy faces of people who have basically what they want in life—enough, at least, to have realized that mere things cannot bring happiness.

Sri Krishna says in the Bhagavad Gita that a fallen yogi, blessed with good karma due to his spiritual practices, is reborn into a good home where his desires can be more easily fulfilled. Thus he gains sufficient freedom, by that fulfillment, to turn again wholeheartedly to God.

Worldly fulfillments lead to entanglements in further desires. One cannot achieve soul freedom until all his desires are fulfilled. Supreme fulfillment comes only in oneness with the Infinite. Worldly disappointment and frustration, on the other hand, bring endless suffering.

It is certainly true that all sensory fulfillments are disappointing in the end. They also, however, carry with them certain positive expectations. The hope they induce—of ever more and better—can thus lead finally to God. In the last analysis it is not the job of an advertiser to worry about his customers' salvation! His function—let's face it!—is to keep the play of *maya* going. If in the process, however, he can uplift people's consciousness even materially, there will be others to take on the duty of pointing out the further path to truth.

It is no accident that in the ashrams in India, and in monasteries and the like, elsewhere, the people who visit them or live in them are not paupers: They all come from well-to-do homes. Poor people are usually too busy sustaining themselves, and perhaps worrying where to find their next meal, to devote much thought to the divine search.

Some Indians have made the statement that India owes her spirituality to the fact of being poor. This is simply not true. Indeed, Marco Polo's description of India when he visited it in the thirteenth century was that India was "the richest country in the world." More people were seeking God then, probably, than today, when India is struggling once again to rise economically and reclaim her rightful place among the world's nations.

The Application

Joy—*Satchidananda*—is the essence of all human seeking. Lasting divine joy can be found only in the higher Self, in God. Yet divine joy will also be found by anyone who, through all life's trials, can maintain a joyful *attitude*. Mere things will never give happiness, but neither will weeping over the lack of things. I have seen no joy in the eyes of people who are destitute. I should qualify that statement, of course, by adding that people who have an inner life, and are free from worldly desires, are far richer than anyone who is rich merely materially. Those with *inner* riches, indeed, aren't really destitute at all even if they own none of the world's "goods."

Joy, however, usually *begins* with outward satisfaction. To have outwardly what one wants may at least give him the incentive to seek beyond material satisfaction until he attains a higher plateau of fulfillment. Advertising can help people to find satisfaction through the senses, at least. That rung is low on the ladder, but at least it leads upward in the direction of fulfillment.

There is nothing wrong, therefore, with advertising that has the purpose of both informing and attracting. We live in an age when spirituality requires a joyful recognition of the good things of life, and not a negation of *everything*.

I've seen too many sadhus in India scorn materiality yet give no evidence of inner joy, and no zeal for the attainment of divine bliss. If this were a higher age, perhaps it would be understood generally that utter simplicity, with ever-fewer possessions, is the best. In such an age, there would be no need for advertising. Mahatma Gandhi's ideal, however, which (it must be said) he practiced conscientiously, is unrealistic today even for most spiritual aspirants. Since no one, realistically speaking, can attain inner freedom without having achieved at least *some* worldly satisfaction first, people with a yogic focus in their lives need to show others also how to combine an inner life with outer competence. Only thus will mankind generally understand that material success matters less than soul attainment, and is even (far more than most people realize) dependent on developing a spiritual consciousness.

Let us consider again the marketing of doughnuts, which I mentioned casually above. If doughnuts happen to be your business, you might suggest "fun" things to do with doughnuts that will catch people's attention and awaken their interest. You could suggest that the buyer hang his doughnut on a little finger while he sips tea or coffee, as a way to save time in taking a quick nibble. You could suggest he use it in a game: tossing doughnuts onto a post at ten meters. Another use for doughnuts might be to use two of them as a mask so as to achieve anonymity in public. He could place a doughnut on the top of his head, creating a flat surface on which to carry things. He could look through a doughnut to give symmetry to his view of things, as one does through the lens of a camera. You could promote doughnuts "To get rid of that hollow feeling" (of hunger).

You could also promote doughnuts in comical self-justification: "See: How can it make me fat? The thing's empty!"

Or you could create a new fancy name for your doughnuts:

1) "The UFO of Baked Goods";

2) "The See-Through Solution";

3) "The Baked Surprise";

4) "The Whodunit (Who Doughnut)"—perhaps with a picture on the package of Sherlock Holmes using his doughnut on a stick as a magnifying glass. In time, this name might be shortened to "The Who."

5) "The Holy One"—perhaps with the caption of a doughnut saying to a slice of bread, "But I *am* holier than thou!" The doughnut could be shown in cartoon fashion, addressing those words to a monk. It could be sold with a thin stick, for the customer to insert and hold above his head like a halo.

6) "The Halo"—the same thing, with that thin stick inserted in the package. The accompanying picture could be of a holy man, or of an angel—the doughnut suspended, shining, above his head. Even a *mala* or garland of doughnuts could be hung around his neck.

Does all this seem sacrilegious? Please don't worry. Real haloes don't look like that anyway!

Advertising, in most business, is a necessity. As the saying goes, "It pays to advertise." Many businessmen are reluctant to spend money on advertising because it isn't easy to tell exactly and to what degree it is effective. The one "statistic" that is common knowledge is that advertising earns you more sales than not advertising. Even Hershey's Chocolates, which for years refused to advertise their product, succumbed finally to this universal modern necessity.

Because advertising is a simple necessity, it might as well be viewed as something right and good. Don't be "of two minds" on the subject. Do what needs to be done in your particular field, and proceed with all joyful energy.

How, then, to advertise? Let your advertising be wholehearted, truthful, but also *joyous*. Joy, and fantasy—these two are important keys to success, especially in advertising. Don't go about your promotions solemnly as if considering it somehow more spiritual to announce with a sad face whatever you have to give.

Joy and fantasy: Let me add another quality: *imagination*. When Kleenex first invented facial tissues, they offered prizes to anyone who could suggest innovative uses for their product. They paid the creator of a famous cartoon character, Little Lulu, to show her putting the tissues to the various uses people recommended. The prizes offered fanned public interest. Since then, many other companies have developed facial tissues, but Kleenex succeeded in conquering the market from the outset; indeed, even today people often refer to facial tissues as "Kleenexes."

What is your own product? Suppose it is a mattress. Well, how much difference can there be between one mattress and another—especially once you're fast asleep on yours? "Beautyrest" mattresses are advertised in what is probably the only way that anyone in this field can be original. They show a side view of the separate-action springs inside the mattress. How, then, to convince people to buy *your* mattress, particularly? It wouldn't be good form, and certainly wouldn't be in keeping with yoga principles, to denigrate other mattresses. Why not, however, get people to connect mattresses *in their minds* with your brand? You could describe your product in some cheerful, imaginative way—depicting your product, perhaps, with even a touch of fantasy.

There are countless ways of doing so. The important thing would be, if possible, to say something fresh and unusual. You could show the sleeper stretched out happily on a cloud, and show far below him a scene of turmoil, and him quite unaffected by it: a battle, perhaps, or a riot, or a Viking invasion, or pirates boarding a ship, or boxers sparring in a ring, or a bumpy terrain. You could show the sleeper drifting happily on a pink cloud into the sunset. You could show him surrounded by a singing choir of angels, or a tree full of nightingales. You could have a special motto such as, "FOR THE REST OF YOUR LIFE!" (This idea seems so obvious, in fact, that I can't help wondering if it hasn't been used already.) You could give your mattress a name—perhaps, "The Restful Solution."

These are suggestions, only. But maybe they'll convey to your mind some notion of the fun and fantasy you could use in your advertising without, in the process, being at all untruthful.

On the other hand, if your product doesn't satisfy in all the ways you've promised, the ads about it might inspire you to improve it until it *does* so. Thus, advertising can help you to clarify your own perceptions concerning what the product offers. If, for example, your mattress *doesn't* give people the perfect rest you've promised them, see that shortfall as a challenge to bring the product to perfection until you've made it the most restful mattress possible. If, on the other hand, what you want is to emphasize the healthfulness of your mattress, take a different line: Find what people want most in that kind of mattress, and what will also benefit them the most, and then emphasize that aspect.

I've no intention of writing a book on this subject, adding to the thousands in the market already. Let it suffice if I urge you to use your imagination. Put yourself in other people's shoes. Try to meet *their* needs. Above all, do whatever you can to lead them in the direction of inner joy and happiness, even if the happiness you are able to deliver is only a hint of the true, spiritual bliss. Advertise joyfully. Have a sense of fun (if it's appropriate) as you do so, of fantasy (again, if it's appropriate), and above all make people associate your product with their own dreams of fulfillment.

Reach out, through your advertising, toward the perfection and clarity you yourself want from life.

I myself have had to advertise many things over the course of years, though my principle effort has been to spread the yoga teachings. I've written books, made recordings, made countless public appearances, tried to interest people in our Ananda products: The list seems virtually endless. I don't supervise very much of what other people do for Ananda; I haven't the time. Whenever I do get involved, however, I try to emphasize the principles outlined above. I try to get people to feel that, in their practice of yoga principles, they will bring greater joy to their lives, greater peace to themselves, deeper understanding and fulfillment to their own lives and to those of others. Well, these aren't material things, but I believe that, if I'd had to be creative in material ways—in fact, many times I've had to be just that—I'd do much of what I've suggested here. Joyful fulfillment is what yoga means to me, personally. I have dedicated my life to finding inner joy and inspiration, and to sharing those benefits with all. Of course, therefore, that is what I emphasize in any advertising I do.

Even serious advertisement on serious subjects can have an element of joy in it. How? Well, isn't there a certain joy in the expectation of finding a solution? Its opposite—expecting only problems—attracts only a grey mist of despair. There is a degree of joy in clear thinking also, and in clear self-expression. Lack of clarity, on the other hand, suggests that perhaps no solution is possible. Firm, positive thinking raises one's consciousness. *Any* uplifting state of mind expresses yoga principles in a very real way, opening up a path toward inner joy.

The wording of an ad should be brief and catchy. It should promise fulfillment in whatever your target audience are seeking. And it should catch their attention as quickly as possible. If you can express yourself colorfully, all the better. Try to appeal to people's imagination. Good grammar is of secondary importance. "Winston tastes good like a cigarette should" ought grammatically speaking to read, "Winston tastes good *as* a cigarette should." The word, "as," however, isn't nearly so catchy as "like." Go with what you think will work best.

Finally, concentrate on the rhythm of your sentences. The rhythm should catch the "mood" of what you want to express. "Be alert! Drink Limca!" (Limca is a "fizzy" soft drink in India.) This would be a far more effective way of expressing the thought than telling people, "Limca will assist you in remaining alert."

Your imagery, too, should be appropriate to the product. Limca, for instance, might be advertised by displaying bubbles that rise gaily upward into a cloudless sky, expanding gradually outward.

MEDITATION

Visualize the bubbles I've just mentioned rising high over the earth. Then see them expand outward to infinity. Think of them as points of light. Then see those points expanding ever outward in all directions—until you see infinite space filled with light.

Whatever your work is in life, see it as a point of light, shedding that light in all directions, everywhere. Think of your work as a service to others. Added to the efforts of many people all of whom follow yoga principles, and all of whom are united in serving humanity, see yourself and them as instruments of the divine light, bringing that light to everyone. Creatures everywhere need to experience that light.

AFFIRMATION

"The work I do is a shining light to all it touches. I do my best to bring light, love, and shining joy into the dark world around me, and into the universe."

POINTS TO REMEMBER

1. Advertising is important for letting people know what *they themselves* want to know. It can offer to others an important service.

2. Advertising your own products or services can also encourage *you* to do better. In fact, the main benefit—as far as you yourself are concerned—may be *increased personal energy*!

3. If you want to achieve material success through yoga principles, the first thing to consider is *your sincerity—above all, before Infinite Consciousness*—that is to say, before God, who ever dwells in your own heart.

4. Don't let your advertising plod along in mere stock phrases. Each time you describe a product, try to say something new about it.

5. If your job is to advertise other people's products, *familiarize* yourself with them.

6. When advertising a product, concentrate on what you yourself like about it, and what you think the customers will like.

7. Exaggerated claims soon lose the power to convince.

8. The first rule in advertising should be, "The truth above all." Facts may indeed be drab and uninteresting, but truth itself can *and should be glorious*! Truth should inspire.

9. Advertising can help you to clarify in your own mind what your goals are.

10. Repetition is often helpful in advertising, but never let a formula that works reach the point of dullness in reiterating it.

11. The results of anything one does seriously should be the joy of offering to others something worthwhile, something to improve the quality of their lives, something which does so in ways which they themselves desire.

12. We live in an age when spirituality requires a joyful recognition of the good things of life, and not a negation of *everything*.

13. Let your advertising be wholehearted, truthful, but also *joyous*. Joy and fantasy are important keys to success, especially in advertising.

14. Use your imagination. Put yourself in other people's shoes. Try to meet *their* needs. Have a sense of fun (if it's appropriate) as you do so, of fantasy (again, if it's appropriate), and above all make people associate your product with their own dreams of fulfillment.

15. The wording of an ad should catch people's attention as quickly as possible. If you can express yourself colorfully, all the better.

16. Concentrate on the rhythm of your sentences. The rhythm should catch the "mood" of what you want to express.

WORKBOOK IDEAS
by Joseph Bharat Cornell

Magnetize Your Product or Service

ACTION IDEAS:

1. Advertising is a way to increase the magnetism of your product. Your ability to attract others will depend first on your own clarity and enthusiasm.

2. Meditate on what your company or organization offers in the following ways:

    a. Ask yourself first, "In my field of endeavor, what do people need?"

    b. Be creative and think of people's "unspoken" needs, too—needs that no one else in your industry has addressed.

    c. Now ask yourself, "What is it that I feel inspired to give?"

    d. Look at the intersection between people's actual needs, and your desire and ability to serve them.

3. Once you've identified what you want to promote, expand your thinking beyond the obvious, mundane needs your product satisfies, and reflect on the universal, higher benefits you can provide. If you own a restaurant, for example, think of what you are giving people besides food. Perhaps you are offering a serene and uplifting atmosphere where your customers can enjoy each other's company. If you are selling tools, feel you are empowering people to build their dreams. The more you appeal to loftier human virtues, even in small ways, the more people will appreciate and value your service.

4. Thinking expansively about your service will inspire you to present your product more energetically and creatively and, thereby, increase its magnetism.

   - Write here the higher or universal needs your product fulfills:

5. While perfecting your product, reflect on the word *usefulness*. Ask yourself, "How can I make my product easier and more enjoyable to use?" Vow to create something genuinely worthwhile. Remember, anything truly useful has its own attractive power.

   - How can I make my product better?

6. In your advertisements, create a sense of joy, or at least a feeling of positive expectation. "Fun is an expression of energy. Any rise of energy will lift people toward a more expansive vision of truth."

It is spiritually wholesome to help people feel that life is good and filled with possibilities. You can do this with integrity if, in your advertisements, you speak of the higher or universal needs your product fulfills.

Think about how you can associate your product with a sense of fun and hopeful expectation. Through surprise, laughter, or inspiration, strive to uplift your customers with the joy of your message.

LESSON NINETEEN

TALK LESS, DO MORE

I do hope that employers . . . will give special thought to the *needs* of the people they employ, and not only to the needs of the work itself. For, obviously, human beings are not machines to be turned on or off, and expected to run automatically without attention to their feelings.

The Principles

A friend of mine, when I sent her the first, unedited version of the last lesson (on advertising), wrote back to say that she imagined me sitting around the table, perhaps at teatime, sharing with friends some of the examples I had come up with. She visualized us all having a merry time together.

The truth was very different. First, I had told no one what I was planning for that chapter. Second, I lay awake in bed late into the night thinking about it and coming up with those examples. Every few minutes I'd get up and write down an idea, or several of them. I don't think I got to sleep that night until after three o'clock.

Did I enjoy the ideas? Yes, of course I did! My enjoyment, however, was mental, not expressed outwardly.

My point here is that mental work is often very different from the act of speaking to others: It demands a different focus of energy. A wagging tongue takes energy away from the brain and makes deep thinking difficult. Hence the saying, "See that your brain is in gear before putting your tongue in motion."

I was struck to learn that P.G. Wodehouse, the British humorist, whom I consider the funniest writer who ever lived, was completely inept as a conversationalist. All those brilliantly comical conversations in his books were hatched entirely in his head. When sitting at the dinner table with guests, he often gave them the impression that he was utterly colorless. His example of vocal ineptitude was the most extreme, perhaps, that has ever come to my notice. But then, he wrote books. Perhaps other dull conversationalists that I've known were as witty and eloquent as he, at least mentally. Perhaps they were simply not able to express themselves outwardly. I say, perhaps!

I remember a time years ago, when I was arranging the music for my oratorio, *Christ Lives*. I became so immersed in the music that it was, for me, as if no other reality existed. I'd invited a group of friends over to a dinner party before I launched into this project, and had to break my seclusion that evening to attend it. A friend of mine told me later, "You seemed so engrossed in your composing that, when I said something to you, I got the feeling from your answer that you were looking at me as though you were thinking, 'Now, is she a B-flat?'"

All of the above is relevant to my subject to this extent: The more people talk, the less energy they have, often, for more mental activity. In offices, it would be good to try to keep all conversations to a minimum. I made the suggestion in lesson seventeen that a room be set aside for any arguments that flair up in order not to disturb the rest of the staff. This room, I said, could be used also for relaxed conversation—a necessity from time to time. Without a modicum of such relaxation the strain of work can become overtiring. I consider such a room important especially for offices in which several people work together. Otherwise, even two people chatting can create a serious distraction for the others. Often, too, everybody gets unnecessarily involved. Long minutes may be required for everyone to settle down and become immersed again in the work.

It can come as quite a revelation to study the amount of time that gets wasted in offices by idle chatting, by unnecessary comments, and by composing clever interoffice memos to one another—all in the name of fun, of course, until the work itself begins to seem like a tea party! I had the job years ago of re-organizing a large office. At one time in the reorganizing process, one of the workers had her job suspended completely for two weeks while I prepared new duties for her. This was a monastery, so the men and women lived separately. That woman's work, therefore, was where she also lived. She was thus able to work late into every evening; often at eleven o'clock she was still at her desk. It amazed me to learn that, during the period when she had been relieved of her work, she was still at her desk till eleven o'clock every evening! This simple fact demonstrated to me eloquently how much of the "hard work" people do is only habit, and is not really productive.

I cannot stress seriously enough the importance of *focused creativity*. I want therefore to emphasize again in this chapter people's need to take occasional breaks from their work. In fact, I recommend that some place be set aside also for silence, where speaking is not allowed: a room to which people can go simply to think things through quietly. I recognize that office space may be at a premium. Please, however, don't dismiss this idea as permanently impractical. Cooperative effort is often necessary in office work, as it is, obviously, in kitchens and other places where people work physically together. More often, however, the cooperation in an office is less overt. Though it involves group effort, the workers may function singly, each contributing in a more general way toward the common goal.

There is a conflict between the exigencies of work and most people's incapacity to work with prolonged concentration. I realize that, realistically speaking, few workplaces can have a room set apart for any of the activities I've recommended: for occasional chatting, for any arguments that erupt, and for silent thinking. I do hope, however, that employers, encouraged by the ideas I've mentioned, will give special thought to the *needs* of the people they employ, and not only to the needs of the work itself. For, obviously, human beings are not machines to be turned on or off, and expected to run automatically without attention to their feelings. Too many offices, in India perhaps especially, are brown, dull, and poorly lighted, with little or no decor beyond the bare minimum needed to keep people plodding away at uninspiring tasks. I've tried in these lessons to set at least a direction. I do say, and I don't think I am impractical: Please look upon these suggestions as what I've said: at least a *direction* for you to move in. The more the conditions in the workplace inspire your staff to take an interest and to feel dedicated to your aims, the better it will be for everything and everyone.

Meanwhile, there are compromise solutions that may work well for you. I've suggested supportive music. Music can help the work in offices, also, where no customers come, but where people need to be kept focused at their desks. One thing is important: If the work is with words, the music played should be instrumental, not vocal. Second, it should be soothing, not restless. I feel awkward in recommending my own instrumental recordings. Still, I use them myself, and find them soothing and relaxing at work. Calming, and perhaps even inspiring music will help to filter out other sounds. So also will recorded environmental sounds, such as flowing brooks, waterfalls, or ocean surf. Recordings of these sounds are available in music stores.

If on the other hand the work people do is not with words, then vocal music need not be obstructive to their work—provided, again, that it is calming. I have the same embarrassment in recommending recordings of my own songs, but in fact they were written to provide uplifting, meaningful thoughts that are easy to understand. They are enjoyable also, and some of them amusing to listen to.

In my early days when I was in SRF, I sometimes visited its Lake Shrine in Pacific Palisades, and meditated there on those beautiful grounds. Heavy traffic passed by on Sunset Boulevard, rushing down the long curve around the property on its way down to the Pacific Ocean. There is a sunken garden on the land, with a continuous waterfall. There, I found the traffic noise so obscured that I almost didn't notice it. The falling water itself, moreover, had a soothing sound. I found meditation there easy. Indeed, it was uplifting even to sit there.

At much less expense than setting aside a room for occasional chatting and relaxation over a cup of coffee, you can place as many dividers as is convenient between the desks, or for separating specifically designated areas. I suggested, earlier, that the color of those dividers be pleasantly neutral: a pale beige, possibly.

Cell phones are a public nuisance nowadays. They must often disrupt the workplace. They are a necessity, I know, but consider the effect of audible conversations on others. One becomes somewhat inured to noise these days—at home, in the streets, in shops, and certainly in offices. Perhaps people imagine they aren't bothered by it. Maybe they aren't, in fact, though I'm highly skeptical. Certainly, when one is concentrating deeply it helps to have as little noise around one as possible.

Another way to create silence for oneself is to insert plugs in the ears, or to have silencing headphones. Even the soothing sounds I've described above can be played through earphones and can assist concentration in a noisy environment—at least when one isn't required to talk with others.

The main point of this lesson is to emphasize a little-known fact: There is a close connection between the tongue and the brain. In yoga there is a technique known as *Kechari Mudra*, in which the tip of the tongue is brought backward in the mouth to touch the uvula, or—better still—brought up behind the nasal passages. Most people find this a difficult practice, and perhaps too strange even to attract them. Considerable mental power, however, can be developed by this practice. Perhaps unfortunately, this lesson is not the place for going deeply into the how-to's and the why's of *Kechari*. The point is, the more one can keep the tongue completely relaxed, the clearer he will find his mind become.

I have been able to take periods of complete seclusion in the mountains—some of them in the Himalayas—and I have found that within a short time my perceptions became so keen that I could feel the thoughts and vibrations of people if I had to be near them. Indeed, it was almost disturbing to have to go down to post letters at the post office, for example in the little village of Lohaghat in the Almora district of the Himalaya, where only one street ran between two rows of little houses.

Sometimes, extreme tests of a truth can help to clarify one's understanding of it. From those times of seclusion—less frequent than I would have liked, in the busy life my Guru had ordained for me—I have come to cherish complete silence.

Curiously, my Guru told me that in past lives I talked "a lot." ("Well," he added, "you were happy in it.") In this life, I have had to use words "a lot" again, but with focus, now—on writing and lecturing. I wanted to be a hermit, but that was not to be. He may have designated this activity for me in order to work out my own tendency toward verbalizing my insights by stating them as clearly as possible.

There is a reason why spiritual initiations are given, traditionally, in secret with a vow usually added to keep them a secret. It isn't, as many may suppose, to keep higher truths from general knowledge. No truly wise person wants to hide wisdom from others, if it can uplift them also. Secrecy is, of course, necessary for preserving the sanctity of truth, which must be held in high regard, and not treated as something common. Worldly people have, for example, made a mockery of the sacred concept of "guru." We hear such expressions these days as "stock market guru," "real estate guru," "financial guru." The list is endless, and makes a travesty of a concept that is holy. No one, not even a spiritual teacher, deserves to be called a guru unless he has achieved deep communion with God. Materialists toss about high concepts like these as though they were playthings. It is well for those concepts to be held sacrosanct.

There is, however, another reason also why initiates are cautioned not to reveal their spiritual practices to others, unless and until they are given permission. When something sacred is spoken aloud to others, the power to succeed in it is diminished. The ramifications of when a truth may be revealed, and to whom, need not concern us here. The important thing is the relevance of this teaching to the workplace.

People love to chatter. A little talk may help them to relieve the tensions built up by too constant mental focus, but too much chatter is detrimental to serious thinking. This principle applies primarily to *mental* effort, but even in physical labor concentration is a great asset.

Many years ago, in the monastery, we had to do a large cement pour. The job took us, if I recall correctly, twenty-three hours. We stopped rarely, to eat, but because focus was necessary—my own job was to shovel sand into the cement mixer—we kept at it virtually the entire time.

One man in the group grumbled, "I didn't come here to this ashram to *pour cement*!" He sat about the whole day, chatting with neighbors and "counseling" them. At the end of the day, only he was tired. The rest of us were filled with joyful energy. Talking, on that occasion, even though the work wasn't mental, would have been distracting to us.

The Application

Habit may make it difficult for you to keep a resolution to "talk less and do more." Like most New Year's resolutions, which often get broken the very first day, you may need a system to help you to be faithful. If so, try coaxing your mind to take only one step at a time. In the case of those "New Year's" resolutions, make a decision that covers, not the whole year, but just one hour. Keep silence at work, similarly, for one hour only, in the morning at the start of the day. Once that hour has become a habit, extend it to two hours; then to three.

Much work necessitates communication with others. If you are the boss, you can let it be known that you can be reached only at certain hours. When something urgent arises, of course, or when the phone rings, you may have no choice but to adjust personal reality to objective demands. Nevertheless, the sterner you can be with yourself, the more others will come to respect it also.

Mahatma Gandhi made a practice of setting aside one day a week, when he simply wouldn't speak. Considering that an entire country depended on him, it must have been a challenge for him to keep that resolution. The result was, however, that he accomplished a great deal more than he could have otherwise. He wrote letters, for instance, and composed public statements. People respected his silence, and accommodated themselves to it. It was his firmness in adhering to resolutions like this that gave him the strength to sway millions to his will, and, in the end, to force the British to withdraw from India.

If you are the boss, it would be good to impose silence on everyone for certain periods at a time. You will find, perhaps to your surprise, that when people can keep silence together for any period of time they become less inclined to speak, afterward. Soon, it won't be as though a dam of silence broke at, let us say, ten or eleven o'clock in the morning! They will *enjoy* the silence.

I had this experience many years ago, when I lived in the SRF monastery. My Guru had placed me in charge of the monks. One of the things he had asked us to do was keep silence at mealtimes. It hadn't been convenient for him to eat with us, however. The rule, in consequence, was honored in the breach. Meals had become an opportunity for exuberant chatter. Most of the monks were young. Getting them to keep silence, after years of undiscipline in the dining room, was more than difficult: it was impossible. I tried, but failed.

And then a solution dawned on me: Why not do it by increments? The first thing we did every morning was meditate together. It proved easy, at least at breakfast time (which came afterward), to enforce complete silence. A night in silent sleep, followed by group meditation, somewhat impeded anyway the men's inclination to chatter. Once they were accustomed to silence at breakfast, it was easier to get them to keep silence in the evenings, after another period of meditation. Still they had the "safety valve" of being able to "talk their heads off" at lunchtime. In time, however, so accustomed did they become to keeping silence at two of the meals, they found themselves somehow out of the habit of speaking during mealtimes at all. I never needed to propose that the silence be extended to lunchtime.

If your response to my first suggestion, that a room be set aside for chatting and another one for silent thinking, was to say, "I can't afford the extra space," then look for some other feasible solution. Since you want your work to be successful, you have all the incentive you need to encourage more silence while working. I myself wasn't in a position to *force* those monks. I tried simply to win them to a way of life they themselves, in fact, wanted. Surely in your workplace, too, everyone really would like the enterprise to succeed. Win them, rather than driving or harassing them.

The expression, "Hold your tongue," doesn't quite do it. *Relax* your tongue! You'll be surprised how little you want to speak, once you've learned to keep that little muscle in your body still and relaxed!

MEDITATION

Tense the muscles in your head: the throat, the tongue, the jaw; then quickly relax them. Repeat this exercise several times. Then relax them consciously, more deeply.

Next, concentrate on the *energy* in those areas where you felt tension. Try to withdraw the energy by visualizing space in your whole head. Withdraw that energy to the medulla oblongata at the back of the head, and then redirect it from there to the point between the eyebrows.

Feel your head surrounded by a bubble of space. Expand that space outward. Let it fill the room where you sit. As you begin enjoying this practice, visualize space expanding in all directions around and beyond you, to the horizon and beyond it; then encompassing the whole world; then spreading beyond our planet to infinity.

AFFIRMATION

"Peace enters me through silence. I enjoy stillness in myself, when I can listen to Thy silent inner whispers."

POINTS TO REMEMBER

1. Mental work is very different from the act of speaking to others: It demands a different focus of energy.

2. The more people talk, the less energy they have, often, for more mental activity. In offices, it would be good to try to keep all conversations to a minimum.

3. The importance of *focused creativity* cannot be stressed seriously enough. Set some place aside for silence, where speaking is not allowed: a room to which people can go simply to think things through quietly.

4. Give special thought to the *needs* of the people you employ. Human beings are not machines expected to run automatically without attention to their feelings.

5. The more the conditions in the workplace inspire your staff to take an interest and to feel dedicated to your aims, the better it will be for everything and everyone.

6. Calming, and perhaps even inspiring music will help to filter out other sounds. So also will recorded environmental sounds, such as flowing brooks, waterfalls, or ocean surf.

7. When one is concentrating deeply it helps to have as little noise around one as possible.

8. There is a close connection between the tongue and the brain. The more one can keep the tongue completely relaxed, the clearer he will find his mind become.

9. Keep silence at work for one hour only, in the morning at the start of the day. Once that hour has become a habit, extend it to two hours; then to three.

10. Much work necessitates communication with others. If you are the boss, you can let it be known that you can be reached only at certain hours.

11. If you are the boss, it would be good to impose silence on everyone for certain periods at a time. You will find that when people can keep silence together for any period of time they become less inclined to speak, afterward. Soon, they will *enjoy* the silence. *Win* them to this idea, rather than driving or harassing them.

12. *Relax* your tongue! You'll be surprised how little you want to speak, once you've learned to keep that little muscle in your body still and relaxed!

WORKBOOK IDEAS
by Joseph Bharat Cornell

The Importance of Listening

Paramhansa Yogananda was once asked why his most advanced disciple, Rajarshi Janakananda, made such rapid spiritual progress. Yogananda replied, "He knows how to listen."

Our minds are like shortwave radios: when the switch is set to "broadcast," all we can hear is our own voice talking. A busy, chattering mind is always in "sending mode," which prevents us from experiencing anything new. We only begin to *hear* when the switch is turned to "receive."

Similarly, true inspiration comes when the mind is calm and listening. Talking less is a marvelous practice for deepening one's receptivity and concentration. Practicing silence also increases productivity, because focused, sustained attention is the key to attracting solutions.

ACTION IDEAS:

1. Paramhansa Yogananda said that most people use only one-tenth of their ability to concentrate. When you restrain your speech and practice silence, the mind becomes less impulsive and centers itself more on what you're *really* doing.

    a. To increase receptivity and concentration: Keep silent for one hour, preferably at the beginning of each workday.

    b. Once that hour has become a habit, extend it to two hours; then to three.

    c. After incorporating silent times at work, ask yourself, "Have I noticed an improvement in the quality and quantity of my work?"

    d. "Do I feel more energy and inspiration?"

    e. Remember, the less you talk, the more energy you will have!

2. It is not always possible, or appropriate, to be silent at work, but we *can* practice being *quiet*. It is estimated that only a tiny part of our speech—some say 1%—is due to the demands of our outer environment. The rest of the time the urge to talk comes from the desire to relate to others.

Conversation in the workplace is not always uplifting or helpful to office harmony and focus. The admonishment given in monasteries, "Do not speak unless you can improve on the silence," is a helpful guideline for appropriate speech.

How to practice the art of being quiet:

- Concentrate more on listening to life. Avoid the sense that you have to direct it.

- Remain centered in yourself.

- When you feel the urge to talk, restrain your first impulse to do so. Ask yourself, "Will

my words contribute to the situation? Improve on the silence? Bless others?"
- When you break your silence, speak as long as you feel inspiration but no longer; then return to the silence.
- Enjoy the tranquility. Express a sense of inner calmness in everything you do.

3. Practice the techniques of silence and quiet regularly. The more you do, the more you will experience their benefits: increased energy, deep concentration, and inner joy and serenity.

LESSON TWENTY

JOY IN BUSINESS

Work with joy. Give back to the world some of the riches it pours out on you, when it does so. In terms of yoga principles, you must give, if you would receive. Give energy to the world, and it will give back energy in return.

The Principles

What is the goal of life? We are not in human bodies by accident, as biologists today insist. They explain evolution in terms of its mere variety. Evolution, however, is a process of reaching out toward ever-greater consciousness. The goal of life is the realization that everything is, in its inmost reality, *Satchidananda*: ever-existing, ever-conscious, ever-new Bliss!

Ego-consciousness takes us outward from that reality. It causes us to seek happiness in things rather than in the Self. *Maya* (delusion) causes us to seek the bliss of our true nature outwardly, as I said, through the senses. Our very bodies might be compared to the little jets on the burner of a gas stove, which, when lit, seem individual, though all of them are expressions of the single supply of gas coming into the burner. We project ourselves outward through the senses, and identify reality itself with the countless objects around us, each one of which seems a separate reality like our own little "gas jet." We hope for happiness through them, but in fact only project our own nature onto them. All they can do for us is reflect back to us our expectations of them. If they make us happy it is because we project happy expectation onto them. And if they make us sad, it is because we project onto them an inner sadness.

"Conditions," Paramhansa Yogananda used to remark, "are always neutral. They seem happy or sad according to the happy or sad attitudes of the mind." In reaching out eagerly toward what we think will be a happy experience, we are disappointed, as the stream of our happiness becomes wasted in desert sands. Indeed, people who think to find in mere things reinforcement of their own happiness will watch it crumble to dust in their hands, and will recoil in disappointment. They do this repeatedly, always with the same result. In time, they begin to develop an *expectation* of disappointment. The smile of confident expectation on a baby's face sometimes grows sour with disillusionment long before old age sets in. Those who expect too much from things, or from other people, end up bitter and disappointed at last. One sometimes sees these attitudes even in children—perhaps as a bitter reflection carried over from a past life. For people's predispositions are carried over from before. One sometimes sees a certain sadness in babies even from birth—an indication of what sort of life they had on earth last time, or in the astral world between physical births.

Other children, on the other hand, more disposed to be *happy in themselves*, smile more often than they cry. Some children, as I said, are born with a negative bias whereas others from the outset have a happy disposition. The predispositions they display speak loudly of a heavy or light karma, brought with them from the past.

An observation I have often made in life, though somehow it always surprises me, is the grim line that tends to form around people's mouths whenever they talk about making money. I noticed it first in my own father's face. He was a good, kind, honest, and truthful man, but whenever he spoke about money or about having a sense of responsibility toward it, that line would appear on his face. With that manifestation came a certain hardness into his voice, as if this particular subject were too grimly *serious* ever to be joked about.

Notice the atmosphere in banks: those temples of modern industry. Doesn't it seem almost church-like? Observe the hushed, almost reverent atmosphere. I've fantasized about approaching the counter of that modern priest, the cashier, with a propitiating check. If he is pleased, he may deign to honor it and give me *prasad*, or holy offering, in the form of paper bills that I can take home with me, fingering them devoutly as if the gods themselves had favored me with a token of their grace.

There is also that inner sanctum into which a favored few are ushered for consultation with one of the high priests—the bank manager or loan officer.

Of course I'm having fun—and, please believe me, not really at anybody's expense. It's the phenomenon that intrigues me, not the individuals who engage in the phenomenon.

Why is money itself treated so grimly—almost with awe? Money has no feature that, in itself, is particularly attractive. If you see a picture of Rama, Krishna, Jesus, or the Virgin Mary you see someone whose image, because of what it represents—goodness, kindness, compassion, wisdom, and divine joy—causes you to feel an inner upliftment. Money has no such attributes. One merely hopes, in the use of it, to buy things he thinks he needs or wants. When you visualize those objects of desire—a beautiful dress perhaps, a handsome suit, succulent fruit, a piece of jewelry, a car—you may smile in anticipation. In fact, there *is* pleasure of a sort—even some *upliftment*—in the anticipation of those purchases. But with money?

When we contemplate the means to satisfaction, the money itself, what actual happiness is there? Shouldn't we find as much pleasure in earning it as we hope for in spending it?

Money itself isn't what awakens people's fantasies, except for the sense of power it may give them. It conveys no immediate delight by its color, symmetry, grace of form, or texture. Once one has submitted the faces and configurations on a bill to superficial study, designed as they are mostly to prevent forgery, one more or less gets the picture and ignores the bill itself. The charm of it, such as it is, revolves entirely around the images one projects upon it: the home, the dress, the food.

When I was recording my daily television series in India, I had to *imagine* my audience through the camera lens. I ignored the lens altogether, and actually visualized the people with whom I was speaking. They were, to my mind, guests in my living room where the recording was being done. Often there were people in the room also, listening, but I myself talked only to the camera lens, and to the imaginary audience *behind* it. The lens was not my reality: the people I imagined behind it were my reality.

Is it like that with money? I don't think so. I would never have fingered the camera lens as lovingly as people finger money! There is in most people's minds a strange, but very real-seeming, delusion attached to money. It isn't the specific things they hope to buy with it. It is the fact that those bank notes can be used to buy *so many different* things! Money assumes an importance for them beyond all hope of fulfillment. It actually is in itself, to their minds, a reality—the more a fetish for them for the very reason that they can give it no clear definition. It is only a lens, so to speak—carrying their hopes beyond it, to a fairyland of (hopefully) realizable dreams.

And yet, the dreams are not, in most people's minds, a part of that reality. They go grimly to their jobs, perhaps laugh a little over some event at work, then return to the thought of the money they are earning.

The nature of desire is the *anticipation* of happiness in the fulfillment in getting what one wants. If that fulfillment is allied to visions of a skiing outing, a trip to some tropical paradise, or—as I said—a beautiful dress or other article of clothing, there is pleasure in the anticipation. There is no such smile in the heart as one thinks of money, merely. Dollar or rupee bills aren't beautiful or attractive in themselves. The best one can do with them, until he uses them, is bank them or hide them out of sight. Thus, no notable happiness is contained in money itself. In fact, money is doubly a delusion: Mostly absent in the first place is the happiness of visualizing specific fulfillments through it; and, in the second place, the *promise* of almost infinite fulfillment by possessing it waves images at one of potential happiness which he sees dimly through alluring mists that seem all the more distant for their very vagueness.

Meanwhile, earning money is not, in itself, a source of happiness. Those grim lines around the mouth are a universal phenomenon. The corners of the mouth turn downward, and the lips compress firmly as the mind affirms, "I'm doing the sensible, the absolutely right and morally proper thing."

In my view, morality should be not a grim obligation, whether social or religious. Since the true goal of life is *Satchidananda* (bliss), that truly is moral which increases true happiness. When a person steals from others, he breaks a law of his own nature, the fundamental urge of which is self-expansion. We attract suffering when we defy that natural law. By stealing, we become self-contractive. By hating others, we narrow our capacity for sympathy inward, upon ourselves. By vengeance, we altogether exclude sympathy from our hearts.

Every moral value can be judged in these simple terms: self-expansive vs. self-contractive. Ultimately, the high commandments of religion are simply expressions of these principles. I don't say of *every* religion, for some people believe in a vengeful, jealous, and angry God—the very opposite of any true saint's experience of Him. Such religion, however, is false. True religion, whatever its images (whether Krishna, Jesus, Mary, Kali, etc.), propounds the expansion from ego-centeredness and petty self-absorption into a universal reality.

Ultimately, God is more even than love: He is bliss. Love is an expression of inner bliss, reaching out from personalized bliss to omnipresent bliss. In bliss there is utter fulfillment—absolute oneness—completion.

Now then, how is bliss to be attained? With grim, joy-withering attitudes? Isn't there something utterly absurd in that concept? A friend of mine told me a story of a man who went to a restaurant, ordered the food, then was furious over the plate he was served. "I know the owner of this establishment. I know"—well, whom? the president of the country, the Pope, the head of the FBI? Anyone! Whatever his amazing influence, the waiters rushed fearfully to the kitchen and urged the cook to make the best meal he could think of. The meal was at last brought to the fuming customer with profuse apologies. At this point the man turned up his nose and cried, "Take it away: I'd rather be furious!"

How can a disgruntled attitude bear fruit in gruntlement? (Yes, that's an invented word, but when writing one wants to have a little fun with words!) It can't, obviously! People work grimly all their lives, thinking to find ease and happiness at least when they retire. How many men I've known who, two years after their retirement, were either senile or dead!

Don't look to the future for happiness. Happiness exists in the present. My Guru once said, "Most people seek happiness in the future, or create a false cloud of nostalgia for the past. When you can be happy *now*, then you have God!"

In his book, *God Is for Everyone*, Yogananda points out, however, that even the happiness people dream of is, finally, only an illusion. Bliss is the reality we all seek.

What people want first, as they set foot on the ladder of upward human evolution, is pleasure. Pleasure is outward, experienced through the senses. In this world of duality, everything reveled in outwardly is tied to its opposite, as a tall wave is accompanied inevitably by a deep trough. Every pleasure is followed by displeasure, or by pain, even as the "pleasure" of drunkenness is replaced by a hangover. Gradually, as people develop greater refinement and spiritual sensitivity, their desire for pleasure becomes a desire for happiness.

Happiness is less directly allied to material things. One can be happy, inwardly, without any obvious reason. Many people cannot understand a happiness that has no external justification. If you ask them, "Are you happy?" they may think, "Well, I'm not ill; I'm not destitute; I'm not aware that I have any enemies; there seems to be nothing wrong in my life. So, yeah, I guess I'm happy."

Still, people seek outward happiness, and imagine they've found it when they attain the desired outward condition: not pleasures, but at least peace. As Krishna states in the Bhagavad Gita, "To the peaceless, how is happiness possible?" Yet peace itself, if not accompanied by an uplifted state of consciousness, causes people finally to ask, "What's wrong with me?" They're happy, so they suppose, but—well, they're just bored!

True happiness can be attained only with a happy attitude. Benvenuto Cellini, a silver worker and sculptor in Renaissance Italy, was employed by the Pope to make a number of ornaments for the Vatican. After a time Cellini demanded payment before he'd begin a new commission. The Pope, who held the reins of power, insisted that the commission be executed. When Cellini continued to refuse, the Pope finally had him thrown into a dungeon. Cellini later described his experience there. Let me paraphrase what he wrote in his autobiography.

"The cell was small, dank, and rat infested. It had a damp mattress that never dried. I was cold and hungry, and had no food except stale bread and water. The cell had one high window that gave enough light for me to read about one hour a day. My reading matter was the Bible. When I was no longer able to read, I prayed.

"After some time, such a deep joy welled up within me that, when the Holy Father finally released me, I said to myself, 'If one wants to know true joy let him arrange to be thrown into a dungeon' "—and he described all the conditions he'd experienced in that dark place.

True happiness is a road to inner joy. And joy wells up from the inner Self. Neither happiness nor joy, however, can be found by merely waiting for it passively. Still less can it be found by waiting with a dour attitude. And least of all can it be found by grim-mouthed determination to *accumulate, accumulate, accumulate* all the money he possibly can.

Why not work joyfully? There was a man—I've written about him elsewhere in these lessons—living in a village in New England. His habit was to snarl at everything and everyone. At work he was dour. At home he was sour. No one liked him. One day, however, he went smiling to work, spent the day at work happily, and returned home with a smile of blessing for everyone. People marveled over this mystery for a week or so. Finally, a committee appointed by the neighborhood paid him a visit.

"Why are you," they demanded, "the town grouch, suddenly such a ray of sunshine? What's happened? What's the matter?"

"Why, nothing's the matter!" he replied. "I just kept waiting for something to make me happy until, finally, I decided nothing was going to do that for me, so I just made up my mind to *be happy!*"

One beautiful thing about a happy outlook is that it tends to be contagious. Whether you are the boss in a firm or an employee, you can affect and possibly change the atmosphere of the place where you work by simply refusing to allow anything to affect your good cheer.

Someone once said to me regarding my songs, "*You* can write happy songs. *You've* never suffered!" I replied, "The very contrary is true. It's *because* I've suffered, and have triumphed over the suffering, that I've earned the right to write happy music."

Don't depend on *anything outward* to make you happy! Be happy inside as a deliberate choice—as a deliberate act of will.

In the Bhagavad Gita Sri Krishna teaches something I've quoted again and again in these lessons: "Act without desire for the fruits of action." A principle of life that few people realize is that when a person develops non-covetousness, he attracts effortlessly to himself everything he needs. As Patanjali wrote, "All jewels are drawn to one."

The secret of wealth is to *be* wealthy, within! Wealth is not money: It is inner completeness and fulfillment. One can be wealthy with very little money, and destitute though he possess millions.

Don't work like a craven! Be contented with what life gives you, then work because work is honorable, whereas sloth is dishonorable. Work with joy. Give back to the world some of the riches it pours out on you, when it does so. In terms of yoga principles, you must give, if you would receive. Give energy to the world, and it will give back energy in return.

Money itself *is* energy. Never think of it as a thing, merely. When you put out the right energy, you will find yourself sustained by the very universe in return. BE RICH, in yourself. Share that wealth with others. This is how to find riches and success pouring out on you from all sides, like showers of gold.

The Application

To find joy in your work, work with joy! You will receive nothing from the world that you do not first give out to it. This is a law of life.

Every day, therefore, when you begin work, determine first to enjoy everything.

I had a relatively bad accident several months ago: I fell in such a way that several stitches needed to be put in my forehead. The doctor who did the stitching commented, "Everybody says when something like this happens, 'Why me?'" I replied, "I *never* say that!" Yes, the blow was painful, and also somewhat messy. Blood was staining a new carpet I'd bought that very day. I said to friends who were helping me, "Let me move over to the floor, so that this new carpet won't get any more blood on it." Through the mess and that moderately severe pain we had a good laugh. Why not enjoy one's self, if one can't enjoy what is happening? I really wasn't concerned. If a thing happens, it happens. If it can't be helped, why lament the circumstance? And why cry out, "Why *me*?" Things are happening constantly in life. Such is the nature of this world. So why not simply shrug it all off, and get on with the business of living?

Declare at the start of every day, "This day I will enjoy my Self!"

George Bernard Shaw, the British playwright, was sitting one evening on the outskirts of a party. His hostess came to him and asked anxiously, "Aren't you enjoying yourself?"

With a wry look Shaw commented, "That's all I *am* enjoying!"

Shaw had a quick wit. He was also cynical. In this case, however, he was right: That's all anyone *can* enjoy: one's own self.

If inner enjoyment—enjoyment in your inner self—is not easy at first, then practice it consciously, deliberately for one hour—or even for a few minutes—at a time. Let no one "get your goat." Let your happiness depend on nothing external to yourself: on no one's attitude toward you, on nothing that happens to you, on no one's behavior around you.

Gradually, when you have "got the hang" of being joyful for one hour, extend that period to two hours, then gradually extend it to the whole day. There is absolutely no reason for being unhappy, no matter what happens.

This attitude, I grant you, is possible only by practicing the presence of God, inwardly. Try it. You will be surprised how wonderful it can be—not because of some emotion you whip up in your own heart, but because of a consciousness that simply wells up within you when you hold your mind up constantly to Him.

Japa, the repetition of God's name, or simply calling to Him inwardly, is a supremely satisfying practice. I know this course of lessons is for everyone, whether believer or unbeliever, but try at least holding your heart and mind up to higher potentials in yourself.

A man approached me once after a lecture I'd given in Australia. "I'm an atheist," he announced. "Can you define what you call God in a way that I can accept?"

I paused briefly, then answered, "Why not think of God as the highest potential you can imagine for your own self?"

"Well!" he replied, surprised at this novel concept, "I can live with that!"

Try it yourself. You are part of a much greater reality than your own little self. Are we all right, so far? Then why not try reaching out to that reality, instead of enclosing yourself tightly in your own thoughts and ideas? Still skeptical? Then look around you and study other people's lives. Who among them seem happier: those who take an interest in life? or those who live, figuratively speaking, with their eyes on the ground, selfish and self-involved? Again, reversing the equation: Who seem happier: those who show no openness to anyone's opinions but their own? or those who listen to others, appreciate them, ask questions, and seek ever to know more?

You can have joy at work. Joy *attracts* joy. Misery attracts only misery. Whatever you want from life, advance toward it in the joyful affirmation of having it already.

MEDITATION

For much of their lives, people live in dread of this thing or that thing going wrong. Think of a potential difficulty, but not one that is crushing in the common view like the death of someone beloved, or utter failure in business, or the loss of everything you hold dear. I won't ask you to try mentally to rise above catastrophes, although life will surely ask you, someday, to transcend everything you really dread, if only because that very dread is a magnet which attracts to itself what it fears, just as a joy-filled expectation *must* be fulfilled, someday.

Concentrate rather then, instead, on some difficulty you think you could handle. Then meditate on facing that difficulty, not with rejection but with an inner joy that can't be touched or affected by that outer circumstance. Suppose you lose an important client. Or supposing a colleague sues you in the courts, or attacks you in the media. Or suppose your income suddenly slips owing to the loss of some investment.

Mentally look that circumstance in the face, and tell yourself, "I am *not* that circumstance! Whatever happens, I am complete and joyful in myself."

The more you practice this attitude of mind, the more you will find it easy and natural. Nothing that can ever happen to you *is* really you, yourself!

AFFIRMATION

"I am complete in myself. Joy is my normal state of mind. No blow of outer circumstance can ever touch me!"

POINTS TO REMEMBER

1. The goal of life is the realization that everything is, in its inmost reality, *Satchidananda*: ever-existing, ever-conscious, ever-new Bliss!

2. "Conditions are always neutral. They seem happy or sad according to the happy or sad attitudes of the mind."

3. Since the true goal of life is *Satchidananda* (bliss), that truly is moral which increases true happiness. Every moral value can be judged in these simple terms: self-expansive vs. self-contractive.

4. Ultimately, God is more even than love: He is bliss. In bliss there is utter fulfillment—absolute oneness—completion.

5. Don't look to the future for happiness. Happiness exists in the present. My Guru once said, "Most people seek happiness in the future, or create a false cloud of nostalgia for the past. When you can be happy *now*, then you have God!"

6. A happy outlook tends to be contagious. You can affect and possibly change the atmosphere of the place where you work by simply refusing to allow anything to affect your good cheer.

7. Don't depend on *anything outward* to make you happy! Be happy inside as a deliberate choice—as a deliberate act of will.

8. The secret of wealth is to *be* wealthy, within! Wealth is not money: It is inner completeness and fulfillment. One can be wealthy with very little money, and destitute though he possess millions.

9. Be contented with what life gives you, then work because work is honorable. In terms of yoga principles, you must give, if you would receive.

10. Money itself *is* energy. Never think of it as a thing, merely. When you put out the right energy, you will find yourself sustained by the very universe in return.

11. To find joy in your work, work with joy! Declare at the start of every day, "This day I will enjoy my Self!"

12. If inner enjoyment—enjoyment in your inner self—is not easy at first, then practice it consciously, deliberately for one hour—or even for a few minutes—at a time. Gradually extend that period to the whole day. There is absolutely no reason for being unhappy, no matter what happens.

13. This attitude is possible only by practicing the presence of God, inwardly. Try it. You will be surprised how wonderful it can be.

14. You can have joy at work. Joy *attracts* joy. Whatever you want from life, advance toward it in the joyful affirmation of having it already.

WORKBOOK IDEAS
by Joseph Bharat Cornell

Joy All the Time

John Muir, the American naturalist and explorer, never let outward circumstances ruin his day. The following passage beautifully describes Muir's contentment even during the most challenging times: *"I was as wet as if I had been swimming after crossing raging torrents and fighting my way through the Alaskan jungle. In the evening I managed to make a small fire out of wet twigs, got a cup of tea, stripped off my dripping clothing, wrapped myself in a blanket and lay thinking of the gains of the day. I was glad, rich, and almost comfortable."*

Muir said that he never felt any real discomfort because he was too busy gazing in wonder at the scenery. Focusing on—and attuning to—that which was positive and uplifting allowed him to transcend any "inconveniences." This was the secret of his strength of mind and constant cheerfulness.

Paramhansa Yogananda said that we take things "too personally." Stay in the flow of inspiration and joy by keeping your "gaze" fixed on higher realities.

ACTION ITEM:
1. During your workday, closely observe your thoughts.
2. Especially note when you react negatively to a challenging situation.
3. Observe how negativity constricts your energy and weakens your enthusiasm.
4. Using dynamic will, redirect your attention from the specific situation to a more expansive, impersonal view of the situation.
5. For the next twenty minutes concentrate on what brings you true joy.

ACTION ITEM:
Whenever you feel overwhelmed at work, do the following to broaden your perspective:
- Take a short break. Go outside, if you can, and breathe deeply.
- Let your eyes feast on the distant horizon. Consciously expand your aura to include everything you see.
- If you find yourself feeling tense about a project or situation, ask yourself, "How will I feel about this in a month?"

ACTION ITEM:
In *The Book of Heroic Failures*, author Stephen Pile writes of a supervisor who insisted that his bus drivers follow precisely their published schedule—a feat they seldom accomplished. One driver had a "creative" solution for staying on time—he simply skipped his busiest stops. It was his passengers, you see, that made him late!

Becoming overly preoccupied with your daily routine can cause you to forget your true purpose.

1. Reflect on why you chose your occupation. What originally inspired you?
2. Now ask yourself, "How can I be more creative and expressive at work? What tasks or roles increase my enthusiasm and serve my deeper goals?"
3. Vow to act more from ideals important to you.
4. Every day, attune to the highest your profession offers—to you, and to others.
5. If you cannot change a difficult situation, concentrate on serving and giving love to others. This will keep your energy expansive and joyful no matter what challenges you face.

> Objective conditions are always neutral. It is how you react to them that makes them appear sad or happy. Work on yourself: on your reactions to outer circumstances. This is the essence of yoga: to neutralize the waves of reaction in the heart. Be ever happy inside. You will never be able to change things outwardly in such a way as to make them ever pleasing to you. Change yourself.
>
> —Paramhansa Yogananda, *How to Face Life's Changes*

LESSON TWENTY-ONE

THE STAGES OF HUMAN EVOLUTION

> The more central a truth is, the greater the number of avenues one can take to reach it. From the center of a wheel outward, the entire wheel can be seen in proportion. From its periphery, the center can be approached from every point of the compass, but every approach is from a different direction.

The Principles

I remember many years ago—I was twenty at the time—entering an informal chess tournament. The man against whom I was pitted was said to be a local chess champion—a title to which I had no claim at all. I'd heard that his specialty was a complicated pawn play. I therefore decided, in a spirit of fun, to "spook" him with an unusual "pawn play" of my own. In truth, I had no system. My only hope of victory lay in bluffing him.

He was a man in his fifties, I'd say, very serious of visage, and bristling with confidence in his own ability. Mine was a sort of "last-ditch" strategy: to confuse the fellow completely by moving my pawns haphazardly without the slightest logic. My only aim was to bewilder him.

Well, he couldn't imagine that I might be playing just for the fun of it. Probably fun was even foreign to his nature. I could almost hear him thinking, "Now, what can the reasoning be behind *that* move?" So perplexed did that brooding make him that I actually checkmated him before he could get any inkling of what I was doing. Still he didn't understand, and came to our second game only slightly better prepared, but insufficiently so. My madcap moves brought him this time to a "stalemate"—which, for those who don't know chess, means that the game was a draw.

At this point, aware by now that I'd been "taking" him, he became furious—more at himself, I suspect, than at me—rose from the table, and stalked fiercely away. Evidently he felt—and quite rightly so!—that it was beneath his dignity to play against such an ignoramus as me!

To succeed in one's work requires a certain expertise, and one not too dissimilar from the skill needed to play a good game of chess. It helps also to have the kind of "skill" that inspired me that day. I hadn't the necessary ability to be expert at the game, but, fortunately for me, I possessed another advantage: I was blessed with a certain creative flair—enough, at least, to see the possibilities of "beating him at his own game," which enabled me to leap, figuratively speaking, left or right as the occasion demanded, and to adjust to the situation at hand.

On many other occasions in my life I've had, similarly, to "tilt" circumstances in my favor by studying a situation, and then taking a new approach to it.

Anyone with a hope of achieving success in life, especially if he is seeking it through yoga principles, must understand that success doesn't always come by plodding along on a predictable course: Often it comes by putting out the mental energy, first, to look for a new way.

Yoga principles might seem to be fixed in an ancient tradition. This is certainly true in the sense that certain realities of human nature never change, and that yoga deals with those realities. It is *not* true, however, in other vitally important ways. The more central a truth is, the greater the number of avenues one can take to reach it. From the center of a wheel outward, the entire wheel can be seen in proportion. From its periphery, the center can be approached from every point of the compass, but every approach is from a different direction.

Really to succeed in life demands a creative outlook. Don't be afraid to develop this gift—for that is what it is, simply: a gift, not a unique quality which only a few individuals possess. Be careful, on the other hand, for others who haven't developed this gift will not appreciate it. If your superior especially prefers the "tried and true" ways, realize that he may consider you a mere upstart. Be careful, and respect him for what he is. Creative arrogance is notorious, and is, in the end, self-defeating. Never allow ability to go to your head. As my Guru said, "A swelled head is the death of wisdom."

People tend to be creatures of habit. Habit, too, is "the death of wisdom." It is amusing, though understandable, to see people in the malls of India who have never before seen a moving staircase or escalator. In Gurgaon, just south of New Delhi, I once tried to assist a young lady who feared to set foot on a downward-moving escalator. Her more enterprising mother had met the challenge and overcome it; she was already waiting at the bottom.

I took pity on the young woman. "Now," I urged her, "set one foot in the middle of a step the moment it appears." After several attempts, she finally "took the plunge" and descended easily to the bottom. Other people whom I've tried to help onto that first step have given up and turned away to take the nearby, and less convenient elevator (or lift).

If you are an employer, recognize that people are like chessmen, in a sense. The bishop in chess can only move diagonally. The castle can only move vertically or horizontally. The knight moves two steps then one step sidewise; he can also leap over other players, something the bishop and castle cannot do. Pawns, of all the pieces, have the most restricted movements.

Obviously, my purpose here is not to teach you chess! I'm using it, however, as a good illustration.

Chess originated in India. The consciousness of Indians can be very subtle, though, as Sherlock Holmes rightly said of chess, exceptional skill in that game suggests a talent for scheming. My point here is that people resemble chessmen in that they, too, each have their limitations. Don't expect the "pawns" in your work force to be able to act like castles or knights. If you are an employee, be tolerant of eccentricities in your fellow workers and even in your boss. Everyone has to work within the limitations of his own nature, which is the result of his own actions in the past. Thus, if you (as an employee) marvel at certain limitations in your co-workers, and if you (as a boss or employer) shake your head at people's inability to grasp something that to you seems obvious, tell yourself that perhaps that person is a knight, not a bishop as you might have wished, and that another person is a castle, not a queen. There must, of course, be pawns also; they will probably be (as in chess) the more numerous. If you, as an employee, find your boss hemmed in by his own limitations—as he almost certainly will be, since he is human—accept that fact good-naturedly. And if you are the boss, don't get impatient with workers on your staff who don't seem to come quite "up to snuff." There are few things more difficult for an intelligent employee than to have an unintelligent boss, or for one who is creative and imaginative to have a boss who is a "plodder." The best thing to do if you find yourself in this position is to see if you can't find some other place of employment. And if you are a boss and a staff member of yours fails similarly, try to fit him into some other position. It may take time to see how a person's talents or abilities can be put to the best use. On the other hand, if his main defect is that he lacks willingness, and if you fail to get him to motivate himself, it may be necessary, after all, to send him on his way.

It is idle to *expect* people to change drastically. It simply doesn't happen. You can't *make* them change, and they themselves, try as they will, can only refine the natures they were born with.

Years ago, while I was writing my autobiography *The Path*, I looked at a photograph of myself at the age of four, and saw in those eyes the same fellow I still was. I've had superiors say about me, "Why must he be like this?" or, "Why can't he be like that?" There is something I might do about it, I suppose—but not as much as might be wished.

The ancient teachings of India make it very clear that there are different lines of human development. Wise gurus see clearly into the uniqueness of each disciple, and encourage his or her development along that line. Such is the way of wisdom.

Some people are more naturally inclined to seek out opportunities. Others wait for opportunity to present itself. Still others would not recognize opportunity if you framed it, wrapped it, and gave it to them as a gift. Many people are too thrustful by nature for their own spiritual good. They may need to be tamed, either by a wise guru or by life itself. Other people are too passive, and need to be spurred to greater activity. Some people are naturally solemn, and cannot be made to laugh even at a good joke. Others react quickly to humor, and can be won best through their sense of fun.

Many years ago, the government of Nevada County, where I founded our first Ananda Sangha community, decided to see us as a threat because we didn't fit into any of their accepted categories. The head of the Planning Department tried to arrange things so that we'd simply blow away. She made things as difficult for us as she could. She insisted, first, that we develop a master plan according to her way of thinking. I think she must have deliberately made it impossible to complete. We presented a plan to her, whereupon she declared that it was too simple. We elaborated it: She then declared that it was too complex. What were we to do? By this time, she'd already been holding up our development for five years.

I decided that the only possible solution was to have her replaced. Obviously, she didn't want to help us to resolve what she saw as our problem. Rather, to her mind, our community itself was the "problem." Her hope was for us simply to fail.

And then came 1976, the bicentennial year of the United States of America. I proposed to our members that year that we form a "Bicentennial Liberty Committee" to publicize America's need for a return to basic liberties. It was my way of protesting official persecution.

The great majority of the Ananda members opposed this idea. To them, it was "goofy" and a conflict with our apolitical nature. "We won't even *have* a community," I replied, "if we don't do *something*! My suggestion isn't immoral: It's *super* moral!" The county officials we had to deal with, I pointed out, had been appointed to their positions and were duty-bound in a democracy to listen to public opinion. Refractory persons at Ananda simply dug in their heels and refused to cooperate.

I myself was busy at the time writing my autobiography, *The Path*, and couldn't go out pamphleteering. At last I managed to interest one member, a woman, by appealing to her lively sense of humor. I figured that if I pitched my appeal to her sense of fun, she might feel inspired to give me the support I needed. She laughed and enlisted a few others.

They distributed handbills outside of supermarkets and in various other public places. She herself spoke in radio news broadcasts about our "Bicentennial Liberty Committee" and what it was all about. Naturally, the literature I wrote for them emphasized the large numbers of people who were seriously concerned. Many people, in fact, had begun to look upon the resistance of the officials as a form of harassment.

We were finally successful. The head of the Planning Department was fired, and a man was brought in from outside who was sympathetic to our needs.

People in the county later tried to get this Ananda member to run for public office, but I discouraged her from that activity. It was, in fact, too different from what Ananda was really all about.

My point here is that one must be flexible in his approach to every situation. Never let any self-definition limit the options before you.

Many years later, that woman member wrote up her recollections of this episode in Ananda's history, centering her recollections of it in the "crazy humor" of the situation. My own intentions, however, had been quite serious from the start (as I reminded her). I'd appealed to her sense of humor only because I considered it the best way to reach her and get her involved.

Any time you find it difficult to get people to do what is needed in some work, consider them from a point of view of their own natures. Work with them *as they are*. If you are the boss, this concept may prove, for you, all-important. If you are an employee, you may find it helpful in your work to take others into account, and to accept them as they are. It seldom works to criticize or judge others. *Go with their reality as it is*. Go with them as they are. And in the process, take your own nature into account!

I remember having to work once with an older woman who insisted on always having the last word. I'd been told simply to try to work *with* her. I wasn't *under* her. Instead, however, of pushing the fact that our responsibilities were supposedly equal, I learned to persuade her to new ideas by reminding her that she had had that idea also. This I was able to do sincerely even if she'd only hinted, once, at the possibility.

Others under me have sometimes tried to use that tactic with me. As I am constituted, however, the tactic doesn't work. If someone tries to tell me that an idea was mine, I am likely to reply, "Did I say that? It seems to me that So-and-so's suggestion is better." People have learned in working with me that my concern is with what will work best, not with who had the idea. I say this not to boast, but simply to urge everyone to recognize the diversity in people's natures, and to try to work with them as they really are.

Anyone who is in a leadership position—and, to a lesser degree, anyone who works *with* others in any capacity—may need to concentrate on deepening his understanding of people—not only of human nature generally, but of the human natures with which he must deal. His understanding, in other words, needs to be not only general, but specific. One thing should be understood above all: There is, for everyone on earth, a specific, clear direction that will lead him or her to highest fulfillment—an apotheosis to which everyone on earth aspires.

Irrespective of the different lines of development people take in the intricate web of possibilities in human nature, there is, as I have said, one basic direction that all must take in their development. The successive stages in that development apply universally. No one can avoid them for the simple reason that all mankind manifests one, universal reality.

This is not the place to argue the doctrine of reincarnation. It is profound, and, in fact—if one will consider it deeply—self-evident. It explains all the differences in human nature, and answers any question that can arise regarding that nature. If you, who study these lessons, believe that a person lives on earth only once, then instead of my trying to win you to this concept let me say only that what follows will make sense to you anyway, though it may be less justifiable philosophically.

The fact is, there *are* differences of refinement and sensitivity in all human beings. Even were I to give the traditional explanation for these differences, as it is presented in the Hindu scriptures, and even if you were to reject that explanation, you would still find yourself facing certain clear and evident realities.

According to the ancient teachings to which I've referred, the manifestations of consciousness in matter evolve upward from lower to higher stages of life. It takes five to eight million incarnations, as I said in an earlier lesson, to reach the human level. At this stage, life has evolved upward to the point where it is fully self-, or ego-conscious. There are lower animals that manifest some degree of ego, but not enough to ask themselves such all-important questions as, "Why am *I* suffering?" Man's ego, too, must evolve before he asks himself that question, and also the next one, which is even more important: "What can *I* do about it?"

A soul newly raised to the human level has all the mental equipment to ask these questions. It hasn't the long memory, however, of repeated suffering for him to give his suffering serious, long-term consideration. Man's natural inclination, earlier on, is to seek gratification through physical sense-pleasures. He is not inclined yet to rely on brainpower to solve any problem more intricate than, "What can I eat today?" or, "How can I fulfill this desire, or that one?" He divides other human beings up into those who please and those who, because they frustrate his desires, displease him. Such a person eats, sleeps, breeds, and dies. His entire life-span might be compared, in its productivity, to a crocodile sleeping on a riverbank.

After a few lives of physical and mental indolence, a person begins to think, "I wish I didn't have to suffer." He then begins to analyze his life. He concludes that suffering comes from not having what he wants. In time, he realizes that even this is not the whole story. Slowly, step by step, he seeks his fulfillments on ever-subtler levels. For a long time, his awareness remains wholly centered in the ego, which causes him to define good and bad in terms of how he himself is affected. He uses his intelligence to ask, of every opportunity, "What's in it for me?"

An individual takes many incarnations to realize that accumulation is not his true goal: that what he wants is that abstraction, happiness. He learns, first, that happiness comes more from sharing his gains with others, including their well-being in his own. Thus, he thinks, "What is best for all concerned?"

Finally, the realization dawns on him that happiness is not a mere thing, but a state of mind. To share his happiness with others is more fulfilling to him than to seek it only for himself. His consciousness becomes focused on becoming a source of happiness for others, and on sharing with them such intangible benefits as peace, love, and understanding.

Everyone wants to expand his self-awareness. Opposing this natural instinct is the ego's desire for self-gratification, which, as long experience shows one, causes self-contraction. The more expansive one's consciousness becomes, the greater his sense of true fulfillment. This truth is universal, because the natural impulse of the soul is to reach toward its origin in God. The more contractive one is, out of ignorance, the more he draws suffering upon himself. Self-limitation contradicts his own inherently expansive urge, which his soul holds up to him constantly, albeit silently.

There are countless pitfalls on the way to Self-realization. Many people, when they first become aware of an expansive urge, want to accumulate wealth. First indeed, I should say, they think to satisfy that urge by indulging in sense-pleasures. Later, others, if they eschew wealth, try to achieve self-expansion by an increase of knowledge. These apparent routes to self-expansion and fulfillment are illusory. At the end of each lies the desire, always, for "something more." One may be wealthy, or absorbed in sense-pleasures, or a veritable paragon of erudition, but everything, in the end, will disappoint him. Wealthy people make the same discovery Howard Hughes made, who was asked toward the end of his life, "Are you happy?" He replied in a thin, cracked voice, "Nah, I can't say that I'm happy!"

There is another type of human being who tries to find happiness by destroying everything he thinks stands in the way to his own fulfillment. He will harm and even kill others, dominate them, trample them underfoot. Is he happy? By no means! Joseph Stalin, ruthless dictator that he was, became paranoid with fear in his last years—as I said earlier—that everyone around him only schemed to do him in, as he himself had "obliterated" so many others.

Kings and emperors dream of ruling over more and more territory, more and more people, and possessing more and more money and power. Are they ever satisfied? The question itself is laughable. Alexander "the Great" sent a drastic summons to a certain yogi he'd heard about in India who slept on a bed of leaves, and whose "roof" consisted of tree branches: "If you come in answer to this summons, and reply to his imperial majesty's questions, he will lavish vast wealth upon you. If, however, you refuse, he will strike off your head!"

The yogi sent back his reply: "What your majesty offers me is of no value to me. I am already wealthy in my few possessions. As for my head, it has served its purpose now that I've realized the Self. If your majesty needs anything of mine, come here and request it of me." Legend tells us that the emperor went humbly to the yogi, and asked for wisdom.

When the vast variety in human nature is reduced to its essentials, we see in the four stages I outlined in an earlier lesson that they define the ego's long journey to Self-realization in the Infinite. Thus did the caste system originally evolve. As I have quoted my Guru, and many other saintly authorities, as saying, caste was not actually a system at all, but simply an explanation of a universal reality. A person's true caste has little to do, except accidentally, with his birth lineage. Often it happens, of course, that people take after their parents. This is because, when a man and a woman unite sexually, their state of mind at that moment emits a light in the astral world; that vibration attracts souls (egos, that is to say) that are ready to be reborn, and who have similar tendencies. This rule is by no means infallible, but the old rule generally applies: "Birds of a feather flock together"! As Krishna states in the Bhagavad Gita, it is difficult for a fallen yogi to be born into a spiritual family, for spiritual people often have few or no children.

A friend of mine once scolded her little five-year-old son, who left the room in a huff. He returned a moment later and announced, "And you weren't my first choice, either!"

Later she asked him, "Who was your first choice?"

"Oh, some woman in the Philippines," he replied. "She was already taken."

The lowest type of human being is defined not only by such qualities as vengefulness and destructiveness, but principally by his nearness to the consciousness of animals. He may even be peaceful by nature, but unless he has self-expansive impulses he may still be a lower type of human being—a *sudra* type.

It is possible for the highest type of human being to sink to the lowest level. The one thing that differentiates man from the lower animals is free will. Self-awareness enables him to rise or fall, as he himself chooses—though few would choose to fall if they understood the consequences of that choice.

It is possible even to sink below the human level. This occurrence is unusual. When it happens, it does so for only one incarnation at a time. If a human being continues to act bestially, he may have to return to that lower state again, and even again repeatedly—for one incarnation, each time. To do so is a great punishment, for there lingers in the subconscious a vague recollection of having been more evolved.

Is it possible to descend even lower than the animal level? Unfortunately, yes, though I am not going to explain that depressing fact here.

The soul's capacity to rise or fall is, indeed—like cosmic consciousness itself—infinite.

A Western visitor to Tibet many years ago wrote of an experience she had heard about in that mysterious land. A certain elderly lama had tried to violate a young maiden sexually. She, being stronger than he, was able easily to fend him off. She ran home and told her mother what had occurred. The older woman, however, replied in astonishment, "But he is such a holy lama! Perhaps you should not have resisted him. He must have had some reason. I suggest you return to him and apologize."

When the girl appeared before him again, the lama told her he wasn't interested. "I was concerned for a certain lama," he explained, "who, owing to his wrong deeds, was destined to take a lower birth in his next life. I saw that he was ready to be reborn, and, out of compassion for him, wanted to help him to achieve at least a human birth. Now conception has occurred anyway. Two asses in that nearby field were copulating at the time, and the ex-lama will be born to the mare."

One naturally wonders: Did the compassion of the lama not extend also to the poor maiden whom he'd intended to burden with this fallen soul? I haven't an answer to that question, and can only be relieved for the sake of the girl herself that he failed in his attempt.

In the normal course of upward human evolution, however, as I have explained earlier, from *sudra* to *vaisya* to *kshatriya* to *brahmin* to Self-realized master, the closer one comes to God, the greater the joy he finds in himself, and the deeper his instinct becomes to share that joy with others. Thus, the saints alone—as distinct from merely religious priests—are the *true* brahmins.

A *jivan mukta*, finally, is a spiritual master. He has attained the highest spiritual state of *nirbikalpa samadhi*, having merged ego-consciousness wholly in the Infinite. Such a one is no longer merely a human being: He has expanded his sense of selfhood to the point where it embraces the Self of all. He is above all the four castes, and beyond the three qualities or *gunas*: *tama* (inertial), *raja* (activating), and *sattwa* (elevating). His nature has no farther to rise, for he has attained the Absolute.

An interesting question was once asked my Guru by a guest at Mt. Washington: "Is there any end to evolution?"

"No end," the Master replied. "You go on until you achieve endlessness."

When working with others, try to see them in relation to the four castes. Never mind what caste their parents seem to be: That is a false categorization, and has been a cause of much social injustice. It has, moreover, excused much unjustified arrogance. See, rather, whether the individuals who work with you have, first, the capacity to think for themselves. In many a business there is a need also for *sudra* types who will not, and should not even be expected to, put their minds to anything. Such persons should be given tasks that require little or no mentation.

My Paramguru, Swami Sri Yukteswar, said that menial positions, far from demeaning such people, are actually helpful to them spiritually owing to their close association with people of higher consciousness. That association raises their consciousness, and thereby improves their karma.

Thus, also, a *vaisya* is raised by mixing with people of a *kshatriya* disposition. A natural *brahmin*, finally, who needs good company as much as anyone, can derive the greatest benefit from mixing with spiritual masters.

Much has been said in popular Hindu tradition about the danger of pollution, from mixing too closely with lower types of humanity than one's own. People have carried this tradition to absurd lengths, creating rules for who pollutes whom. They have made people the prisoners of their own culture. My Guru pointed out that fear itself *attracts* the objects of its fears. If you fear pollution, you may actually draw occasions of pollution to yourself. Moreover, my Guru said that, in any exchange of magnetism, it is the stronger that influences the weaker, not the reverse. When faith in God is strong, *no negativity* can touch you.

I remember once sitting out of doors with a group of monks in the company of our Guru. We were eating. Someone dropped a piece of food onto the ground, and our Guru warned, "Don't eat it!" Then he added, "But if you declare with faith, 'All is Brahman!' it won't matter if you eat it." Accordingly, we all chanted, "All is Brahman!" Whoever it was that had dropped the food picked it up solemnly and put it in his mouth. It was an occasion of amusement.

An attitude very often encountered in offices, or wherever groups of people work together, is one of behaving slightingly toward others. Egoism is strongly rooted in human nature. Many would define virtue itself in terms of the sort of people they are, themselves. "I may be a slow worker, but *at least* I don't leave my desk cluttered as you do!" Or, "I may not be neat, but *at least* I get things done quickly." Which way is better? To be both neat and efficient is best of all, of course, but neither quality deserves special placement in any gradation of virtue, until other factors have been taken into consideration. The ancient system in India was supreme in that it provided a reasonable guideline to excellence. That person is best who is the least centered in the common attitude of, "What's in it for me?"

We cannot leave the subject there, however. To do so would be too simplistic. Every organization, every office, every group of people who work together has specific needs that may have nothing to do with caste refinements. A man who lays bricks needs, from his employer's point of view, to be skilled only at laying bricks. He may be of any caste: all that matters to his employer is that he lay the bricks straight, well, and true. Although these considerations are important, they have little or nothing to do with our course on yoga principles. On the other hand, efficiency also is a yoga principle, and is more likely to be found in persons of greater intelligence, and therefore is more likely to exist in people of a naturally higher caste, where the brain gets some employment, at least.

What I am saying, in practical terms, is that an efficient bricklayer may find himself forever confined to that kind of work—much to his own detriment in terms of his spiritual growth. Look at those who work for you—and, for that matter, at those also who work *with* you—and see what might be done to raise them higher than their present position, and not keep them doing the same thing adequately. In this way you will—if your position is that of leader—improve your business in the highest way, by producing other leaders.

Several times in my own life I have felt that I must sacrifice an excellent secretary, simply because he or she was ready to serve in some other and perhaps higher way. For me, personally, to do so was a setback, but it meant a gain for the over-all work I was developing.

Understanding that the different castes are a valid way of separating people into self-determined categories will help you to direct your entire work force along yoga principles, for it will mean keeping in mind, and helping to advance, everyone's evolution. This system will help you to think not only of developing people's natural skills, but also of unfolding their natures to their own highest effectiveness in the organization.

This lesson may help you above all by getting you to stop judging people (if this happens to be your fault) in terms of what you think they *ought* to be, and to work with everybody, instead, *as he is*.

The Application

Ultimately, the quest for material success through yoga principles must be related to the kind of success you yourself desire in life. Everything you seek is, if you will analyze it deeply, something that you hope will increase your happiness. Why aspire to be as wealthy as Howard Hughes, who was possibly the wealthiest man in the world, but who never found happiness?

I myself turned to God only after realizing that what I thought I wanted—namely, intellectual understanding—couldn't give me the simple, heartfelt joy I remembered having as a child. I decided that that simple joy was what was lacking in my life. It is that realization which, in the end, turns everyone to God. People may hope, for the present, to find the end of their "rainbow" in lesser fulfillments. Whatever that hope, their hearts will be dry and unfulfilled until they turn back toward their own true Source, within.

You may think of that Self as God. You may think of it in more personal, or more abstract, terms. Still, there is something within you that will never let you rest until you've found the joy of your own being.

So—you may wonder—is this not also a "principle," rather than an "application" of the teachings in this chapter? No, for what I've pointed out to you as the end you are already seeking is the essence of your own nature. Now you must *do* something about it! What you must do is *expand* your self-identification.

You've been seeking self-expansion already, by developing your brain and nervous system. You've sought it also, presumably, by expanding from selfish accumulation and self-indulgence to helping others. You must have done so; otherwise, you would not be studying these lessons!

What you need, now, is to continue to expand your sympathies *consciously*. Try to *feel* other people's joys and sorrows as your own. When you take a solitary walk, try to *feel* the breeze that moves the leaves of the trees around you. Try to *feel* the atmosphere that encircles you. When traveling, try to *feel* the vibrations of the places you visit. Should you enter a holy shrine, try to feel the blessings it emanates. Indeed, the holier the place, the more its vibrations will uplift you.

You are so much more than you know! Direct your quest for success *through* normal goals in life to ever-higher levels of fulfillment in your own Self. It is for that fulfillment that you will always long, until you achieve your destiny at last—endless, eternal bliss!

MEDITATION

Sit in meditation. Try to *feel* the world around you. As you apply yourself to this practice you will develop a real intuition of it as a conscious reality.

In business, or when contemplating an investment, or a new direction of activity, try to *feel* whether or not it is right for you. That kind of intuition will appear in your heart center, the *anahat chakra*. Concentrate, first, at the point between the eyebrows, and visualize clearly there what it is you contemplate doing. Then "listen" in the heart: see whether the response you get there is "Go!" or "Stop!" A "Go" feeling will uplift you; it will be accompanied by a certain flow of energy. A "Stop" feeling will produce a sort of nervousness, of rejection; there will be no flow in it at all. Rather, you will feel the energy blocked. Try it!

Years ago, the owner of a bookstore in Menlo Park, California, asked me if I would like to buy her out (she was growing old and wanted to retire). It took me hardly a moment to decide. I simply practiced what I've written above: Standing before her desk, I inwardly asked myself the question: "Should I?" Suddenly I felt a "Go!" response in my heart. I didn't have the money, nor anything close to it, at the time. Nor did our Ananda community. Even so I felt to say, "Yes." The money came—miraculously, and within the two weeks I'd promised!

AFFIRMATION

"Of the two choices before me—to move downward in consciousness, or upward—I choose with all my heart to rise toward inner joy!"

POINTS TO REMEMBER

1. Everyone must work within the limitations he himself has placed on his own nature, by his past actions. It is idle to *expect* people to change drastically. They can only refine the natures they were born with.

2. Any time you find it difficult to get people to do what is needed in some work, consider them from a point of view of their own natures. Work with them *as they are*.

3. Anyone who works *with* others may need to concentrate on deepening his understanding of people—not only of human nature generally, but of the human natures with which he must deal.

4. The natural inclination of a soul newly raised to the human level is to seek gratification through physical sense-pleasures. Slowly, step by step, a person seeks his fulfillments on ever-subtler levels. For a long time, his awareness remains wholly centered in the ego, which causes him to define good and bad in terms of how he himself is affected.

5. An individual takes many incarnations to realize that accumulation is not his true goal: that what he wants is happiness. He learns that happiness comes more from sharing his gains with others. Thus, he thinks, "What is best for all concerned?"

6. Finally, the realization dawns on him that happiness is not a mere thing, but a state of mind. His consciousness becomes focused on becoming a source of happiness for others, and on sharing with them such intangible benefits as peace, love, and understanding.

7. The more expansive one's consciousness becomes, the greater his sense of true fulfillment.

8. Caste was not originally a system at all, but simply an explanation of a universal reality. A person's true caste has little to do, except accidentally, with his birth lineage.

9. Self-awareness enables man to rise or fall, as he himself chooses.

10. In the normal course of upward human evolution from *sudra* to *vaisya* to *kshatriya* to *brahmin* to Self-realized master, the closer one comes to God, the greater the joy he finds in himself, and the deeper his instinct becomes to share that joy with others.

11. When working with others, try to see them in relation to the four castes.

12. The association between different castes helps to raise the consciousness of the lower-caste person. In any exchange of magnetism, it is the stronger that influences the weaker, not the reverse. When faith in God is strong, *no negativity* can touch you.

13. That person is best who is the least centered in the common attitude of, "What's in it for me?"

14. Look at those who work for you—and *with* you—and see what might be done to raise them higher than their present position. In this way you will—if your position is that of leader—improve your business in the highest way, by producing other leaders.

15. Understanding the different castes will help you to direct your entire work force along yoga principles, for it will mean keeping in mind, and helping to advance, everyone's evolution. This system will help you to think of unfolding people's natures to their own highest effectiveness in the organization.

16. The end you are already seeking is the essence of your own nature. What you need, now, is to continue to expand your sympathies *consciously*. Try to *feel* other people's joys and sorrows as your own.

17. You are so much more than you know! Direct your quest for success *through* normal goals in life to ever-higher levels of fulfillment in your own Self. It is for that fulfillment that you will always long, until you achieve your destiny at last—endless, eternal bliss!

WORKBOOK IDEAS
by Joseph Bharat Cornell

In the 1890s, American scientist George Washington Carver landscaped the barren campus of Tuskegee University. The newly planted trees and flowers were a joy to behold, but no matter how carefully Carver laid out his footpaths, the students and faculty ignored them and walked in a direct line to their destination, trampling and killing the new grass.

Carver removed his ineffective pathway signs and took a fresh look at the problem. He realized that people would walk in a logical way, no matter how hard he tried to persuade them otherwise. A better idea for laying out the paths came to him; soon the grass began to flourish. The university president was so impressed that he asked Carver, "How did you manage it?" Carver replied, "I spent a few days observing where people naturally walked, then I put my paths under their feet."

When working with others, work *with*, not against, their natures, and you'll be much more successful. People's characters develop over lifetimes of repeated responses to other people and circumstances. They have a tremendous amount of momentum invested in their way of coping with life, and it isn't easy for them to change drastically or embrace ways foreign to their nature. In fact, people usually can only *refine* the natures they were born with.

ACTION ITEM:

It is a common—although unrealistic—human trait to think that others should behave in specific ways. Judgment implies condemnation, or at least a preference that someone be other than he *is*.

1. When you notice that you are mentally criticizing someone, immediately stop yourself.
2. Remember that what you dislike in others is usually what you dislike in yourself. Their behavior would not upset you unless it found a place to resonate inside of you.
3. As you think of the criticism you were making, substitute your own name for that of the other person.
4. See how your desire to criticize that person vanishes.

Accept and be patient with the eccentricities of others. Deepen your understanding of human nature by observing how different people respond to the same situation. Look for natural opportunities to help others broaden their perspectives and expand their sympathies.

"The best leadership," Swami Kriyananda says, "is rooted in compassion, in kindness, in deep concern for the welfare of others. But to be most effective it must at the same time be liberated from personal likes and dislikes."

LESSON TWENTY-TWO

DHARMA VERSUS ADHARMA: TRUTH VERSUS UNTRUTH

The businessman's self-assumed duty in the great scheme of things is not only to earn money, but to learn the deeper, spiritual purpose of all labor, which is self-expansion through service to others.

The Principles

I have once before told the story of when I was with my Guru at his retreat in Twenty-Nine Palms, California, and he came out of doors to work alongside a small group of us who were shoveling sand in the hot sun. At one point I noticed him panting slightly from the exertion.

"It's hot work!" I exclaimed sympathetically.

A little sternly he replied, "It is *good* work!"

I understood his meaning at once. He was emphasizing the dignity of labor, whether physical, mental, or spiritual. Work, he implied, is ennobling, and becomes doubly so when it is given to God. As Swami Sri Yukteswar had said to him as a boy, "So long as you breathe the free air of earth, you are under obligation to render grateful service." The particular way of serving opens up for each person according to the energy he puts out, which is dictated by his own nature, and is the product of his own karma, or past actions, and of the attitudes he brought to bear on them. His nature may be primarily spiritual, mental, or physical.

The businessman's self-assumed duty in the great scheme of things is not only to earn money, but to learn the deeper, spiritual purpose of all labor, which is self-expansion through service to others.

Those who see the present life as their entire reality are blind. In the third passage of my book *Conversations with Yogananda*, the Master says, "[Man] is not important for his body, ego, or personality. His constant affirmation of ego-consciousness is the source of all his problems."

In China, scholars, intellectuals, and aristocrats considered it a mark of high breeding to let their fingernails grow to such a length that they couldn't do ordinary physical activity. In other countries, too, aristocrats have sometimes looked down on manual labor and gainful employment of any kind, considering it beneath their station. This world—to paraphrase Swami Sri Yukteswar—is inconveniently arranged for this exquisite attitude.

The Fiji Islands offer perhaps the closest thing on earth to a stress-free existence: no poisonous snakes or insects, no dangerous animals, no pollution. The inhabitants might have survived comfortably on the fruits and vegetables that grow abundantly, without help, in that perfect climate. The seasons are equable. Nature shines on one and all. Life, for the islanders, should have been ideal. But they found it too easy. What could they do for excitement? Their solution was to make war on one another. And what to do with all those dead bodies? What to do with them . . . what to *do*? Why, of course, eat them! According at least to the missionaries (who, perhaps, were seeking more support from the home church) the Fiji islanders were cannibals. It may of course be that the natives restricted their non-vegetarian diet to missionaries!

At any rate, the human condition demands that everyone put out some kind of energy. Not to do so causes one to sink into *tamas*. The more energetic one is, the sooner he can rise spiritually.

Energy is something I have emphasized repeatedly in these lessons. In studying, you may have formed the impression from the saying I've quoted often, *yato dharma, tato jaya*—"where adherence to truth exists, there is victory"—that business or any other kind of success follows automatically from being truthful, fair-minded, kind, and from entertaining all the attitudes that lead upward, spiritually. It is time I explained that the victory I mean is, above all, dharma itself. We might even change that saying to read, "Where there is dharma (adherence to truth), bliss itself becomes one's definition of success." What I am saying is that even if one fails outwardly, by clinging to dharma he achieves the only victory worth having. As Krishna states in the Bhagavad Gita, "It is better to fail doing one's own duty than to succeed, doing someone else's."

I hope you don't feel that I have lured you down a false trail: promising material success, then suddenly whipping off the mask and saying, "Actually, yoga principles define success itself as very different from anything you imagined!" What I'm really saying is that there are varying *degrees* of success. If you are a grocer, a baker, or a dry goods merchant, and want only a stress-free existence with a moderate income and a moderate flow of customers, then everything I have written so far will come to you if you follow the principles stated so far. *Maya* (delusion) will resist you, of course, but the way to win out over its opposing force is to adhere to truth and honesty.

There is, however, another and less beautiful—or at least more difficult-to-accept—side to this picture. Normal resistance from *maya* can be like the bushes on a hillside, past which one can thread his way to the top. But what about other people's deliberate *adharma*: their untruthfulness, their desire to injure, their determination even to destroy you? The unfortunate truth is, the more energy you put out to achieve a high and noble success, the more *maya* will use other people to put forth an opposite energy.

One would think, on reading about Paramhansa Yogananda's amazingly successful career in America, that he more or less slid down an easy slope to victory by simply loving everyone, and by his joyful, positive attitude of service to all. The truth, however, must be told: He faced constant, determined opposition. A very small example is one time when two gunmen were sent to Mt. Washington Estates to murder him. They waited for him at the basement elevator door, where he was scheduled to emerge. God warned him in time, however, and he changed his plans.

Well, one might say, God came to his rescue, so where's the stress involved? Most of his stress was not physical, but mental and spiritual. Still, he had to face hate-filled opposition through lawsuits, constant calumny, and dishonesty. One time his closest co-worker betrayed him, absconding with almost all of the money the Master had been sending back from his lecture tours and classes around the country. The man then tried to sue him. One might ask, "Didn't Yogananda, being a master, recognize that danger and do something in advance to prevent it?" Yes, he'd known about it. It came out years later that he'd predicted many years earlier to a boyhood friend that this person would someday betray him. To him, life was a movie. He accepted its ups and downs as the features of this world, where he'd been sent by God to guide people *out of maya*, not to make their delusions more comfortable for them.

My Guru achieved stunning success in his life, but the way was never easy for him. The important lesson his life teaches is that he *never* cut moral corners in striving for success, and never compromised in his absolute, unswerving adherence to right action. Disciples like me don't want to frighten people from embracing spiritual principles by emphasizing the difficulties even a true guru faces in life. I admit frankly that I don't emphasize them.

It is natural for us to do what we can to stress the joys, not the difficulties. The higher one aspires, however, the more *maya* itself intervenes to prevent one from changing the ways of this world.

Don't be afraid. A boxer, my Guru used to say, doesn't become strong by fighting children. He must spar with strong men, who might even knock him down. The plain truth is, though the tests do become greater as one advances spiritually, one also develops the inner strength to conquer them. All his consciousness is of joy, not of suffering and sorrow.

The popular image in Christianity is of Jesus suffering for mankind. In a shop in Greece I saw a painting of the crèche scene showing the Virgin Mary holding the baby Jesus. "Why on earth," I exclaimed in dismay to the shopkeeper, "is Mary depicted as miserable?!"

"That," he explained, "is because she knows her child will someday be crucified on the cross." What a gloomy picture to keep in one's home! The Jewish historian Josephus wrote much later of Jesus Christ that he was "a man never known to smile." What utter nonsense! Can you imagine anyone attracting thousands by weeping for their sins? People seek others who may be able to give them what they all want: joy! Jesus knew God, which is to say, he knew perfect bliss. It was bliss that everyone hoped for through him, not his pain.

I'm a very small example of the truths I teach in my Guru's name—at least, I try to be an example. Yet even I have experienced some of the joy behind difficulties, not their horrors. Many years ago, shortly after founding the first Ananda community, I was discussing with a new friend the hardships so many people face in life. At one point I said to her, "You know, it's strange, but I don't seem to have had any such problems!"

"*No problems!*" she exclaimed, flinging a hand to her forehead. She then reminded me of what I'd had to face in just the short year she had known me: a serious attempt by the trustees of our land to foreclose on us; the opposition of new members within the community; gossip and mockery from others; the destruction of our new temple by fire; opposition and calumny from my fellow disciples; numerous other financial tests; a constant barrage of criticism for anything I did. After listening to this litany I replied, "Well, yes, I suppose you're right. I just hadn't put my mind there." I promptly dismissed the memories again from my mind.

The lesson I want to emphasize in my Guru's life is not that he was spared tests and difficulties, but that he always faced them with honor, charity, truthfulness, and the highest spiritual consciousness. Moreover, however much people tried to hurt him he always forgave them. Indeed, one time, in his role of Guru, he scolded someone for something that person had done. The disciple asked, "But will you forgive me, Sir?" Our Guru replied in astonishment, "Why, what else can I do?"

Another popular image of Jesus Christ is expressed in the hymn, "Gentle Jesus, meek and mild." What a travesty of a true master! One who has achieved oneness with God is *powerful*. Yogananda responded dharmically to everything, but that doesn't mean he ever responded weakly. His was a force to be reckoned with! The important thing is, he never wished harm to anyone. Still, he was very firm, when the circumstances called for strength over sweetness.

One time at Mt. Washington he was sitting on his bed upstairs when, as he put it later, "God showed me that a certain young man was coming up the stairs to punish me physically.

The voice told me, 'Defend yourself for the sake of this work.' That young man wanted to spread the word that he'd shown this 'charlatan' a thing or two." When the man reached the threshold of Yogananda's room, the Master opened his eyes.

"I know why you've come," he said. "And I want you to know, first, that I'm physically very strong. It would be easy for me to beat you in bodily battle. I will not use physical force, however. Nevertheless, I warn you: Don't cross that threshold."

"Go on, prophet!" sneered the other. "What can you do?" Crossing the threshold with a stride, he immediately fell to the floor crying, "I'm on fire! I'm on fire!"

Leaping up, he rushed down the stairs and ran out of doors, where he rolled over and over on the lawn outside, trying to ease the burning on the cool grass. The Master came down and touched him lightly, healing him.

"Don't come near me!" shouted the man fearfully. He wouldn't even enter the building again, but asked his sister, who was living there, to bring him his belongings, whereupon he left immediately.

The young man had resented his sister's discipleship to this "Hindu prophet." (The sister, Durga Mata, went on to become one of the Guru's foremost disciples.)

Opposition of all kinds, including lawsuits, defamation, and other attacks, is, of course, a recognized feature of worldly existence. The strange thing is that *goodness* should attract such opposition, and that common persecution should be intensified so far beyond the norm. Many people—criminals usually, of course—were crucified before Jesus Christ, but the fact that he himself was so treated for doing only good in the world seems extraordinary. Yet it is an example of something that happens constantly. The stronger the light, the stronger also the contrasting darkness.

If you want to avoid attracting opposition, the easiest way is simply to do nothing. Success of any kind will attract animosity to varying degrees, its intensity depending on the amount of good one does. Some people will hate you because they themselves are failures in life. Even mediocre success on your part may attract a few envious grumbles. I don't think you'd be taking this course, however, if all you wanted was the pale satisfaction of a mediocre success. The steepest slope may lead you most quickly to the top, but that climb will, at the same time, be more demanding.

Past karma is also a major factor, of course, in any opposition confronting you. The spiritual hero wants to pay off that karma as soon as possible. Even a liberated master like Paramhansa Yogananda, however, who had no karma of his own left to work out, meets opposition for the good he does in the world. Opposing him is *maya* itself. The world flounders in a mire of desires, selfishness, and inertia. A master's struggle is to lift people out of that mud of worldliness.

One who is content to follow well-worn trails won't need to blaze new ones on his own. Such a life will be relatively easy. Let us say one has an ordinary business—perhaps like the one I mentioned earlier: plumbing. Or let us take home building, or stock investing, or banking, or starting a secretarial firm. Even in such work, all that I've taught in these lessons will prove helpful. Especially if one adds the burden of novelty, however, he will encounter more resistance. In every walk of life one encounters difficulties, naturally, but everything I've written so far will help you to conquer them. Moreover, yes, you must face, pay off, or cancel out whatever karmas are blocking your present efforts. Most people's reaction even to life's perfectly normal problems is to lament, "Why me?" If the success you dream of is more outstanding, or even heroic, the burdens you will have to shoulder will not be your own, only, but the opposition of delusion's inertia itself.

No matter what opposition or even outright persecution you encounter, never let it cause you to be negative. The ultimate reason for being kind and forgiving to all may be described, in a sense, as selfish! For you will be happier when you can direct your heart's energy upward to the brain, and not let it sink down in the spine to the darker consciousness of anger, resentment, or vengefulness. When you can return love for hatred, calm acceptance for anger, and kindness for persecution, you yourself will find happiness.

When I was still a relatively young man—thirty-six years old—my fellow disciples became furious with me over my "independent" nature. I was serving my Guru as he himself had told me to do. Seeing me as a threat, however, they dismissed me from his organization (this was long after he'd left this world) with a harshness I could hardly believe, hurling imprecations and telling me I wasn't fit even to call myself a disciple for I had failed to support them in the directions they themselves wanted to take his work. Well, that story is well known, in consequence of the publicity they generated and of their efforts to destroy me through the law courts. The treatment was unjust, as has been amply proved by my continued service to my Guru both before and since then.

Thank God, I wasn't even *tempted* to turn against them. Since my dismissal I've stated that my rationale for remaining loyal and loving toward them was that I felt happier loving than I would have been by hating them or seeking vengeance against them. In truth, however, I needed no such rationale: I simply wasn't tempted to respond with negatively. I've offered that rationale rather in the hope of helping others, in similar circumstances, to respond positively.

The most important decision all of us must face in life is, always, how to react in the highest way, from a standpoint of our own spiritual growth.

Years ago, when I was an eleven-year-old schoolboy in England, one of the boys there once addressed me, as an American, with contempt. "You dirty foreigner!" he sneered. Such a comment, I decided, could mean only that he didn't think I'd had a bath recently. With that thought, then, and not with the intention of insulting him, I replied pleasantly, "Well, in that case maybe you're a dirty Englishman."

Furious with me at this imagined insult (though certainly he'd invited one), he leapt for my throat. I was stronger than he, fortunately, and simply wrestled him to the floor on his back, holding him there while I waited for him to stop trying impotently to strike me. He lay there spitting up at me, but couldn't reach me; probably his spittle only wet his own face! Still, I waited for him to calm down. When finally he did so, reluctantly, I let him get up. This was one occasion when the gym, where fights were supposed to be conducted, was a distant reality: We were both in the sick rooms.

Why take people's deliberate insults personally? If they are valid, the best reaction is to accept them gratefully, as any constructive criticism should be. Try, at least in private, to correct yourself. But why get angry? You'll be the greater loser if you do.

I was in a courtroom some years ago. Some people—incited by my fellow disciples—were doing their best to harm and, if possible, to destroy me. Their lawyer did everything he could in the courtroom to make me angry. In response, I simply didn't respond! Inwardly I prayed, "Divine Mother, everything I've done can be taken away from me, but no one can rob me of my one real treasure: my love for Thee."

Well, we survived, and are thriving now more than ever. But it is something to remember: Everyone must be ready for attacks of some kind in life. And calm forgiveness has this one compensation, apart from the fact that it preserves your own peace of mind: Forgiveness without personal motive completely *infuriates* those who have defined themselves as your enemies.

Maybe my own reactions in such matters "run in the family." As my father liked to put it humorously, "You've come by it honestly." I remember us boys going to a circus with him in Grand Haven, Michigan, when I was nine years old and we were visiting America. My father bought the entry tickets to the circus, and we went inside. There, however, the man in charge told him he'd have to pay extra for the privilege of sitting down. This, clearly, was chicanery. My father calmly refused to pay more. We therefore stood through the entire performance. I remember the manager shouting at him furiously, "I hope you die!" My father didn't answer. We were the only ones present who would not submit to this sharp practice; everyone else paid extra for a seat.

Try always to react *appropriately* in every circumstance. As my Guru used to say, "Don't be a doormat." This means you may sometimes have to be stern. Strange to relate, I can recall only twice in Ananda's history when I had to *demand* that someone behave as he should. I prefer to be gentle, but no one can push me away from my purpose—a fact which has awakened enmity throughout my life in certain people, who, generally, *want* you to agree with them. The less you give in to their insistence, the angrier, often, they become. In both of the cases when I've had to demand obedience at Ananda, those people did their best later on to avenge themselves on me. I would not, in retrospect, have behaved any differently.

On one of those occasions (I'll describe only this one, here) a young man in our community had got a young woman pregnant. The woman herself was a "charity" case—not a member, and a little slow-witted, whom her mother had sent to us as a child, paying her tuition. After the girl finished high school (I'm not sure she graduated), I felt a certain responsibility for her, hesitating to send her out into the world to seek a job.

The young man insisted, after he'd broken the news of her pregnancy to me, that what he wanted to do now was to enter our monastery. I firmly ordered him, instead, to marry the girl. He did so, then left Ananda, thoroughly "disillusioned" with me. Since then, he has done his best to turn people against me. The popular expression comes to mind regarding him, "Get a life!"

Maya has many ways of opposing positive energy. One way is not to offer harsh opposition, but simply to dilute it. I gave the example of that sincere minister-disciple of my Guru who couldn't match Yogananda's high energy in demanding of his audiences, "How is everybody? . . . How *feels* everybody?" (To which the answer in both cases was the shouted reply: "AWAKE AND READY!") The minister to whom I refer told me one Sunday before the service, "I do things a little differently here." At the start of the service he said quietly, "I trust everyone here is awake and ready?"

A prayer followed, and then the service was "up and running."

I am, as you've read already in these lessons, a composer of some sincerity, whatever my merit. Whether my music will "live" must await the unwinding scroll of destiny. Still, what I've written is definitely a new kind of music: not classical, not popular, not folk or ethnic or regional, and not "modern" in any sense of the word. It is simply itself. I've never pushed it, and though I myself enjoy it and consider it good, I haven't put the kind of energy into it that attracts opposition. Indeed, there's nothing about it to oppose. The only danger to its eventual popularity is public indifference. So far, this music has made its impact more or less without effort. It has, perhaps uniquely out of everything I've done, attracted no hostility that I'm aware of. All I've had to combat with regard to it is occasional attempts to dilute it.

If your work is new and different, and if the energy you put into it is in no way forceful, you may attract no hostility, but people may very well try to "translate" it into terms with which they feel comfortable, as that minister-doctor-disciple did with our Guru's "Awake and Ready!" Don't be upset. Dilution normally happens to everything new, especially if it takes a step upward in consciousness. Simply return the focus calmly to your original intentions. I've had to do that repeatedly with my music, quietly reiterating to people the rhythm, melodic patterns, chords, and lyrics I wanted when I found them inclined to change things. Sometimes, though not often, I've approved a new idea. Don't be dogmatic: Listen to the voice of reason. State reasons, if you can verbalize them, for wanting things the way they are. It has taken me many years, but, in most things anyway, I've managed in the end to win out by calm persistence. I wouldn't have won if I'd allowed myself to become upset. The temperamental artist of legend only upsets people; he never *wins* them.

When people get upset or angry, or when they experience pain and suffering, it is only because they want something different from what life has given them. The most important point I want to make in this lesson is, learn to accept what *is*. It is only from that preliminary recognition that you can improve anything.

The Application

Because the obstacles one faces in life can be multifarious, let me list a few of them only, and suggest certain basic attitudes that may help you to sail past them.

1. *Intolerance*: People have their own views on how things ought to be or how they should be done. Don't allow yourself to be swayed by opinions, even your own. Mostly, people allow themselves to be ruled by habit. There is a common saying in America: "They laughed at Fulton." Robert Fulton was the inventor of the steel ship. His detractors laughed because, as they pointed out, metals sink in water. They will float, however, if the amount of water displaced is heavier than the metals used. Fulton calmly proceeded to construct his hollow-hulled vessel. When the ship actually floated, all criticism ceased.

2. *Anger*: Anger, as the Indian scriptures point out, is created by thwarted desires. You will encounter anger when you don't do as others want. They have no right, however, to want anything of you. Be your own master. A spiritual master is one who has, simply, mastered

himself. Such a one has no desire to control others. He desires nothing of others but their own true fulfillment. Those who follow him do so simply because they know he is pointing out the way to their own spiritual freedom. If you encounter others' anger, react calmly and you'll never need to fear them.

Once, when I was thirteen and weighed only 106 pounds, a classmate of mine who was fifteen and weighed 230 pounds became furious with me. Why? Perhaps because of the English accent I had then. Perhaps because I didn't "kowtow" to him. He attacked me one day in my room. There was no way for me to defend myself. I simply lay on the bed with my arms over my head, while he pummeled me, working himself up to such a fury that, after a few minutes, he cried panting, "I'm going to throw you out the window!" The window was behind the building, three stories above the ground. At last he'd worked out his anger, and left me in not very good shape.

A friend of mine asked me later, "Why didn't you shout for help? We'd all have come at once."

"Because," I said, "I wasn't afraid." I never deferred afterward to this bully. As for him, his force had been spent as far as I was concerned. There was nothing more for him to do. From then on, he left me strictly alone. Others, in fact, also threatened retribution if he didn't.

Defend yourself when you can. If you cannot, accept what happens, and don't let yourself be upset by it. After all, this sort of thing happens anyway in this world. Be inwardly non-attached.

Still, if you *can* defend yourself you must do so — calmly, not with anger, but always with inner firmness.

When SRF sued me, hoping to get the court's approval of their monopoly over our Guru's name, image, likeness, and words, critics asked me, "Why do you fight back?" A ridiculous question! To have remained silent would have meant ceasing the work to which I'd dedicated my life. I *had* to fight back.

Never, however, did I try to harm *them*. It would have been normal, I suppose, for someone in my position to accuse them, as they accused me; to abuse them as they abused me; to mount a press campaign against them, as they had done against me. The legal firm they chose was the third largest in the world. I could afford no such expertise. I didn't want it anyway. I chose a lawyer who was *dharmic*. To make a long story short, though it took us twelve years and over ten million dollars, Ananda Sangha won on virtually every issue. In consequence, we are much stronger than before, whereas I do not think the same can be said of them.

Stick, therefore, to your principles. If you must contest angry opposition, do so calmly and with never failing goodwill.

3. *Lies*: It is not easy to bear it when people tell lies against you. I wrote many years ago to those who had been doing so, "Every time you tell a lie against me, remember, the truth *has* to come out eventually. Your lies will only make me stronger, whereas they will weaken you." I was ignored, but my words proved true.

Never tell a lie against anyone. A lie is a *conscious* untruth. It is, of course, always possible to tell an untruth without realizing it. The best solution is never to speak unkindly of anyone. Wish everyone well.

Sri Krishna made it clear to Arjuna that it was dharmically right to fight injustice. The way of *ahimsa*, or harmlessness, is not by any means to *submit to* injustice. Even if you haven't the power to defend yourself effectively, in your mind you should constantly resist aggression. As a boy, I found on more occasions than one that bullies left me strictly alone once they saw I would never give in to them, mentally.

4. *Sneers, disdain, and disrespect*: Because I've always been something of an outsider, even in my own country, I've had to learn to put up with attitudes like these. What do people's opinions of you really matter? Most people are wrong most of the time! (That, in fact, is the weakness of democracy.) Be strong in your own truths. To do so, without becoming bigoted, keep your mind always in a state of reason. Listen to what people say. Accept their reasons if you consider them right. The solution is always to be inwardly non-attached, and even indifferent, to the constantly fluctuating waves on the ocean of life.

5. *Unkindness, malice, or hatred*: Ask yourself simply, "When am I happier? When hating—or when loving?" For *your own peace of mind*, then, be kind to everyone. Even if they are determined to harm you, respond with kindness, for the simple reason that this is how to be happy.

Many years ago, there was someone at Ananda Village whom I'd allowed to get by without paying the usual monthly maintenance fees. After twelve years, someone whom I'd made the Village manager decided it was time to ask this member to shoulder this responsibility like everyone else. He gave the non-payer a simple choice: Either accept your responsibility to the community, or else leave Ananda. The recalcitrant member not only chose to leave, but came to me before doing so to vent his spleen on me. He spent at least an hour telling me everything I'd done and was still doing wrong in my life. Evidently, I'd done nothing right, and was bound to fail at everything I tried. I heard him out without comment. It seemed useless to defend myself.

I simply thanked him and wished him well. Since then, he has made himself one of my most vocal enemies.

My calmness in the face of his diatribe inspired me, afterward, to compose what I have always considered one of my best songs. Here are the lyrics:

I Live Without Fear

Though green summer fade,
    And winter draw near,
My Lord, in Your presence
    I live without fear.

Through tempest, through snows,
    Through turbulent tide,
The touch of Your hand
    Is my strength, and my guide.

I ask for no riches
    That death can destroy:
I crave only Thee,
    Your love and your joy!

The dancers will pass,
    The singing must end.
I welcome the darkness
    With You for my Friend.

Thus, my nonresistance helped to inspire something worth more to me than any defense would have done.

No matter what contretemps you suffer, you can gain from them if you keep your energy determinedly uplifted.

6. *Threats to destroy you*: Make no self-defined success your absolute goal. Who knows what karmic law will impose upon you, or what God will ordain for you? Sainte Thérèse de Lisieux, a French nun, expressed complete willingness even to be sent to Hell after death. "I would even like it!"

she exclaimed. "For then I could show that it is possible to love God no matter what the outer circumstances."

I read a story years ago about a man who was an inspiration to one much younger than himself for his calmness and wisdom. The younger one once asked him his secret. For his reply, the other showed him a small, very fragile seashell.

"This is my secret," he said. He then explained:

"I used to be very wealthy. then I lost everything in the stock market crash of 1929. I decided the only solution was to commit suicide. I packed my family off on a vacation, then rented a small cabin by the ocean. My plan was to walk out into the water until the waves took me.

"I began walking out, but my plan was thwarted repeatedly by strong waves that beat me back to shore. The last time I fell, beaten down by a wave, I saw this little shell swirling close to me. It was completely unbroken. I picked it up. How, I asked myself, was it possible for this fragile thing to go churning safely through the waves when I myself was thrown back by them every time I tried to go forward? The answer was obvious: The seashell hadn't resisted the flow! Might this, I reflected, be a lesson pertinent to my own case? Perhaps I'd been *resisting* the waves of my own destiny!

"I decided from then on that I would live, and that I'd go with the waves instead of resisting them. You see me now: successful again in business, but even more than that, happy and at peace."

MEDITATION

Contemplate that last thought, and make it your meditation. Think of life's circumstances as waves over which you have no direct control. Meditate on the thought of riding them. Don't fight or resist them. Be a mental surfer, going with the currents of life, but seeking always, as you ride them, to select the best wave, and the best current. You can ride wisely or foolishly, but you can never command the waves to be as you want them to be, or to go where you want them to go. Learn to flow *with* life, not against it, if you want to win through to freedom.

AFFIRMATION

"I am the master of my fate, for I realize my place in the great ocean of life and flow willingly with its mighty currents."

POINTS TO REMEMBER

1. The businessman's self-assumed duty is to learn the deeper, spiritual purpose of all labor, which is self-expansion through service to others.

2. "Where there is dharma (adherence to truth), bliss itself becomes one's definition of success."

3. The more energy you put out to achieve a high and noble success, the more *maya* will use other people to put forth an opposite energy.

4. Though the tests do become greater as one advances spiritually, one also develops the inner strength to conquer them. All his consciousness is of joy, not of suffering and sorrow.

5. Yogananda was not spared tests and difficulties, but he always faced them with honor, charity, truthfulness, and the highest spiritual consciousness.

6. The stronger the light, the stronger also the contrasting darkness.

7. No matter what opposition you encounter, never let it cause you to become negative. When you can return love for hatred, calm acceptance for anger, and kindness for persecution, you yourself will find happiness.

8. The most important decision all of us must face in life is how to react in the highest way from a standpoint of our own spiritual growth.

9. Try always to react *appropriately* in every circumstance. Don't be a doormat. You may sometimes have to be stern.

10. When people get upset, it is only because they want something different from what life has given them. Learn to accept what *is*.

How to Meet Specific Obstacles

11. *Intolerance*: Don't allow yourself to be swayed by opinions, even your own.

12. *Anger*: Anger is created by thwarted desires. You will encounter anger when you don't do as others want. React calmly, and you'll never need to fear them. Defend yourself when you can. If you cannot, accept what happens. If you *can* defend yourself you must do so—calmly, but always with inner firmness and with never failing goodwill.

13. *Lies*: Every time someone tells a lie against you, remember, the truth *has* to come out eventually. Never tell a lie against anyone. Never speak unkindly of anyone.

14. *Sneers, disdain, and disrespect*: Be strong in your own truths. Listen to what people say. Accept their reasons if you consider them right. The solution is always to be inwardly non-attached.

15. *Unkindness, malice, or hatred*: For *your own peace of mind*, respond with kindness for the simple reason that this is how to be happy. No matter what contretemps you suffer, you can gain from them if you keep your energy determinedly uplifted.

16. *Threats to destroy you*: Make no self-defined success your absolute goal. Think of life's circumstances as waves over which you have no direct control. Don't fight or resist them. Learn to flow *with* life, not against it, if you want to win through to freedom.

WORKBOOK IDEAS
by Joseph Bharat Cornell

See Only Goodness

When facing negativity, Paramhansa Yogananda's way was if possible to emphasize something positive. One of his disciples, a prominent Indian yogi, motivated by envy, turned against the Master. Later, during a public lecture in Arizona, he angrily denounced Yogananda. Several of Yogananda's students telephoned the Master that evening in Los Angeles and reported this outrage.

"Thank you for telling me," the Master said. "I will take care of the matter." Thus, he relieved them of any further responsibility in the situation. Next, he telephoned the errant disciple. What he said to him, however, was not at all what anyone expected.

"God bless you," he said, "for the good that you are doing. I bless you; our gurus bless you." He said nothing about the episode of the previous evening.

Maya is a conscious force, which seeks to separate mankind from Spirit. Evil, however, influences us only to the degree we let it. We can lessen its power by training ourselves to see the highest good in every situation.

ACTION ITEM:
1. When negativity is directed at you, don't react in kind.
2. Never let anger or ill will from others cause you to become negative.
3. Use such challenging situations as opportunities to affirm your belief and commitment to the goodness in others, and in Life itself.
4. For your own salvation—and for the upliftment of others—express kindness and goodwill always, no matter how difficult the circumstances.

ACTION ITEM:
Observe how *maya* manifests itself in human nature by paying close attention to your interactions with others. Identify the universal causes behind any inharmonious human behavior you experience—whether in yourself or in others. If you remember that negative behavior is *maya*, or lower consciousness expressing itself, you will feel more impersonal and compassionate toward others.

Look for these ways that *maya* manifests in human nature:
- *Intolerance:* People often have fixed views on how things ought to be. When one is too self-centered, he tries to control the free will and discrimination of others with the attitude: "*My* reality should be *your* reality." Don't allow yourself to be swayed by opinions, even your own.

- *Anger:* Anger is created by thwarted desires. You will encounter it when you don't do as others want. They have no right, however, to control you. Be your own master. If you encounter others' anger, react calmly, and you'll never need to fear them.

- *Lies:* People tell lies for two reasons: because they perceive the "truth" as being inconvenient, and because they have a feeling of ill will toward others. Avoid telling *conscious* untruths by making it your practice never to speak unkindly of anyone, and to ask yourself the question, "What is true?" Then align your actions to this truth.

In challenging situations, concentrate more on raising your energy level, and therefore your consciousness.

LESSON TWENTY-THREE

GOD'S PLACE IN THE BUSINESS WORLD

[All] businessmen should be able to embrace an *uplifted* consciousness in their work. God . . . represents a *direction*, not a definite goal. My Guru's answer to the question, "Is there any end to evolution?" was in this context a classic of clarity. "No end," he said. "You go on until you achieve endlessness."

The Principles

I used to smile, in high school, when our football team prayed for victory over the opposition. It seemed absurd to think that God's favor could be enlisted in a partisan cause. Good and evil were not at stake. It was, I supposed, a question of who got to Him first.

We've all seen examples of the all-too-human tendency to humanize God. The Greeks had a veritable pantheon (meaning, "all gods"), each god acting in an extremely human way—with lust, anger, jealousy, and other emotions mimicking the likes and dislikes of humankind. The Greek, Roman, and Norse pantheons probably all got their mythology from the Hindu gods and goddesses. I remember a lady who guided a small group of us through the Acropolis in Athens. She asked suddenly, as if expecting to surprise us, "Where do you think the Greek myths came from?"

"From India," I replied, surprising her in turn.

"Very few people know that!" she commented.

Thus, in this discussion of God's place in the business world, I want to plead with you not to attribute your own emotions to the Divinity. God transcends time and space. He is impersonal and impartial, and not susceptible to appeasement or flattery.

I suppose the first point to be considered in these modern times is the question whether God even exists. Most businessmen, I imagine, see no connection between spiritual and business considerations. Probably most of them don't even see a relation between them. It is easy to see why they create this separation. If God exists, He couldn't possibly be in there rooting like a cheerleader for the success of the human ego.

Yet there are many who believe, more sensitively, that God should be loved all the time. I was in a printshop in Calcutta many years ago, talking to one of the managers, when an errand boy passed by. I noticed that he paused briefly before a niche in the wall, placed his hands together and bowed, then moved on about his duties. I looked at the niche and saw within it an image of some Indian deity: Durga, Krishna, or Ganesha (I forget which it was). How charming, I thought, how inspiring and beautiful that in this place of worldly activity God should be remembered.

God, my Guru said, is formless and eternal, but *as* God He is more personal, in a sense, than the Supreme Spirit. We can think of God as He, or She. God, though an abstraction, is that aspect of Spirit which relates to cosmic creation. He is *Ishwara*, the Lord. The Supreme Spirit, on the other hand, exists in "that watchful state," as Paramhansa Yogananda described it: aloof from Its creation. People cannot even visualize that state of total disinterest and noninvolvement. It has even been said that many people never have an abstract thought in their lives. They cannot imagine how it is possible even to love a reality completely abstract. Most of them feel a need to personalize the object of their devotion in some form: as Krishna, Durga, Ganesha; as Jesus or Mary. It is not that God, who created everything, has any such form. He also, however, became personal in creating us, in giving us ego-consciousness, and in creating the conditions that would awaken in us human desires. His love for us is impersonal in the sense that He wants nothing from us, but it is also personal in the sense that He loves each of us as we are, and wants for us only the best.

Let me tell you of an evening, many years ago in Charleston, South Carolina, where I lived for nearly a year at the age of twenty-one. I had always thought *about* God. In my search for truth, however, I simply couldn't visualize Him in personal terms. The vastness of the universe meant, to me, that His consciousness could only be infinite. It was, to me, inconceivable that He could have any interest in little "insects" like us. Yet all my philosophical probing lead me irresistibly toward a *spiritual*, not a material, reality. I simply hadn't yet been able to expand my understanding of the vastness of infinity to the inclusion also of *infinitesimal smallness*.

I had tried to leave the Deity out of my reckoning, simply because I could see no way that He could be relevant to human affairs. At first, when I was thirteen, I had wanted to become an astronomer. With the passing years, however, I realized that any truth worth knowing for human beings had to be personally meaningful for them. Exactly how many galaxies the universe holds had no relevance except, perhaps, in the general sense that the vastness of reality is expanding to our own consciousness. I found that vastness inspiring rather than daunting or overwhelming, but what seemed important, to me, was the inspiration and not the mere fact of universal vastness.

I wanted *inner* inspiration, however: joy, peace of mind, a more personally meaningful understanding of life. I sought that inspiration in music, in the arts, in literature and drama, in learning, perhaps even in some better political system. I wanted anything that offered promise in these directions. Wherever I sought, however, I found only dead ends.

In college I had asked myself, "Is there really life after death?" I'd tried to imagine what that life would be. The conclusion I'd reached was life after death had to be conscious, but that it could only be an extension of whatever consciousness we'd developed here on earth. Perusal of the scriptures and attending church regularly seemed to me useless, for I had never met anyone, whether in religion or out of it, who inspired me as *knowing* anything, really, that I wanted to know. The churchmen I'd met seemed, if anything, less convincing than many others, for they seemed hemmed in by fixed sets of dogmas, outside of which they refused even to peer.

At last, desperate for an answer, I realized that without God, and without spiritual understanding, no answer was available. Every other line of inquiry led to materialism and mindlessness or else to insights that inspired only because they tickled a few nerves, merely!

Thus, that evening in Charleston I went out for a long walk, alone. Earnestly I asked myself, "If God exists, what must He be?" It seemed ridiculous to think that He could be like some cosmic policeman, looking down to see that we behaved, and, when we didn't, punishing us—perhaps with hell, or with suffering. My questioning turned from God to man: "Who and what *are* we? Have we *any* connection to God, if He exists?" Then I answered my own question: "If He made us, there *must* be a connection!"

How, then, could He have made us? Could it have been in some way like a sculptor carving a statue—from without, inward? Absurd! For nothing existed out of which to carve or mold anything. He can only, in some way, have *become* us. In what way, then?

That which is most real to us is our consciousness: Whence, then, came this consciousness? If God exists, then obviously He, too, is conscious. Our very human awareness, in that case, can only derive from Him, even as existence itself has to derive from Him. Conscious beings could not have come into existence were not consciousness itself an already-existing, universal reality. Man can only *manifest* consciousness: he cannot create it.

Human consciousness, then, can only be a limited manifestation of infinite consciousness.

I thought of the vast variety in the manifestations of intelligent awareness in mankind. All of us, I realized, must belong to an infinite and forever conscious reality. We have sprung from that. The criminal, the drunkard, those who debase themselves and lessen their awareness by wrong living, are no different from me. The saints, too—if they exist—express potentials that must be within all humanity—indeed, also within me!

Who has the clearest understanding of things as they really are: fools? drunkards? people of lower consciousness? Or the saints? My answer, without even knowing what a saint was, was simple: the saints, surely!

Looking back now, I remember my father telling me how as a child of nine, owing to delirium which accompanied a serious illness, I had tossed back and forth in a desperation of anxiety. He had been reading Mark Twain's *Huckleberry Finn* to me, and I'd evidently been deeply impressed by the bouts of drunkenness Huckleberry's father had experienced. What a terrible state to fall into! In my delirium I cried out over and over again, "I don't *want* to be a drunkard! I don't *want* to be a drunkard!"

On my long walk that evening in Charleston I thought, "How terrible, to *fall away from* joy! Joy and inspiration are something all men are seeking, though most of them unconsciously! I am no different from the worst human being on earth, but, O God, let me not fall away from the ideal! Out of compassion for others also, let me find a way to uplift myself and also them.

"What is God?" I asked urgently. "What is man? *What am I?* My very awareness can only be a limited expression of His consciousness. Obviously, however, I can rise or fall in clarity of consciousness. The joy and inspiration I long for must depend, then, on the degree to which I absorb His consciousness into myself.

"My duty in life," I resolved, "is somehow to become ever more receptive to His consciousness! I must absolutely reject in myself my own downward potential. I must try to raise myself toward infinite awareness!"

I determined in that instant to seek God. My first thought was to become a hermit. I had decided, previously, to become a playwright, but I'd already reached the conclusion that, ignorant as I was, it would be wrong to impose that ignorance on others. I couldn't really believe that God, in His infinite awareness, could be conscious of any prayer of mine, but I was resolved to try to live more in the consciousness of Him. A deep longing was also born in me to help everyone on earth to see that what all are seeking is not self-forgetfulness—drunkenness and endless, trivial distractions—but *joy* absolute!

Thank God He did hear and listen to my desperate prayer. It was not consciously even a prayer, but my desperate longing reached out to, and touched, that Infinite Consciousness. Only six months later I was led to my Guru, and was able, through Him, to understand what divine truth and the path to God are all about.

In this chapter's discussion of God in the workplace, I want to make it very clear that the God to whom I refer does not require that we hold a pious attitude. He is no mere image of which to stand in awe. He is *our own highest Self*. This Self stands transcendent above the ego. It is absolute joy—*Satchidananda*: conscious, eternal bliss. Love itself is, in its highest expression, the longing in all hearts for perfect bliss.

My Guru defined divine vision as, "center everywhere, circumference nowhere." The God I say should be brought into the workplace can have that as one of its myriad centers of awareness. The devotional attitude of that errand boy in the Calcutta printshop, and of the shop's owner who had placed that sacred image there, was valid and beautiful. Sacred images, however, are not by any means the essence of what I am trying to explain in this lesson.

God is *within you*. Every human being must choose for himself whether he would be a saint or a sinner. A saint is one whose energy moves upward, toward the higher, more spiritual part of his own being. A sinner is one whose energy and consciousness move downward in the spine and outward from the spine through the senses to the world. Most people's energy moves indecisively in both directions. In the "dedicated" sinner much more of that energy flows downward, leading to unhappiness, sorrow, and a dimmer awareness. An upward flow, on the other hand, produces happiness, expansive joy, and ever-expanding awareness. Again, it is *your* decision. To bring God into the workplace means to have not so much a *religious* attitude as an *aware* one.

That printshop in Calcutta exemplifies the usual approach to religion—a perfectly justifiable approach, as I'll explain later on. Yoga, however, emphasizes going within. Jesus Christ also said in words that few Christians know what to do with, "The kingdom of God is *within you*." Some people think yoga has nothing to do with devotion. They are mistaken. Swami Sri Yukteswar, in *The Holy Science*, makes the statement that without devotion ("developing the natural love of the heart," as he puts it) one cannot take a single step toward the realization of God.

Still, what I want to emphasize here is something that all businessmen should be able to embrace: an *uplifted* consciousness in their work. God, for this purpose, needs no definition for He represents a *direction*, not a definite goal. My Guru's answer to the question, "Is there any end to evolution?" was in this context a classic of clarity. "No end," he said. "You go on until you achieve endlessness." He didn't describe God as having any particular form. Of course he subscribed to Shankaracharya's definition of the Infinite: *Satchidananda* (which I've defined more than once, so won't explain here again). The important thing, however, is the direction our consciousness takes in the spine.

A fascinating feature of the ancient teachings of *Sanatan Dharma* is their *directional* nature. Both the caste system and the three gunas might be compared to a bar magnet, which has a north and a south pole, but which, when cut at any point in its length, produces a north and a south pole in each section. Thus, in the caste system, although there are gradations toward perfection, within each caste the same direction can be observed. A *sudra* is not a fixed quantity, so to speak. A somewhat developed *sudra* may be a *vaisya-sudra*; an even more developed *sudra* may be a *kshatriya-sudra*; one most highly developed, but still a *sudra*, would be a *brahmin-sudra*.

Among *brahmins* also *sudra-brahmins*, *vaisya-brahmins*, etc., may be discerned. One's position in his own natural (as opposed to genetic) category is determined also by the degree he manifests of that category's lower or higher potentials. Man likes to cast things firmly as if in concrete. Spirit expresses Itself in Nature very differently. Both its progress toward higher perfection and its regression toward ever-lower consciousness are unlimited.

There is a story (I hope it is only mythical) of Krishna speaking to a disciple of his named Uddhava. Looking down, he said, "You see that beetle, Uddhava? In the dim past it was Indra (king of the gods)." It is indeed true that even the gods can fall, though the thought that Indra can fall so low is appalling. Nevertheless, the struggling ego reaches spiritual safety only when it achieves *nirbikalpa samadhi*—complete oneness with God. My Guru even spoke to me of certain people who had attained *sabikalpa samadhi*—qualified oneness with God—who, for one reason or another, had fallen from their high state.

The *gunas* can be described, similarly, as directional rather than as fixed states. Higher and lower levels exist within each of them. Yogananda described *Rajo guna* particularly as "*Rajo-rajas*" and "*Sattwa-rajas*." In every case, those aspects within each *guna* which lead toward higher or toward lower consciousness are what really count for every individual. *Direction of movement* is the defining factor. Static definitions are much less important than the direction one is moving.

Thus, in business, or in any effort to achieve success, don't limit your notion of God. Most people who define themselves as atheists do so, I think, because they can't accept someone else's notion. In Lesson Twenty I told the story of that man in Australia who came up to me after a lecture and said, "I noticed that you referred quite often in your talk to God. As it happens, I'm an atheist. Can you define God in such a way as to be meaningful to me?"

I paused a moment as I pondered this challenge. Then I suggested, "Why don't you think of God as the highest potential you can imagine for yourself?"

He was surprised. He then answered with that quizzical expression so many Australians so often assume. "Well, yeah," he said, "I can live with that!"

Many people would never dream of equating material success with anyone's search for God. Few, however, would *exclude* greater concentration, more energy, increased creativity, and a flow of consciousness toward greater awareness from their quest for success. Few, besides, would exclude their own native desire for happiness. The highest potential you can imagine for yourself forms part, surely, of your own ideal of success. And that's all I'm really talking about in urging you to include God in the workplace.

Well, I've done what I could to invite atheists and agnostics on board! I've shown that this subject is a matter of sheer common sense. I would like to show, furthermore, that it is common sense also to include God Himself as a conscious reality in the workplace.

It is all very well to think that the only thing needed for raising one's consciousness is to uplift the energy and consciousness, particularly in the spine. The process is very different from—let us say—mountain climbing. A mountain climber's efforts depend wholly on his own skill and energy. The mountain, moreover, is not conscious of his efforts. In the effort to raise one's *consciousness*, one rises to greater heights within a consciousness that exists already. From above, that consciousness will cooperate in our struggle. Why do we call that consciousness, God? It is because it is a higher consciousness than what we know at present. We can appeal to it. God, in turn, responds, if we invite Him with magnetic love. An "endlessly" higher consciousness is our own highest potential. That potential is not like an unknown continent, waiting to be discovered and explored. It is aware of us as we reach toward it. In response, it reaches down willingly to help us in our ascent.

Mankind is by nature goal-oriented. A sports race that has a direction, but no goal, will not inspire runners to give of their best. They are helped in their efforts if they have a clear idea of the exact location of the finishing line. It is helpful in the divine quest, similarly, to have a concept—even a limited one—of what divine attainment entails. *Limitless bliss, Satchidananda, is the goal of all striving.* That goal seems distant, however, to most people. They need to be able to visualize it in terms of something they can understand.

God, in other words, although He is formless, manifests all the forms in the universe. There is a problem, moreover, with using *ego-consciousness* to try only to raise one's own awareness. The ego is inclined to see all things in relation to itself. Thus, a businessman who tries to include God in the workplace by thinking, "I must uplift *myself*," is likely to strengthen, not transcend, his ego.

When my Guru introduced me to the concept of God as the Divine Mother, I knew that he was speaking of an infinite consciousness, not someone feminine in form. Ramproshad, the devotional singer/saint of Bengal who worshiped God as the Divine Mother, stated in one of his songs, "Oh, a thousand scriptures declare it: My Divine Mother has no form. Yet She is also in all forms: She is everywhere! O blind ones, behold our Mother's form in all things!" To think of God as Father, Mother, Divine Friend, Beloved is one way of invoking a conscious response from the Infinite One, who can be, for you, whatever form will uplift your mind. I began by visualizing Her as resembling the wife of my godfather, whose compassionate, motherly smile I had always found uplifting. I soon "graduated" from that visualization to imagine the Divine Mother in every tree, every rock, in every radiant sunset.

The point is, to project onto God a loving human image helps one to avoid concentrating on ego-consciousness. My Guru said that even liberated saints often take a step down the ladder of consciousness to enjoy an I-and-Thou relationship with God.

Ego-consciousness has a tendency to be centripetal: focused inward upon itself. Devotees praying to God often mistakenly think, "How can God be of help to *me*?" Thus, someone seeking material success may ask God for assistance toward that goal. No harm, so long as success for you doesn't mean failure for someone else. Personal aspiration is limited because circumscribed by the ego, however, and limited aspiration can only bring limited results. It is always better to ask God for help in a righteous cause. In such a cause—in a war, for example—it is all right to pray for victory. There is a more exalted view in such matters, however. It is given in the *Mahabharata*.

Prior to the Kurukshetra war, both Arjuna (the leader of the Pandavas, the side of righteousness) and Duryodhana (the leader of the Kauravas, the evil side) went to Krishna (who in that epic represents God Himself) to solicit his help. When they come, Krishna is asleep. They wait, therefore. When he awakes, he first sees Arjuna, who is seated humbly at his feet. Since both men are together, however, Krishna must (according to the ethics of those times) offer his help to them both.

He resolves the dilemma by giving them a choice: either his entire army, or his presence but nonparticipation in the battle. He then asks Arjuna, whom he saw first upon awaking, to choose first.

"I choose Thee, Lord," was the reply. "Wherever Thou art, there must be the outcome I seek."

Duryodhana was very pleased with the alternative: Krishna's entire army, with or without their commander. "What kind of a bargain would that be, anyway," he thought, "if their commander didn't even take part in the fighting?" Both men went away happy and satisfied, therefore.

Arjuna, however, was the wiser of the two, for he realized that where God is, there alone is victory! And so it proved.

When you pray to God, your prayers will be more effective if you don't ask anything of Him, but simply give Him yourself, and your love.

The Application

What is the best way to bring God into the workplace? The answer depends on you—on what most awakens in your heart a feeling of reality.

If I have opened your mind to the merits of including God in the workplace, it may still be a stretch for you also to love Him. Have you only just brought yourself to believe in Him at all? Does He still seem to you, therefore, merely an abstract state of consciousness? In whatever way you approach Him, He will come to you in that aspect. Nevertheless, as your closeness to Him increases, you will feel joy constantly increasing in your heart.

Patanjali gave a fascinating definition of yoga: *Yogas chitta vritti nirodha*: "Yoga is the neutralization of the vortices (*vrittis*) of feeling." This definition clarifies consciousness in a way that many commentators have misunderstood. *Chitta* is not "mind-stuff," as Swami Vivekananda called it. Nor is it merely consciousness, as many translators aver—many of them describing it as the "lower aspects of consciousness." It is consciousness itself, defined as *feeling*. Feeling, my Guru stated, is the very essence of awareness. Without feeling, intelligence is something even computers can be programmed to do. Computers, however, are not conscious: they cannot *feel*.

Thus, to *think* one's way to truth is forever to try to approach the center of reality from its periphery. Science can never give us truth. Not only can it never plumb the depths of consciousness, but it insists on reason alone for its proofs. It can tell us *about* truth, but it can give us no *perception* of truth.

The quest for truth needs to be accompanied by a longing for direct experience. So long as there is no actual feeling involved, one is like a man who lived next door to a famous restaurant, knew the bill of fare, could describe the menu and tell how the best dishes were made, but was not hungry enough to go there and eat. Devotion is no mere excitation of feeling: It is the *hunger of the heart* to experience truth. Without that hunger, we can only "philosophize."

Sukdeva, a great saint of ancient India, stated, "All time is wasted that is not spent in seeking God." This advice, which may seem tenable only for hermits, can become acceptable to everyone if it is understood that "seeking God" means any activity that expands one's sympathies, raises one's consciousness, and fires the heart with enthusiasm for useful service to society. Granted, the strict definition of the meaning is stretched, but, as in the case of a bar magnet, *wherever* one stands at present in his spiritual evolution, activities that point his energies in the right direction may be included, if broadly, within the meaning of the term.

The great obstacle to worshiping God in the workplace is that of sectarianism. Can Hindus, Christians, Muslims, Buddhists, and Jews see themselves as all worshiping the same God? Whether they should be sectarian or not begs the point: The fact is, either most them are, or some of them could be. How, then, to introduce God into an environment where religious differences may surface in response to any such attempt? In such cases, it will be important to make issues of worship as broad as possible. Even to speak of God may be offensive to some Buddhists, and is likely to create hostility in communists and others who consider themselves atheists. The definition I have given of God—the joy that all men seek, though by countless different paths—is very well for this lesson, but would hardly be acceptable to people to whom philosophy seems a foreign language.

One thing you can do is emphasize periodic silence as a proved means of inducing greater harmony in the workplace. A friend of mine told me recently that the people in his office practice brief periods of group meditation at the beginning of every workday. If you have a room set aside for any of the purposes I have suggested before, your staff could also gather there for a brief period of meditation every morning. The idea could be introduced as a means for everyone to become attuned in harmony together before work begins.

What should they think about? It could be suggested to them that they watch the breath, concentrating particularly on the pauses between the breaths. Try to feel expansive calmness during those pauses, while trying to bring the consciousness of everyone there to a state of peace and harmony.

They can be encouraged to think of God as possessing those states to an infinite degree. Whether He be Jehovah, Ishwara, God, Allah, or the compassion of the Buddha, peace and harmony must accompany attunement with Him, and if one believes in no God, even so the concept of bringing greater peace and harmony to the workplace and to the workers' lives must be universally acceptable.

MEDITATION

Place those two concepts (peace and harmony) mentally on the altar of your own consciousness. Think not of what God, or of what those concepts, can do for you. Think, rather, that you are offering yourself up to them. Attunement with higher consciousness demands giving of one's self more than asking for one's self.

Whether you think of God in abstract terms, or in more personal, human terms, you will receive much more if your entire flow of concentration and devotion is made an offering, and not turned inward toward yourself by demanding anything.

AFFIRMATION

"In loving Thee, I offer Thee the peace and harmony of my own being."

POINTS TO REMEMBER

1. God is no mere image of which to stand in awe. He is *our own highest Self*. This Self stands transcendent above the ego. It is absolute joy—*Satchidananda*: conscious, eternal bliss. Love itself is, in its highest expression, the longing in all hearts for perfect bliss.

2. Every human being must choose for himself whether he would be a saint or a sinner. A saint is one whose energy moves upward, toward the higher, more spiritual part of his own being. A sinner is one whose energy and consciousness move downward in the spine and outward from the spine through the senses to the world. Most people's energy moves indecisively in both directions. An upward flow produces happiness, expansive joy, and ever-expanding awareness. To bring God into the workplace means to have not so much a *religious* attitude as an *aware* one.

3. Swami Sri Yukteswar, in *The Holy Science*, makes the statement that without devotion ("developing the natural love of the heart," as he puts it) one cannot take a single step toward the realization of God.

4. Many people would never dream of equating material success with anyone's search for God. Few, however, would *exclude* greater concentration, more energy, increased creativity, and a flow of consciousness toward greater awareness from their quest for success. Few, besides, would exclude their own native desire for happiness. The highest potential you can imagine for yourself forms part, surely, of your own ideal of success. And that's all I'm really talking about in urging you to include God in the workplace.

5. God is a higher consciousness than what we know at present. We can appeal to it. God, in turn, responds, if we invite Him with magnetic love. An "endlessly" higher consciousness is our own highest potential. It is aware of us as we reach toward it. In response, it reaches down willingly to help us in our ascent.

6. It is helpful in the divine quest to have a concept—even a limited one—of what divine attainment entails. To think of God as Father, Mother, Divine Friend, Beloved is one way of invoking a conscious response from the Infinite One, who can be, for you, whatever form will uplift your mind.

7. A businessman who tries to include God in the workplace by thinking, "I must uplift *myself*," is likely to strengthen, not transcend, his ego. To project onto God a loving human image helps one to avoid concentrating on ego-consciousness.

8. When you pray to God, your prayers will be more effective if you don't ask anything of Him, but simply give Him yourself, and your love.

9. What is the best way to bring God into the workplace? The answer depends on you—on what most awakens in your heart a feeling of reality.

10. In whatever way you approach Him, He will come to you in that aspect. As your closeness to Him increases, you will feel joy constantly increasing in your heart.

11. Devotion is no mere excitation of feeling: It is the *hunger of the heart* to experience truth.

12. Suk Deva, a great saint of ancient India, stated, "All time is wasted that is not spent in seeking God." This advice can become acceptable to everyone if it is understood that "seeking God" means any activity that expands one's sympathies, raises one's consciousness, and fires the heart with enthusiasm for useful service to society.

13. The great obstacle to worshiping God in the workplace is that of sectarianism. It will be important to make issues of worship as broad as possible.

14. One thing you can do is emphasize periodic silence as a proved means of inducing greater harmony in the workplace. Your staff could gather for a brief period of meditation every morning. The idea could be introduced as a means for everyone to become attuned in harmony together before work begins.

15. It could be suggested to them that they watch the breath, concentrating particularly on the pauses between the breaths. Try to feel expansive calmness during those pauses, while trying to bring the consciousness of everyone there to a state of peace and harmony. They can be encouraged to think of God as possessing those states to an infinite degree.

16. Place those two concepts (peace and harmony) mentally on the altar of your own consciousness. Think that you are offering yourself up to them. Attunement with higher consciousness demands giving of one's self more than asking for one's self.

WORKBOOK IDEAS
by Joseph Bharat Cornell

Experience Universal Consciousness

ACTION ITEM:
1. Go to a quiet, serene place, preferably outdoors.
    a. Begin by meditating a few minutes to calm your thoughts.
    b. Open your eyes and gaze around you. Note the many forms of Life who share this place with you.
    c. Look intently at a tree, flower, rock, or cloud. As you observe your subject, honor it as a fellow expression of Life—which has also created *you*. Repeat this exercise two more times.
    d. Now expand your awareness to include everything around you.
    e. In the vibrant calmness you feel, *sense* the unifying energy that animates all things.
2. Make this Universal Consciousness more immediate to your own consciousness by practicing the following walking meditation:

Imagine that you and the Creator are walking together. Share with the Creator every impression you see and hear, just as you would with a treasured friend. Gaze at the clouds and enjoy them together. Take delight in the birds singing all around, and bask in the sun's warm rays. Thank the Creator for every joy and inspiration you feel.

ACTION ITEM:
Harmony and unity are said to be defining characteristics of God. Every office staff can benefit from greater group harmony. When employees act from *universal*, not *limited*, consciousness, they become more creative, cooperative, and productive.
1. Encourage an uplifted consciousness at work: When your colleagues have different religious or even nonreligious allegiances, focus on sharing qualities associated with Higher Truth, such as inner calmness, selflessness, love, and impartial wisdom.
2. Choose one of these qualities to practice this week. End your morning meditation by attuning to the quality and how you can express it at work.

God is in money. . . . God is in business. God is in the banks just as much as He is in the mountains and the clouds, and in temples and churches. And though it is, I grant you, more difficult to see Him in the marketplace, nonetheless, He is there. If you look deeply enough, you *must* find Him, wherever *you* are.

—Swami Kriyananda, *Money Magnetism*

LESSON TWENTY-FOUR

WHAT SHOULD YOUR LINE OF WORK BE?

One's attitudes are more important than any specific thing one does. The attitudes one should develop are above all those which lead to superconsciousness.

The Principles

Think of a world where everyone wanted to be a streetcar conductor. The variety of jobs available on this Earth, and the number of people capable of handling them, is inconceivably large. An astrologer I knew in America told me she had once studied the horoscope of a young man who had come to her for advice on what line of work he should follow. She saw indications in his chart that pointed toward his becoming an undertaker. Years later she said to me, "I was hesitant to tell him so, but because all the aspects pointed that way I finally told him what I saw. To my relief he exclaimed, 'That is exactly what I've been feeling! What I hoped you'd give me was corroboration!'"

When the soul first manifests itself outwardly on the material plane, it enters upon a vast number of possibilities. Long before reaching the human level, it passes through countless lower forms. It can amuse one to look at human beings and try to imagine what lower forms they might have inhabited previously. Some of them may have a certain resemblance to rabbits. Others have a decidedly equine appearance. Many of them look intriguingly like erstwhile dogs or cats. The variety is endless, and can give one much amusement, in a friendly spirit, while sitting in a park, a restaurant, or a hotel lobby.

Even after the soul reaches the human level, its evolution is by no means near finality; indeed, it may be said to have hardly begun. Man, of all the animals, has the free will to co-operate with the process of natural evolution, or to counteract it by creating endless desires that cluster around the ego. Many lifetimes are needed for the ego, which is first manifested strongly at the human level, to develop sufficient refinement to "graduate" to higher levels of existence. Through all one's lower manifestations, and for countless lifetimes as a human being, one follows innumerable trails as he threads his way to the soul's final destination: oneness with God. All of us develop certain tendencies over these incarnations, the sum total of which makes us each, with our own special tastes and distastes, different from anyone else on earth.

I remember a picnic outing at the Downs School in England. The outing was close to a river. One of the boys decided to have fun by throwing mud at the others. Soon everyone was gleefully throwing mud—everyone but me, that is to say. I was horrified by this pastime. So much did I abhor it that a few of the boys, noticing my aversion, focused with particular delight on plastering mud on me. I suppose they were determined to make me a "good sport." I was so covered over that it was months before I was able to get the last mud clot out of my ears.

I see now, from a yogic viewpoint, that my aversion was wrong. A yogi in search of inner freedom must overcome all likes and dislikes, all desires and aversions.

Years later I enrolled in a course on auto mechanics. Again, I recoiled from getting my hands greasy from the machinery. After one or two attempts, I stood around a car engine with other students, listening politely as the teacher explained to us how a car works. Automobiles, to me, are still magic conveyances. One propitiates them by turning on the ignition. If the engine is pleased, it will hum with satisfaction, at which point one is free to engage the clutch and drive off, commending his soul to the automobile devas.

"What comes of itself," my Guru used to say, "let it come." Perhaps, nowadays, I would simply not respond if people tried to involve me in a mud fight. Indifference would have been, even in my childhood days, a better defense.

What remains with me from that somewhat faded, but never attractive memory is the reinforcement it gave my self-knowledge that the realities I would deal with in life were more in the direction of trying to understand life than toward getting a grip on mechanics.

I relate these stories in order to suggest that you, too, have a nature of your own to contend with. Try to find work that is compatible with that nature.

Many years ago, when I lived at the SRF headquarters, the president of the organization informed me that our printer wanted me to help him in the printshop. This was very different work from what our Guru had told me to do: namely, lecturing, writing, and editing. I said as much to her, as tactfully as I could without seeming to offer a correction. Hintingly I replied, "I don't think that is what I am meant to do."

"Why *not*?" she demanded, exasperated at what she perceived as my unwillingness. Obedience was fundamental to our way of life—a fact which has led me to question the very merits of monastic obedience, if to someone who is only one's superior but not one's guru. The point which that episode began to raise in my mind was: obedience to *whom*? One's guru is one thing, but a monastic superior, something very different. This dilemma was to become crucial for me in years to come. I knew what my Guru had given me as my duty in this life. He was no longer in the body now, however. My superior wanted to take me in a very different direction. I explained truthfully, "Any machinery I work with is certain to break down in a matter of days!"

Before he assigned me those duties, however, I had cheerfully mixed cement and done other self-dirtying jobs, because I saw them as a way of serving God. In God's work, all work is noble and uplifting. This did not mean, however, that I ever became skillful at such jobs. When I was helping to build India Center, which stands on the same grounds as our church in Hollywood, I clearly (and not happily) remember my almost hopeless inadequacy as a carpenter. I would hammer a nail, missing it altogether nine times out of ten, then finally hit the nail only to see it bending at a ninety-degree angle as it stuck out from the board. After we finished the job, I remarked enthusiastically to our foreman, "I sure learned a lot on this job, Andy!" Andy stared at me a moment unbelievingly, then had the tact not to say anything!

My point here is that most people have only certain skills, if any, and are simply not adapted to other kinds of work. Sometimes, they are not even adaptable. It is good to have skills, but it is quite unnecessary to be skilled at everything.

There is an assertion to which I've occasionally been exposed in my life: namely, that if there is something you're not good at—assuming of course that you have enough intelligence for the job—you should try to become good at it in order to "perfect" your personality. The motivation behind this advice is that perfection of the human personality is a goal toward which every idealistic person should aspire. Not a few times in my life I've encountered people who insisted that one must strive to become good at anything one considers difficult. One lady I knew determined, when she was in her late sixties, to become a millionaire. Her justification was the belief that, in order to become perfect spiritually, one must achieve material perfection. Her attempt to become wealthy—apart from the fact that she failed at it—became her greatest obstacle on the spiritual path!

I am writing this lesson partly to address that thought. Perfection lies not in what one does, but *in what one IS*, in consciousness. It is a foolish waste of energy to try to bring to perfection one's human personality. Energy devoted to one achievement is so much energy withheld from other achievements. This I found out years ago, when in desperation I realized that I needed a guru.

Mahatma Gandhi was a great national leader, but his focus on that essential role is said to have prevented him from being a good father. One reason for Ananda Sangha's success is that I was determined from the start that I was not going to try to create a perfect community. Improving on the possible has proved more effective than trying to impose ideals that were impossible, even for idealists. An article in a communities magazine in the early 1970s took me to task for my compromise with idealism. Every community they praised for its high ideals, however, failed within a year, whereas Ananda has developed far beyond those very ideals by simple realism concerning human nature.

The ancient Greek philosopher Longinus, in his famous essay "On the Sublime," declared that excessive effort to achieve perfection in a work of art is itself an imperfection. The arms of Krishna at Jagannath Temple in Puri are truncated deliberately in order to show the futility of attempting to capture the Infinite in a material form. The best man can do when carving a statue is only to hint at the divine truths one desires to express.

The work you do, considered in light of the goals of yoga, should be that which can help you to grow, spiritually. What should that work be? It depends on your nature. What is right for one person would be wrong for another. One's attitudes are more important than any specific thing one does. The attitudes one should develop are above all those which lead to superconsciousness.

What is the difference between superconscious and conscious awareness? The superconscious mind sees things as a unity. The conscious, rational mind on the other hand analyzes things to see how they can be distinguished from one another. The conscious mind, because of the analytical quality of the intellect, tends toward problem-consciousness. The superconscious mind, on the other hand, because it is unitive, is solution-oriented. The way to approach the question of what work is right for you is to *expect* solutions. Don't wrestle with the problems that the question itself may pose for you.

Again and again in my life I have found that answers came to me when I brushed aside any doubt in my mind that muttered, "You've got a problem!"

Here is a truth to ponder: *Where there's a problem, there has to be a solution.*

Another essential attitude is *willingness*. To reject any suggested solution means, self-evidently, to deny what may have to be done. One must be ready for *anything*. Had I accepted that mudslinging "game" in England, accepting others' reality as their own even though it was not mine, I would have instantly perceived the solution: to remain centered in myself; to accept the excitement around me neutrally, as a simple fact. Probably, in that case, they'd have left me alone. No one would have felt I was being judgmental.

Another attitude, important to the selection and pursuit of the right course in life, is *calmness*. Some work is by its very nature agitating to the heart and the mind. Consider the madness on the floor of a commodities exchange. There, people shout and scream agitatedly, waving paper notes desperately to attract attention. To participate in such a swirl of desperate emotions makes it impossible to have mental clarity. Greed, competition, anger at being thwarted, fear of losing out on what looks like a golden opportunity: these and similar emotions can only undermine any true success one might achieve. One becomes a successful moneymaking machine, perhaps, but one loses all chance of happiness in this life. As Sri Krishna says in the Bhagavad Gita, "To the peaceless person, how is happiness possible?" There is much in the process of moneymaking that creates nervousness. Avoid such work as you would the plague.

Joy and calm enthusiasm, then, are states of mind to be sought in any work one accepts. Don't look upon employment as a means merely to make money. If you do so, no matter how much you earn, the money itself will buy you only suffering in the end. Seek work, rather, that—at least according to your present understanding—promises happiness.

An important attitude is *ahimsa*: harmlessness. Seek never to harm anyone. Be conscious rather of how the work you do might affect others. The more you can put yourself in their shoes, the more rapid will your spiritual progress be. Seeing one's work as a service to others will also bring blessings to yourself.

Do not work under anyone who asks you to be untruthful. One who is strictly truthful finds the divine law itself directing him into activities that are aligned with dharma. If, on the other hand, you seek an excuse in the fact that you are only obeying someone else's request, when he tells you to be adharmic, yours, too, will be the sin.

I noticed when I first lived in India in 1958 that many people I met, still under the influence of Mahatma Gandhi's utter truthfulness, were often deliberately rude to others in the thought that to do so was to be sincere. Truthfulness, however, should always be combined with kindness and consideration for others. Another person's understanding of what is true may be different from your own, after all. Respect others, even if you don't see eye-to-eye with them.

My Guru pointed out that there is a difference between truth and fact. It may be a fact that someone you know is in the hospital and direly ill. To tell him he looks terrible, however, may make him worse! Since well-being is an aspect of soul-consciousness, you will be speaking the truth if you can find a valid reason for telling him he "looks good."

Do not allow the company of others where you work to lower your principles. Seek work, indeed, where the people themselves are, as far as you know, honorable.

Seek work that will, if possible, give you a sense that you are serving others. Serviceful work is expansive. Anything that takes you toward greater expansion will help you as well as others. (We'll go further into this aspect of work in the last lesson.) Most activities take people in circles, as regards any progress they make. Since self-interest might be described as their only actual religion, everything they do will revolve about their egos. It is like passing from room to room in the same building without ever going out the front door. Seek to become skillful at whatever work you want to do. What is skill, however, if it only encourages pride?

Motives are more important than deeds. There is a well-known saying, "The road to hell is paved with good intentions." My Guru often quoted those words; he meant that one should never make good intentions an excuse for passivity. To do so is rather like saying, "I'm a sinner": a statement usually meant to sound humble, but often made as an excuse to go right on sinning! Have good intentions, but also put out the energy to *fulfill* those intentions by right action.

A good motive sometimes begets wrong deeds. When Yogananda was a young man, the ideal of freedom from foreign rule was beginning to fire Indians' imagination. Yogananda had a dynamic, even fiery, personality. One could easily visualize him as a great warrior of the past. Certain young men in Calcutta approached him one day and asked him to lead them in a revolution against the English.

"India," the young yogi replied, "will be freed in my lifetime, by peaceful means." Those youths still insisted on revolution, whereupon the Master told their spokesman, "You lead it."

An armaments shipment was stopped outside Calcutta, and those men were caught. Their leader was executed.

"Why, Sir," I asked my Guru, "did you advise him to lead the revolution, since you knew it wouldn't work and that he would fail?"

"It was his karma," was the reply. According to my understanding, it was the young man's persistence that had invited that response from Yogananda. The young men hadn't come asking for advice. They were already determined to go the way of violence.

I should add that death, to a spiritual master, is not something to be avoided at all cost. What seems to worldly people an extreme punishment, owing to their body-attachment, is really only a kind of migration.

I remember my Guru telling me another somewhat similar story. "A woman disciple of Swami Shankara's," he said, "was eaten up mentally by doubts. One day she said to him [speaking, I presume, of her own desire for salvation], 'But—what if I die?'

"'All right,' was his response, 'then die!' The woman fell over immediately, dead."

Death itself is not the tragedy it may seem. It is something all of us have experienced many, many times in the past. Sometimes death comes to teach us an important lesson. In that woman's case, the lesson was that anything one fears, especially if that fear is expressed in the presence of an enlightened master (before whom a person's thoughts gain added power), will attract the very things one fears.

Whatever path you follow in life, and whatever work you do, try always to relate it to a broader reality. Thus, your job may be something quite simple like selling groceries. If so, be conscientious in the selling. Look for the best food available, within your economic capabilities. Make a study of what makes some foods more healthful, or taste better than others. Become knowledgeable, so you can advise your customers on the esoterica of right diet. Know more, if possible, than they themselves know. They will be much more likely to continue shopping with you, and to urge their friends to patronize your store. If job promotion is possible where you work, you will be among the first to be considered for a higher position.

In choosing, or in developing, a work, look for enough variety in it to keep you energetic and interested. Don't seek a merely comfortable niche. The more energy the work demands of you, and the greater its challenge to you, the more greatly you will benefit from it.

In emphasizing the importance of energy, I want to urge you not to make investments your principal source of income. Investments are, for the investor himself, a dead energy. You pay others to be creative, rather than trying, yourself, to be creative. I've known people who became wealthy by making clever investments, but what I've observed is that their own energy became increasingly contractive. I urge you to get into work where you can apply energy directly. The money you make will be left behind when you die, but the energy you invest in your work will ensure you an ever-more-shining future.

One question you should face when selecting a line of work concerns also the karmic debts remaining for you to work out. You probably have no idea what they are. That is one reason why it is important to have a wise guru. A guru, however, is a rare find, and a blessing that must be earned. Many people do have at least some intuition as to what may be blocking their further progress.

Another question to ponder must certainly relate to the kind of good karma you specially need—karma that will help you in terms of your happiness, and also your spiritual development. An important consideration would be to divert harmful tendencies into constructive channels which will clear away those blocks. If you feel an impulse, for example, to deprive people of anything, look for ways of *giving* to them. If you have an urge to compete against them, look for ways of giving them the victory.

I have already suggested a key to understanding the basic nature with which you were born, as opposed to those inclinations which present environment has instilled in you: Look back to your childhood; reflect on your earliest tendencies and see how they might fit into your present realities. These memories will give you clues to the personality traits and skills you developed in other lifetimes—especially the last one—and therefore to what is most likely to bring you success in this life.

I remember when I was first learning to write. I was six years old, and was asked to write the kind of brief paper first graders may reasonably be expected to handle. I showed my parents what I'd written, and they commented that I had overused the word, "and." Unquestionably they were right; both of them were, in fact, good writers. The odd thing was my own unvoiced reaction. I still remember my thought: "When it comes to writing, who is there that can teach me?" A ridiculous idea, but the fact that it even came to me suggests that I probably wrote for a living before. In little hints like these we may get an inkling of what we did in the past, and of options open to us in the present.

When I was sixteen, my father offered to buy me a tuxedo—the elegant suit that Western men wear on formal occasions like weddings or first nights at the opera. I replied, "Please don't bother, Dad. I'll never wear it. In fact, I'll never earn enough money even to pay income tax." My father smiled. He must have thought I was going through some "adolescent phase." My words were consciously prescient, however. Six years later I became a monk in my Guru's ashram. My path in this life has never been what most people would call normal, though as far as moneymaking is concerned I have probably earned millions for the work to which I've dedicated my life.

Above all, if you sincerely want to find truth, even while working to earn a living, ask for divine assistance. It isn't only the saints whose prayers are answered. Of supreme importance is the *attitude* you hold while praying. Don't ask God to help you: rather, ask Him what you can do to *serve* Him. Self-giving prayer is much more effective than a beggarly attitude.

There is a beautiful prose poem by Rabindranath Tagore. I included it in a small book of mine, *Money Magnetism*. Let me quote it again here for you:

> I had gone a-begging from door to door in the village path, when thy golden chariot appeared in the distance like a gorgeous dream and I wondered who was this King of all kings!
>
> My hopes rose high and methought my evil days were at an end, and I stood waiting for alms to be given unasked and for wealth scattered on all sides in the dust.
>
> The chariot stopped where I stood. Thy glance fell on me and thou camest down with a smile. I felt that the luck of my life had come at last. Then of a sudden thou didst hold out thy right hand and say, "What hast thou to give me?"
>
> Ah, what a kingly jest was it to open thy palm to a beggar to beg! I was confused and stood undecided, and then from my wallet I slowly took out the least little grain of corn and gave it to thee.
>
> But how great was my surprise when at the day's end I emptied my bag on the floor to find a least little grain of gold among the poor heap! I bitterly wept and wished that I had had the heart to give thee my all.

The Application

Avoid setting unnecessary and useless precedents in your life. Live creatively in the present. Habit, at work, can be anathema to real success. Flexibility is essential if you want to address new situations appropriately.

A fellow disciple of mine—Dr. Lewis, the first to meet Paramhansa Yogananda in America, in 1920—once told me, "The Master never did anything out of habit."

I was astonished. "You mean, not even when he was tying his shoelaces?"

"Not even then," Dr. Lewis responded.

I still find his statement difficult to believe. As the Master himself wrote, "Habits are a convenient mechanism of the mind to prevent one from having to exercise his will for actions that are repeated frequently." Whether or not "Doctor's" statement was literally true, however, it still bore remarkable testimony to the freedom of Master's will—a feature of his life in any case that always seemed to me extraordinary. One could never predict with certainty what he would say or do in any circumstance. Others of my fellow disciples have made such statements as, "Master would *never* have said that!" when a remark attributed to him concerned not dharma or truth, but something the one negating the statement had never, in years of association with him, heard him say. I was with him fewer years, certainly, than many of them, but I myself heard him make statements that those same people later rejected as impossible. I submit that the error was theirs. They had channeled their memories of him into a narrow riverbed of their own thinking. A master lives his life, however, ever afresh and ever in the present.

When groups of people live or work together, a certain number of rules are necessary for the over-all harmony and efficiency. Rules might be described as "group habits." They are necessary, but even so, the rules should be kept to a minimum.

When our Guru placed me in charge of the other monks, he told me, "Don't make too many rules: it destroys the spirit." There come to my mind images of traditional monasteries where the monks and nuns are bound by such a plethora of rules that it is difficult, if not impossible, for them to develop their own free will, a complete necessity on the spiritual path. I saw, after Paramhansa Yogananda left his body, how eagerly some of my fellow disciples embraced rules as a replacement for his active guidance. I confess that atmosphere became more and more suffocating for me.

If you want to be creative and happy, seek work where *sensible* innovation is appreciated. If you have inherited a work that was started by someone else, and you want to honor its principles and traditions, try to discriminate between the way things are done and the spirit that first animated them. The surest way to mummify an organization is to bind it to the wheel of "what is done," rather than being guided creatively in response to new needs and to new realities as they confront one.

To be creative and happy requires that you live more by inspiration, and guided less by institutional habit. My Guru, when he gave me advice on how to lecture, emphasized spontaneity over preparation, and attunement over giving intellectual discourses. Over the years, this advice has resulted in my seldom needing to prepare for a lecture I must give. I have learned to tune in to the audience, as well as into divine inspiration, and thereby to give them what they themselves need at the time.

Sometimes, when I have been invited to speak as part of a conference, I've been asked to submit a written text of my speech for later publication. I've regretfully had to deny every such request. I never form a fixed plan of what I'm going to say. After a lecture, moreover, I simply wipe the slate clean so that, if I have to speak again on the same subject, I will be able to address it creatively, as though for the first time. Often, I haven't known what I would say until I took my first breath to begin speaking. Sometimes during a talk I've surprised myself by announcing, "Now, here's an important point to bear in mind," when I hadn't the slightest notion what that "important point" was! The guidance for what to say next, in fulfillment of that promise, has never yet failed me in all my "career" of public speaking. Always, what I should say next has appeared instantly in my mind. And always it has, indeed, been important in the context of my talk.

It would be foolhardy for most people to take such a chance. Though it works for me, I don't suggest that you go at it the same way. I do, however, urge you to try to live more in the moment, and to seek guidance from God or from your higher Self, rather than trying to figure everything out in advance, intellectually. The more you learn to depend on higher guidance, even though taking only little steps at a time, the more you will find intuition flowing. Intuition is an aspect of normal human awareness of which most people are entirely ignorant.

Similarly, when others ask you for advice, and particularly if they are depending on your wisdom, don't rely on what you've said to anyone previously. Your wisdom will thus tend to be both apposite and helpful. Try to tune in to the realities of the person you are counseling. Remember, everyone is, in a way, unique. I've said this in these lessons before: Try to reach them at their center from your own inner center.

A famous author in America once told me that she was working on a new book. Then with unaccustomed frankness she added, "Of course, it's always the same, anyway!" I smiled encouragingly, not wanting to tell her that, with me, it is *never* the same. As often as I've expressed myself in writing or in lecturing, it is always as if for the first time. I grant you that more energy is required this way: It is always easier to rely on what one has said or done before than to seek guidance ever anew, especially in familiar matters. That is the way, however, to mental ossification.

Allow no self-image to build up in your mind. I grant you here, also, that if one has a negative self-image it will help him to substitute for it a positive one. Nevertheless, I've found it an even greater help not to hold any image at all. Respond sensitively to each new situation as it arises, as if you'd never faced that situation before. In this way your responses will be always fresh, as well as particularly meaningful.

A corollary to this thought is the following: Don't be ruled by any image others hold of you. I don't mean in any way to suggest you outrage their sensibilities by trying to be "original." Respect others, even for any exaggerated image they hold of you. Be guided, however, by your own conscience from within.

Originality is popularly misunderstood to signify a work that has never been done before. In the name of "originality," many people try to do what the French call "*épater les bourgeois*: shock the middle classes." They try to be so different from everyone else that they become a class to themselves. Some people might even call them mad!

In truth, originality means to come from one's own inner *point of origin*. Just think how many millions of people, speaking every language known to man, have said the equivalent of those English words, "I love you."

No sensible person would ever scoff at those words, or call people trite for making that statement, if it is made sincerely. It isn't what one says or does that spells either triteness or originality. It is the *sincerity* of one's expression. Be, in that sense, original: That is to say, be completely true to yourself.

I've often thought that unappreciated genius in any field is not so unfortunate as it is often thought to be. The person of genius is free to create as he feels to do, inwardly, if he is not tempted to accede to public demand. If he is truly a person of genius, what will matter to him will be the joy of creating something meaningful, and not the plaudits of any mob.

Another way to apply the principles I've been describing is to be willing to laugh with good cheer at yourself. Having no self-image to live up to will keep you from becoming a pompous ass! On the plus side of the ledger, you will then find it easier to be original in the true sense, and to be guided by your own understanding.

Ask God to inspire you in what you say or do. Never tell yourself, "I can't do that," if what you'd like to do seems to you impossible, particularly if the job is important to you. (I say that because the memory comes to me of a time, nearly sixty years ago, when I said to someone, "I can't do that." He replied, almost as if by rote, "There's no such word as *can't*!" I don't consider it important, however, to be good at *everything* one does. "All right, then," I replied: "I *won't*!") If something is important to you, it is no sign of humility to claim inability. Tell yourself, rather, "I certainly couldn't do it, myself, but God *through* me can accomplish anything." Indeed, everything on earth is created by God through instruments—usually, human ones.

MEDITATION

Reflect on the following lines from Paramhansa Yogananda's poem "*Samadhi*":

> Present, past, future, no more for me,
> But ever-present, all-flowing I, I, everywhere. . . .
> I swallowed, transmuted all
> Into a vast ocean of blood of my own one Being!

Meditate on the phenomenon of Time—Time not as a continuum, but as nonexistent. Space and time are products merely of consciousness in motion.

The more clearly you can live in the thought of stillness, the more you will find yourself at the center of all creativity.

AFFIRMATION

"I am no free man or free woman merely: I am a free soul."

POINTS TO REMEMBER

1. Try to find work that is compatible with your nature. Most people have only certain skills and are simply not adapted to other kinds of work.

2. Perfection lies not in what one does, but *in what one IS*, in consciousness. It is a foolish waste of energy to try to bring to perfection one's human personality.

3. The work you do should be that which can help you to grow, spiritually.

4. One's attitudes are more important than any specific thing one does. The attitudes one should develop are above all those which lead to superconsciousness.

5. The way to approach the question of what work is right for you is to *expect* solutions. *Where there's a problem, there has to be a solution.*

6. An essential attitude is *willingness*. To reject any suggested solution means, self-evidently, to deny what may have to be done. One must be ready for *anything*.

7. Another attitude, important to the selection and pursuit of the right course in life, is *calmness*. There is much in the process of moneymaking that creates nervousness. Avoid such work as you would the plague.

8. Joy and calm enthusiasm are states of mind to be sought in any work one accepts. Seek work that—at least according to your present understanding—promises happiness.

9. Be conscious of how the work you do might affect others. Seek never to harm anyone.

10. Do not work under anyone who asks you to be untruthful. Do not allow the company of others where you work to lower your principles. Seek work where the people themselves are, as far as you know, honorable.

11. Seek work that will give you a sense that you are serving others. Serviceful work is expansive. Anything that takes you toward greater expansion will help you as well as others. Seek to become skillful at whatever work you want to do.

12. In choosing, or in developing, a work, look for enough variety in it to keep you energetic and interested. The more energy the work demands of you, and the greater its challenge to you, the more greatly you will benefit from it.

13. What kind of good karma do you especially need? Divert any harmful tendencies in yourself into constructive channels which will clear away your karmic blocks.

14. Look back to your childhood; reflect on your earliest tendencies and see how they might fit into your present realities. These memories will give you clues to the personality traits and skills you developed in other lifetimes and therefore to what is most likely to bring you success in this life.

15. If you sincerely want to find truth, even while working to earn a living, ask for divine assistance. Don't ask God to help you: rather, ask Him what you can do to *serve* Him.

16. If you want to be creative and happy, seek work where *sensible* innovation is appreciated.

17. Try to live more in the moment, and to seek guidance from God or from your higher Self, rather than trying to figure everything out in advance, intellectually. The more you learn to depend on higher guidance, the more you will find intuition flowing.

18. Originality means to come from one's own inner *point of origin*.

19. Be willing to laugh with good cheer at yourself. Having no self-image to live up to will help you to be original in the true sense, and to be guided by your own understanding.

20. Ask God to inspire you in what you say or do. Never tell yourself, "I can't do that," but say, rather, "I certainly couldn't do it, myself, but God *through* me can accomplish anything."

WORKBOOK IDEAS
by Joseph Bharat Cornell

Follow Your Dharma

John Muir (1838–1924), America's most renowned and influential conservationist, is revered today as the "Father of the National Parks." Muir's writing and enthusiasm inspired the modern conservation movement, and "all other torches," it was said, "were lighted from his."

As a young man, however, Muir was a source of embarrassment to his family. They worried about him spending so much time wandering through the countryside looking at plants. His family wanted him to choose a profession—the more socially acceptable, the better. During this time, John received lots of "helpful" suggestions on what he should do with his life. But John stayed true to his inner calling. Responding to the admonishments from others to follow a more respectable profession, Muir wrote, "I will follow my instincts—be myself for good or ill—and see what will be the upshot."

"It is better to fail attempting to follow one's own dharma than to succeed in following the dharma of another," says the Bhagavad Gita. The more you act in harmony with what your nature calls you to do, the happier you will be. The purpose of life is to learn to direct your life force energetically. Work that brings out the highest within you awakens the enthusiastic support of your whole being.

ACTION ITEM:

The time spent at work comprises half your waking hours, so choosing harmonious and enjoyable work is crucial to your well-being.

Examine your present occupation and how it affects your attitudes and level of energy. Ask yourself the following questions:

- Am I happy to go to work each day?
- Do I perform my tasks with attention and loving interest?
- Is the over-all quality of my energy positive, willing, and cheerful?
- Can I be creative? Is there enough variety to keep me interested?
- Am I providing a meaningful service for others?

No job will be perfect until we reach perfection ourselves. If you find, however, that your job suppresses your energy and enthusiasm, you should try to find another position in your company, or perhaps even in another profession. If this is impossible, try to find volunteer work or a hobby that allows you to express a more fulfilling part of yourself.

ACTION ITEM:
1. Look back at your childhood. Try to recall your earliest tendencies. What were your interests? What were you drawn to? What did you have a natural flair for?
2. Analyze your present-day tendencies and interests.
3. Can you see how your natural tendencies might give you clues for your choice of profession?

ACTION ITEM:
- Once you have determined the kind of job you want, employ your will power, creative ability, and steadfast patience to materialize your work or service. "Opportunities in life come by *creation*, not by chance," said Paramhansa Yogananda.

LESSON TWENTY-FIVE

CREATING OPPORTUNITIES

If you expect the worst, the worst is most certainly what you'll attract, eventually. But if you expect the best, then that is what will appear, as if unbidden, on your doorstep.

Thoughts are things. Their power is far greater than any mechanism for accomplishing things.

The Principles

I have often thought about the subject of creating opportunities in life. As I sat down to begin work on this lesson, a childhood recollection came to me—perhaps because in the last lesson I'd just written about that mudslinging episode during our Downs School outing in England. This new recollection was of comic books I used to read at the barbershop when I was a teenager in Scarsdale, America. The "books" featured impossibly great heroes—Superman, Batman, Spiderman—each with a special gift for handling a special kind of villain. The hero was always on the scene with his gift, and—lo and behold!—a villain always appeared whom only this hero could handle! In real life, of course, neither such heroes nor such villains exist.

Opportunity is often like that: What comes to you is, generally, that for which you yourself are prepared! The most important thing, then, is to be *prepared* for the opportunities that come your way. In a way, you *create* them. Karma is certainly a part of that process, but even more important, because immediately useful to you, are right attitude, right expectations, right use of energy.

Here are a number of thoughts to help you prepare. All of them center in how you present yourself to the world, and in how you *relate* to the world.

Your voice can and should be one of your chief assets. Many people however, unfortunately for them, never take the trouble to develop magnetic voices that express warm feeling and other uplifting qualities of the heart. Some people croak at others like frogs. When they announce, "It's *great* to see you!" your instinctive reaction, often, is to ask yourself, "What do they want from me?" Voices like that repel; they do not attract. Their friends will make excuses for them, perhaps by explaining, "He really has a heart of gold." ("Yeah, sure," we mutter silently to ourselves.)

To bring magnetism to your voice, learn first to breathe properly. Think of a garden hose for an analogy. There are two ways to strengthen the flow of water passing through it. One is to tighten the nozzle; the other is to increase the flow at the tap. "Tightening the nozzle" is also a very common way of increasing the power of one's voice. What people do is squeeze the throat, which enables them to produce a thin, crackling noise that may, for some things, be effective, but that cannot but be unattractive also, and sometimes even offensive. Instead of trying to squeeze the vocal cords to increase the volume of sound coming through them, try to increase that volume by using the diaphragm as a bellows from below. Relax the throat; don't tense it. Lift your breath upwards, past the vocal cords, like a violin bow stroking the strings.

I studied singing when I was eighteen. My singing teacher, an old lady, told me at our first lesson, "The voice is the one instrument you can't see. I can show you how to hold your hands over the keyboard of a piano. I can show you how to stroke a violin bow. But I can't *show* you how to use your voice. The only way I can help you is by example. I will sing a note as it should be sung, and then ask you to listen sensitively and imitate the way I placed my voice."

She proceeded to sing a note. I tried to repeat it as she had done it. Her training was so sensitive that only six months later, during a song I was singing to her piano accompaniment, she stopped me at a certain point and cried, "That note! That's just how all of them should sound."

By this time she began to have ambitions for me. As she announced, "I'm living for only one thing now: to see you become a *great* singer! It isn't only your voice. Lots of people have good voices. But *you understand*." When she said that, I realized I simply could not continue our lessons. I'd been studying for the sheer fun of learning to sing well, but I'd never had the slightest ambition of taking up singing as a profession. All I really wanted was to find truth. I'm afraid I did no more studying with her.

I did learn, however, that one can inject much more power into the voice, and do so quite effortlessly, by simply relaxing the vocal cords and "lifting" the voice up through them to the lips and the forehead, which soon were vibrating with the sound of my voice.

I went beyond her teaching, eventually, by discovering that the "violin bow" of the breath can also stroke the heart strings to bring warmth, rather than a pure operatic tone, to the voice. I can't easily explain this discovery through this medium of the written word, but in classes I have worked with people on their voice production, and have found that within very few minutes they were, virtually all of them, singing—audibly so—from the heart. To the extent that you can understand these written words, experiment with what I am saying. You will find that if you can infuse *consciousness* into your voice, people will *want* to hear you, and will feel even before they get to know you that you are (as you must in fact *feel* yourself to be) their friend.

The better placed your voice is, the better your own individuality will come out. It will be like your "calling card." Often, when I return to some city where I have spent time in the past, and phone a friend after reaching there, I may only say, "Hello," and a pleased voice over the wire exclaims, "Swami! When did you arrive?" Sometimes I get to say nothing but, "Uh," and the same thing happens.

Many years ago, in 1959, at the airport in Patna, India, I was transiting to another city, and was talking English with a small group of Indian friends. I was well "disguised": hair halfway down my back, a beard, and a geru (saffron) robe. Just then, an elderly American gentleman came over to our table and addressed me: "From your voice, you must be one of the Walters boys!" This man's name was Harry Gibbon. He and his wife had been friends of my parents in Scarsdale, N.Y. They knew us "boys," too—rather abstractly, as parents tend to do with their friends' children. Even in those years, I had been away from Scarsdale most of the time, whether at school or traveling, Our family name, I should add, was Walters. How did he recognize my voice, "disguised" as I was, after the more than fifteen years that we hadn't seen each other?

Your *accent* when you speak is another very important point in any effort you make to reach people and thus to attract opportunities to yourself that might, otherwise, prove elusive. Many people keep their mouths almost fixed in one, basic position, and find it next to impossible to speak with an accent different from the one they've developed, usually by imitating their peers. You can often tell just by looking at a Texan, with his slight smile at the corners of his mouth, that that is, in fact, his home state. That position enables him to speak with a Texan accent.

Another example: About sixty years ago, I was sitting with a friend in a New York restaurant when a young woman came in with an escort. I said to my friend, "I'm sure she's English."

"How can you possibly tell?" he demanded, almost dismissively.

I replied, "She just looks it." Just then, she turned to her escort and spoke with a clear English accent. *How* did she "look it"? It may have been something about the mouth, or the eyes—or possibly it was the hairdo, though in such matters I am no expert.

I am sensitive to accents, having grown up with several languages, some of which I spoke almost as well as English. I used as a child to enjoy imitating people's accents: for instance, when I was in school in England I heard a story about an American and a Cockney meeting in a London Pub. The Cockney announced his name as, "'Arrison."

"Say, you must mean *Harrison*, don't you?" replied the American, speaking with a nasal twang.

The Cockney, outraged by this evidence of stupidity, said, "Wha'? A haitch, a hoy, two hars, a hi, a hess, a ho, and a hen: If that don't spell ''Arrison'!" It's always been fun to tell that story.

My point here is that accents are not only widely diverse, but that they can also be quite unattractive—or, alternatively, attractive. When visiting Texas some years ago, I noted that radio announcers spoke with a universal American accent, which people define as more from the north. Evidently, even Texans felt that this accent was less "down-home," and more "sophisticated."

A general belief is that an accent is created by climate. In the colder northern climes, for instance, the air induces people to speak through lips that are stiff and almost closed. In the warmer southern climes, people tend more to open their mouths to let the air in. Considerations like these have little bearing on the present lesson. I am more interested in what is revealed by people's mental attitudes in their accents. These often override to some extent the influence of their environment.

I have come to realize that there are universal aspects to people's accents. People with a stronger feeling quality will tend to emphasize their vowels more than their consonants, regardless of their basic environmental accents. People with a strong will power often tend to emphasize their consonants. In Mexico I noticed that, although their language tends to be a little lip-lazy (reflecting a "*mañana*" consciousness), macho young men, when coming to the letter *r*, roll it with gusto. I've enjoyed listening to them pronounce the *r* in Monterrey, for example, making it sound almost like "Monterrrrey."

A nasal accent is a sign either of arrogance, if people speak loudly, or of aloofness or a shyness that borders on self-preoccupation.

I've told a story from my childhood in this lesson, and another in the last one. Here's another that might be from those years but that in fact, despite its childhood origins, took place quite recently. Just two evenings ago a few friends and I watched the Walt Disney movie *Bambi*. In passing I have to say that I consider that movie a true work of art, inspiring as well as beautiful. I have a special "accentual" memory of that movie, however. There is a rabbit called "Thumper." The slightly swallowed, American *r*, as pronounced by the rabbit, comes across as friendly and charming in his first declaration, "I'm Thumper!" Later, this thought came to me: How would the rabbit have come across if he'd announced, with the accent of an English schoolboy, "I'm Thumpah." The feeling would have been altogether different: slightly off-putting, perhaps, instead of warm and friendly.

Accents have been, as I said, a particular fascination of mine throughout my life. In several countries where I speak the language fluently people think I'm "almost" a native. In Paris, they think perhaps I'm from Geneva; in German Switzerland I've been asked if I was from Germany; in America, many (foreigners especially) have wondered if I was English; in Spain, they've thought perhaps I was Mexican. In Italy, as I've commented before, I am often taken for an Italian—though that may be because many Italians are new even to their Italian language, having grown up speaking one of the many dialects. In Calcutta, one day, someone asked my driver incredulously (as he later told me), "Is he *Bengali*?!" My Bengali accent didn't go with my white skin!

From experience, then, I can say that it is possible to change your accent if you want to. Do you consider your speaking voice less attractive than it might be? If so, work on it. It is important to speak with a pleasing accent. People will often categorize you, for instance as cultured or rustic, refined or poorly unlettered, and will treat you accordingly.

Here are several things that will help you when speaking:

1) Don't speak in a monotone. It will lull people to sleep. Your voice will be much more magnetic if it has a certain melody to it. Melody should be very individual, not the product of a socially recognized pattern. Americans tend to speak in a monotone. The English often infuse an attractive melody into their speech—until one realizes that the melody is culturally induced, and hasn't creative feeling behind it.

2) Avoid the common practice of dropping your voice at the end of a sentence. Imagine someone saying to you, "I find it simply amazing!" but reducing that last word to a mumble or a whisper!

3) The beginning and ending of a sentence are vital to the impact it has. Your voice will be more magnetic if you can inject extra energy into those first and last words. (When writing, also, how you end a sentence is important. If I had cast that sentence to read, "How you end a sentence is important also, when writing," it would have been perfectly grammatical to do so, but notice how such a sequence lowers the impact.)

Words are expressions of consciousness. Be conscious of every word you utter. Speak it with concentration. Infuse the tone of your voice with the feeling you want to convey. The tone of voice, more than any musical instrument, can evoke the feeling intended in a composition.

Many years ago at Mt. Washington, the new monks' ashram was being built on a corner of the property that was situated on a lower level than the main building. One late afternoon, while the site was still open to possible marauders, I saw a group of neighborhood boys clambering around the premises. As I went down to tell them to leave, I was still some distance away when I called out to them in a deliberately harsh tone, "What are you doing down there?" As the boys ran away fearfully I heard one of them cry to another, "God, what a wicked voice!"

Listening to the tones your own voice expresses can afford you an excellent means of self-analysis. After that last-mentioned episode I had a good laugh with my friends, but notice how instantly any mood of anger, for example, is reflected in the voice—even before you yourself are even aware of that sudden spurt of emotion in your heart. Try especially to keep your vocal cords relaxed. The very practice will help you to feel an expansion of consciousness.

One way to make your voice more magnetic is to use the breath consciously to project the vocal tone upward, through the heart, then on through the *bishuddha chakra*, or cervical center, then projecting it outward through the *Kutastha* between the eyebrows. When your voice is really well placed, you will feel a vibration in the forehead, and in the lips also.

Calmness is expressed more through keeping the voice steady than by tones spoken softly. Expansive calmness radiates upward and outward when it is consciously centered in the *bishuddha* (the cervical).

When expressing your thoughts to others, remember that the heart is more important than the head. Perfectly clear logic is less important than deep feeling—as opposed to the excitement of emotion.

Keep your consciousness centered in the higher *chakras* of the spine. The lower the center of energy, the weaker—or else, the darker—will be your magnetism. (For remember, there is also negative magnetism. You yourself, if that is what you project, will be the greatest sufferer.)

Similarly, sit, walk, or stand with a firm, upright posture.

I myself speak English deliberately the way I like it to sound. You might let your own preference be a factor in how you speak, instead of making your words merely beasts of burden to carry your ideas. Notice little things: In the movie *Bambi*, for example, the way the little rabbit pronounces "Thumper"—with the tip of the tongue curled slightly back in the mouth—seems to invite others to one, whereas "Thumpah," with the tongue flat and the mouth opened more widely, would have subtly expressed a preference for keeping others at a distance.

The way to create opportunities involves, first, attracting them to you by projecting the right magnetism. Voice is only one aspect of that process, but from all that I've written on that subject it must be apparent that other aspects are involved also: posture, general physical appearance, the clothing one wears, neatness: From everything above I think you yourself can apply many of these principles to other aspects of your life.

The second thing necessary is to be alert enough to *recognize* opportunity when it appears. Many discoveries have been made, as I remarked earlier in these lessons, not when new facts appeared, but when people were ready to recognize their usefulness to mankind.

George Washington Carver was a black man in America, of low birth, a scientific disposition, and a desire to serve humanity. God told him in prayer that He would show him hundreds of uses for the humble peanut. Carver became, in his way, a great inventor. You, yourself, could discover wonders in everything if you would keep your eyes open to that possibility. Henry David Thoreau was walking with a friend across a field in Massachusetts when the friend remarked what a pity it was that the old American Indian culture had died out so completely.

"And yet," said Thoreau, "there are signs of it all around us."

"What signs?" challenged the friend. "I never see any."

At that moment, Thoreau stooped down and picked up an arrowhead from the ground. Like Sherlock Holmes he said something like, "You see, but you do not observe."

Be more observant. The successful person is one who *looks*, and who *expects* opportunities to appear in his life. Many others receive countless opportunities in life, yet pass them by as though they wore blinders and dark glasses. They see what lies straight ahead of them, but see even that only dimly as far as opportunity is concerned.

Face life with expectation. Wonderful adventure awaits you practically underfoot. Thoreau's answer to people who boasted of their "continental tours" was, "I, too, have traveled extensively—around the city of Concord" (where he lived).

One aspect of being expectant and observant is, as I've stated repeatedly in these lessons, *energy*. I should repeat here a simple principle that I've explained before: *Energy, projected with will power, can project a ray of consciousness that will generate a magnetic field around it, strong enough to attract to itself anything desired.*

Another point I have touched on before is *positive expectation*. If you expect the worst, the worst is most certainly what you'll attract, eventually. But if you expect the best, then that is what will appear, as if unbidden, on your doorstep.

Thoughts are things. Their power is far greater than any mechanism for accomplishing things. There was an episode in my life that I love to dwell on. This was in 1972. I had felt directed by the Divine Mother to return, for the first time in ten years, to India. In India I visited my old "stomping ground," Calcutta. One disappointment I felt was that a certain Indian friend of mine, a Dr. Mishra, had returned from America to Bubaneshwar in the Indian State of Orissa, and I didn't have his address. I landed at Dum Dum airport in Calcutta, expecting to find a couple of Bengali friends of mine waiting for me. They'd been delayed by heavy traffic, however (as I learned later). Not knowing what to do, I simply asked Divine Mother with complete acceptance of Her will, "What do You want?" If I'd rushed off to telephone for explanations as to what was happening, I'd have missed what I have always thought of as a miracle. Instead, as I stood there waiting inwardly for guidance, a passenger hurrying by from another plane stopped in front of me, paused, and then asked, "What is your good name?" (This is a common way in India of putting this question.)

"Swami Kriyananda," I replied.

"Ah, I thought you must be he. A friend of mine, a Dr. Mishra in Bubaneshwar, has shown me photographs of you. I've been longing to meet you!"

"And I," I replied, "have been wishing I could meet him. Can you please give me his address?"

"There's no need for me to do so," was his answer. "He happens to be staying in Calcutta, and I've come here especially to meet him!"

I got not only to see Dr. Mishra, but to stay in the same house for the night.

The Application

A classmate of mine once showed me a story he had written. It was about a young, aspiring violinist whose talent went unrecognized until one day a famous orchestra conductor happened to walk by his house. He heard the young man's music through an open window, was amazed by its beauty, knocked on the front door and asked to see "this great genius." Before long, the discovered artist was thrilling audiences around the country, then internationally.

It was, in other words, a very typical "wish fulfillment" story. Did the writer himself play the violin? Probably, though he may have had the decency to project that dream onto some other profession than the one he himself contemplated.

My mother's comment, when I told her the story, was to exclaim pityingly, "Oh, how pathetic!"

Most people's dreams of success, probably, revolve around unexpected offers, sudden recognition, unheard-of opportunities. "How pathetic," indeed! All of us have of course heard of blessings suddenly being poured on someone: amazing recognition of talent or ability that has rocketed someone, who seemingly had done little or nothing to deserve it, to fame and fortune. What people don't realize is the role past karma plays in everyone's life. We can't alter what has been done. The important thing is to understand that we *can*, in the present life, generate the energy to offset failure karma and develop success karma.

Karma is not what many people think it: fate, carved in stone. Stanza 51, in *The Rubaiyat of Omar Khayyam*, states:

> The Moving Finger writes; and, having writ,
> Moves on: nor all thy Piety nor Wit
>   Shall lure it back to cancel half a Line,
> Nor all thy Tears wash out a Word of it.

Paramhansa Yogananda wrote, in his explanation of this quatrain, or "*rubai*," that in the context of the other stanzas what this one offers is hope, not hopelessness. In Yogananda's words, "Omar's warning that fate's decrees are inexorable was given so as to draw our attention the more forcefully to the way of escape from destiny, emphasized elsewhere in this poem.

"Karma's unalterable decrees govern human destiny only as long as man continues to live through his senses, in reaction to outer events. For such a person, moral reasoning is centered in ego-consciousness. Scriptural learning is centered in ego-consciousness. Self-pitying tears are centered in ego-consciousness. Ego-consciousness is the problem. The greater its hold on the mind, the greater karma's hold on our lives."

My next and final lesson is titled, "The Right Use of Ego." Even in ego-consciousness one can improve on his karma by right action, and cancel out bad karma, not by trying to "cancel out" the past, nor by weeping and pleading for divine mercy, but by the right use of will. Were this not the case, there would indeed be no exit. The way out for the ego is to go out the front door, and not roam about through the house, or try to beat the walls down. Learn correct ways—not by mere "wit," or cleverness, but by devotional *attunement* with the divine will.

Bad karma is simply the result of wrong use of one's will in the past. Develop strong, positive will power in the present, and if your will is attuned to a higher Will you can at least move through the rooms in your house *toward* the front door!

It is not an easy point to understand. Where does personal will enter the picture, and how much of what happens in our lives is due merely to past karma? My Guru's comment on this question was, "Only free souls can really understand." Nevertheless, he repeatedly urged right attitude as a means of changing one's destiny. One time he said, "Karma! Karma! I'm tired of people lamenting about their karma! This is a weakness of India's culture. Just say to yourself: 'I *have* no karma.' Attune yourself to God, live more in His consciousness, and you yourself will be free!"

So then, when it comes to creating opportunities, never cower before the decrees of fate! Don't wait for others to give you success on a silver platter! As Yogananda said during the depression of the 1930s, "If I needed a job, and couldn't find one, I would shake the world until it *had* to give me work!"

MEDITATION

There is a story in the Christian New Testament of the Bible which tells of the disciples in a boat on the Sea of Galilee when, suddenly, a fierce storm threatened to upset the boat and drown them. Of a sudden, Jesus Christ appeared walking over the water. "Peace!" he declared to the wind. "Be still!"

There is a somewhat similar story about Paramhansa Yogananda, in which he stilled a sudden, mighty wind. He and a woman disciple had just returned to Mt. Washington when the wind hurled itself upon the building. The Master said it was a consequence of the karma of World War II. He told the woman to take off one shoe and strike it with the heel three times on the porch, uttering a mantra he gave her. On the final blow, the wind suddenly ceased.

The following day, in the Los Angeles Times, there was a report of a freak wind that had appeared suddenly, then as suddenly had ceased.

In this meditation, think of calming the waves, or the mighty winds, of *maya*. Visualize yourself standing in the midst of all the turmoil, and addressing it calmly from your own center. Say to it, "Peace! Be still!" Feel an aura of calmness emanating from you and calming all the waters of delusion.

AFFIRMATION

This is an affirmation recommended by Paramhansa Yogananda: "I stand unshaken amidst the crash of breaking worlds!"

POINTS TO REMEMBER

1. The most important thing is to be *prepared* for the opportunities that come your way. In a way, you *create* them. Karma is certainly a part of that process, but even more important, because immediately useful to you, are right attitude, right expectations, right use of energy.

2. Your voice can and should be one of your chief assets.

3. To bring magnetism to your voice, learn first to breathe properly. Try to increase the volume of sound by using the diaphragm as a bellows from below and relaxing the vocal cords.

4. The "violin bow" of the breath can also stroke the heart strings to bring warmth to the voice. If you can infuse *consciousness* into your voice, people will *want* to hear you, and will feel that you are their friend.

5. One way to make your voice more magnetic is to use the breath consciously to project the vocal tone upward, through the heart, then on through the *bishuddha chakra*, or cervical center, then projecting it outward through the *ajna chakra* between the eyebrows. When your voice is really well placed, you will feel a vibration in the forehead, and in the lips also.

6. The better placed your voice is, the better your own individuality will come out.

7. Your *accent* when you speak is another very important point in any effort you make to reach people and thus to attract opportunities to yourself that might, otherwise, prove elusive. Accents can be quite unattractive—or, alternatively, attractive.

8. When speaking: Don't speak in a monotone; your voice will be much more magnetic if it has a certain melody to it. Avoid the common practice of dropping your voice at the end of a sentence. Your voice will be more magnetic if you can inject extra energy into the first and last words of a sentence.

9. Be conscious of every word you utter. Speak it with concentration. Infuse the tone of your voice with the feeling you want to convey.

10. Try especially to keep your vocal cords relaxed. The very practice will help you to feel an expansion of consciousness.

11. Calmness is expressed more through keeping the voice steady than by tones spoken softly. Expansive calmness radiates upward and outward when it is consciously centered in the *bishuddha* (the cervical).

12. When expressing your thoughts to others, remember that the heart is more important than the head. Perfectly clear logic is less important than deep feeling.

13. The way to create opportunities involves, first, attracting them to you by projecting

the right magnetism. Voice is only one aspect; other aspects are posture, general physical appearance, the clothing one wears, neatness. Sit, walk, or stand with a firm, upright posture.

14. The second thing necessary is to be alert enough to *recognize* opportunity when it appears.

15. Be more observant. The successful person is one who *looks*, and who *expects* opportunities to appear in his life. Wonderful adventure awaits you practically underfoot.

16. *Energy, projected with will power, can project a ray of consciousness that will generate a magnetic field around it, strong enough to attract to itself anything desired.*

17. If you expect the best, then that is what will appear, as if unbidden, on your doorstep.

18. Thoughts are things. Their power is far greater than any mechanism for accomplishing things.

19. The greater the hold of ego-consciousness on the mind, the greater karma's hold on our lives. Even in ego-consciousness one can improve on his karma by right action, and cancel out bad karma, by the right use of will. Learn correct ways—by devotional *attunement* with the divine will.

20. Yogananda repeatedly urged right attitude as a means of changing one's destiny: "Just say to yourself: 'I *have* no karma.' Attune yourself to God, live more in His consciousness, and you yourself will be free!"

WORKBOOK IDEAS
by Joseph Bharat Cornell

Generate a Flow of Positive Energy

A teacher at a children's museum loved his work, but he noticed that sometimes his classes were successful and sometimes they were lackluster. At first he thought this depended on how well prepared the students were for their visit to the museum. As he thought more carefully, however, he realized that when *he* felt inspired and enthusiastic the children had a wonderful time, and on days when he felt low energy, the tour wasn't particularly special—no matter how good the group of children.

Henry David Thoreau said, "There must be the generating force of love behind every effort destined to be successful." The world responds in kind to our energy and expectations. More than we realize, all success and failure is a result of right or wrong magnetism. If we generate a strong flow of positive, loving energy, we will attract positive energy in return.

ACTION ITEM:
1. Pay attention to the quality of your energy today. What is the underlying tone of that energy: positive or negative, hopeful or hopeless, courageous or fearful?
2. If you find that you are holding negative expectations about a project, practice the following exercise to attract the outcome you truly desire:
    a. Hold an image of your project at the point between the eyebrows.
    b. Then send a strong a ray of positive intention—from your heart and through the spiritual eye—to your project.
    c. Think of the energy you're sending as a ray of light. Rotate around that ray the magnetism you want to create.

Repeat this exercise when you feel the need to create a more positive outlook or magnetism for your project.

3. Repeat every day: "Everything that comes to me is a reflection of my energy, so I choose to have only positive thoughts and expectations."

LESSON TWENTY-SIX

THE RIGHT USE OF EGO

The more we manifest the spiritual light from within, the more, in a sense, we lose our egoic individuality. . . . As individuality becomes less and less centered in the ego, a deeper sense of who we really are begins to manifest.

The Principles

There is a children's story—perhaps you know it?—about a mother frog and a little baby frog just out of the tadpole stage. In the baby's view, its mother was surely the largest creature in existence.

One day the baby frog hopped a little distance from their home pond, and came upon a country lane. There, taking up most of the lane as it lumbered along it, was a cow. In amazement, the little frog gazed for a moment, then hopped and hopped frantically home to tell its mother about this incredible phenomenon.

"You say it was large?" said the mother, not at all liking this demotion to a relatively small size in her baby's mind.

"Oh, Mummy, it was *enormous*!"

"Do you mean it was *this* big?" asked the mother as she inhaled deeply, puffing out her chest.

"Oh, Mummy, it was *much* bigger!"

"Was it *this* big?" asked the mother grimly as she took an even deeper breath.

"Oh, it was much, much bigger, Mummy! I can't even begin to describe its hugeness."

"Do you mean your monster *dared* to be . . ." the mother tried to take as deep a breath as she could, but never finished her sentence. Suddenly, there was a loud "POP!"

The mother—or, to paraphrase the title of a Hitchcock movie, the lady—had vanished.

I have written many times in these lessons about the need for self-expansion. An expansion of ego-identity, however, is very different from what I wanted to convey.

Isn't it curious, the way so many people boast of their accomplishments—when nobody likes a boaster? The phenomenon is self-contradictory: How to explain it? Do people merely dislike having their own egos "crowded to the wall"? Surely it is more than that. Sensitive people, especially, can't help sensing that there is something wrong about emphasizing one's own ego at the expense of other people's. As I have often remarked in these lessons, people are wiser than they know. Many know themselves also to be greater than what they seem, objectively. Intuitively they know that, whatever their human foibles, they have at least the potential for true greatness. As Emerson put it, "Men descend to meet." When people boast, they—and, perhaps even more so, their listeners!—feel in some way degraded by the self-promotion.

"Who is he to talk like that?" is a normal reaction when others try to set themselves above the common ruck of humanity. Their displeasure is motivated only partly by self-interest. They are also intuitively aware that their hidden greatness defies competition; it simply *is*.

Where your own work is concerned, remember, *Maya* will always try to trick you into seeking self-gratification by ego-affirming means. In the process, *Maya* will carefully avoid the only thing that will ever really work for you: offering yourself into a greater reality. The way to defeat *Maya*'s ego-narrowing arguments is to remind yourself constantly that happiness and fulfillment come through self-expansion—a kind of expansion that is unattainable by the ego, but that comes inevitably to one who achieves release from the ego.

It is no easy task to overcome the ego! Can anyone really do so, as long as he sees his ego as his own self? The answer is, no, he cannot! The ego is, in fact, indestructible. It can only be transcended in the realization that we are much more—when the little self expands to become, in time, the overarching, omnipresent, divine Self.

I myself, after meeting my Guru, worked hard to overcome what he described as my tendency toward "intellectual aloofness." After months of effort, I awoke one morning to the dismaying realization that I was becoming proud of my humility!

On what firm ground can we stand, to lever *ourselves* up to higher levels of understanding? Archimedes stated, "Give me sufficient leverage and I will raise the very earth!" Is there a "ground" firm enough for the ego?

What, essentially, *is* the ego? What, essentially, *are* we? This lesson will address three important aspects of the subject: 1) the unreality of the ego in the context of infinite consciousness; 2) the need to shoulder responsibility for one's own part in the great "drama" of life; and 3) the desirability of keeping ourselves open, when working, to the inspiration of higher consciousness.

Each of us, considered singly, is infinitesimal compared to the great scheme of things. That fact, however, doesn't excuse dysfunction on our part. Each of us is important, within his closely circumscribed circle of influence.

There is a story of a Jewish rabbi who, at the Sabbath service in his synagogue, knelt before the altar and cried out in a loud voice, "I am nothing, Lord! Nothing!"

The assistant rabbi, observing this inspiring act of humility, imitated it and, like the rabbi, knelt before the altar and cried out, "I am nothing! nothing!"

The janitor, on observing these wonderful acts of self-abnegation, rushed down the aisle from the back of the hall, threw himself on his knees before the altar, and cried out, "I am nothing, Lord! nothing!"

The rabbi, seeing this (to him) ridiculous display of the janitor's, declaring what seemed to him an obvious fact, turned to his assistant with raised eyebrows and exclaimed, "So look who thinks he's nothing!"

To know who and what we really are, we must first of all know in what manner we were created, and in what manner the universe was created.

Let us begin by discussing the second of the points mentioned above: How did God create the universe?

Twice previously in these lessons I have alluded to a statement of my Guru's in *Autobiography of a Yogi*. Here I quote it exactly: "The divine eye is center everywhere, circumference nowhere." The Infinite doesn't *create* in the manner you and I do when making things. We can go out and buy the materials for our creation: the stone, the wood, the paints and brushes, the ink and paper we need. God had nothing "on hand" but His own consciousness. In creating, He could only *become* His creation. Consciousness itself could not be created, for the Spirit already *was* consciousness! The nature of Spirit is absolute and perfect bliss.

Hence Swami Shankara's definition of the Supreme Spirit: *Satchidananda*, which my Guru translated to mean, "ever-existing, ever-conscious, *ever-new* Bliss." Most translations of that Sanskrit word read more abruptly: "Existence, Consciousness, Bliss." The words my Guru added, "ever-" and "ever-new," were appended by him so as to clarify the eternal nature of Divine Bliss, and to suggest that ever-newness is an aspect of the divine nature. He added "ever-new" to emphasize that, in eternity, Bliss never becomes boring or "old hat" (as all things do that we enjoy through the senses). "Ever-new" suggests also that the Spirit, in its own "ever-newness," naturally "spills over" into the inconceivably diverse manifestations that form the universe. "The Spirit wanted to enjoy Itself through many": so state the Hindu scriptures.

God's creation was projected as movement, or vibration: that which the scriptures call AUM, the Amen, the Ahunavar of the Zoroastrians, the Amin of the Moslems. At first, creation was in idea only. Ideation formed the "blueprint" of what was yet to come. After this phase of creation had been projected in its unimaginably vast diversity, its idea-forms were vibrated more grossly to become energy. Divine Consciousness *thought* energy into being. Thus, energy was the second phase of creation. It was an appearance, only, for everything actually exists only in consciousness.

The first phase of creation—that is to say, the first outward manifestation of God's consciousness—is called the ideational, or causal plane. The ideational plane, or causal universe, cannot be conceived of in terms of size, for time and space at this stage of manifestation are not yet well-defined realities.

The second phase, the astral universe is—so my Paramguru Swami Sri Yukteswar explained—"hundreds of times" larger than our material universe, which, to our understanding, is itself incomprehensibly vast.

The third phase, the material universe, is the last stage of creation. Why is it the last? Because nothing can become more solid. Everything in existence manifests what it has ever been in essence: consciousness, whether silent or vibratory. There can be no opposite to absolute consciousness. The appearance of solidity, therefore, can be only that: a mere seeming.

These truths can be declared openly nowadays, since science has discovered that energy is the key to matter. Matter, in other words, *is* energy, which in turn—so the wise have declared—is a vibration of ideas, which are vibrations of absolute, motionless consciousness. What appear to be hard rocks, metals, and crystals are only energy in gross rates of vibration. Nowhere in creation is anything really solid. In cases where material forms manifest consciousness—the brain, for example—consciousness manifests *through* those forms: it cannot be *created* by matter. Not even the most wonderfully constructed brain could produce genius. It is man's consciousness, manifested through the brain, which sometimes reveals genius. A great actor displays his extraordinary skill out of his subtle awareness. No gesture or expression, merely imitated by another actor, could ever reproduce the same level of genius. Consciousness can manifest itself effectively through matter, but nothing material can possibly, in itself, ever create consciousness.

Thus, the ego is not *created* with human birth. Rather, the ego is only an "element"—my Guru used this word—of the astral body. The ego is that consciousness of individuality which spins a "cocoon" of energy about itself. Only in the astral or energy body does an entity become clearly differentiated and individual.

The causal body contains the essence of our individuality, but its state of awareness is so subtle that it is also deeply conscious of its oneness with all existence. Separate existence, at that level, is only an idea: a thin veil lightly covering the soul.

In the astral body, the veil of separateness is thicker, or denser. Energy and the multicolored expressions that energy manifests, determined by various states of consciousness, creates the illusion of a definite and separate individuality.

Finally, on the material plane, the physical body in its apparent denseness is so clearly differentiated from everything else that the indwelling ego cannot easily see everything as merely a manifestation of the unifying consciousness of Spirit.

Paramhansa Yogananda described our apparent individuality with the illustration of countless tiny slivers of glass, each of us being one sliver. The light reflected from the sun of Spirit seems, in every sliver, individual. It is only a reflection, however, of the one sun. As the sun sets for us here on Earth, the slivers of glass grow gradually dimmer and, with nightfall, become invisible.

Every sliver of glass, considered individually, seems distinct and separate. The less light is reflected in it, however, the more clearly its unique form becomes visible. Each sliver, when not reflecting any light, can be seen as wide, narrow, thick, or long, and in other ways as uniquely contoured. What makes it attractive to our eyes is the light reflected in it. As a rule, no sliver will be, in itself, beautiful.

If, moreover, you pick up a sliver of glass and examine it closely, it may cut you. Similar is the case if you examine your ego too closely. Self-absorption may cut you—or cause you in some way to suffer—owing to your indifference to other, broader realities. The secret of a happy life is—well, not exactly self-forgetfulness, but a minimum of self-preoccupation.

The more we manifest the spiritual light from within, the more, in a sense, we lose our egoic individuality. No analogy is perfect, of course. As individuality becomes less and less centered in the ego, a deeper sense of who we really are begins to manifest. Every apparently separate point in God's creation, though all reflect His consciousness, is unique. No two snowflakes, so science tells us, are exactly alike. No two egos, similarly, are completely alike. Every one of us, throughout eternity, is different from every other. Even stripped of the *koshas*, or sheaths, within which human consciousness is enclosed, every soul is uniquely itself.

Human egos, generally speaking, undergo countless similar experiences through all their incarnations, but no two lives are ever exactly alike. You and I may have been pirates in the past, or emperors, or warriors, or lowly street sweepers, but never have we played any role as anything other than ourselves. Always, we've been *our own special kind* of pirate, emperor, warrior, or street sweeper. We have even gone through what may have seemed identically the same experiences as other egos, but we've gone through each of them in our own way. It is a mistake—indeed, one might almost call it a slight upon God's ingenuity!—to reduce anyone, as astrologers often try to do, to a type.

The intricacies of the cosmic "show" are amazing, and seemingly they are never ending. Every atom manifests itself from its own center. Any change that it undergoes is outward from that center. Certain realities never change, however. All of us must, for example, cooperate with cosmic law; we cannot safely ignore it. Anything that will help us to expand our *consciousness*, rather than narrow it in egoic self-importance, will bring us the happiness and fulfillment we all crave. Anything, on the other hand, that shrinks our awareness into a narrower identity squeezes upon our happiness, deprives us of the fulfillment we dream of, and increases our suffering.

It is quite normal for businessmen and for anyone striving for success in life to feel a need for self-esteem. Low self-esteem is an obstacle to success, obviously. If, however, a person wants true happiness, it is also necessary for him to eliminate any relish in his self-importance.

I suggest that the modern-day emphasis on self-esteem be changed. *Self-respect*, surely, would be a better concept; it is less susceptible of misunderstanding. The problem with self-esteem is that it blocks higher creativity. The highest kind of creativity flows down to us from the superconscious. In that context, high or low self-esteem are no different from each other: both of them arise from excessive ego-consciousness.

When I was nine or ten years old, living in Bucharest, Romania, I made a trip from Teleajen to Bucharest with a few American businessmen. Their very voices conveyed vibrations of self-importance. Mere child that I was, and certainly only that in their eyes, I was more or less ignored. The car windows were tightly closed. The men puffed on thick cigars the whole way. As for me, I suffered in silence. At last, however, the air was so suffocating I could bear it no longer. In desperation I rolled down my window and leaned out, gasping for air.

"Shut the window, son," said the man seated beside me. "You'll catch cold." I wonder now, in retrospect, if he didn't treat everyone under him at the office with similar lack of concern. That ride lingers in memory even today, seventy years later, as one of the worst experiences of my life.

Most people equate the word *ego* with arrogance. A friend of mine once announced to me, "I have no ego." I wondered how he, an intelligent man, could make such an absurd statement. And then it occurred to me that all he could have meant was, "I am not arrogant." He corrected his own statement later, when we talked again. Arrogance had indeed been his true meaning.

It is important to understand that those two words, *arrogance* and *ego*, have very different meanings. Arrogance means to have a superior opinion of oneself. I remember with amusement someone once saying to me, "I'm not conceited: I'm just *aware*!" To be "aware" of one's own superiority to others is not genuine awareness: it reeks of delusion. The more competent one actually is, the more his pride in the fact, if he feels it, disturbs his mental equilibrium. For, as I shall explain shortly at some length, ego-consciousness is centered in the medulla oblongata at the base of the brain. Creative energy needs to flow freely up the spine, through the brain, becoming focused at the point between the eyebrows. When that flow is blocked in the medulla, the seat of ego, a strong energy-flow may cause the mind itself to become unbalanced.

When Yogananda was a young man, he applied to the Maharajah of Kasimbazar for help in founding a boys' school for the all-rounded spiritual, mental, and physical education of the young. The maharajah decided to put the young yogi to the test, first, in order to see how competent he was to teach spiritual truths.

He called in several pundits, or scriptural scholars, to conduct the test. My Guru told me many years later what happened next.

"I saw," he said, "that they were prepared for a spiritual bullfight. So I blocked their intention by stating at the outset, 'Let us base our discussion, not on scriptural authority, but on direct experience. Knowledge,' as I reminded them, 'is not the same as wisdom, which may tell us, among other things, what to do with knowledge.'

"Well, it was obvious to me that none of them was Self-realized. My approach put them at a disadvantage from the start! Their knowledge of scripture was limited to what they had learned intellectually, and consisted of passages they had memorized.

"I then said to them," my Guru continued, "'The scriptures tell us there are four divisions of human consciousness: *mon, buddhi, ahankara*, and *chitta* (mind, intellect, ego, and feeling). They also say these four divisions, or aspects, have their corresponding centers in the body. Can you tell me where those centers are located?' I knew they would not be able to answer, for that answer isn't contained in any scripture.

"'Can *you* describe those locations?' they demanded.

"'I can indeed,' I replied, 'and from experience. *Mon* (mind) is centered at the top of the head. *Buddhi* (intellect) is centered between the eyebrows. *Ahankara* (ego) is centered in the medulla oblongata at the base of the brain. And *chitta* (the feeling aspect of consciousness) is centered in the *anahat*, or heart region.'" The Master finished his story with the declaration, "I got my school!"

Here I should explain the way these different divisions function. My Guru's guru explained it in this way:

Mon (the mind) is like a mirror: it merely reflects what is perceived through the senses. Mind alone, therefore, has no discrimination. If one sees reflected in a mirror the image of a horse, his first impression, if he doesn't know what it is, will be only of that image.

Next what is needed is *buddhi*, intellect, to discriminate among the various known objects to determine, "That's a horse."

Ahankara (the ego) then steps in, perhaps to say, "That is *my* horse." So far, delusion has not yet entered one's consciousness. For even the realization that it is your horse doesn't necessarily bind you with attachment. So masters, too, need to be aware, in order to function in this world, of those things for which they are responsible. That knowledge need not create in them the slightest attachment.

Then, however, what appears on the scene is the faculty of *chitta* (feeling), which at that point may cry exultingly: "How *happy* I am to behold my horse!" Because feeling is primarily that aspect of consciousness which binds us to delusion, Patanjali defined yoga (as I've mentioned before) by the words, "*Yogas chitta vritti nirodha* (Yoga is the neutralization of the larger vortices and smallest eddies of feeling)."

Mon (mind) is the most difficult to locate in the body, for few have any direct experience of it.

The location of *buddhi* (intellect) is easier to recognize. For example, notice how, when you think deeply, you tend to knit your eyebrows. Men's intellects are uppermost; their feeling quality is somewhat in abeyance. They often have what I call, in humorous allusion to my own forehead, a "Neanderthal ridge" beneath their eyebrows. They also have a somewhat square, "no-nonsense" forehead. (In women, on the other hand, feeling is uppermost, and intellect, somewhat in abeyance).

Ahankara (ego-consciousness), being centered in the medulla oblongata, reveals itself as physical tension when there is an excess of energy in that region. Proud people tend to draw their heads back, seeming to "look down their noses" at others. The man who, during that car ride to Bucharest, told me to shut the window spoke with his head habitually tilted back a little. That position alone would have been enough to reveal his sense of self-importance. Notice also how public performers—actors, pop singers, and the like—often toss their heads left and right as if wanting to say, "Look at me. Listen to me. Aren't I good?"

Chitta is centered in the heart. Women's breasts grow in that region instead of in the lower abdomen, like the udders of lower animals. The feeling quality in women is, generally speaking, more developed than in men. Indeed, women's breasts serve not only the function of giving milk. From the same region also the feelings radiate outward—whether in emotional excitement, or in calm intuition. Because of this location, women's breasts serve a further purpose apart from that of giving milk: they also indicate sensitivity of feeling.

Men who are somewhat spiritually developed—saints and yogis—also develop slight breasts—rather like the small, still-forming breasts of a young adolescent girl. Men give no milk, obviously; they are not mothers. Even so, small breasts may appear beneath the nipples of those who are saintly in consequence of having more sensitive feelings. The feeling quality in saints is an expression of divine love and devotion. In men who have reached this level of development, the feelings are not emotional, but calm and dispassionate.

Women saints, on the other hand, retain a woman's normal forehead, the bone structure being unsusceptible of alteration, but they reveal their balance of feminine and masculine qualities by their firm tread and decisive gestures. Saint Teresa of Avila was once described by a Catholic bishop as a "bearded man"—not because she had hair on her face, but because she displayed a decidedly masculine style of behavior when discussing business matters.

How many novels, plays, and works of short fiction of our times depict the typical lives of individuals as pathetic or degraded! On the one hand, we recognize ourselves in those pitiless exposures. On the other hand, we reject them as false and unfair. What are we, really? Are we great, or mean? The soul intuits a divine greatness which the ego rejects in its search for merely competitive self-importance.

People, again, see the stars in the vastness of space, and marvel at that immensity. Some people see it as reducing them in significance. Others, wiser than most, recognize themselves as participants in that vastness and recognize themselves as actually *enhanced* by it, not belittled. For the latter group, infinity is like the sounding board of a musical instrument. As wood is built into a piano, violin, or guitar to enhance the volume of the strings, so the great reality to which all of us belong *enhances* the meaning of our own lives: it doesn't render human life petty or without meaning, as modern scientists often insist. If we will allow our awareness to expand beyond limitations of our egos, infinite consciousness itself will lift us, giving us the power to reach out and embrace the universe.

When people first contemplate the vastness of the universe—though one wonders how many of them ever indulge that thought seriously—their first reaction may well be to think, "How *tiny* I am!" When they first contemplate the great deeds of human beings in history, their first reaction may well be similar: "I could never do that!" When we refer this greatness back to ourselves, we may feel helpless. Unless we expand our consciousness and think rather of impersonal greatness than of greatness referred back to our littleness, we think, "What can I myself ever accomplish?" Many religious people do in fact become passive in depending supinely on God. How much, they ask, should man seek to accomplish on his own, and how much should he leave to God to accomplish? This has been a dilemma, through the ages, in all religions.

Confronted with an awareness of infinity—an awareness that modern science is constantly expanding—how ought we to react? Is it even worthwhile to ponder our own littleness? Even if we can forget how puny we are compared to the greater, divine realities, the plain fact is, we have to begin *somewhere*. Tiny or not, we are *responsible* for that little atom which is our own ego. If we don't use will power and energy to act, we'll accomplish *nothing*. Our minds, when we contemplate the universe, are exalted, but we need also to act, ourselves. The best way to do so is, while acting, to expand our consciousness from our inner center by those acts.

Ego is the subject of this lesson. Ego-consciousness is not the same as arrogance, which is perhaps the ego's least attractive manifestation. Because many prominent people, however, are arrogant, let us consider pride first, as a negative aspect of ego-consciousness.

Many people *desire* to seem important in the eyes of others. It pleases them to look down aloofly on their fellow creatures, and to treat them slightingly. Those who have this tendency focus more on things than on people. Those "things" include their own position in the world. Snobs enjoy anything that feeds their sense of self-importance. What this lesson teaches is diametrically opposite to that all-too-common failing. People whose focus is especially on themselves will often seek justification for any weakness by saying, "After all, I'm only human." The truth is, they view themselves as *better* than human! The answer they deserve, however, is, "No, you are *not yet* human!"

Lalla Yogishwari, a woman saint, lived as a hermit centuries ago in Kashmir. She wore no clothes, a fact which caused some people, scandalized, to ask her why she didn't display enough feminine modesty to wear at least *something*.

"Why should I dress?" she retorted. "I see no men around!"

One day word reached her that a famous male saint was coming to see her. Hastily, then, she clothed herself, exclaiming, "At last I'm to see a true man!" According to her rather drastic point of view, no one deserves full consideration as a human being until he has realized the fullness of his human potential!

Never excuse yourself with the words, "I'm only human." Failings that are common to the human herd do not belong to man's higher nature. As the *adi* (first) Swami Shankara said, "It is very hard to reach the human level. Don't pass over that great blessing!" I quote Shankara, as my Guru did, but I feel a little hesitant in doing so for the word "hard" suggests effort, and self-effort begins only at the human level. "Hard," however, also means hard *experience*—in other words, suffering, which living creatures experience again and again at every level of existence.

If you yourself balk at the idea of ego-transcendence, I have no choice but to defer to your free will. In that case, indeed, I must tell you, "Go right ahead! Become quite as self-important as you desire. Seek name, fame, a surfeit of riches, and overweening power—if those baubles still attract you. They attract most human beings. Seek those 'satisfactions,' therefore, until you grow sick of them—as you certainly will do, someday!"

A young man living among the gangs of New York City told a woman I met later in California, "It gives me a real feeling of power to carry a gun when I walk the streets of New York. I know, then, that *nobody* can mess with me!"

That man I've described in that car ride to Bucharest exuded a consciousness of power and self-importance. Had I told him it was a mistake to feel that way, he'd only have laughed and called me crazy.

The daughter of another prominent businessman went years later to Vassar College. When she returned to Scarsdale for a vacation, she saw herself as a queen. At a party I attended she made a show of pulling elbow-length velvet gloves from her arm, lingering impressively on the movement until she'd released all her fingers. If the thought of impressing others appeals to you, join the hordes who see nothing better in life. I doubt in that case, however, that you'd have come as far as this with these lessons!

A man who was on the board of directors of my father's company boasted to a family friend of ours concerning the many oil discoveries he'd made. Our friend retorted humorously, "Why, M——, you must be just about the greatest geologist in the whole world."

"Oh, no," replied the other with hastily assumed modesty. "In oil, maybe."

People don't realize the extent to which self-importance invites gentle mockery from others, and doesn't by any means attract their awe and respect! The essence of yoga principles is to emphasize the need for transcendence over ego in oneness with infinite truth. If people want egoic self-importance; if they want power over others; if they hunger for name and fame; if they hope to radiate self-esteem to everyone around them; and if they like to manipulate others—they might do well to study Niccolò Machiavelli's classic book of self-help, *Il Principe*. It has, I understand, been well received. Hitler kept a copy of it on his night table. Napoleon had a copy, discovered in his carriage after the Battle of Waterloo. The only trouble with Machiavelli's principles, and with the delusions I've briefly described here, is that they never fail to disappoint their votaries in the end.

If, on the other hand, you equate success with happiness for yourself and others, and not with the ability to exert power over anyone, then know that self-importance, power over others, and a desire to manipulate *are* delusions—dreams that are eventually succeeded by a rude awakening. The awakening may take time, owing to what my Guru called "the thwarting crosscurrents of ego." When retribution comes, however, it no longer awaits us in some dim future: It is very much right here and now—this very minute.

It is more difficult for those who are in fact great in the eyes of the world to ponder their own insignificance before the universe. Emperors, generals, and people who have achieved worldly fame or other kinds of success are more inclined to preen themselves on their importance than to reflect on how little they are before the cosmic verities. Their objective circumstances soon condition them to the assumption of a smug downward gaze upon the human "*canaille*"—"the great unwashed" in seething masses beneath them.

Most people, however, gaze on ambitious, struggling, sweating humanity about them and think, "Am I so different in my ignominy?" Unless they, like that mother frog at the beginning of this chapter, want to inflate themselves and look bigger than all the other beasts of pond and meadow, the very fact that their lot is so similar to that of most others can hardly fail to awaken in them a sneaking suspicion: "Are we not all poor, stressed toilers in the field—wholly insignificant?"—and then the thought, "No, it can't be true! I'm small, yes, but I am in fact more than I seem."

Even as individuals we are more than we seem.

The nature of duality provides for everything a compensating opposite. Power and self-importance become balanced out, in time, by nullifying impotence and disgrace. Even *you* yourself may—according to something my Guru wrote many years ago—have a dual balance to your own being which, in this case, increases your reality. In one of his commentaries on the Bible, Paramhansa Yogananda wrote that everyone has a soul mate. Unity with that other being, the compensating half of ourselves, must come before completion can be achieved in God. One reason people are drawn to marriage is that they feel a subconscious need for unity with some *one* other. The soul-union must be on a spiritual level, however. Paramhansa Yogananda wrote in that article that the union can take place in the form of a vision—even with someone inhabiting another planet.

A final, and seemingly supernal, objection to overcoming ego-consciousness is a thought that comes naturally to everyone: "I don't want to cease to exist! If cessation of my own individual existence is the goal of yoga, I consider that no fulfillment at all!"

Paramhansa Yogananda explained a final, supremely inspiring point in the endless debate between the advantages and disadvantages of ego-consciousness: *The ego*, he said, *is never destroyed. Indeed, nothing can be destroyed except attachment to ego-limitation!*

What happens, he explained, is that, once the soul achieves Self-realization, it discovers that God alone was, in fact, the only Actor of every role the ego ever played. In divine omniscience, once it is attained, there remains the *memory* of all one's prior, individual existences. In cosmic memory, then, your own ego itself will continue to exist forever. You will also be able to re-manifest yourself whenever the need arises—if ever, for example, someone prays to you for your blessings. In such cases, it is not that the Infinite Consciousness recreates something resembling you: It will be you, yourself, who re-manifests—that very ego with which your being was once identified.

There are several practical ways of expanding your consciousness even while living and working in this body. These methods can be practiced anywhere. I shall try in the next section to offer a few.

The Application

1) Tell yourself that anyone who works under you is working *with* you. He is your co-worker in the same enterprise.

2) Share with others the credit for any success you achieve. Resist the temptation to call attention to any part you played in that success.

3) Try not to defend yourself against people's accusations. Accept them silently, instead, with good cheer. The ability to bear the negative opinions of others against you will be a feather in your cap. That very thought will make you aware of a growing freedom and happiness within.

4) Try not to create a mental image of yourself that you will then feel that you have to defend.

5) Don't meet praise with denial. To do so might be construed by others as impugning the other person's good taste! Instead, say, "You know, we all have within us a power, if we keep ourselves open to it, that will work *with* us. God alone is the Doer. I appreciate what you've said, but the credit really belongs only to Him."

6) When circumstances prove you to have been right in some matter, never announce smugly, "I said so, didn't I?"

7) Don't point out to others their flaw of ego-centeredness, unless you can do so with wisdom. To challenge others is to expose

yourself to their almost-inevitable counter-challenge: "*You* are the one with the ego problem!" That, of course, might not be a bad thought to ponder. Inviting it, however, can bring harmful consequences to yourself: Negative reminders can become negative *affirmations* in your own mind.

8) In answer to anyone who criticizes you, never justify yourself by quoting favorable remarks made by others about you.

9) Never say, "Everyone says so" in justification of any statement of yours that others have rejected. Since most opinions have little value anyway, try rather to seek justification by emphasizing the good sense of any proposal you make.

10) Give to God everything you do, even if the profits of that action accrue to you, personally. In this practice lies the secret of "*nishkam karma*"—action without desire for the fruits of action. That advice of Sri Krishna's leads to liberation and perfect fulfillment.

11) Whatever happens to you outwardly, remain inwardly non-attached and even unaffected. Remember, nothing can touch the eternal YOU, which is your soul.

12) When people accuse you of anything for any reason, whether fairly or unfairly, don't let your feelings become ruffled. If those people are in the right, don't be ashamed. Shame will only affirm your ego-consciousness—which is usually in the wrong, anyway! (After all, your ego, like everyone else's, is under the sway of delusion.) And if others are in the wrong, ask yourself: "What does it matter, anyway?" Yes, their opinions may matter in the effect they have on your work, but you will win a better opinion from others if you take their accusations cheerfully, and reply with a smile, "I'll try to do better next time."

13) If someone sets himself up as your rival at work, don't respond with antagonism. The petty, competitive spirit others may demonstrate cannot be avoided; it is part of the "play" of life, which becomes actually enjoyable once one learns non-attachment. Remember the saying, "What comes of itself, let it come." You will always be the gainer if you offer everything up to God.

14) Office politics are simply power games. Avoid them whenever possible. The best "power game" of all is to befriend everyone. What need have you, after all, to judge anyone? Everyone's karma is his own. The responsibility for working it out is his also.

15) Be truthful, sincere, and ever kind.

16) Don't hesitate to say "I can," if you think you might succeed at some task. It is no sign of humility to tell others, "I can't do that." Remember: *God, through you, can do anything!*

17) Ambition can be a fault if it is harbored for personal ends. If your ambition is for a project, however, or if it is to help others, or to serve God, it may be considered a virtue.

18) People often try to manipulate others, or the circumstances around them. Live, rather, by that oft-stated principle, "What comes of itself, let it come." You will find that, if you can reject completely the tendency to manipulate others, things will somehow flow well and smoothly for you.

19) Laugh *with* people, never *at* them.

20) Never call anyone—particularly never a subordinate—"stupid." Even if you feel so inclined, remember that non-judgment will help to release you forever from ego-involvement.

21) That victory is best which is won through the use of will power, and through having faith in goodness as a greater power, ultimately, than evil.

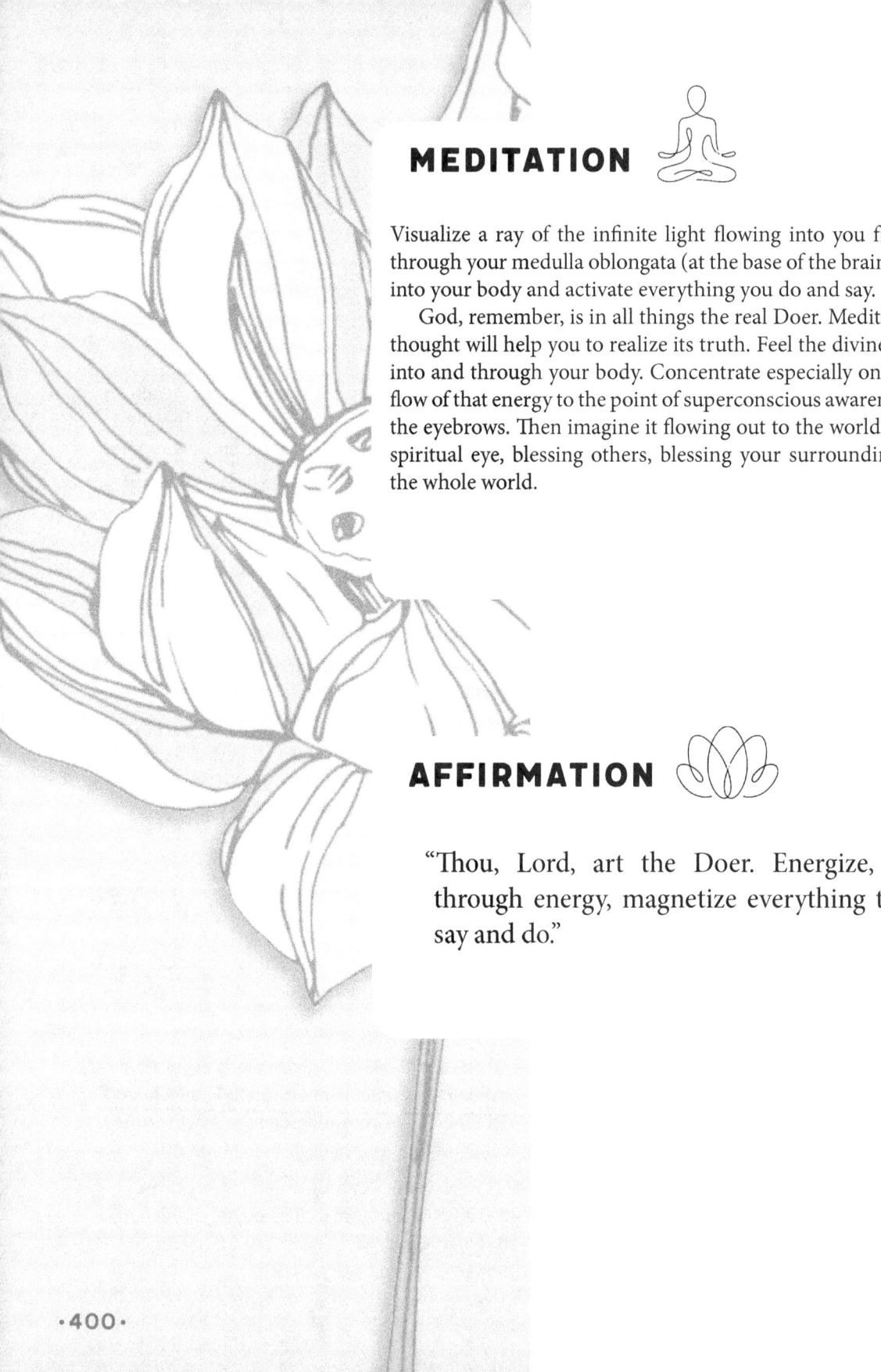

MEDITATION

Visualize a ray of the infinite light flowing into you from behind, through your medulla oblongata (at the base of the brain). Let it flow into your body and activate everything you do and say.

God, remember, is in all things the real Doer. Meditating on this thought will help you to realize its truth. Feel the divine ray flowing into and through your body. Concentrate especially on the forward flow of that energy to the point of superconscious awareness between the eyebrows. Then imagine it flowing out to the world through the spiritual eye, blessing others, blessing your surroundings, blessing the whole world.

AFFIRMATION

"Thou, Lord, art the Doer. Energize, and, through energy, magnetize everything that I say and do."

POINTS TO REMEMBER

1. The ego can only be transcended in the realization that we are much more—when the little self expands to become, in time, the overarching, omnipresent, divine Self.

2. As individuality becomes less and less centered in the ego, a deeper sense of who we really are begins to manifest. Every apparently separate point in God's creation, though all reflect His consciousness, is unique.

3. Anything that will help us to expand our *consciousness*, rather than narrow it in egoic self-importance, will bring us the happiness and fulfillment we all crave.

4. The highest kind of creativity flows down to us from the superconscious. In that context, high or low self-esteem are no different from each other: both of them arise from excessive ego-consciousness.

5. Ego-consciousness is centered in the medulla oblongata at the base of the brain. Creative energy needs to flow freely up the spine, through the medulla and the brain, becoming focused at the point between the eyebrows.

6. Because feeling is primarily that aspect of consciousness which binds us to delusion, Patanjali defined yoga by the words, "*Yogas chitta vritti nirodha* (Yoga is the neutralization of the larger vortices and smallest eddies of feeling)."

7. If we will allow our awareness to expand beyond limitations of our egos, infinite consciousness itself will lift us, giving us the power to reach out and embrace the universe.

8. Paramhansa Yogananda said: *The ego is never destroyed. Indeed, nothing can be destroyed except* attachment *to ego-limitation!*

9. There are several practical ways of expanding your consciousness even while living and working in this body:

- Tell yourself that anyone who works under you is working *with* you. He is your co-worker in the same enterprise.

- Share with others the credit for any success you achieve. Resist the temptation to call attention to any part you played in that success.

- Try not to defend yourself against people's accusations. Accept them silently, instead, with good cheer.

- Don't meet praise with denial. Instead, say, "I appreciate what you've said, but the credit really belongs only to Him."

- Give to God everything you do. This leads to liberation and perfect fulfillment.

- Whatever happens to you outwardly, remain inwardly non-attached and even unaffected. Remember, nothing can touch the eternal YOU, which is your soul.
- Remember the saying, "What comes of itself, let it come." You will always be the gainer if you offer everything up to God.
- Avoid office politics whenever possible. Befriend everyone.
- Be truthful, sincere, and ever kind.
- Don't hesitate to say "I can," if you think you might succeed at some task. Remember: *God, through you, can do anything!*
- If your ambition is for a project, or if it is to help others, or to serve God, it may be considered a virtue.
- That victory is best which is won through the use of will power, and through having faith in goodness.

> **Money is not a curse. It is the manner in which you use money that is important. . . . When you use it rightly, it gives you happiness.**
>
> —PARAMHANSA YOGANANDA, *How to Be a Success*

WORKBOOK IDEAS
by Joseph Bharat Cornell

Expand Your Self-Awareness

A rabbit and beaver were looking at a huge concrete dam when the rabbit, greatly impressed, asked the beaver, "Is that your work?" "No," replied the beaver, "but it *was* based on an idea of mine."

The ego's tendency is to refer everything back to itself to inflate its own importance. Yet the more we feel separate from others, the smaller and unhappier we are. The secret to fulfillment lies in expanding our *consciousness*, not narrowing it in egoic self-importance.

During the early years at Ananda Village, a few friends joined together informally in a club they called "The Great Life Society." They encouraged each other to look at life expansively and not to be trapped in egoic preoccupation. A member caught by self-interested thinking, for example, would immediately direct his attention away from himself to expand his perspective and sympathies.

Attuning to a larger reality harmonizes us with God and the rest of creation. Our ability, then, to receive inspiration, manifest ideas, and work with others is tremendously enhanced. The key to a successful life—and the central theme of this course—is *being expansive* at all times.

ACTION ITEM:
Practice the following exercise:
1. Ask yourself often during the day: "Where is my attention?"
2. If you find that you are thinking too much about yourself: Go on a "self-involvement" fast.
3. Vow to live in greater awareness. Remind yourself constantly that happiness and fulfillment come through self-expansion.
4. Center yourself in the spine. Relate from your center to the center of the people around you (or the project you're working on). This practice will help you appreciate the realities of others.
5. Keep your awareness expansive by asking: "How can I *give* to this situation, to this person?"
6. As you give to others or to your work, feel God's love and energy flowing through you.

ACTION ITEM:
- Take advantage of small quiet moments to center yourself and affirm your desire to live expansively. Begin by telling your mind firmly to be quiet—right now. *Feel* a sense of deep stillness within and all around you. Become aware of things in your environment that you haven't noticed before. Experience yourself living and moving in them. Enjoy the contrast between being self-absorbed, and embracing a larger world.

About Swami Kriyananda

"Swami Kriyananda is a man of wisdom and compassion in action, truly one of the leading lights in the spiritual world today."

—Lama Surya Das, Dzogchen Center, author of *Awakening the Buddha Within*

A prolific author, accomplished composer, playwright, and artist, and a world-renowned spiritual teacher, Swami Kriyananda (1926–2013) referred to himself simply as a close disciple of the great God-realized master, Paramhansa Yogananda. He met his guru at the age of twenty-two, and served him during the last four years of the Master's life. He dedicated the rest of his life to sharing Yogananda's teachings throughout the world.

Kriyananda was born in Romania of American parents, and educated in Europe, England, and the United States. Philosophically and artistically inclined from youth, he soon came to question life's meaning and society's values. During a period of intense inward reflection, he discovered Yogananda's *Autobiography of a Yogi*, and immediately traveled three thousand miles from New York to California to meet the Master, who accepted him as a monastic disciple. Yogananda appointed him as the head of the monastery, authorized him to teach and give Kriya initiation in his name, and entrusted him with the missions of writing, teaching, and creating what he called "world brotherhood colonies."

Kriyananda founded the first such community, Ananda Village, in the Sierra Nevada foothills of Northern California in 1968. Ananda is recognized as one of the most successful intentional communities in the world today. It has served as a model for other such communities that he founded subsequently in the United States, Europe, and India.

FURTHER EXPLORATIONS

CRYSTAL CLARITY PUBLISHERS

If you enjoyed this title, Crystal Clarity Publishers invites you to deepen your spiritual life through many additional resources based on the teachings of Paramhansa Yogananda. We offer books, e-books, audiobooks, yoga and meditation videos, and a wide variety of inspirational and relaxation music composed by Swami Kriyananda.

See a listing of books below, visit our secure website for a complete online catalog, or place an order for our products.

crystalclarity.com
800.424.1055 | clarity@crystalclarity.com
1123 Goodrich Blvd. | Commerce, CA 90022

ANANDA WORLDWIDE

Crystal Clarity Publishers is the publishing house of Ananda, a worldwide spiritual movement founded by Swami Kriyananda, a direct disciple of Paramhansa Yogananda. Ananda offers resources and support for your spiritual journey through meditation instruction, webinars, online virtual community, email, and chat.

Ananda has centers and meditation groups in over 45 countries, offering group guided meditations, classes and teacher training in meditation and yoga, and many other resources.

In addition, Ananda has residential communities in the US, Europe, and India. Spiritual communities are places where people live together in a spirit of cooperation and friendship, dedicated to a common goal. Spirituality is practiced in all areas of daily life: at school, at work, or in the home. Many Ananda communities offer internships during which one can stay and experience spiritual community firsthand.

For more information about Ananda communities or meditation groups near you, please visit ananda.org or call 530.478.7560.

THE EXPANDING LIGHT RETREAT

The Expanding Light is the largest retreat center in the world to share exclusively the teachings of Paramhansa Yogananda. Situated in the Ananda Village community near Nevada City, California, the center offers the opportunity to experience spiritual life in a contemporary ashram setting. The varied, year-round schedule of classes and programs on yoga, meditation, and spiritual practice includes Karma Yoga, personal retreat, spiritual travel, and online learning. Large groups are welcome.

The Ananda School of Yoga & Meditation offers certified yoga, yoga therapist, spiritual counselor, and meditation teacher trainings.

The teaching staff has years of experience practicing Kriya Yoga meditation and all aspects of Paramhansa Yogananda's teachings. You may come for a relaxed personal renewal, participating in ongoing activities as much or as little as you wish. The serene mountain setting, supportive staff, and delicious vegetarian meals provide an ideal environment for a truly meaningful stay, be it a brief respite or an extended spiritual vacation.

For more information, please visit expandinglight.org or call 800.346.5350.

ANANDA MEDITATION RETREAT

Set amidst seventy-two acres of beautiful meditation gardens and wild forest in Northern California's Sierra foothills, the Ananda Meditation Retreat is an ideal setting for a rejuvenating, inner experience.

The Meditation Retreat has been a place of deep meditation and sincere devotion for over fifty years. Long before that, the Native American Maidu tribe held this to be sacred land. The beauty and presence of the Divine are tangibly felt by all who visit here.

Studies show that being in nature and using techniques such as forest bathing can significantly reduce stress and blood pressure while strengthening your immune system, concentration, and level of happiness. The Meditation Retreat is the perfect place for quiet immersion in nature.

Plan a personal retreat, enjoy one of the guided retreats, or choose from a variety of programs led by the caring and joyful staff.

For more information or to place your reservation, please visit meditationretreat.org, email meditationretreat@ananda.org, or call 530.478.7557.

The Original 1946 Unedited Edition of
Yogananda's Spiritual Masterpiece

AUTOBIOGRAPHY OF A YOGI
Paramhansa Yogananda

Autobiography of a Yogi is one of the world's most acclaimed spiritual classics, with millions of copies sold. Named one of the Best 100 Spiritual Books of the twentieth century, this book helped launch and continues to inspire a spiritual awakening throughout the Western world.

Yogananda was the first yoga master of India whose mission brought him to settle and teach in the West. His firsthand account of his life experiences in India includes childhood revelations, stories of his visits to saints and masters, and long-secret teachings of yoga and Self-realization that he first made available to the Western reader.

This reprint of the original 1946 edition is free from textual changes made after Yogananda's passing in 1952. This updated edition includes bonus materials: the last chapter that Yogananda wrote in 1951, also without posthumous changes, the eulogy Yogananda wrote for Gandhi, and a new foreword and afterword by Swami Kriyananda, one of Yogananda's close, direct disciples.

Also available in Spanish and Hindi from Crystal Clarity Publishers.

The Original Writings of Paramhansa Yogananda

SONGS OF THE SOUL
Paramhansa Yogananda

Yogananda preferred to express his wisdom not in dry intellectual terms but as pure, expansive feeling. To drink his poetry is to be drawn into the web of his boundless, childlike love. In one moment his *Songs of the Soul* invite us to join him as he plays among the stars with his Cosmic Beloved. Then they call us to discover that portion of our own hearts that is eternally one with the Nearest and Dearest. This volume is a bubbling, singing wellspring of spiritual healing that we can bring with us everywhere.

METAPHYSICAL MEDITATIONS
Paramhansa Yogananda

Metaphysical Meditations is a classic collection of meditation techniques, visualizations, affirmations, and prayers from the great yoga master, Paramhansa Yogananda. The meditations given are of three types: those spoken to the individual consciousness, prayers or demands addressed to God, and affirmations that bring us closer to the Divine.

Select a passage that meets your specific need and speak each word slowly and purposefully until you become absorbed in its inner meaning. At the bedside, by the meditation seat, or while traveling — one can choose no better companion than *Metaphysical Meditations*.

SCIENTIFIC HEALING AFFIRMATIONS
Paramhansa Yogananda

Yogananda's 1924 classic, reprinted here, is a pioneering work in the fields of self-healing and self-transformation. He explains that words are crystallized thoughts and have life-changing power when spoken with conviction, concentration, willpower, and feeling. Yogananda offers far more than mere suggestions for achieving positive attitudes. He shows how to impregnate words with spiritual force to shift habitual thought patterns of the mind and create a new personal reality.

Added to this text are over fifty of Yogananda's well-loved "Short Affirmations," taken from issues of *East-West* and *Inner Culture* magazines from 1932 to 1942. This little book will be a treasured companion on the road to realizing your highest, divine potential.

The Wisdom of Yogananda *series*

Paramhansa Yogananda's timeless wisdom is offered here in an approachable, easy-to-read format. The writings of the Master are presented with minimal editing to capture his expansive and compassionate wisdom, his sense of fun, and his practical spiritual guidance.

HOW TO BE A SUCCESS
The Wisdom of Yogananda, Volume 4

The Attributes of Success, Yogananda's original booklet on reaching one's goals, is included here along with his other writings on success: how to develop habits of success and eradicate habits of failure; thriving in the right job; how to build willpower and magnetism; and finding the true purpose of one's life.

HOW TO HAVE COURAGE, CALMNESS, AND CONFIDENCE
The Wisdom of Yogananda, Volume 5

A master at helping people change and grow, Yogananda shows how to transform one's life: dislodge negative thoughts and depression; uproot fear and thoughts of failure; cure nervousness and systematically eliminate worry from life; and overcome anger, sorrow, oversensitivity, and a host of other troublesome emotions.
Winner of the 2011 International Book Award for Best Self-Help Title

HOW TO AWAKEN YOUR TRUE POTENTIAL
The Wisdom of Yogananda, Volume 7

With compassion, humor, and deep understanding of human psychology, Yogananda offers instruction on releasing limitations to access the power of mind and heart. Discover your hidden resources and be empowered to choose a life with greater meaning, purpose, and joy.

HOW TO FACE LIFE'S CHANGES
The Wisdom of Yogananda, Volume 9

Changes come not to destroy us, but to help us grow in understanding and learn the lessons we must to reach our highest potential. Guided by Yogananda, tap into the changeless joy of your soul-nature, empowering you to move through life fearlessly and with an open heart. Learn to accept change as the reality of life; face change in relationships, finances, and health with gratitude; and cultivate key attitudes like fearlessness, non-attachment, and willpower.

HOW TO LIVE WITHOUT FEAR
The Wisdom of Yogananda, Volume 11

Yogananda said that one of the greatest enemies of willpower is fear. Avoid it both in thought and in action. Fear doesn't help you to get away from the object of fear, it only paralyzes your willpower. Here the great yoga master, Paramhansa Yogananda, teaches us how to: eliminate the mental bacteria of fear, rid the mind of worry poisons, overcome stage fright, use chants and affirmations to overcome fear, and much more!

THE NEW PATH
My Life with Paramhansa Yogananda
Swami Kriyananda

Winner of the 2010 Eric Hoffer Award for Best Self-Help/Spiritual Book
Winner of the 2010 USA Book News Award for Best Spiritual Book

The New Path is a moving revelation of one man's search for lasting happiness. After rejecting the false promises offered by modern society, J. Donald Walters found himself (much to his surprise) at the feet of Paramhansa Yogananda, asking to become his disciple. How he got there, trained with the Master, and became Swami Kriyananda makes fascinating reading.

The rest of the book is the fullest account by far of what it was like to live with and be a disciple of that great man of God.

Anyone hungering to learn more about Yogananda will delight in the hundreds of stories of life with a great avatar and the profound lessons they offer. This book is an ideal complement to *Autobiography of a Yogi*.

THE ART OF SUPPORTIVE LEADERSHIP
A Practical Guide for People in Positions of Responsibility
J. Donald Walters (Swami Kriyananda)

A Proven Approach to Successful Leadership

Do you want to improve your leadership skills and learn how to bring out the best in your employees, co-workers, or students? Then *The Art of Supportive Leadership* can help you! Organizations of every kind—well-established industrial corporations, pioneering tech firms, schools, nonprofits, the military—all are using this proven approach to leadership with great success.

The Art of Supportive Leadership is defining the new cutting edge of leadership training. The author has drawn on his many years of successful leadership to offer clear, practical techniques that produce results quickly—even if you're new to leadership, and even if you can only devote limited time to improving your skills. Each chapter ends with concise summaries that serve as quick reference guides when you need them.

MONEY MAGNETISM
How to Attract What You Need When You Need It
J. Donald Walters (Swami Kriyananda)

Winner of the 2010 USA Book News Award for Best Spiritual Book

With *Money Magnetism* you will unlock the hdden secrets of *true* abundance. This book can change your life by changing how you think and feel about money. Offering simple, powerful techniques for attracting material and spiritual success, *Money Magnetism* is a practical, easy-to-understand guide that will help you quickly realize results. With its fresh, new insights this book goes far beyond the scope of other "money" books.

According to Swami Kriyananda, anyone can attract wealth—"there need be no limits to the flow of your abundance." Through numerous stories and examples from his own life and others', Kriyananda vividly—sometimes humorously—shows you how and why the principles of money magnetism work, and how you can immediately start applying them in your own life.

www.ingramcontent.com/pod-product-compliance
Lightning Source LLC
Chambersburg PA
CBHW060333010526
44117CB00017B/2819